Mrs. (Anna) Jameson

Memoirs of the Beauties of the Court of Charles the Second

Mrs. (Anna) Jameson

Memoirs of the Beauties of the Court of Charles the Second

ISBN/EAN: 9783744678797

Printed in Europe, USA, Canada, Australia, Japan

Cover: Foto ©ninafisch / pixelio.de

More available books at **www.hansebooks.com**

MEMOIRS

OF

THE BEAUTIES

OF THE

COURT OF CHARLES THE SECOND,

WITH

THEIR PORTRAITS,

AFTER SIR PETER LELY AND OTHER EMINENT PAINTERS:

ILLUSTRATING

THE DIARIES OF PEPYS, EVELYN, CLARENDON,

AND OTHER CONTEMPORARY WRITERS.

BY MRS. JAMESON.

FOURTH EDITION.

LONDON:
HENRY G. BOHN, YORK STREET, COVENT GARDEN.
MDCCCLXI.

ADVERTISEMENT.

In offering to the public a new edition of Mrs. Jameson's popular biographies of the "Beauties of the Court of Charles the Second," the publisher has endeavoured, in every possible way, to make it worthy of a still more extended patronage than that which has been already accorded to it. With this view, he has not only printed it in a more convenient form, but has caused it to be enlarged by considerable additions, both to the notes and text, and by an introductory Essay on the reign and character of Charles II. The Portraits have for the most part been re-engraved, and are restored to their original brilliancy. He trusts that the efforts thus made, will be received with the favour which it has been his object to merit.

PORTRAITS AND MEMOIRS.

	PAGE
QUEEN CATHERINE OF BRAGANZA	53
THE DUCHESS OF CLEVELAND	78
THE COUNTESS DE GRAMMONT	102
THE COUNTESS OF OSSORY	110
LADY DENHAM	138
NELL GWYNN	146
THE DUCHESS OF SOMERSET	167
THE DUCHESS OF RICHMOND	173
MRS. LAWSON	186
THE COUNTESS OF CHESTERFIELD	189
THE COUNTESS OF ROCHESTER	201
MISS BAGOT	212
MRS. NOTT	220
THE COUNTESS OF SOUTHESK	223
LADY BELLASYS	230
THE COUNTESS OF SUNDERLAND	237
MRS. MIDDLETON	252
THE COUNTESS OF NORTHUMBERLAND	259
THE DUCHESS OF PORTSMOUTH	271
THE DUCHESS OF DEVONSHIRE	304
MISS JENNINGS	314

EDITOR'S INTRODUCTION

TO

THE SECOND EDITION.

"A prince like a pear, which rotten at core is,
With a court that takes millions, and yet as Job poor is."
                                                    OLD SONG.

THE Court of Charles the Second is very properly illustrated by the portraits of his ladies. It was by their secret influence that the most important affairs of state were directed, at their all-powerful nod ministers rose or fell, by their contrivance were effected foreign treaties, and the most weighty decisions of war or peace were determined by their intermediation. In the weak mind and hollow heart of Charles, a Castlemaine or a Portsmouth might always gain the mastery over the integrity of a Clarendon or an Ormond. It happens but too frequently, that when female influence is thus predominant in the cabinet, it is exercised by the worst portion of the fairer sex, and this was eminently the case in Charles's days, the avarice of whose mistresses robbed the country of its resources, and reduced the king himself to a disgraceful dependency on France. Along with foreign finery came in foreign licentiousness, and the court of Charles the Second, in this latter respect, presents a strong contrast to the stern morality of that of Cromwell. Fortunately, the debauchery of the gay cavaliers, and the lax virtue of the dames of Louis XIV., were too grating to the public feelings to take firm root in England; and, whilst the nation went on gradually increasing and improving upon the refinements which were now introduced, a few years saw the more objectionable fashions which had accompanied them, disappear.

The joy which seemed to hail the accession of Charles to the throne of his father, was but the gleamy sunshine which often ushers in a gloomy overclouded day. Many people, tired of the uncertainties which had for some time filled their minds, hailed a change which seemed to promise them some settled government. The King was not brought in by the strength of his own party, but rather by the dissatisfaction of those unquiet people, who, irritated because the government was not moulded according to their own ideas and influenced by themselves, hastened the recall of the exiled monarch, that they might at least see the overthrow of the party of which they were jealous. They bore no love to Charles in their hearts, but they shouted at his elevation, because it was the downfall of the Protectorate. The leading men seized the occasion which they saw presented, and made their own advantage of it, by making their peace with the exile, and hurrying his restoration. But many of his best friends, who knew well his incapacity for the throne to which he was called, were not without their fears of the future. Yet there were not wanting many also, who, in the warmth of their zeal, thought the joy of every body was as sincere as their own.

"This day," (29th May,) says Evelyn, "his majestic Charles the Second came to London, after a sad and long exile and calamitous suffering, both of the King and church, being 17 years. This was also his birth-day, and with a triumph of above 20,000 horse and foote, brandishing their swords and shouting with inexpressible joy; the wayes strew'd with flowers, the belles ringing, the streetes hung with tapistry, fountaines running with wine; the maior, aldermen, and all the companies in their liveries, chaines of gold, and banners; lords and nobles clad in cloth of silver, gold, and velvet; the windowes and balconies all set with ladies; trumpets, music, and myriads of people flocking, even so far as from Rochester, so as they were seven houres in passing the citty, even from 2 in the afternoone till 9 at night.

"I stood in the Strand and beheld it, and bless'd God. And all this was don without one drop of bloud shed, and by that very army which rebell'd against him; but it was the Lord's doing, for such a restauration was never mention'd in any history, ancient or modern, since the returne of the Jewes from the Babylonish captivity; nor so joyfull a day and so bright ever seene in this nation, this hapning when to expect or effect it was past all human policy."*

The night of this day, which drew forth so abundantly the pious thanksgivings of John Evelyn, the King passed in the company of Mrs. Palmer, so soon afterwards notorious as the Duchess of Cleveland; and immediately after, he issued a proclamation against debauchery. Pepys observes on the 4th of June, "This morning the King's proclamation against drinking, swearing, and debauchery, was read to our ships' companies in the fleet, and indeed *it gives great satisfaction to all.*"

The members of Charles's first administration were partly his staunch friends, who had followed him in his misfortunes, as Ormond, Hyde, (created soon after Earl of Clarendon,) and partly some of his new friends, who had at least the reputation of having been chiefly instrumental in his restoration, such as Monk, whom he created Duke of Albemarle, and Montague, created Earl of Sandwich. They were generally men who possessed, in comparison with his other favourites, and of those who succeeded them, a considerable degree of integrity or ability. Pepys gives us a curious insight into the temporizing policy of Sandwich ("his lord," as he styles him,) during the negotiations for the King's return, and

* Evelyn's Diary, vol. ii. p. 148.

confesses that he learnt, in a conversation with him, that as to religion he was "wholly sceptical." On another occasion Pepys speaks of him as going further than became him in flattering the King's vices. There can be no doubt, however, that Sandwich possessed sufficient virtue to render him obnoxious to the King's more immediate companions, and he gradually fell into disfavour and disgrace, till at last he was slain, fighting bravely, in the great sea-fight in the May of 1672. On this occasion, Evelyn bursts into a flood of eloquence in lamenting the loss of his friend: "My Lord Sandwich was prudent as well as valiant, and always govern'd his affaires with successe and little losse; he was for deliberation and reason, they (Monk and Lord Clifford) for action and slaughter without either; and for this, whisper'd as if my Lord Sandwich was not so gallant because he was not so rash, and knew how fatal it was to loose a fleete, such as was that under his conduct, and for which these very persons would have censur'd him. Deplorable was the losse of one of the best accomplish'd persons, not onely of this nation, but of any other. He was learned in sea affaires, in politics, in mathematics, and in music; he had been on divers embassies, was of a sweete and obliging temper, sober, chast, very ingenious, a true nobleman, an ornament to the court and his prince, nor has he left any behind him who approach his many virtues."*

Edward Hyde, created soon afterwards Earl of Clarendon, was certainly a man of great ability; but he was not popular, and in the political songs of the day he is accused of unbounded avarice. Charles supported him, both in gratitude for a long series of faithful services, and because he thought that no other person was so capable of supporting the Restoration, and of enlarging the limits of his regal power.

Clarendon was virtually the head of the administration with which Charles began his reign, and which was indeed kept together

* Evelyn's Diary, vol. ii. p. 370.

almost entirely by his influence, for the King's favour was bestowed secretly on men of a very different character and reputation. Charles had become gradually more and more the slave of Lady Castlemaine, and left his ministers to follow their own counsels whilst he spent his time with buffoons and debauchees; and his courtiers, who were preparing under female influence to stand at the head of the government, thought of nothing but fine clothes and petty intrigues. The want of personal security which every body felt under the Restoration, drove even the best men to consider only of making their profit of the present moment. Who can help smiling at the fears of Pepys, which he avows with so much *naïveté* in the November of 1660, on the occasion of a dinner at Sir William Batten's?—" Here dined with us two or three more country gentlemen; among the rest Mr. Christmas, my old school-fellow, with whom I had much talk. He did remember that I was a great Roundhead when I was a boy, and I was much afraid that he would have remembered the words that I said the day the King was beheaded, (that, were I to preach upon him, my text should be, 'The memory of the wicked shall rot ;') but I found *afterwards that he did go away from school before that time !*"

In the August following, Pepys, who had hailed with so much satisfaction the blessings which at its outset, little more than a year before, the Restoration seemed to promise, observes of the state of things,—" At court things are in a very ill condition, there being so much emulacion, poverty, and the vices of drinking, swearing, and loose amours, that I know not what will be the end of it, but confusion. And the clergy so high, that all people that I meet with do protest against their practice. In short, I see no content or satisfaction any where, in any one sort of people."

In the October of 1662, when the Chancellor (Clarendon) had lost not a little of what popularity he had, by the marriage of his daughter with the Duke of York, and by the part he had taken in the marriage of the King and in the reconciliation of the Queen with Lady Castlemaine, and when the influence of this termagant lady had been doubly strengthened by the Queen's submission, the administration which had been formed around Lord Clarendon began to give way. The Secretary of State, Sir Edward Nicholas, a man of great integrity, and one of the faithfullest friends of the King as well as of his father, was sacrificed to make place for Sir H. Bennet, afterwards known as the Earl of Arlington, a creature of Lady Castlemaine. The privy-purse was at the same time given to the custody of Sir Charles Berkeley, "a most vicious person, and one," says Pepys, "whom Mr. Pierce, the surgeon, did tell me that he offered his wife 300*l.* per annum to be his mistress. He also told me, that none in court had more the King's ear now than Sir Charles Berkeley, and Sir H. Bennet, and my Lady Castlemaine."

In its foreign negotiations, the government of Charles the Second made a very different figure from that which had always been sustained by England during the Protectorate. Early in the new reign, the advantages which had been obtained by the latter were sold for money to supply the extravagance of the court. The parliament, at first so compliant with the King, became soon dissatisfied with his conduct, and distrustful of him, and gave him but small supplies, and that not without making many difficulties; the more so, because they saw that the ministers themselves were intent only upon filling their own purses as quickly as possible. It was observed in 1665, "for my Lord Treasurer, he minds his ease, and lets things go how they will; if he can have his 8000*l.* per annum and a game at l'ombre, he is well. My Lord Chancellor, he minds getting of money and nothing else; and my Lord Ashly (the Chancellor of the Exchequer) will rob the devil and the altar, but he will get money if it be to be got." The mass of the people was equally distrustful as the parliament, and the assessments were collected with difficulty;* so that between the extravagant profusion

---

* On the 9th November, 1663, Pepys gives an interesting account of the difference between Cromwell's soldiery, who had been disbanded, and those of the

of the King and the unwillingness of the people to pay, the revenue of the kingdom was in a very low condition. The ministers therefore dreaded a war, when they had not sufficient money even to supply the private expenditure of the King, and the debts of the court were becoming continually heavier and more galling.

In 1665, the Dutch war broke out. The people of England were extremely irritated against the Hollanders, and a very large supply was voted by the parliament for the carrying on of the war. On the part of the English, the war was ill managed in every department. The court was too busy about its own pleasures to

King, and describes the difficulties of getting in the revenue. "He (Mr. Blackburne) tells me, that the King, by name, with all his dignities, is prayed for by them that they call Fanatiques, as heartily and powerfully as in any of the other churches that are thought better: and that, let the King think what he will, it is them that must help him in the day of warr. For so generally they are the most substantiall sort of people, and the soberest; and did desire me to observe it to my Lord Sandwich, among other things, that of all the old army, now you cannot see a man begging about the streets; but what? You shall have this captain turned a shoemaker; the lieutenant, a baker; this, a brewer; that, a haberdasher; this common soldier, a porter; and every man in his apron and frock, &c., as if they never had done anything else; whereas the other go with their belts and swords, swearing, and cursing, and stealing; running into people's houses, by force oftentimes, to carry away something; and this is the difference between the temper of one and the other; and concludes (and I think with some reason) that the spirits of the old parliament soldiers are so quiet and contented with God's providences, that the King is safe from any evil meant him by them, one thousand times more than from his own discontented cavaliers. And then to the publick management of business: it is done, as he observes, so loosely and so carelessly, that the kingdom can never be happy with it, every man looking after himself, and his own lust and luxury; and that half of what money the parliament gives the King is not so much as gathered. And to the purpose he told me how the Bellamys (who had some of the northern counties assigned them for their debt for the petty-warrant victualling) have often complained to him that they cannot get it collected, for that nobody minds, or if they do, they won't pay it in. Whereas (which is a very remarkable thing) he hath been told by some of the treasurers at warr here of late, to whom the most of the 120,000*l.* monthly was paid, that for most months the payments were gathered so duly, that they seldom had so much or more than 40*s.* or the like, short in the whole collection."

allow its attention to be given to public business: the money was ill applied; and, after the King had squandered the enormous sum of 2,390,000*l.* amongst his mistresses and favourites, the war ended, in 1667, with disgrace. It is recorded, that when the Dutch fleet was employed in destroying the shipping in the Thames and the Medway, and threatened a still more serious invasion, Charles was employed with Lady Castlemaine in the interesting sport of hunting a moth!

Much of this waste of resources and ill management, was laid to the venality of Sir William Coventry, the treasurer of the navy. Denham, in one of his political poems, describes him as—

> "Cerulian Coventry,
> Keeper, or rather chancellor, of the sea. . . . .
> To pay his foes the silver trumpet spends,
> And boatswain's whistle for his place depends;
> Pilots in vain repeat their compass o'er,
> Until of him they learn that one point more,
> The constant magnet to the pole doth hold,
> Steel to the magnet, Coventry to gold.
> Muscovy *sells* us pitch, and hemp, and tar;
> Iron and copper, Sweden; Munster, war;
> Ashly, prize; Warwick, custom; Carteret, pay;
> But Coventry doth sell the fleet away."

But the tide of unpopularity, raised by the disadvantageous peace, after so much money and blood had been expended, fell heaviest on Lord Clarendon. Lady Castlemaine, who hated him because he had obstructed some of her extravagant whims, gave the King no rest till the Chancellor was dismissed from his office; and then Charles's worthless companions congratulated him on being, at last, *his own master.*

Pepys has entered in his Diary a conversation with Evelyn in the spring of this year, (1667,) before the peace and the fall of the Chancellor, which gives a curious picture of the weak conduct of the "merry King."*

* Pepys, vol. iii. p. 201.

"Then," says he, "I took a turn with Mr. Evelyn; with whom I walked two hours, till almost one of the clock: talking of the badness of the government, where nothing but wickedness, and wicked men and women, command the King: that it is not in his nature to gainsay any thing that relates to his pleasure; that much of it arises from the sickliness of our Ministers of State, who cannot be about him as the idle companions are, and therefore he gives way to the young rogues; and then from the negligence of the clergy, that a bishop shall never be seen about him, as the King of France hath always; that the King would fain have some of the same gang to be Lord Treasurer, which would be yet worse, for now some delays are put to the getting gifts of the King, as Lady Byron, who had been, as he called it, the King's seventeenth mistress abroad, did not leave him till she had got him to give her an order for 4000*l.* worth of plate to be made for her; but by delays, thanks be to God! she died before she had it. * * * And Mr. Evelyn tells me of several of the menial servants of the court lacking bread, that have not received a farthing wages since the King's coming in. He tells me the King of France hath his mistresses, but laughs at the foolery of our King, that makes his bastards princes, and loses his revenue upon them, and makes his mistresses his masters. And the King of France did never grant Lavaliere any thing to bestow on others."—" By the way," adds Pepys, " he tells me that of all the great men of England there is none that endeavours more to raise those that he takes into favour than my Lord Arlington; and that on that score, he is much more to be made one's patron than my Lord Chancellor, (Clarendon,) who never did, nor never will do any thing, but for money."

After the fall of Clarendon, all who would obtain great places were obliged to conciliate " Bab May, my Lady Castlemaine, and that wicked crew." The King was, however, in a difficult position; his parliament had been called together, and dismissed with the greatest dissatisfaction, and the whole country was in a ferment. Everybody disliked the peace; but no one wished for the continuation of war, because they saw that it was so ill managed that it could bring nothing but disgrace. The government was deeply in debt; and the King was distressed for want of money; yet he dared not to call a parliament to vote supplies. At the same time, he loved too much his ease and his pleasures to take any decisive steps to make himself independent of his parliament, and he was continually vacillating between different counsels. Sometimes he was determined to send away Lady Castlemaine with a pension, and to conciliate the parliament; at others, his turbulent mistress hectored him into obedience to, and his heartless courtiers laughed him into acquiescence in, worse advice. The sacrifice which he pretended to make to the parliament, but which in reality arose from other feelings, the disgrace of the Lord Chancellor, only served to render himself contemptible. Yet amid all this public dissatisfaction, and much public misery, the King was still "merry." Pepys, the valuable and amusing commentator on this reign, tells us a story in September, 1667, " how merry the King and Duke of York and court were the other day, when they were abroad a-hunting. They came to Sir G. Carteret's house at Cranbourne, and there were entertain'd, and all made drunk; and being all drunk, Armerer did come to the King, and swore to him by G—, 'Sir,' says he, ' you are not so kind to the Duke of York of late as you used to be.'—' Not I ?' says the King, ' why so ?'—' Why,' says he, ' if you are, let us drink his health.'— ' Why let us,' says the King. Then he fell on his knees and drank it; and having done, the King began to drink it. ' Nay, sir,' says Armerer, ' by G—, you must do it on your knees!' So he did, and then all the company: and having done it, all fell a-crying for joy, being all maudlin and kissing one another, the King the Duke of York, and the Duke of York the King; and in such a maudlin pickle as never people were: and so passed the day."*

Up to this period, the public advisers of the King had been constantly changing for the worse; and at the time of Clarendon's impeachment, even Arlington and Coventry had fallen into some

* Pepys, vol. iii. pp. 362, 363.

disfavour, and Buckingham and Bristol, two men devoid equally of principle or ability, were his chief counsellors. Buckingham had but recently been liberated from the Tower, at the command rather than persuasion of Lady Castlemaine, who called his sacred majesty a fool; but it was no long time after this that the minister showed his gratitude, by exerting all his power against the imperious mistress; and she also fell into disfavour, though it was only to make way for a still more shameless successor.

The cabal which governed after Clarendon's fall, was composed of men entirely unfit for any other business but that of administering to the King's pleasures. The Diary of Pepys contains many sneers at the ignorance and imbecility which they exhibited in council. In proportion with the weakness of the court, the boldness and resoluteness of the House of Commons increased, and the session in which Clarendon was banished struck such a fear into all the courtiers, that they did not dare to face another for a long time, and were in continual apprehensions.* Multitudes of people, who had been the warmest advocates of the Restoration, began to regret the days of the Commonwealth, and the very members of the House of Commons, in their speeches, frequently contrasted the acts of Charles's government with those of Cromwell.†

---

* In 1668, Pepys observes, " It is pretty to see how careful these great men are to do every thing so as they may answer it to the parliament, thinking themselves safe in nothing but where the judges (with whom they often advise) do say the matter is doubtful; and so they take upon themselves then to be the chief persons to interpret what is doubtful." — Pepys, vol. iv. p. 119.

† Feb. 14, 1667-8. " Secretary Morrice did this day, in the House, when they talked of intelligence, say that he was allowed but 700*l*. a-year for intelligence: whereas, in Cromwell's time, he did allow 70,000*l*. a-year for it; and was confirmed therein by Colonell Birch, who said that thereby Cromwell carried the secrets of all the princes of Europe at his girdle."—*Pepys*, iii. 41. Feb. 17. "Great high words in the House. . . . The King's bad intelligence was mentioned, wherein they were bitter against my Lord Arlington, saying, among other things, that whatever Morrice's was, who declared he had but 750*l*. a-year allowed him for intelligence, the King paid too dear for my Lord Arlington's, in giving him 10,000*l*. and a barony for it."—iii. 42. Feb. 21. " The House this

Buckingham, now the King's favourite and chief minister, was a mad debauchee, as destitute of ability as of conduct. While Prime Minister of the crown, he had seduced the Countess of Shrewsbury, and kept her as his mistress. The earl challenged him, and each came to the field with two companions, one of whom was killed on the spot, and Shrewsbury received a wound of which he died shortly after. From this time he lived publicly with the countess. In the May of 1668, Pepys notes that " the Countesse of Shrewsbery is brought home by the Duke of Buckingham to his house; where his duchesse saying that it was not for her and the other to live together in a house, he answered, ' Why, madam, I did think so, and therefore have ordered your coach to be ready to carry you to your father's:" which was a devilish speech, but they say, true; and my Lady Shrewsbery is there, it seems." Four months after this, we have an anecdote highly characteristic of the unbounded arrogance and insolence of this minister, then in the plenitude of his power. "Buckingham now rules all; and the other day, in the King's journey he is now in, at Bagshot and that way, he caused Prince Rupert's horses to be turned out of an inne, and caused his own to be kept there, which the prince complained of to the King, and the Duke of York seconded the complaint; but the King did over-rule it for Buckingham, by which there are high displeasures among them; and Buckingham and Arlington rule all."

Amidst the senseless measures of his ministers, and the increasing indignation of his people, Charles still lived easily and "merrily" with his vicious and debasing companions. The squabbles of his mistresses caused more troubles than the dangers of the state. A ridiculous circumstance happened at court in the

day is still as backward for giving any money as ever, and do declare they will first have an account of the disposals of the last Poll-bill and eleven months' tax. And it is pretty odde, that the very first sum mentioned in the account brought in by Sir Robert Long of the disposal of the Poll-bill money, is 5000*l*. to my Lord Arlington for intelligence; which was mighty unseasonable, so soon after they had so much cried out against his want of intelligence."—Vol. iii. 46.

beginning of 1669, which caused hot blood, and raised high factions, "even to the sober engaging of great persons."—" It is about my Lady Harvy's being offended at Doll Common's acting of *Sempronia*, to imitate her; for which she got my Lord Chamberlain, (the Duke of Buckingham,) her kinsman, to imprison Doll: upon which my Lady Castlemaine made the King to release her, and to order her to act it again worse than ever, the other day, where the King himself was; and since it was acted again, and my Lady Harvy provided people to hiss her, and fling oranges at her; but it seems the heat is come to a great height, and real troubles at court about it."

The ambition of the King's ministers, and the apprehensions of future retribution for the many extravagant and criminal measures of which they had been the authors, drove them to seek gratification and safety by desperate projects. The invaluable Diary of Pepys, which throws so much light both on the temper of the people, and on the secret intrigues of the court, closes with the year 1669; but during that year we find several notices, which show that the measures which were only fully developed a few years later, had already been privately resolved. The King and his ministers had conciliated no party in the state; the latter could only escape punishment so long as they kept the power to avoid, or rather delay it, in their own hands, and there was nothing they feared so much as the meeting of parliament. On the 21st of April, Pepys observes, "Sir H. Cholmley told me that now the great design of the Duke of Buckingham is to prevent the meeting, since he cannot bring about with the King the dissolving of this parliament, that the King may not need it; and therefore my Lord St. Albans (the ambassador in France) is hourly expected, with great offers of a million of money, to buy our breach with the Dutch; and this, they do think, may tempt the King to take the money, and thereby be out of a necessity of calling the parliament again, which these people dare not suffer to meet again: but this he doubts, and so do I, that it will be the ruin of the nation if we fall out with Holland."

On the 28th of the same month, Pepys learned in conversation with the same person, " that it is brought almost to effect, the late endeavours of the Duke of York and Duchesse, the Queene-mother,* and my Lord St. Albans, together with some of the contrary faction, as my Lord Arlington, that for a sum of money we shall enter into a league with the King of France, wherein he says, my Lord Chancellor† is also concerned ; and that he believes that in the doing hereof, it is meant that he shall come in again, and that this sum of money will so help the King, as that he will not need the parliament; and that in that regard, it will be forwarded by the Duke of Buckingham and his faction, who dread the parliament. But hereby we must leave the Dutch, and that I doubt will undo us."

That Louis XIV. was at this time preparing to make Charles an instrument of his all-grasping ambition there is no doubt, and it was not many months after that a secret treaty was entered into, by which the King and his ministry hoped to make themselves independent of the parliament. Yet the only thing which Charles really gained by the alliance was a new mistress, the too celebrated Duchess of Portsmouth. Besides the prospect it afforded of the ultimate gratification of their ambition, the English courtiers seem pretty generally to have filled their pockets with French money, and a war with Holland was resolved on. The first act of hostilities was an unprovoked and disgraceful aggression on the part of the King of England. In the beginning of 1672, before any war had been commenced or proclaimed, the King sent out what can be considered as no better than a piratical expedition to seize on the Dutch Smyrna fleet, which was said to be worth a million and a half of money. The avarice of the King was excited by the richness of the prize; and so little scrupulous was he or his agents in the means they employed to effect their purpose, that the Dutch officers were invited on board the English fleet to a friendly repast,

---

* Henrietta Maria, who is said to have been secretly married to the Duke of St. Albans.

† Clarendon, who was living in banishment.

that their convoy might be seized with the less difficulty. But the latter were on their guard, the English were repulsed, and the expedition ended in nothing but disgrace. Another arbitrary measure to obtain money, the closing of the Exchequer, ruined thousands of his subjects, and destroyed entirely the confidence of the merchants and moneyed men.

"Now," says Evelyn, (a zealous royalist,) on the 12th of March, "was the first blow given by us to the Dutch convoy of the Smyrna fleete, by Sir Robert Holmes and Lord Ossorie, in which we received little, save blows and worthy reproach, for attacking our neighbours ere any war was proclaim'd; and then pretending the occasion to be, that some time before, the Merlin yacht chancing to saile thro' the whole Dutch fleete, their Admiral did not strike to that trifling vessel. Surely this was a quarrel slenderly grounded, and not becoming Christian neighbours. We are like to thrive accordingly. Lord Ossorie several times deplor'd to me his being engaged in it; he had more justice and honour than in the least to approve of it, tho' he had been over persuaded to the expedition.* There is no doubt but we should have surpriz'd this exceeding rich fleete, had not the avarice and ambition of Holmes and Sprag separated themselves, and wilfully divided our fleete, on presumption that either of them was strong enough to deale with the Dutch convoy without joyning and mutual help; but they so warmly plied our divided fleets, that whilst in conflict the merchants sailed away, and got safe into Holland.

"A few daies before this, the Treasurer of the Household, Sir Tho. Clifford, hinted to me as a confident, that his majesty would

* Evelyn has again, on another occasion, recorded the indignation of the gallant and virtuous Earl of Ossory at this action. "One thing more let me note, that he often express'd to me the abhorrence he had of that base and unworthy action which he was put upon, of engaging the Smyrna fleete in time of peace, in which tho' he behav'd himself like a greate captain, yet he told me it was the onely blot in his life, and troubled him exceedingly. Though he was commanded, and never examin'd further when he was so, yet he always spoke of it with regret and detestation."—Vol. iii. p. 31.

shut up the Exchequer, (and accordingly his majesty made use of infinite treasure there, to prepare for an intended rupture); but, says he, it will soone be open againe and every body satisfied; for this bold man, who had been the sole adviser of the King to invade that sacred stock, (tho' some pretend it was Lord Ashley's counsel, then Chancellor of the Exchequer,) was so over confident of the successe of this unworthy designe against the Smyrna merchants, as to put his majesty on an action which not onely lost the hearts of his subjects, and ruined many widows and orphans whose stocks were lent him, but the reputation of his exchequer for ever, it being before in such credit, that he might have commanded halfe the wealth of the nation.

"The credit of this bank being thus broken, did exceedingly discontent the people, and never did his majesty's affairs prosper to any purpose after it, for as it did not supply the expense of the meditated war, *so it mealted away, I know not how.*"

With the exception of Buckingham, the King's ordinary companions, such as Rochester, Killigrew, &c., were men who never troubled him with business, or meddled in it themselves, and their names seldom appear in history. Charles was a man who cared too much for his own interest to think for a moment of that of any body else, but he was too intent on his pleasures even to take the trouble to look after his interest. Hence he left all to the management of his favourites. When, however, to secure his own ease, he found it necessary to conciliate his parliament, he never scrupled a moment to sacrifice his best favourite to attain his end. The cabal which governed after Clarendon's fall, hoped to secure themselves by rendering the King absolute and independent of the parliament. It was certainly a wild scheme, and rather a dangerous one, but they trusted much in the aid of France, whom they were to appease by the sacrifice of Holland. The Dutch war was carried on with ill success on the part of England, although Louis XIV. was gaining great advantages by it. In the great naval fight of Solebay, 1672, was lost the Earl of

Sandwich; and shortly after, the want of money and the discontent
of the people, obliged the King to make a separate peace with the
Dutch, which he excused to Louis, whose pensioner he was become,
as well as he could. In the session of parliament, which was now
called together, the expression of discontent and indignation was
so unanimous and so formidable, that the King, who was now
arrived at the point where he must either be master of the parliament or give in, slunk from the struggle in defeat. The ministers
were in dismay, and began to think of saving themselves by joining
the popular party. The history of the remainder of his reign, till
the secret treaty with France, presents one series of attempts by
the King, not to awe the parliament, but to cheat it by every
species of falsehood and duplicity possible. The parliament, however, had no longer any faith in his promises; they were well
aware, that when he came to them and asked for supplies,
promising them *on his royal word and honour* that it was to support
a war against France, he was secretly making a league with
France to use the money in subverting the best interests of his own
country. Every trifling circumstance raised the suspicion of the
popular party, and new heats were blown up continually; until at
last, when his own constitution was beginning to give way by his
irregular life, and he was not able to live and enjoy the advantages
of it, he went so far as to sell the freedom of his country to the
French King for a pension, which would enable him to go on
without calling a parliament at all. The first part of Charles's
reign, which may rather be called the reign of Lady Castlemaine,
was fruitful enough in calamities to the country, when the resources
of the state were consumed in waste and debauchery; but the
reign of the Duchess of Portsmouth struck more deeply at the
roots of English liberty and independence, though happily the
folly of the court party was itself continually thwarting and
rendering inefficient the blow.

A great cause of the violent heats and factions which arose
during the latter part of Charles's reign, was the discovery that
the Duke of York and several of the ministers had turned to the

c

Catholic religion, and the not ill-founded suspicion that there was a plot to change the religion, as well as to overthrow the liberties of the country. The bloody proceedings on Titus Oates's plot are now scarcely conceivable; but if we consider the extreme apprehensions under which every body then laboured, we shall have no difficulty in accounting for their having been thus carried away by the passion of the moment. It is probable, however, that the violence of these proceedings contributed, more than any other thing, to the patience with which the nation bore the tyrannical proceedings of the court during the King's last years, and to the quiet accession of the Duke of York.

The period of arbitrary government which followed Charles's last parliament, was distinguished by a plot not much less sanguinary than that of Titus Oates's, which afforded the court a pretence for making away with some of the most influential of its opponents.

"After the Popish plot," observes Evelyn on the 28th of June, 1683,* "there was now a new, and (as they called it) a Protestant plot discover'd, that certaine lords and others should designe the assassination of the King and the Duke as they were to come from Newmarket, with a general rising of the nation, and especially of the citty of London, disaffected to the present government; upon which were committed to the Tower the Lord Russell, eldest son of the Earle of Bedford, the Earle of Essex, Mr. Algernon Sydney, son to the old Earle of Leicester, Mr. Trenchard, Hampden, Lord Howard of Escrick, and others. A proclamation was issued against my Lord Grey, the Duke of Monmouth, Sir Thomas Armstrong, and one Ferguson, who had escaped beyond sea. . .

. . . The Lords Essex and Russell were much deplor'd, few believing they had any evil intention against the King or the church; some thought they were cunningly drawn in by their enemies, for not approving some late councils and management

* Evelyn, vol. iii. pp. 85, 86.

relating to France, to popery, to the persecution of the dissenters, &c."

The pretended plot was discovered by Lord Howard, a man of no principle, who was supposed to have shared in their councils. There was no evidence of any value against them; but Jeffreys was the judge, and they were persons whom the King wished to be rid of. Essex was found in the Tower with his throat cut; Russell was first executed, and afterwards Sydney, who was convicted on his reputation of a republican, and on a piece of paper found in his study, written long before, and said to contain republican doctrines. Monmouth surrendered himself shortly after, and was persuaded by the King and the Duke of York to confess a plot before the council; on which condition he received his pardon, but he immediately made public declaration that there was no plot at all.

Most people lamented the fate of Russell and Sydney. Of the many libels against the court, composed and distributed on this occasion, the following '*new song of the times*' is a fair specimen, and is not devoid of wit.

"'Twere folly for ever
The Whigs* to endeavour
Disowning their plots, when all the world knows 'em:
Did they not fix
On a council of six,†
Appointed to govern, though nobody chose 'em?
They, that bore sway,
Knew not one who'd obey,
Did Trincalo make such a ridiculous pother?

---

* *Whig* was the term by which the party opposed to the aggressions of the court began now generally to be designated.
† The council of six were Monmouth, Russell, Essex, Howard, Sydney, and John Hampden, the latter being the grandson of the parliamentary leader.

Monmouth's the head,
To strike monarchy dead,
They chose themselves viceroys each o'er one another.

Was it not a damn'd thing,
That Russel and Hambden
Should serve all the projects of hot-headed Tony?
But much more untoward,
To appoint my Lord Howard
Of his own purse and credit to raise men and money?
Who at Knightsbridge did hide
Those *brisk boys* unspy'd,
That at Shaftesbury's whistle were ready to follow;*
But when aid he should bring,
Like a true Brentford king,
He was here with a whoop, and there with a hollo.

Algernon Sydney,
Of Commonwealth kidney,
Composed a damn'd libel, (ay, marry was it,)
Writt to occasion
Ill blood in the nation,
And therefore dispers'd it all over his closet.
It was not the writing
Was prov'd, or inditing;
And though he urg'd statutes, what was it but fooling?
Since a new trust is
Plac'd in the Chief-justice,
To damn law and reason too by over-ruling.†

And what if a traitor
In spite of the state, sir,
Should cut his own throat from one ear to the other?‡

---

* The Earl of Shaftesbury is said to have been the first instigator of the plot, but, irritated and in despair at the dilatoriness of the conspirators, to have fled to Holland, where he died. But, in remonstrating, he had previously "threatened to commence the insurrection with his friends in the city alone; and he boasted that he had ten thousand *brisk boys*, as he called them, who, on a motion of his finger, were ready to fly to arms."—*Hume.*

† Whenever the prisoners made legal objections, the plea was invariably *over-ruled* by the judge.

‡ From the extraordinary manner in which the Earl of Essex's throat was cut,

  Shall then a new freak
  Make Braddon and Speak
To be more concerned than his wife or his brother?
  A razor all bloody,
  Thrown out of a study,
Is evidence strong of his desperate guilt, sir;
  So Godfrey* when dead,
  Full of horror and dread,
Run his sword through his body up to the hilt, sir.

  All Europe together
  Can't show such a father,
So tenderly nice of his son's reputation,
  As our good King is,
  Who labours to bring his
By tricks to subscribe to a sham declaration.
  'Twas very good reason,
  To pardon his treason,
To obey (not his own, but) his brother's command, sir,
  To merit whose grace,
  He must in the first place
Confess he's dishonest under his hand, sir."

  The Rye-House conspiracy, for so this plot was called, was made to appear far more than it really was. The illegal and unjustifiable manner in which the trials of the prisoners were carried on, seems to shew that the court was aware that there was no legal evidence whatever to condemn them: people in general beheld the executions with distaste and indignation, and six years afterwards,

it was believed by many that he had been murdered. "Yet it was wondered by some," says Evelyn, "how it was possible he should do it in the manner he was found, for the wound was so deep, and wide, that being cut through the gullet, wind-pipe, and both the jugulars, it reached to the very vertebræ of the neck, so that the head held to it by a very little skin as it were; the gapping, too, of the razor, and cutting his owne fingers, was a little strange; but more, that having pass'd the jugulars, he should have strength to proceed so far, that an executioner could hardly have done more with an axe. There were odd reflections upon it." —Vol. iii. p. 87. "Two children affirmed that they heard a great noise from his window, and that they saw a hand throw out a bloody razor."—*Hume*.

 * Sir Edmondbury Godfrey, who was found murdered with his sword run through his body, at the beginning of the trials about the plot of Titus Oates.

when the bigotry and tyranny of Charles's successor had paved the way to the revolution, the judgment was reversed, and the whole declared a murder. Evelyn, who was equally bigoted in his hatred to catholics and dissenters as in his loyalty, expresses the same incredulity in the Rye-House Plot, as in that of Titus Oates. "The public," he observes on the 14th July, 1683, "was now in greater consternation on the late plot and conspiracy; his majestie very melancholy, and not stirring without double guards; all the avenues and private dores about White-hall and the Park shut up, few admitted to walke in it. The papists in the meane time very jocond, and indeede with reason, seeing their own plot brought to nothing, and turn'd to ridicule, and now a conspiracy of protestants as they call'd them."

The King lived scarcely two years after the discovery of this plot, and three after the infamous bargain with France, whereby he had sold the liberty of his country in exchange for a pension for himself. During that period, all the acts of the court were directed to the same point at which James the Second aimed more openly, the establishment of the Popish religion and arbitrary government. Charles the Second ended his reign as he began it, —a heartless libertine and a hypocrite. On the twenty-fifth of January, 1685, when he was fifty-four years old, Evelyn was at court, and, it being a Sunday, was shocked at the debauchery and profaneness which was there exhibited. "I saw this evening such a scene of profuse gaming, and the King in the midst of his three concubines (Portsmouth, Cleveland, and Mazarine,) as I had never before seen. Luxurious dallying and prophaneness." On the 6th of February the King died, in the profession of the Roman Catholic religion, to which, up to the last moment, he had made a public show of being averse.

The numerous libels published during the latter part of Charles's reign, point to the Duke of York as the chief abettor of the arbitrary and tyrannical proceedings of the court, and, to all appearance, not without good reason. In his mind, the Popish religion seems to have planted all its worst principles, without intermixing with them any of the good Christian feelings of which every sect possesses its share. On his accession to the crown, all the evil tendencies of the faith which he had embraced began to show themselves still more openly. During a reign of three years and a few months, he contrived to insult and despise every party, to interfere with every body's privileges and rights, and so entirely to lose the love of his own subjects, that when the revolution broke out, there was not a person to hold up a hand in his favour.

INTRODUCTION.

> "In days of ease, when now the weary sword
> Was sheathed, and luxury with Charles restor'd,
> In every taste of foreign courts improved,
> All by the King's example lived and loved.
> The soldier breathed the gallantries of France,
> And every flowery courtier writ romance:
> Lely on animated canvass stole
> The sleepy eye, that spoke the melting soul."—POPE.

IT is the peculiar privilege of the Portrait-painter to immortalize BEAUTY, to give duration to the most perishable of Heaven's gifts, and bestow upon the Fair "a thousand years of bloom." When the poet has done his utmost to describe the charms which kindled his fancy and inspired his song; when, in the divine spirit of his art, he has arrayed

> "The thing he doats upon with colouring
> Richer than roses, brighter than the beams
> Of the clear sun at morning;"

when he has decked out the idol of his imagination in all the pomp of words, and similes culled from whatever is sweetest and loveliest in creation—the bloom of flowers, the freshness of the dawn, the breathings of the spring, and the sparkling of the stars,—he has but given us the elements out of which we compose a Beauty, each after a fashion and fancy of our own. Painting alone can place before us the personal identity of the poet's divinity,—made such by the superstition of love. When the historian has told us that Mark Antony lost the world for a woman, and sold an empire for Cleopatra's smile, his eloquence can go no further: the record of her beauty lives upon his page,—her beauty itself only in the faith of our imagination. What would we not give to gaze indeed upon that " brow of Egypt,"—

"The love, the spell, the bane of Antony,"

such as the pencil of Arellius might have transmitted it to us!

It is true, that when the personage is purely ideal and poetical, we do not willingly part with the imaginary form which has been stamped upon our individual fancy, for any imitative semblance. We have no desire to see a portrait of the lady in *Comus*, or the Jewess Rebecca, or Gulnare, or Corinne, or Mignonne. In these and similar instances, the best of painters will scarce equal either the creation of the poet, or its vivid reflections in our own minds: but where the personage is real or historical, the feeling is reversed; we ask for truth even at the risk of disappointment, and are willing to exchange the vaguely beautiful figure which has dwelt upon our fancy, for the defined reality, however different and, in all probability, inferior.

When lingering in a gallery of pictures, with what eagerness of attention do we approach a portrait of Mary Stuart, or Lucrezia d'Este, or Tasso's Leonora! Lady Sunderland* and Lady Bridgewater might have hung and mouldered upon the walls of Blenheim, of no more regard than other dowagers of quality, if Waller had not sung the disdainful charms of the first, and Pope celebrated the eyes and the virtues of the latter. Yet, on the other hand, were it not for Vandyke and Kneller, we should scarce have sympathized in Waller's complaints of "Sacharissa's haughty scorn," or understood the influence of "Bridgewater's eyes." If the portrait sometimes derives from the poet or historian its best value, the beauty of the portrait as often makes us turn with redoubled interest to the page of the poet. After looking at the picture of Hortense Mancini in the Stafford Gallery, we take down St. Evremond with added zest: and who has not known what it is to pause before some beautiful 'portrait unknown' of Titian or

* The *elder* Lady Sunderland, Lady Dorothea Sidney.

Vandyke, with a sigh of baffled interest? calling upon our imagination to supply the lack of tradition, and asking such questions as Lord Byron asks of Cecilia Metella, with as little possibility of being satisfied,—

> "Was she chaste and fair?—
> What race of chiefs and heroes did she bear?
> What daughter of her beauties was the heir?
> How lived, how loved, how died she?"

Or, who ever gazed upon the portrait at Windsor of Venetia Digby, without a devouring but vain curiosity to pierce the mystery of her story and her fate? The silence of the grave rests upon both. A few scattered and contradictory notices, and all that painting could express of the matchless beauties of her face and form, remain to us: dust and an endless darkness have swallowed up the rest!*

"Lely alone," says Walpole, "can excuse the gallantries of Charles: he painted an apology for that Asiatic court:"—bear witness these lovely forms, which his pencil has rescued from death and fate, and preserved to us even in the loveliest looks they wore on earth:—

> "Redundant are those locks, those lips as fair,
> As when their breath enriched Thessalian air."

But, says Morality, and frowns, How is the world or posterity benefited by celebrating the charms and the errors of these fair

---

* Venetia Digby was the wife of Sir Kenelm Digby: the emblematical accompaniments of her picture cannot now be explained or understood. She was of noble—of the noblest blood: her father was a Stanley; her mother, Lady Lucy Percy: yet Aubrey calls her a *courtesan*. She married Sir Kenelm Digby while yet very young; and at the age of thirty was found dead, her head resting on her hand, in the attitude of one asleep. Some said she was poisoned by her husband through jealousy; others that her death was caused by certain medicaments and preparations he had administered to enhance the power of her charms, of which he was enamoured even to madness.

Sir Kenelm Digby was not only the handsomest man and most accomplished cavalier of his time, but a statesman, a courtier, a philosopher, and a dabbler in judicial astrology and alchymy.

pieces of sin and mischief, who ought rather to do penance with their faces to the wall, than thus boldly attempt to dazzle and blind our severer judgment by the blaze of their attractions! Or if they must needs be preserved as valuable works of art, why should we not gaze upon them merely as such? While thus they smile upon us from the almost breathing canvas, serene in their silent beauty, why should we be forced to remember that faces so fair were ever stained by passion, or clouded by grief, or wrinkled by time? If the severe historian must needs stain his page with that disgraceful era of profligacy and blood, as a record and a warning to future ages, let the poet forget it,—let the lover forget it; above all, let women forget the period which saw them degraded from objects of adoration to servants of pleasure, and gave the first blow to that chivalrous feeling with which their sex had hitherto been regarded, by levelling the distinction between the unblemished matron and her who was the "ready spoil of opportunity." Let them be the first to fling a veil over what woman should shrink to look upon, and exclaim, like Claire when she threw the pall over the perishing features of Julie,—" Maudite soit l'indigne main qui jamais soulevera ce voile!"

This would be well, if it were possible; but it is not. Of late a variety of causes have combined to fix the public attention upon the age of Charles the Second; and to render interesting every circumstance connected with his court and reign. Common gallantry requires that we should no longer suffer the Beauties of that day to be libelled by the caricature resemblances which have hitherto, by way of illustrating, deformed the editions of De Grammont; it is due to the good taste of Charles, to give him the full benefit of the excuse which Lely's pencil afforded him; and, lastly, common justice, not only to the dead, but the living, requires that the innocent should not be confounded with the guilty. Most of those who visit the Gallery of Beauties at Windsor, leave it with the impression that they have been introduced into a set of kept-mistresses. Truly, it seems hard that such women as Lady Northumberland, Miss Hamilton, Lady Ossory, whose fair reputations no slanderous wit dared to profane while living, should be condemned to posthumous dishonour, because their pictures hang in the same room with those of Middleton and Denham.

It is difficult to touch upon the female influence of Charles's reign, without being either betrayed into an unbeseeming levity, or assuming a tone of unseasonable severity: yet thus much may be said; the Memoirs, which have been collected to illustrate these beautiful Portraits, have been written without any design of raking up forgotten scandal, or varnishing over vice; and equally without any presumptuous idea of benefiting the world and posterity; but certainly not without a deep feeling of the lesson they are fitted to convey. Virtue is scarcely virtue, till it has stood the test: a woman who could pass through the ordeal of such a court as that of Charles the Second unstained in person and in reputation, may be supposed to have possessed a more than common share of innate virtue and feminine dignity; and she who stooped to folly, at least left no temptation to others to follow her example. When, from the picture of Castlemaine, in her triumphant beauty, we turn to her last years and her death, there lies in that transition a deeper moral than in twenty sermons: let woman lay it to her heart.

* * * * *

But a lighter and gayer subject demands the pen. The obvious connexion between beauty and dress, and the influence of the reigning fashions upon the style of the portrait-painter, render it necessary to say a few words of the costume of Charles the Second's time, as illustrative of the following Portraits and Memoirs.

At the period of the Restoration, and for some years afterwards, the style of dress retained something of the picturesque elegance of Charles the First's time. French fashions prevailed indeed, more or less, during the whole of the succeeding reign: French tailors, milliners, hairdressers, and tire-women were then, as now, indispensable; but it was not till a later period, after a secret and disgraceful treaty had made Charles a pensioned creature of France, that the English court became in dress and manners, a gross and caricatured copy of the court of Louis the Fourteenth. Before the introduction of perukes, men as well as women wore their hair long and curling down their shoulders: the women, in particular, had their tresses artfully arranged in elaborate ringlets, partly loose, or confined to the back of the head by jewels or knots of riband, as in the portraits of Lady Northumberland and Lady Rochester. The general effect was graceful and feminine; till, like other fashions, it was carried to an excess, and artificial curls were worn to supply the want or scarcity of natural hair. The men wore coats of cloth, velvet, or serge; and, in full dress, of gold and silver tissue, richly slashed and covered with embroidery: large bows of riband of various colours, wherever they could be placed—on the shoulders, at the breast, at the knees, at the sword-hilt, distinguished the "ruffling gallants" of the court.* The dress of the ladies was, in material, rich silk or satin, sometimes brocaded with gold and silver;† and consisted of a long boddice fitted to the shape, and cut low in the bosom, a tucker or laced chemise appearing above. This boddice was open down the front, and fastened with brooches of jewels, or knots of riband, or *crevés*, as in the portraits of the Duchess of Richmond and Lady Sunderland. The skirt was worn full with many plaits, and sufficiently short to shew the ankles: the sleeves were generally full, long, and very wide, gathered and looped up high in front with jewels; and shewing beneath a white sleeve of fine linen or cambric,

---

* Evelyn humorously alludes to this extravagant fashion. "He met," he says, "a fine thing in Westminster Hall, that had as much riband about him as would have plundered six shops, and set up twenty pedlars: a frigate, newly rigged, kept not half such a clatter in a storm as this puppet's streamers did, when the wind was in his shrouds."—*Tyrannus, or the Mode—Evelyn's Memoirs,* vol. ii.

† Pepys mentions, that his wife and Lady Castlemaine purchased a dress off the same piece of silk, for which they paid 15s. a-yard: this is, as if a lady of these days were to pay three guineas a-yard for a gown.

embroidered or trimmed with lace. This must have been rather an inconvenient fashion; but very graceful in appearance, and calculated to set off a beautiful arm to the greatest possible advantage.

The custom of patching the face prevailed about this time, and continued till the days of the *Spectator*; when, as we are told, the Tory ladies patched on one side of the face, and those of the Whig persuasion on the other; till Addison's exquisite raillery rendered both patching and party-spirit unfashionable. Shoe-buckles were now first introduced, instead of the large roses of riband formerly worn; and green stockings were affected by some of the court ladies, for reasons which politeness forbids us to mention—except in a note.* Every one who has read De Grammont, will recollect the green stockings of the beautiful Lady Chesterfield, which made the Duke of York swear so gallantly, that there was "point de salut sans des bas verts."

In 1666, the King, in order to repress the increasing luxury of dress, and, as Mr. Pepys expresses it, "to teach the nobility thrift," declared in council his design of adopting a certain habit, which he was resolved never to alter. It consisted of a long close vest of black cloth or velvet, pinked with white satin; a loose coat over it of the Polish fashion; and, instead of shoes and stockings, buskins or brodequins.† Some of the young courtiers, aware of the King's versatility, laid wagers with him that he would not

* Elle l' a (la jambe) grosse et courte, poursuivit-il, et pour diminuer ses défauts autant que cela se peut, elle ne porte presque jamais que des bas verts.— *De Grammont.*

† See Echard's History of England, vol. ii. p. 836, and Evelyn's Memoirs.

"Oct. 8th. The King hath yesterday in council declared his resolution of setting a fashion for clothes, which he will never alter; it will be a vest: I know not well how, but it will teach the nobility thrift, and will do good."

"17th. The court is all full of vests, only my Lord St. Albans (Jermyn) not pinked, but plain black; and they say the King says that the pinking upon white, makes them look too much like magpies; so hath bespoke one of plain velvet."—*Pepys' Diary,* vol. i. p. 171.

continue in this fashion beyond a certain time, which proved to be the case. "It was," says Evelyn, "a comely and a manly habit, too good to hold, it being impossible for us to leave the Monsieur's vanities long."

The use of ladies' riding-habits, or Amazonian habits as they were termed, was introduced in this reign. It was the custom for the Queen and the Maids of Honour to accompany the King in his hawking parties, mounted upon fine horses, and attended by the courtiers. To ride well, was then an admired female accomplishment; it appears that the peculiar grace with which Miss Stewart sat and managed her horse, was one of her principal attractions in the eyes of the King; and that Miss Churchill had nearly lost the heart of the Duke of York by her equestrian awkwardness.

Cocked hats, laced with gold, and trimmed with white, black, and red feathers were worn by both sexes. Pepys records his admiration of Miss Stewart in her " cocked hat and red plume," as she returned from riding. A particularly smart and knowing cock of the hat was assumed by the young gallants, called the " Monmouth cock," after the Duke of Monmouth.

In the latter part of Charles's reign, the close and disgraceful connexion between the French and English courts delivered us up to French interests, French politics, and French fashions. This was the era of those enormous perukes, which in the succeeding reigns of William and Anne attained to such a preposterous size.* Mustachios on the upper lip disappeared from court, but were not finally abolished till the succeeding reign. At this time, the exposure of the neck and shoulders was carried to such a shameless

---

* They were first worn by a Duke of Anjou, to conceal a personal deformity, and adopted by the court in compliment to him. In the same spirit, when Philip of Macedon was wounded in the forehead, all his courtiers walked about with bandages round their heads.

eme, that even women of character and reputation scarcely affected a superficial decency of attire. Painting the face, which had declined since Queen Elizabeth's time, was again introduced from France, and became a fashion. Hoods of various colours were worn, and long trains, which caused, very unreasonably, almost as much scandal as the meretricious display of the person.* Women, instead of wearing long ringlets clustering down the neck, began to frizzle up their hair like periwigs, as in the portrait of the Duchess of Portsmouth. It is remarkable, that the elevation, decline, and fall of the female coiffure, comprised exactly a century. It began to rise between 1680 and 1690; rose gradually for the next fifty years; and reached its extremest height toward the end of George the Second's reign, when it absolutely emulated the Tower of Babel: from that time it declined by slow degrees, and about the period of the French Revolution, the heads of our women began to assume their natural shape and proportion.

Other fashions and tastes of Charles's time may be dismissed in a few words. The King, from spending his youth abroad, and perhaps in earlier years from his mother, had imbibed a decided

* In the Preface to a curious religious Tract, entitled " A just and seasonable reprehension of the enormity of naked breasts and shoulders," published by a Non-conformist Divine, but translated, as the title sets forth, from the French of a grave and learned Papist, these long trains are censured, with much spiritual indignation, as " a monstrous superfluity of cloth or silk, that must be dragged after them, or carried by another, or fardelled behind them." There is an anecdote of a lady of that time, who being forbidden, by court etiquette, to bring her train-bearers into the Queen's presence, had her train made long enough to reach into the ante-chamber.

[The inconvenient fashion of long trains belonged properly to an earlier, more stiff and formal, and less civilized period. During the fourteenth, and part of the fifteenth centuries, they were most enormous, both in France, England, and Scotland, if we may judge by the paintings on the manuscripts of that period, and by the allusions by contemporary writers. The puritans, and particularly the reformers in Scotland, had too much zeal to be reasonable; and among the numerous writings of the latter which remain, we find invectives against these long trains so virulent and so gross, as is not easily to be conceived.—ED.]

partiality for the language and literature of France; and after he return to the throne, French became the fashionable language at court. The patriotic Evelyn inveighs against this innovation; and only excuses the King as having " in some sort a right to speak French, he being King of France."* There are some lines in Andrew Marvel's Works, in allusion to this fashion, so beautiful and so little known, that I cannot deny myself the pleasure of quoting them:—

> " Cœlia, whose English doth more richly flow
> Than Tagus—purer than dissolved snow,
> And sweet as are her lips that speak it, she
> Now learns the tongues of France and Italy;
> But she is Cœlia still; no other grace
> But her own smiles commend that lovely face!
> Her native beauty's not Italianated,
> Nor her chaste mind into the French translated;
> Her thoughts are English, though her speaking wit
> With other language doth them fitly fit."

Here compliment and reproof are exquisitely blended: but Dryden, in the comedy of *Marriage à-la-Mode*, has rallied the same fashion with more severity, and infinite comic humour. Melantha, the fine lady of the piece, most industriously interlards her discourse with French phraseology. " No one can be so curious of a new fashion, as she is of a new French word: she is the very mint of the nation; and, as fast as any bullion comes out of France, coins it immediately into our language."† Her waiting-maid, who is the " heir of her cast words as well as of her old clothes," and supplies her toilet every morning with a list of new French words for her daily conversation, betrays her vocabulary to her lover, who

---

* Preface to the Essay in Evelyn's Works, entitled " Tyrannus, or the Mode."
† Marriage à-la-Mode, Act i., Scene 1. In a subsequent scene Melantha thus expresses her admiration of a French, and her contempt for an English beau:—How charming is the French air! and what an *étourdi bête* is one of our untravelled Islanders! When he would make his court to me, let me die but he is just Æsop's Ass, that would imitate the courtly French in their addresses; but, instead of those, comes pawing upon me, and doing all things so *mal-a-droitly*.—Act ii., Scene 1.

us enabled to attack her with her own weapons, and wins her by out-doing her in affectation, and overpowering her with her own nonsense.* The character of Melantha in this play, or rather the admirable performance of the part by the celebrated actress, Mrs. Montfort, is considered by Cibber as a most lively and just representation of a fantastic fine lady of Charles's time. His sketch is so very amusing, and so à propos to our subject, that it is given in his own words. " Melantha," he says, " is as finished an impertinent as ever fluttered in a drawing room; and seems to contain the most complete system of female foppery that could possibly be crowded into the tortured form of a fine lady. Her language, dress, motion, manners, soul, and body are in a continual hurry to be something more than is necessary or commendable. The first ridiculous airs that break from her, are upon a gallant never seen before, who delivers her a letter from her father, recommending him to her good graces as an honourable lover. Here now, one would think, she might naturally show a little of the sex's decent reserve, though never so slightly covered. No, sir, not a tittle of it: modesty is a poor-souled country gentlewoman; she is too much a court lady to be under so vulgar a confusion. She reads the letter, therefore, with a careless dropping lip and erected brow, humming it hastily over, as if she were impatient to outgo her father's commands by making a complete conquest of him at once; and that the letter might not embarrass the attack,—crack! she crumbles it at once into her palm, and pours down on him her whole artillery of airs, eyes, and motion: down to the ground goes her dainty diving body, as if she were sinking under the weight of her own attractions; then she launches into a flood of fine language and compliment, still playing her chest forward in fifty falls and risings, like a swan upon waving water; and, to complete her impertinence, she is so rapidly fond of her own wit, that she will not give her lover leave to praise it. Silent, assenting

* In the list of Melantha's modish and new-fangled French words, the reader is surprised to find several which are now so completely naturalized, that the date of their introduction is only thus ascertained; as *figure, conversation, grimace, embarrassed, ridicule, good graces, &c.*

bows, and vain endeavours to speak, are all the share of be conversation he is admitted to; which, at last, he is removed from, by her engagement to half a score of visits, which she swims from him to make, with a promise to return in a twinkling."*

This spirited sketch is possibly dashed with some little caricature and exaggeration, but it is evidently from the life: and we are tempted here to pause, and consider the revolutions in taste and manner, and contrast the tawdry affectation, the flaunting airs, the fluttering movements, the laborious volubility,—in a word, the intolerable vulgarity of a fine lady of Charles's court, with the calm, quiet elegance, the refined and unobtrusive simplicity, which distinguish the really well-bred woman of our time. Notwithstanding what De Grammont says of the *politeness* of the English court, the general profligacy of morals was accompanied by a grossness of manners and language, in both sexes, scarcely to be credited in these days. Women of condition scrupled not to swear " good mouth-filling oaths," such as Hotspur recommended to his wife. The licence introduced and endured upon the stage, was not certainly borrowed from the French theatre; but, encouraged by the depraved taste of the King, and supported by the prostituted talents of Dryden, and the wit of Etheridge, Davenant, Killigrew, Wycherly, it spread the contagion far and wide, where the influence and example of the court could not otherwise have extended. Women of reputation and virtue, married and unmarried, frequented the theatre, which was then a favourite and fashionable place of amusement; from which, in summer, they adjourned to the Park or Spring Gardens,—the performances being over about the time they now begin. How any woman, not wholly abandoned, could sit out one of the fashionable comedies of those days, appears incomprehensible: most of them, indeed, paid so much external homage to modesty, as to appear in masks; which from the facilities they afforded to intrigue, were then a useful appendage to the female costume. To this Pope alludes:—

* Cibber's Apology, 99.

> " The fair sat panting at a courtier's play,
> And not a mask went unimproved away;
> The modest fan was lifted up no more,
> And virgins smiled at what they blushed before."

The fashionable poetry and light literature of the day, consisted chiefly of love-songs, epigrams, epistles, and satires; all tinged, more or less, with the same perverted and licentious spirit. Well might Dryden, in self-humiliation, exclaim,—

> " O gracious God! how oft have we
> Profaned thy sacred gift of poesy,
> Made prostitute and profligate the muse!"

A vicious taste for personal scandal was one of the most marked characteristics of that period. The age deserved the lash of satire; but they who coarsely satirized it, often committed " most mischievous foul sin, in chiding sin." There is, however, a wide difference between the spirit and talent of the various satirists then in vogue: some, like Marvel, Denham, and Rochester, mangled their prey like " carcases for hounds;" others, like Dryden and Butler, " carved it as a dish fit for the gods." In those days newspapers were not, as now, the vehicles for fashionable chit-chat and satire. Coffee-houses,* which had lately been established, were the resort of the gallants, the poets and wits of the times; and the usual method of circulating a court lampoon, or any piece of malicious or political wit, was by transcripts handed about in the coffee-houses, till they fell at last into the hands of some obscure printer, who loved his profit better than his ears; and by dashes and stars, (another invention of that time,) contrived at once to fix the scandal and elude the law.

The last successful play of Dryden, the last court lampoon of Dorset, or the last new love-song of Sedley, then comprised the

---

* I believe it is scarce necessary to notice, that tea, coffee, and chocolate were all introduced into England in the reign of Charles the Second; the first from Holland, the second from France, and the last from Portugal, by the Queen and her Portuguese attendants.

light reading of a fine lady. As yet novels were not: the
and prolix romances in folio of Calprenede, Scuderi, and Durfey,
—Clèlie, and the Grand Cyrus, were the only works of fiction then
fashionable; and in their pictures of pastoral purity, and exalted
love, and high-wrought tone of impossible heroism and double-
refined sentiment, formed so strong a contrast to the prevailing
manners and tastes, that one wonders how the gay gallants and
court dames of that period could ever have had patience to pore
over them: but thus it was.

Charles loved and patronised music;* and the germ of the
Italian Opera may be traced to his reign.† Killigrew, who had

* But—he neglected Purcell, and rewarded Grabut!

† [The origin of the Opera in England is a subject that has been as yet very
imperfectly known. We may, perhaps, consider as its first form the Masques
which were so common during the reigns of Elizabeth and the two first Stuarts.
However, we are certain that there was an Opera in England under the Commonwealth. Old Anthony Wood, mentioning a piece of Sir William Davenant's
which was performed at Rutland House, May 23, 1656, calls it an *Italian* Opera;
but with as little reason, apparently, as Dr. Burney had for supposing that the
name *Opera* was only applied to these performances by Wood. The piece to
which he alludes was probably the one printed the following year (1657) under
the title of " The First Dayes Entertainment at Rutland-House by Declamations
and Music; after the manner of the Antients;" in the Prologue to which it is
said, in apology for the smallness of the stage, (" our cupboard scene,")—

" Think this your passage, and the narrow way
To our Elisian field, the *Opera*."

And again, in one of the 'Declamations,'—" Poetry is the subtle engine by
which the wonderful body of the *Opera* must move." The name is here introduced as though it were by no means new. It must be confessed that this
'Entertainment' bears no great resemblance to the Operas of the present day;
but another piece, by the same author, comes somewhat nearer to our notion of
an Opera: it was printed in 1658, with the title " The Cruelty of the Spaniards
in Peru. Exprest by instrumentall and vocall Musick, and by Art of Perspective
in Scenes, &c. Represented daily at the Cockpit in Drury Lane, at three after
noone punctually."

Wood says, that the Opera went on with tolerable success for some years at
Drury Lane. Sir William Davenant afterwards obtained a patent for a theatre
in Lincoln's Inn Fields, (we believe in Great Queen-street,) where, soon after

resided some time at Venice, brought over a company of Italian singers, who sang in dialogue and recitative, with accompaniments, and excited great admiration at court. A young Italian,

the Restoration, he was busy performing his Operas, and particularly this one of the "Cruelty of the Spaniards in Peru." In a rare volume of Songs, printed in 1661, with the title "Choyce Poems, by Wits of both Universities," we find "a Ballad against the Opera," whose satire is directed against this identical piece :—

> " Now heaven preserve our realm,
> And him that sits at th' helm,
>   I will tell you of a new story,
> Of Sir William and his apes,
> With full many merry japes,
>   Much after the rate of John Dorie.
>
> This sight is to be seen
> Near the street that's called Queen,
>   And the people have call'd it the *Opera*,
> But the devil take my wife!
> If all the dayes of my life
>   I did ever see such a fopperie."

And so our satirist goes on to tell us, how one of the performers comes forward with a speech to inform his hearers of the subject of the piece, of which he declares " 'Tis two hours of I know not what."

> " Neither must I here forget
> The musick there, how it was set,
>   Dise two ayers and half and a Jove;
> All the rest was such a gig,
> Like the squeaking of a pig,
>   Or cats when they'r making their love.
>
> The next thing was the scene,
> And that, as it was layne,
>   But no man knows where, in Peru,
> With a story for the nones,
> Of raw head and bloody-bones,
>   But the devil a word that was true."

The subject of Davenant's Opera was, indeed, one by no means proper for stage representation. Among other stage directions in the printed edition, we have "Two Spaniards are discovered,—the one turning a spit, whilst the other is basting an Indian prince, which is rosted at an artificial fire." ! ! On which the writer of the song says,—

named Francesco Corbetta,* whose performance on the guitar was much admired and patronised by the King, first made that elegant instrument fashionable in England; and it became such a mania, that, either for show or use, it was as indispensable upon a lady's toilet as her rouge and patch-box. A beau of that time was little thought of, who could not write a song on his mistress, and sing it himself to his guitar. Lord Arran, a younger son of the great Duke of Ormond, was the most admired amateur performer at court; and his beautiful sister, Lady Chesterfield, gloried in possessing the finest guitar in England: but it sounded discord in the ears of her jealous lord, according to the story in De Grammont. The following passage in Pepys' Diary is characteristic of the time: he went to pay a visit of business to Lord Sandwich, on board the *Royal James*; " and there spent an hour, my lord playing on the gittarr, which he now commends above all musique in the world." Lord Sandwich was a distinguished and veteran commander, admiral of the fleet, and at this time a grandfather, or old enough to be one.

"Oh! greater cruelty yet!
Like a pig upon a spit
Here lies one, there another boyl'd to a jellie."

The Opera ended by a dance of the Indians, who had been delivered from Spanish cruelty by the bravery of the English,—

"But which was strange again,
The Indians that they had slain
Came dancing all in a troop.
But, oh! give me the last!
For as often as he past,
He still tumbled like a dog in a hoop."

English Operas were common enough during the reign of Charles II. Pepys (Jan. 12, 1667,) mentions "Signor Baptista, (Draghi,) who had proposed a play in Italian for the Opera, which Sir T. Killigrew do intend to have up."—Ed.]

* There is a print of him by Gascar with this inscription:—
"Francesco Corbetta
Famosissimo maestro di Chitarra
Qual Orfeo nel suonar ognun il narra."

INTRODUCTION. 41

Painting was neglected in this reign, except as far as it flattered and was subservient to personal vanity. Accordingly we do not find the name of a single good painter of history; while portrait-painters abounded. Those who were chiefly employed by the court, during the reign of Charles the Second, were Sir Peter Lely, Huysman, Wissing, and Sir Godfrey Kneller.

Sir Peter Lely was a native of Soest, in Westphalia, where his father, a captain of horse, was then in garrison. After studying some time under an obscure painter of the name of Grebber, he came to England in 1641. Though he painted Charles the First, a short time before his downfall,* and Cromwell more than once, it does not appear that Lely enjoyed much celebrity till after the Restoration. The gay cavaliers and beautiful women of Charles the Second's court were better suited to his taste, and more appropriate subjects for his delicate and graceful pencil than the stiff figures and stern puritanical visages of the Commonwealth. The first Duchess of York, Anne Hyde, though a fine woman, was not remarkable for her personal attractions: she was, however, content to gratify the taste of the King and her husband in this particular; and, in forming her court, after the acknowledgment of her marriage, took pains to surround herself with all that was most brilliant and fascinating in youth and beauty. Miss Jennings,† Miss Temple,‡ and Miss Hamilton, were among the most conspicuous ornaments of her court. She began the collection now known as the "Beauties of Windsor," by commanding Sir Peter Lely to paint for her the handsomest women of the time, commencing with her own lovely Maids of Honour. The success with which he executed this charming task, raised him at once to reputation and to fortune. Every woman was emulous to have her charms immortalized by his beauty-breathing pencil; and lovers and poets were, for the first time, gratified by beholding

---

* This remarkable picture is now at Sion-House.
† Afterwards Duchess of Tyrconnel.
‡ Afterwards Lady Lyttelton.

their mistresses on Lely's canvas, scarce less enchanting than they existed in their own imaginations.

Lely has been severely criticised as an abandoned mannerist; and, it must be confessed, that the languid air, the sleepy elongated eyelids, and loose fluttering draperies of his women, have given a general character to his pictures, which may be detected almost at the first glance. "Lely's nymphs," says Walpole, "are far too wanton and magnificent to be taken for any thing but Maids of Honour." In another place he says, " Sir Peter Lely's women trail fringes and embroidery through meadows and purling streams." This is surely hypercriticism; and, in fact, through the whole of his observations, Walpole seems determined to undervalue Lely in comparison with Kneller. The *clinquant* of which he accuses him, and justly, was equally the characteristic of the latter painter; and, in Lely, is redeemed by a brilliance of colouring, and a thousand graces in style and composition, which Kneller never equalled, except in one or two of his very best productions. Neither, it is true, can he compared to the great classic-painters; but some of Lely's heads are exquisite in tone of colour and expression: his airy, graceful, and floating draperies certainly bear no traces of having been trailed through purling streams; and what true judge or real lover of painting, could wish away those charming snatches of woodland landscape, those magical glimpses of sky and masses of foliage, with which he has so beautifully—so poetically relieved his female figures; or choose to substitute for these rich effects of scenery, the straight lines of architecture, or the folds of a curtain? Why may not a lovely woman be represented, without any intolerable violation of taste or probability, in a garden or a bower, as well as in a saloon at Whitehall? or seated beneath a tree, or beside a fountain, as well as before a piece of red drapery? In other respects, there can be no doubt that the manner of the painter was in a great measure caught from the prevailing manners, fashions, and character of the times in which he lived. He painted what he saw, and if he made his nymphs "wanton and magnificent," we have very good authority for believing in the accuracy of his likenesses. The loose undress in which many of his female portraits are arrayed, or rather disarrayed, came into fashion as modesty went out, and virtue was voted " une impertinence." The soft sleepy eye,—

" Seeming to shun the rudeness of men's sight,
And shedding a delicious lunar light,"

appears to have been natural to one or two distinguished beauties of the time, who led the fashion, and carried to an extreme by others, who wished to be in the mode. We are told that the lovely Mrs. Hyde* had, by long practice, subdued her glances to such a languishing tenderness, that her eyes never opened more than those of a Chinese. We may imagine the fair and indolent Middleton, the languishing Miss Boynton, or the insipid Miss Blague, " aux blondes paupières," with these drooping lids and half-shut glances; but it must have cost the imperious Castlemaine, the brilliant Jennings, and the sprightly Hamilton, no small effort to veil their sparkling orbs in compliance with the fashion, and affect an insidious leer or a drowsy languor. With them it must have been an exquisite refinement of coquetterie, a kind of *demi jour*, giving to the raised lid and full soul-beaming eye an effect like that of unexpected light—dazzling, surprising, overpowering.

Sir Peter Lely painted some history pieces, which have the same merits and defects as his portraits: the defects, however, predominate. He also drew finely in crayons: some exquisite pieces of his, in this style, are still extant. He was knighted by Charles the Second; and, like his predecessor Vandyke, married a beautiful English woman of high family: like him, too, he was remarkable for his graceful and courtier-like manners, for the splendour of his house and equipage, and for keeping a sumptuous table. He spent thirty-nine years in Engand, and during twenty he was confessedly at the head of his profession. He died suddenly in 1680, while painting that beautiful Duchess of Somerset, whose portrait is in this collection.

* Theodosia Capel, afterwards Lady Clarendon.

Wissing was a Dutch painter, who came over to England after having obtained some celebrity at the French court: he was much patronised during the short time he was here, and painted most of the royal family. The portraits of Lady Ossory and Mrs. Nott, in this collection, are by Wissing: he was especially in fashion among the ladies, for he was sure to catch the best and most advantageous expression of every face. If it happened that one of his lovely models grew pale, and looked fatigued during a long sitting, he would take her by the hand and dance her about the room, to restore bloom to her complexion and spirit to her countenance: it was a specific which never failed. Wissing died young, at Lord Exeter's seat at Burleigh. He has been celebrated by Prior.

James Huysman, or Houseman, was a native of Antwerp, who came over to England when Lely was in the zenith of his reputation, and had nearly rivalled him: and not without reason. Huysman had studied in the school of Rubens, and formed his taste and style after the model of Vandyke. Some of his pictures which I have seen, have something of the power and freedom of the latter painter, blended with the sweetness and grace of Lely. His beautiful portrait of the Duchess of Richmond, (Miss Stewart,) as a young cavalier, is at Kensington. Whether the fine picture, which hangs over the door in the Beauty Room at Windsor, be the work of Huysman or Vandyke,—whether it represent a Lady Bellasys, or a Lady Byron, are points which will be discussed and settled in their proper place.

Huysman constituted himself the Queen's painter, and made her sit for all his Madonnas and Venuses. He might have chosen a better model, and more munificent patroness: Catherine had no predilection for the fine arts. Huysman died in 1696: his death left Kneller without a rival.

Sir Godfrey Kneller was by birth a Saxon. His first success in England is connected with a very characteristic anecdote. He came to this country in 1674, without any intention of residing here, having resolved to settle at Venice, where he had already received great encouragement. Soon after his arrival, he painted the Duke of Monmouth for Secretary Vernon ; and the duke was so charmed by the resemblance, that he engaged the King, his father, to sit to the new painter. At this time Charles had promised the Duke of York his portrait by Lely; and disliking the trouble of sitting, he proposed that both the artists should paint him at the same time. Sir Peter was to choose the light and point of view he thought most advantageous; the stranger was to take the likeness as he could: he performed his task with so much expedition, that he had nearly finished his head of the King, when Lely had only just begun his. Charles was pleased: Lely generously owned the abilities of his competitor, and the justice of the resemblance; and this first success induced Kneller to settle finally in England. After the death of Sir Peter Lely, in 1680, he became the court and fashionable painter, and was for nearly fifty years without a competitor; during which time, he painted all the distinguished characters of the age, both English and foreign. William the Third knighted him, George the First made him a baronet, and Leopold created him a knight of the Roman Empire. Ten sovereigns sat to him ; but we owe him a far deeper debt of gratitude for the likenesses of Dryden, Pope, Newton, Locke, Addison, Congreve, and Wortley Montague, which his pencil has transmitted to us.

The well-known "Beauties" at Hampton Court, were painted by Sir Godfrey Kneller for William the Third. As paintings, they are decidedly inferior to the Windsor Beauties; and, with due deference to the virtues of the ladies they represent, are, as subjects, not to be compared in interest and beauty, to their naughty mammas and grandmammas of Charles the Second's time. There is a chalkiness in the flesh, and a general rawness in the tints, which will not bear a comparison with the delicacy of Lely's carnations, and the splendour of colouring in his landscapes and draperies; and they have all a look of studied stiffness and propriety, which, as it is obviously affected, is almost as bad as the voluptuous negligence of Lely's females.*

Kneller's powers as a wit almost equalled his talents as a painter, and his vanity appears to have exceeded both. Pope, who was his personal friend, and who has given him in his verses a surer immortality than the pencil ever conferred, has left us a characteristic anecdote of him: it is thus related in Spence:—" I (it is Pope who speaks) was sitting one day by Sir Godfrey Kneller, whilst he was drawing a picture: he stopped and said, ' I can't do so well as I should do, unless you flatter me a little; pray flatter me, Mr. Pope; you know I love to be flattered!' I was for once willing to try how far his vanity would carry him; and, after considering a picture he had just fin'shed for a good while very attentively, I said to him in French, (for we had been talking for some time before in that language,) 'On lit dans les Ecritures Saintes, que le bon Dieu faisait l'homme après son image; mais, je crois, s'il voudrait faire un autre à présent, qu'il le ferait après l'image que voilà.' Sir Godfrey turned round, and said very gravely, 'Vous avez raison, Monsieur Pope; par Dieu, je le crois aussi.'" The gross folly and profaneness of this answer, seem inconsistent with the wit Sir Godfrey really possessed: possibly he was playing off the poet's trick upon himself, and the reply was only ironical; for he seems, from the first part of the story, to have been quite aware of his own foible. His answer to his tailor was in better taste; the man had proposed his son to him as an apprentice, and begged he would make him a painter: " Dost thou think, man," exclaimed Sir Godfrey in a rage, " that *I* can make thy son a painter? No; only God Almighty makes painters!"†

[* Seven of the heads in the gallery of Admirals, were done by Kneller, and the portraits of the Kit-cat Club were his. Kneller had an elder brother, who was also distinguished as a painter, and is said to have studied under Bol and Rembrandt. He came to England, and died in 1702. ED.]

† Walpole.

Sir Godfrey Kneller died in 1723, and left £300 to erect a monument to himself in Westminster Abbey, which was executed by Rysbrach. Pope said the epitaph he composed for this monument was the worst thing he ever wrote,* and he was not far mistaken. The thought in the concluding lines,

> "Living, great Nature feared he might outvie
> Her works, and dying, fears herself may die,"

is borrowed from Cardinal Bembo's epitaph on Raphael in the Pantheon at Rome; but the hyperbole does not sound so ill in Latin, as in plain homely English; and is, besides, most clumsily translated. It may be added, that a compliment which, paid to the divinest of painters, was only a poetical licence, has become burlesque and absurd when applied to one so immeasurably his inferior. One would almost think, that the vanity which Pope had flattered and ridiculed when living, he meant to stigmatize on the tomb, by praise at once so affected and poor in its expression, so exaggerated and misapplied in its meaning.

It will not be out of place here to continue this slight sketch of portrait-painting and portrait-painters, as connected with female beauty and the English Court, down to our own time.

Jervas succeeded Sir Godfrey Kneller as court-painter. In spite of the poetical flattery of Pope,† who embalmed his name in

---

* "I paid Sir Godfrey Kneller a visit but two days before he died, and I think I never saw such a scene of vanity in all my life: he was lying in his bed, and contemplating the plan he had made for his own monument. He said many gross things in relation to himself, and the memory he should leave behind him; he said he should not like to lie among the *rascals* in Westminister: a memorial there would be sufficient, and desired me to write an epitaph for it. I did so afterwards; and I think it is the worst thing I ever wrote."—*Pope – in Spence.*

† Pope spared not to flatter his friend in prose as well as in verse. In one of his letters to him, he writes, "Every body here has great need of you: many faces have died for want of your pencil; and blooming ladies have withered in expecting your return." In another, he says, "I long to see you a history-

the "lucid amber of his lines," and his immense reputation when living, Jervas is now almost forgotten as a painter. His portraits being without intrinsic merit as paintings, without even the value which just likeness could give them, have long ago been banished into garrets and housekeepers' rooms, or turned with their faces to the wall, or exiled into brokers' shops, to be sold for the value of their frames. Jervas had formed his taste on two of the worst models a painter could select,—Carlo Maratti and Sir Godfrey Kneller: he contrived to exaggerate the faults of both, without possessing any of their merits; and while his success equalled that of the former, his vanity even exceeded the conceit of the latter.*

At this time also lived Dahl, a Swede by birth, who came over to England about the time of the Revolution. He was a portrait-painter of considerable merit, and patronised by William the Third, for whom he painted the Gallery of Admirals at Hampton Court. He appears, however, to have painted few female portraits; the ladies being engrossed by Kneller and Jervas.

The reigns of George the First and Second present not one name of eminence in portrait-painting: the arts had sunk to the lowest possible ebb; and the absurd and ungraceful fashions, which prevailed in dress and manners at this time, are perpetuated in the stiff, homely, insipid portraits of Richardson and Hudson. "Kneller," as Walpole pleasantly observes, "had exaggerated the curls of full-bottomed wigs, and the tiaras of ribands, lace, and hair, till he had struck out a graceful kind of unnatural grandeur." Not so his immediate successors: they, destitute of taste or imagi-

---

painter: you have already done enough for the private; do something for the public," &c. Jervas would have made a rare history-painter!—so much is there in a fashion and a name, it could dazzle even Pope.

* Jervas was supposed to have indulged a presumptuous passion for Lady Bridgewater, the loveliest of the four lovely daughters of the great Marlborough. Hence the frequent introduction of her name into Pope's Epistle to Jervas, and the exquisite character he has drawn of her: he calls her in one place, "thy Bridgewater."

nation, have either left us hideous and literal transcripts of the awkward, tight-laced, be-hooped, and be-wigged generation of belles and beaux before them; or, quitting at once all nature, grace, probability, and even possibility, have given us Arcadian shepherdesses, and Heathen goddesses, and soi-disant Greeks and Romans, where wigs and flounces, and frippery mingle with crooks, sheep, thunderbolts, and Roman draperies. But it is out of the last abasement of hopeless mediocrity, that original genius most frequently rises and soars; where there is nothing to imitate, nothing to rest upon, a reaction takes place: and while Hudson was painting insipid faces, in powdered side-curls and white satin waistcoats, the genius of Gainsborough and Sir Joshua Reynolds was preparing a new era in the history of art. Gainsborough is chiefly celebrated as a landscape-painter; yet what truth of character, what vigour of touch, what free, unmannered simplicity of style in some of his portraits!—his BLUE BOY at Grosvenor-House, for instance, equal to any thing of Sir Joshua's. But the bland and graceful pencil of the latter was calculated to please more generally, and he was soon without a competitor. If court patronage make the court-painter, Sir Joshua has little claim to the title: it was impossible to owe less than he did to *royal* favour: but if the presence of high-born loveliness in attendance upon Majesty constitute a court, he whose pencil has immortalized two generations of English beauties, may well be styled the court-painter of England. Among his pupils and successors, Hoppner imitated him, and caught something of his style and feeling: Sir Thomas Lawrence has *not* imitated him, and has inherited his genius and his fame. It is therefore easier to contrast, than to compare them. Thus, the excellencies of Sir Joshua Reynolds are more allied to the Venetian school, those of Sir Thomas Lawrence to the Flemish school. Sir Joshua reminds us more of Giorgione and Titian, Sir Thomas of Vandyke and Lely. Both are graceful; but the grace of Sir Joshua Reynolds is more poetical, that of Sir Thomas Lawrence more *spirituel;* there is more of fancy and feeling in Sir Joshua, more of high bred elegance in Sir Thomas Lawrence. The first is the sweeter colourist, the latter the more vigorous draughtsman. In the portraits of Sir Joshua there is ever a predominance of sentiment; in those of Sir Thomas a predominance of spirit. The pencil of the latter would instinctively illuminate with animation the most pensive face; and the genius of the former would throw a shade of tenderness into the countenance of a virago. Between both, what an enchanting gallery might be formed of the Beauties of George the Third's reign,—the Beauties who have been presented at St. James's during the last half century! Or, to go no further back than those painted by Lawrence, since he has been confessedly the court-painter of England—if the aërial loveliness of Lady Leicester—the splendid beauty of Mrs. Littleton—the poetical sweetness of Lady Walscourt, with "mind and music breathing from her face,"—the patrician grace of Lady Lansdowne—the pensive elegance of Mrs. Wolfe;—the more brilliant and intellectual graces of Lady Jersey,—Mrs. Hope, with eyes that anticipate a smile, and lips round which the last bon-mot seems to linger still, —the Duchess of Devonshire, the Lady Elizabeth Forster, Miss Thayer, Lady Blessington, Lady Charlotte Campbell, Mrs. Arbuthnot, &c.—if these, and a hundred other fair "stars," who each in their turn have blazed away a season on the walls of the Academy, "the cynosure of neighbouring eyes," and then set for ever to the public—if these could be taken from their scattered stations over pianos and over chimney-pieces, and assembled together for one spring in the British Gallery, an exhibition more interesting, more attractive, more dazzlingly beautiful can scarcely be imagined: but if the pride of some, and the modesty of others, would militate against such an arrangement, we know nothing that could prevent the Directors of the British Institution from gratifying the public with a regular and chronological series of British historical portraits; beginning with the age of Henry VIII. and Elizabeth, as illustrated by Hans Holbein, Antonio More, Oliver, &c., and bringing them down to the conclusion of the last century. The royal palaces, Knowle, Burleigh, Blenheim, Dunham, Hinchingbroke, Tabley, Castle-Howard, &c. contain treasures in this department, which the noble proprietors would proudly contribute:

and such a collection or selection of "gorgeous dames and statesmen old," would not only comprise many curiosities and chefs-d'œuvre of art, but form a most interesting and instructive commentary on the biography and history of our country.

The only substitute for such an exhibition is a Gallery of Engraved Portraits. This brings us back at last to the peculiar subject of this work, "THE BEAUTIES OF CHARLES'S DAYS," and the Queen leads the way, by right of etiquette and courtesy, if not by " right divine" of Beauty.

QUEEN CATHERINE

OF BRAGANZA.

QUEEN KATHERINE.—Bring me a constant woman to her husband;
One that ne'er dream'd a joy beyond his pleasure;
And to that woman, when she has done most,
Yet will I add an honour,—a great patience.
KING HENRY.   Go thy ways, Kate.
That man i' the world, who shall report he has
A better wife, let him in nought be trusted,
For speaking false in that.

CATHERINE OF BRAGANZA was the only daughter of that celebrated Duke of Braganza, who, by one of the most bloodless and most patriotic revolutions ever recorded, was placed upon the throne of Portugal in 1641, with the title of Don Juan the Fourth. Her mother, Louisa de Guzman, a daughter of the Duke of Medina Sidonia, was a woman of great beauty and spirit. On the death of her husband in 1656, she was left Regent of the kingdom; and, during the minority of her weak and worthless son, she maintained the national independence against Spain with equal ability and success.

Catherine, the eldest of her children, was born just before the Duke of Braganza's elevation to the throne. She was brought up, according to the custom of her age and country, within the strict bounds of a convent: her society confined to her confessor, and a few simple-minded, fanatic nuns; her reading, to her

Breviary and the Lives of the Saints. Such was the society and such the education from which she was called at the age of three and twenty to share the throne of England, and rule the most licentious court in Europe: a court in which her ignorance and innocence rendered her ridiculous, her religious bigotry contemptible, and her high spirit and fresh and unworn affections only made her feel more acutely the mortifications to which she was hourly exposed, both as a queen and as a woman.

The first overtures for the marriage of Charles with the Infanta of Portugal were made by the Portuguese ambassador, Don Francisco de Melo, in 1661, through the medium of the Earl of Manchester, then Lord Chamberlain. It was at first privately represented to the King, that "it was time for his majesty to think of marriage, from which he had hitherto been withheld by the extreme difficulty of finding, among the issue of the royal houses of Europe, a consort in all respects suited to him :* that there was in Portugal a princess, whose youth, beauty, and large portion, rendered her a desirable match for the King of England: she was, indeed, a Catholic, and would never forsake the religion in which she had been bred up; but she was without any meddling activity of mind, and had been educated by her mother, the Queen Regent, in total ignorance of politics and business; and being of a gentle and submissive disposition, would be satisfied with the undisturbed exercise of her own religion, without concerning herself with that of others."

Finding these representations graciously received, the ambassador proceeded, still with the utmost secrecy, to explain the offer he

* The King, guided by his mother, had early resolved not to marry a Protestant. When the matter was debated by the privy council, and some of his best friends strongly advised him to unite himself with a Protestant princess, he asked petulantly where there was a Protestant for him to marry ? Several of the German princesses were mentioned. "Odds-fish !" says the King impatiently, " they are all foggy ; I cannot like any one of them for a wife !"—*Carte's Life of Ormond.*

was authorized to make. Portugal was to pay down in ready money five hundred thousand pounds sterling, as the marriage portion of the Infanta; and to assign over to the crown of England the fortress of Tangier, on the African coast, and the island of Bombay in the East Indies, with full liberty to the English of trading to the Brazils. To the profuse and needy Charles, the offer of half a million of money, placed at his sole disposal, was a tempting consideration: the religion of the Infanta was no objection to *him*, and he hoped that the advantageous conditions annexed to the treaty would render it palatable to his people.

When it was laid before the council, Clarendon, whose influence was then at its height, eagerly supported the measure; partly from a conviction of its political utility, partly to prevent the suspicion that he had been privy to the marriage of his daughter* with the Duke of York, in the hope of her offspring succeeding to the crown: perhaps, also, he thought to make the young Queen his friend, in opposition to the mistresses and profligate courtiers, whom his natural timidity of disposition made him fear, but whom the inborn integrity of his character would not allow him to court. Supported by his credit, and the evident wishes of the King, the treaty met with no opposition from the council. The Portuguese ambassador returned to his country to make known the favourable sentiments of the King, and to bring back full powers for the ratification of the treaty: he carried with him also a letter from Charles to the Infanta, written with his majesty's own hand, in which he addressed her as his wife.

Even when matters had gone thus far, and the King's honour was in some degree pledged, the treaty was nearly broken off by the intrigues of the Earl of Bristol, who was devoted to the Spanish interest, then in direct opposition to that of Portugal. Bristol,† the most crack-brained of political profligates, whose

* Anne Hyde.
† George Digby. See more of him in the Memoir of Lady Sunderland.

inconsistency made him a by-word and a mockery, had rendered himself pleasing to the King by his convivial qualities, which were unrestrained by principle or decency, and obtained a strong influence over him by being privy to some important state secrets.* He now employed all that influence to break off the intended marriage, and was zealously supported by the ambassador of Spain, (Don Louis de Haro,) a man of high passions, and more than Spanish pride. Portugal, they insisted, was then in such a state of poverty, that all her finances were inadequate to pay the promised portion: Spain was collecting all her power to crush the family of Braganza; who, unable to cope with the immense expedition arrayed against them, would have no other resource than "that of transporting themselves and all their adherents to Brazil:"† and the ambassador added, with characteristic audacity, that "really he had too high an opinion of his majesty's good sense to believe that he would incur the resentment of Spain, by allying himself with a family and a nation of rebels."

The Earl of Bristol, who knew the King's ruling foible, drew a most odious picture of the Infanta's person, and asserted her incapacity of becoming a mother: he then reverted to the charms and accomplishments of the Italian women. His majesty, he said, had only to take his choice among the princesses of Italy; and the King of Spain would adopt her, and dower her as a daughter of Spain.

These artful suggestions had their effect upon the versatile and susceptible mind of Charles. He began to cool upon his intended marriage; and, at length, to view it even with a degree of disgust. When the Portuguese ambassador returned from Lisbon, the changes which had taken place during his short absence, and his cold reception at court, so astonished and affected him, that being

---

* It is said, that he was one of the witnesses to the King's formal abjuration of the Protestant religion.

† It is a curious coincidence, that the expedient here anticipated should have been actually resorted to within our own memory.

"something of a hypochondriac," he took to his bed, and felt or feigned sickness.*

But, just at this crisis, fortunately (or should we not rather say, *unfortunately?*) for Catherine, the levity of Bristol, and the unexampled audacity of the Spanish ambassador, defeated the effect of all their past intrigues. The latter behaved with such rash insolence, that the King, with a spirit he seldom asserted on such occasions, commanded him to depart the kingdom instantly, without seeing his face again; and sent the Secretary of State to inform him " that a complaint of his conduct would be made to the King, his master, from whom his majesty would expect that justice should be done upon him." The ambassador, full of alarm and resentment, withdrew from court, and quitted the country in a few days. The Chancellor, and others of the council, seized this moment to represent to Charles, that his honour was too far pledged to retreat. A private intimation was delivered from the French government, through the envoy Bastide, that the King could not bestow himself better in marriage than with the Infanta of Portugal, who was styled, in courtly phrase, " a lady of great beauty and admirable endowments;" offering assistance in money in case of a rupture with Spain. The King's wavering resolution was at length fixed by a sight of a miniature of the Infanta, which the Portuguese ambassador had brought with him. It represented a young person, not indeed strikingly or regularly beautiful, but whose delicate features, soft expression, clear olive complexion, and fine dark eyes, were at least attractive. The King, gazing on it with complacency, declared "*that* person could not be unhandsome," and, with little more deliberation, the famous treaty was concluded which has bound England and Portugal in strict alliance ever since.

The Earl of Sandwich was immediately despatched with a fleet to take possession of Tangier, and bring home the new

* Clarendon's Life.

Queen.* Her embarkation and arrival in England were attended by some curious circumstances, which influenced her future life. The portion of £500,000 which the Queen-mother had with difficulty

* [The circumstance of a person of so good reputation as the Earl of Sandwich having been employed on this service, might almost have been looked on as a favourable omen for the new Queen, and as a pledge that her cause, had she herself possessed the spirit to support it, would have been that of the better party, though not always the stronger party, in the state. The character of this nobleman, as left us by his contemporaries, shines much above the generality of the courtiers of the reign of Charles II. Clarendon says of him, "that he was a gentleman of so excellent a temper, that he could make himself no enemies; of so many good qualities, and so easy to live with, that he marvellously reconciled the minds of all men to him, who had not intimacy enough with him to admire his other parts; yet was, in the general inclination of men, upon some disadvantage. They who had as constantly followed the king, whilst he as constantly adhered to Cromwell, and knew not how early he entertained repentance, and with what hazards and dangers he had manifested it, did believe the King had been too prodigal in heaping honours upon him. And they who had been familiar with him, and of the same party, and thought they had been as active as he in contributing to the revolution, considered him with some anger, as one who had better luck than they without more merit, and who had made early conditions: when, in truth, no man in the kingdom had been less guilty of that address; nor did he ever contribute to any advancement to which he arrived by the least intimation or insinuation that he wished it, or that it would be acceptable to him. Yet, upon this blast, the winds rose from all quarters; reproaches of all sorts were cast upon him, and all affronts contrived for him."—*Continuation of the Life of the Earl of Clarendon*, p. 303. He fell in the famous engagement with the Dutch off Southwold Bay, 28th May, 1672, and it was observed of him, that he was always on the victorious side in the many actions in which he had been engaged, even in this in which he died. "So that," says the elegant historian of the British Peerage, "we may say of this noble earl, that as he was the chief cause of the defeat given to the Hollanders, in the first fight of the second war, so he was a principal occasion of preventing the ruin of the English and French in this remarkable engagement, which was the first of the third war." Gerard Brandt acknowledges, in his Life of De Ruyter, that the squadron of Van Ghrut entering into the action, several men of war fell upon the earl; that however he contrived to maintain himself, and give the last proofs of an unfortunate valour, till noon, when a fireship took hold of his ship. "Such," says Brandt, "was the end of this earl, who was vice-admiral of England, valiant, intelligent, prudent, civil, obliging in his words and deeds, who had performed great services to his king not only in war, but also in affairs of state, and in his embassies."—ED.]

provided, by selling her jewels and much of her plate, and borrowing the jewels and plate of several churches and monasteries, had been employed on some sudden emergency in fitting out forces against Spain, and was not forthcoming. The Queen-mother made the best apology she could for a step to which she had been driven by the cruel necessity of her situation: she proposed to put on board the fleet the amount of one-half the portion in jewels, sugar, cotton, silk, and other commodities, and pledged herself to the payment of the other half within a year. Lord Sandwich was much embarrassed; but found it necessary to acquiesce, having no instructions provided against such a dilemma: and the King, who expected the arrival of half a million in gold, with at least as much impatience as that of his bride, was equally enraged and disappointed at the non-payment. Even Catherine herself was made to feel the effects of his ill-humour on this occasion.

The other circumstance above alluded to, was more important in its effects. Though Catherine assumed state in Portugal, and held a court as Queen of England, she was suffered to embark without the performance of any of the rites of marriage, or any of the ceremonies usual among crowned heads on such occasions. The cause of this extraordinary, and even unparalleled proceeding was this:—The power of Spain at the court of Rome was so predominant, that the title of the Braganza family to the throne of Portugal had never yet been acknowledged there. Without a dispensation from the Pope, the Infanta could not be married to a heretic in her own country, and the papal dispensation, if granted at all, would have styled her simply the daughter and sister to a Duke of Braganza. Rather than submit to this apprehended insult, her proud and jealous relatives chose to trust unreservedly in the honour of England.* The fleet, with the princess and her retinue, sailed from Lisbon the 13th of April, and arrived at

---

* Secret History, vol. i. In the Stuart Papers it is said, that Catherine " would not be married by a Protestant proxy." Was she then in the secret that her husband was a Catholic?

Portsmouth the 14th of May. But though suffering severely from the effects of her voyage, Catherine remained on board till the 20th, from a point of etiquette which did not allow her to land, or be seen by any but her women, till met by the King, who was detained in London. Immediately on his arrival the marriage ceremony was performed according to the Romish rite, by the Lord Aubigny,* almoner to the Queen, in the presence of the Portuguese ambassador, and two or three of her women. They were afterwards married according to the Protestant church, by Dr. Sheldon, bishop of London: but, on this occasion, Catherine, as simple-minded as bigoted, refused to repeat the words of the ritual, turned away her head poutingly, and would not even look the bishop in the face. She insisted, however, on his solemnly pronouncing her the *wife* of the King before he quitted her chamber.†

This hasty and imperfect marriage was subsequently the occasion of much scandal, and tended to embitter the after-life of Catherine. Many affected to regard it as a mere contract, not binding upon the King; and even to found on it additional reasons for the divorce, which, in 1669, was seriously agitated; and would probably have been carried into effect upon slighter grounds, if Charles had resembled his bluff ancestor Harry the Eighth.

It does not appear that the King was disappointed in the person

---

* Brother to the Duke of Richmond.

† [The Earl of Sandwich gave the following account of the manner of the Protestant marriage:—" May 21, 1662, in the afternoon the King and Queen came into the presence-chamber (at Portsmouth) upon the throne, and the contract formerly made with the Portuguese ambassador was read in English by Sir John Nicholas, in Portuguese by the Portuguese secretary De Saire; after which, the King took the Queen by the hand, and (*as I think*) said the words of matrimony appointed in the Common-Prayer, the Queen also declaring her consent. Then the bishop of London (Sheldon) stood forth, and made the declaration of matrimony in the Common-Prayer, in the name of the Father, Son, and Holy Ghost."—*Kraket's Chronicle*. See Harris's Life of Charles the Second, 2 vols. 8vo. 1757.—ED.]

of his young Queen;* in a letter to Lord Clarendon, dated from Portsmouth, he expresses his satisfaction in strong terms;† and Clarendon says, "it is certain she had wit and beauty enough to have pleased the King, if bigotry and an ill education had not spoiled her." Pepys, describing her in his Diary, says, "For the Queen, though she be not a very charming, yet hath she a good, modest, and innocent look, which is most pleasing." Catherine's defects seem to have been those of manner, rather than person; her disposition was not sprightly, nor her deportment dignified. It would be unjust to attribute the moody pettishness and melancholy, which she betrayed soon after her marriage, to a natural gloominess of disposition; for it only proved that she was not absolutely insensible. Charles, whose powers of captivation few women could withstand, had, in the commencement of their intercourse, won her whole affections; and she could not see herself neglected by her husband, and brow-beat by insolent rivals, without the discontent and anger natural to a fond, jealous, and high-spirited woman.

When Catherine first arrived in England, she was dressed after the antiquated fashion of Portugal, in a high boddice, ruff, and

---

* "The Queen is brought a few days since to Hampton Court, and all people do say of her to be a very fine and handsome lady, and very discreet, and that the King is pleased enough with her, which, I fear, will put Madam Castlemaine's nose out of joynt."—*Pepys' Diary.*

"Portsmouth, 21 May, 8 in the Morning.

† "I arrived here yesterday, about two in the afternoon; and as soon as I had shifted myself, I went to my wife's chamber. * * * * * Her face is not so exact as to be called a beauty, though her eyes are excellent good, and not any thing in her face that in the least degree can shock me. On the contrary, she has as much agreeableness in her looks, altogether, as ever I saw; and if I have any skill in physiognomy, which I think I have, she must be as good a woman as ever was born. Her conversation, as much as I can perceive, is very good; for she has wit enough, and a most agreeable voice. You would much wonder to see how well we are acquainted already. In a word, I think myself very happy; but I am confident our two humours will agree very well together. I have not time to say any more. My Lord-Lieutenant will give you an account of the rest."

farthingale, which excited some insolent merriment in her new court, and which the King *obliged* her to alter.* She had brought with her from Lisbon a bevy of Portuguese attendants, of whom De Grammont has left us a ludicrous description. Six "monsters," alias Maids of Honour, ruffed and farthingaled like their mistress surrounded her person: they were governed by an old duenna (or *guarda damas*,) more hideous than all her damsels, as stiff as pride and buckram could make her, with, we may suppose, double solemnity of ruff, and treble expansion of farthingale. Besides these, Catherine had in her retinue six almoners, a confessor, a Jewish perfumer, and an officer, whose function seems to have puzzled the whole court, entitled the "Queen's barber." These foreigners, by their ignorance, bigotry, and officiousness, caused as much confusion as the French attendants of her predecessor, Henrietta Maria; and Charles soon followed the example of his father, by shipping the whole cargo back to their own country, and surrounded the Queen with creatures of his own.† In the list of her new attendants laid before Catherine for her approbation, Charles had the effrontery to include Lady Castlemaine, his acknowledged mistress. Catherine instantly drew her pen across the name, and when the King insisted, she replied haughtily, "that she would return to her own country, rather than be forced to submit to such an indignity." Her spirit however availed her

---

* There is a fine print of the Queen in her Portuguese costume by Faithorne; in which her hair is dressed out like a full-bottomed wig. Catherine was very reluctant to change her style of dress: her Portuguese attendants had endeavoured to persuade her that she should neither learn the English language, nor use their habit; which they told her would be for the dignity of Portugal, and would quickly induce the English ladies to conform to her majesty's practice. The result, however, was just the reverse. Evelyn speaks of the excessive ugliness and "monstrous fardingals" of the Portuguese women: and Pepys (who was very sensitive to personal appearance) seems to have been horrified both by their hideous persons and dresses.

† The Countess of Penalva, "by reason of the Queen's tender attachment to her, and her own infirmities, was suffered to remain on the Queen's earnest entreaty, that she might not be left wholly in the hands of strangers."—See Clarendon.

little: Charles, spurred on by the female fury who governed him, was steady to his cruel purpose. On one particular occasion, when the Queen held what we should now call a Drawing-room, at Hampton Court, Lady Castlemaine was introduced in form by the King. Catherine, who did not know her, and heard the name imperfectly, received her with as much grace and benignity as the rest:—but in the next moment, recollecting herself, and aware of the public insult which had been offered to her, all her passions were roused: she started from her chair, turned as pale as ashes; then red with shame and anger; the blood gushed from her nose, and she swooned in the arms of her women. The court was immediately broken up: but Charles, though probably touched with some compunction, had been persuaded by some of the profligates about his person, that the Queen wished to govern him; that his dignity and authority would be compromised if he gave up the point; and fancying he was imitating his model, Louis Quatorze, by forcing his Queen to acquiesce in her own dishonour. Lord Clarendon, during this degrading contest between the wife and the mistress, had vainly opposed the King's intention; and at length, in disgust, absented himself from court: upon which the King wrote to him a letter of which the following is an extract:—

"I wish I may be unhappy in this world, and in the world to come, if I fail in the least degree of what I have resolved, which is of making my Lady Castlemaine of my wife's bed-chamber; and whosoever I find use any endeavours to hinder this resolution of mine, except it be only to myself, I will be his enemy to the last moment of my life. You know how true a friend I have been to you. If you will oblige me eternally, make this business as easy to me as you can, what opinion soever you are of; for I am resolved to go through this matter, let what will come on it, which again I swear before Almighty God: therefore, if you desire to have the continuance of my friendship, meddle no more with this business, except it be to beat down all false and scandalous reports, and to facilitate what I am sure my honour is so much concerned in; and whosoever I find to be my Lady Castlemaine's enemy in the matter, I do promise upon my word to be his enemy as long as I live."

Whatever may be thought of the style and reasoning of this notable epistle, it had its effect. Lord Clarendon labours to excuse the part he took in this wretched business, of which he has given us a very particular account: but it must be allowed that it ill became the gravity of his place and character to stoop to be the King's instrument on such an occasion. He allows that, after having represented to Charles "the hard-heartedness and cruelty of laying such a command upon the Queen, which flesh and blood could not comply with;" and reminded him of the difference, in this respect, between the French and English courts; "that in the former, such connections were not new and scandalous, whereas in England they were so unheard of, and so odious, that the mistress of the King was infamous to all women of honour;"* he yet undertook to persuade the Queen to bear this indignity, which was "more than flesh and blood could comply with," and to receive into her society—nay, into an office of honour and trust about her person, a female held "infamous by all women of honour," and whom he would never suffer his own wife to visit.

When the Chancellor first addressed himself to the Queen upon this delicate subject, she broke out into such a passion of grief and indignation, that he was obliged to quit her. The next day she asked his pardon "for giving vent to the passion that was ready to break her heart;" and desired his advice, and to hear the truth with all freedom. He began by excusing the King: he told her "he doubted she was little beholden to her education, that had

* Charles the First and James the First were models of conjugal fidelity; and Henry the Eighth never thought of any other resource in his amours, but the desperate one of divorcing, or cutting off the head of one Queen to marry another.

given her no better information of the follies and iniquities of mankind, of which he presumed the climate whence she came could have given her more instances than this cold region would afford (*though at that time it was indeed very hot*): and if her majesty had been fairly dealt with in that particular, she could never have thought herself so miserable, and her condition so insupportable, as she seemed to think; the ground of which heavy complaint he could not comprehend." The poor Queen, with many blushes and tears, acknowledged that " she did not think she should have found the King's affections engaged to another lady ;" and then she stopped abruptly, unable from the excess of her emotion to say more. The Chancellor continued the conference with true diplomatic art; paid her some compliments, and assured her, that if she made use of her own powers of charming, she need fear no rivals. He ventured to ask her, " whether, if it should please God to give a Queen to Portugal, she would find that court so full of chaste affections?" and this allusion to the notorious gallantry of her brother Alphonso, made the Queen smile. But, when he touched upon the hated point of contention, and named Lady Castlemaine, it called forth all the rage and fury of yesterday, with " fewer tears and more fire ;" and she declared with passionate vehemence, that rather than submit, she would embark for Lisbon in " any little vessel."

"That night," adds Lord Clarendon, " the fire flamed higher than ever. The King reproached the Queen with stubbornness and want of duty; she him with tyranny and want of affection." The next day, they neither spoke nor looked at each other. The Queen sat " melancholick in her chamber, all in tears." The King sought his diversions elsewhere; never, however, sleeping out of his own apartment. After a few days, the Chancellor again waited on the Queen by the King's command; but with no better success than is usual with those who interfere in matrimonial squabbles. After exhausting all his arts of diplomacy, and employing such arguments as would have come better from any other lips than those of " my grave Lord Keeper," he could not, though the Queen listened to him with edifying patience, draw from her any other reply than "that the King might do as he pleased, but that she never would consent to it." The Lord Chancellor at length withdrew himself from a contest, in which he had cut such a sorry figure, making it his humble suit to the King, that he might no more be consulted nor employed in an affair, in which he had been so unsuccessful; at the same time, advising him strongly to desist from an intention at once cruel and unjust.

But Charles had not studied women to so little purpose: he knew there is one method of crushing down a female heart that never fails: and better than the Chancellor he knew, that possessing his wife's unbounded affection while he cared not for her, he had the game in his own hands: and well he understood how to play it effectually. He no longer insisted, or met violence with violence; but he treated Catherine with a cold and scornful neglect, assuming to others a more than usual gaiety and complacency of manner. She was left out in all the mirth and parties of pleasure going forward. Charles studiously proved to her that his happiness in no respect depended on her, nor on her acquiescence in his wishes. The courtiers, having their cue from their master, forsook her to crowd round Lady Castlemaine; and she was reduced to a mere cypher in her own court. It was too much to bear: Catherine had strong passions, but no real strength and magnanimity of character: after a short struggle, in which her pride, her spirits, her heart, were broken down and subdued by continued mortifications, she yielded,—and gained nothing by the concession, but the contempt and mistrust of those who had hitherto pitied her ill usage, honoured her firmness, and confided in her principles.[*] Even the King, who had affected throughout more displeasure than he really felt, and could not but respect the cause from which her opposition sprung, now contemned her for her weak submission, and imputed her former resistance to pride and petulance, rather than to affection and female dignity.

[*] Clarendon's Life, folio, pp. 169, 180.

In the month of August following her marriage, Catherine was induced to receive Lady Castlemaine as one of the ladies of her bed-chamber, and to allow her all the honours and privileges attending that office.* It happened, on one occasion, that Lady Castlemaine came into the Queen's closet, while she was under the hands of her dresser: "I wonder," said she insolently, "your majesty can have patience to sit so long a dressing!" "I have so much reason to use patience," replied the Queen, pointedly, "that I can very well bear it!" This was the retort courteous, such as became a Queen: but Lady Castlemaine was not one to be easily abashed by a repartee.

From this time we do not hear of any open misunderstanding between the King and Queen. Charles, who was good-humoured and polite, treated his wife with an easy complaisance, which, without satisfying her tenderness, left her nothing to complain of. She even assumed a gaiety of manner which she thought would be agreeable to the King, and encouraged the festivities, the masques, and banquets in which she knew he delighted: but this struggle to subdue herself, the continued indifference of her husband, the presence of more than one insolent favourite, who braved her in her own court,—above all, her excessive anxiety to have children, which was increased by the prevalent belief that she was incapable of producing heirs to the crown, seem to have preyed upon her mind, and, at length, threw her into a dangerous fever, in which she was twice given over by the court physicians.† In her delirium she raved in the most affecting manner of *her children*, fancying she had three; "but was troubled lest her boy should be but an ugly boy; upon which the King, who was present, in order to soothe her, said, 'No, he was a very pretty boy.'—' Nay,' replied the poor Queen, distractedly, 'if he be like you, he is a very

* "They went away—the King and his Queen, and my Lady Castlemaine and young Crofts (the Duke of Monmouth) *in one coach*, and the rest in other coaches."—*Pepys' Diary.*

† In October, 1663.

pretty boy indeed, and I would be very well pleased with it.' "*
In one of her lucid intervals she expressed a thankful sense of the
King's affectionate attentions, which, indeed, ceased not during her
illness; and told him that the sight of his affliction would have
made her regret life, but for the conviction that she had never
possessed his love; and that in dying, she should make room for a
successor more worthy of him, and to whom Heaven would perhaps
grant the blessing denied to her: and taking his hand while she
spoke, she bathed it with tears. The King, who was naturally
soft-tempered, was utterly subdued; he wept and entreated her to
live for his sake. His endearing expressions had more effect than
all the prescriptions and cordials of Dr. Prujeon, and it was
believed at that time were the real cause of her recovery: at all
events, her disorder from that moment took a favourable turn, and
she was shortly afterwards pronounced out of danger. An incident
so romantic, and so well known, was not likely to be passed over
in silence by the poets in those days. Waller, the prince of courtly
rhymsters, has made the best use of it, in his Address to the Queen
on her Birth-day, soon after her recovery: it is not the happiest of
his occasional pieces, but the concluding lines are not without
elegance:

> "He that was never known to mourn
> So many kingdoms from him torn,
> His tears reserved for you, more dear,
> More prized, than all those kingdoms were;
> For when no healing art avail'd,
> When cordials and elixirs fail'd,
> On your pale cheek he dropp'd the shower,
> Revived you like a dying flower."

There are some other trifling pieces among Waller's Miscellanies,
in which Catherine is flattered with much courtly *savoir faire*.

---

* *Pepys' Diary*, vol. i. 255, 256.—"This morning, about five o'clock, the
physician feeling the Queen's pulse, thinking to be better able to judge, she being
still and asleep, waked her; and the first word she said was, "How are the
children?"—Poor Queen!

The little poem of "Tea commended by her Majesty," is one of the best. There is also an epigram, not very pointed or significant, "Upon a Card which her Majesty tore at Ombre,"—whether in petulance or playfulness, we are not told.

The remainder of Catherine's life affords little to interest. She not only never interfered in politics, but did not even attempt to serve or countenance those who were inclined to be her friends; and who, by rallying round her, might have formed a counterpoise to the party of Lady Castlemaine. Lord Sandwich, who brought her over from Portugal, and at first attached himself to her, gave as a reason for his dereliction, that he did not choose "to fall for her sake, whose wit, management, or interest, was not likely to hold up any man." It was, indeed, sufficient for her to distinguish any of the courtiers in particular, to mark them at once as objects of the King's displeasure. Thus, young Edward Montagu, the son of Lord Manchester, was disgraced and turned out of the court, for no other fault than the pride he took in the Queen's favour. Not that Charles either valued her affections or doubted her discretion; but merely from a love of contradiction, a petty jealousy of power, or a fear of the raillery of such profligates as Rochester, Buckingham, and Killigrew, his "all-licensed jester." But Catherine allowed him few opportunities of thus mortifying her.

After having suffered in the first years of her marriage from every passion that could distract a female mind, she appears to have been at length wearied into perfect indifference; and not only endured her husband's licentious conduct with equanimity,* but even took pains to reconcile him, on some notable occasions, with his perverse and capricious mistresses. She endeavoured to please the King, by encouraging every species of dissipation and

* "Mr. Pierce told me, that the good Queene will, of herself, stop before she goes sometimes into her dressing-room, till she knows whether the King be there, for fear he should be, as she hath sometimes taken him, with Miss Stewart."— *Pepys' Diary*, vol. i. p. 277.

gaiety; and even entered into the extravagant masquerading frolics, then so fashionable, with more spirit than success.* "Once," says Burnet, "the Queen's chairman, not knowing who she was, went from her; so she was alone, and much disturbed, and came to Whitehall in a hackney-coach, some say in a cart."

Another of Catherine's masquerading whims is recorded in Ives's Select Papers. There being a fair at Audley-End, where the court then was, the Queen, the Duchess of Richmond, (Miss Stewart,) and the Duchess of Buckingham, disguised themselves as country lasses, in red petticoats, &c. &c., and so went to see the fair; Sir Bernard Gascoigne riding before the Queen on a sorry cart-horse. But they had so caricatured their disguises that they "looked more like antiques than country-folk," and the country people began to gather round them :—" The Queen going into a booth to buy a pair of garters for her sweete harte, and Sir Bernard asking for a pair of gloves stitched with blue for his sweete harte, they were betrayed by their gebrish and their exaggerated rusticity; and the Queen being recognised, the whole fair flocked about them. They at length got to their horses; but as many of the fair as had horses got up with their wives, children, neighbours, and sweete hartes behind them, to get as much gape as they could, 'till they brought them to the court-gate. Thus, by ill conduct, was a merrie frolic turned into a penance."

It should be observed, that nothing worse than frolic was ever imputed to Queen Catherine, even by the scandalous court in which she lived. Buckingham, who offered to carry her off to the Plantations, out of the King's way, to give colour to a divorce and make room for Miss Stewart, would not have spared her fair fame, had it not been unimpeachable. The King rejected this idea with horror, saying, " it was a wicked thing to make a poor lady

---

* " In the hall, to-day, Dr. Pierce (one of the court physicians) tells me that the Queene begins to be briske and play like other ladies, and is quite another woman from what she was. It may be, it may make the King like her better," &c.—*Pepys' Diary*, vol. i. p. 225.

miserable, only because she was his wife and had no children, which was not her fault." In that age, when satire was "worn to rags and scribbled out of fashion," she did not wholly escape the "fangs of malice;" but the most coarse and violent lampoons of which she was the subject, could not attack her on any other score than her popish education, and her inordinate passion for dancing.*

When the question of a divorce was afterwards more seriously debated, and even some preliminary steps taken in the House of

---

* It seems incredible how a woman, who did not aspire beyond the passive, insignificant, inoffensive part Catherine was content to play in her own court, could ever have provoked the grossness and bitterness of invective which appears in some of these productions. One entitled "The Queen's Ball," which was several times reprinted, and widely circulated, begins thus:—

> "Reform, great Queen! the errors of your youth,
> And hear a thing you never heard, called Truth!
> Poor *private* balls content the Fairy Queen;
> You must dance (and dance damnably) to be seen,
> Ill-natured little goblin! and designed
> For nothing but to dance and vex mankind!
> What wiser thing could our great monarch do,
> Than root ambition out by showing you?
> You can the most aspiring thoughts pull down;
> For who would have his wife to have his crown?"

The next lines seem to refer to some particular trick, or habit, which Catherine had of holding jewels in her mouth:—

> "See in her mouth a sparkling diamond shine;—
> The first good thing that e'er came from that mine.
> Heaven some great curse upon that hand dispense,
> That for the increase of nonsense takes it thence."

After a great deal in the same strain, this polite effusion concludes:—

> "What will be next, unless you please to go
> And dance among your fellow-fiends below!
> There, as upon the Stygian lake you float,
> You may o'erset and sink the laden boat;
> While we the funeral rites devoutly pay,
> And dance for joy that you are danced away!"

Lords,* and Dr. Burnet employed to write in favour of it; the King then said publicly, "that if his conscience would allow him to divorce the Queen, it would suffer him to dispatch her out of the world;"† and Buckingham, and his worthy coadjutor, Lord Bristol, found themselves opposed in a quarter where they certainly little expected opposition. Affection for his brother might possibly have influenced Charles in this instance, as well as justice to his Queen.

In the same year, 1668, the elder brother of Catherine, Don Alphonso VI., a contemptible and dissolute monarch, was deposed by his Queen and council, and his brother, Don Pedro, a man of courage and talent, placed upon the throne of Portugal. This revolution in no other respects affected the situation or happiness of the Queen of England, than as it probably furnished an additional reason against the meditated divorce. Some attempts were made, on the King's part, to induce her to go into a nunnery of her own free will; but, with all her bigotry, she had no vocation that way.‡

In 1679, during the sanguinary farce of the Popish Plot, the wretches Oates and Bedloe accused the Queen of being privy to the pretended conspiracy against her husband's life. Animated by a belief that this would be agreeable to the King, Oates had the boldness, at the bar of the House of Commons, to utter these words in his affected phraseology:—"Aye, Taitus Oates, accuuse

---

* In the divorce-bill of Lord Roos, afterwards Earl of Rutland, which was passed through the House to serve as a precedent.

[It is curious that the Duke of Buckingham opposed somewhat violently the progress of this bill, and only desisted after concessions had been made to him by Lord Roos. The lady was first cousin to the Duchess of Cleveland.—ED.]

† James II.—*Vide* "Stuart Papers."

‡ "This being St. Catherine's day, the Queene was at masse by seven o'clock this morning; and Mr Ashburnham (groom of the bedchamber) do say, that he never saw any one have so much zeale in his life as she hath; and (the question being asked by my Lady Carteret) much beyond the bigotry that ever the old Queene-mother had."—*Pepys.*

Catherine, Queen of England, of Haigh Traison!" The grounds of his accusation are stated in the trial of Wakeman, the Queen's physician; who, he alleged, was bribed with £15,000 to poison the King, in case he should escape the poniard of a Jesuit named Coniers, and the pistols of Pickering and Groves. Oates then swore, "that three Jesuits carried him with them to Somerset-House, where they were summoned to attend the Queen; that he remained in an anti-chamber, when they were ushered into her presence; that he heard a female voice say, that she would assist Sir George Wakeman in his project, and would no longer bear these repeated violations of her bed. When the fathers came out, he desired to see the Queen; and when admitted into the anti-chamber, whence the female voice had proceeded, he saw the Queen, who smiled graciously on him, and there was no other woman present." These impudent stories, with some blunders into which the best-breathed witness may fall, saved Sir George Wakeman's life.*

In the commencement of this affair the Commons, maddened with rage and terror, sent up a petition to the King to have the Queen removed from Whitehall, and her household arrested, or dispatched out of the country; and Charles had now an opportunity of ridding himself legally of a wife he had never loved. Such a measure, though it would have consigned him to the abhorrence of posterity, would at the moment have been in the highest degree popular; but, shocked at the audacity of such a monstrous fabrication, and touched with pity for his defenceless and inoffensive Queen, he crushed the accusation at once, observing to those about him, "They think I have a mind for a new wife; but, for all that, I will not stand by and see an innocent woman abused."

In February 1685, the King was seized with apoplexy, and the Queen hearing of his danger, but that he was still sensible, sent an earnest request to be admitted into his presence, at the same

---

* See Dryden's Works (Sir Walter Scott's Ed.) vol. ix. p. 204.

time entreating his forgiveness for any offences she might have ignorantly committed. Charles refused to see her, but sent her a message, couched in the most affectionate terms, assuring her he had nothing to forgive, but requesting her pardon for the many wrongs he had done her. At this time the Duchess of Portsmouth was seated by his pillow, and she took care that none should approach whose interests were likely to counteract her own. The King, after lingering a few days, died in her arms—a hypocrite to the last. It is remarkable, that Charles II., with all his popular qualities, so beloved, so regretted by the nation he had sold, cheated, impoverished, misgoverned, and enslaved, possessed not one personal friend: and the disgusting negligence with which his last remains were treated, strengthened the false report that he had been poisoned.* He captivated all who approached him occasionally by his amiable manners; but only those who were at a distance were deceived by his hollow and heartless courtesy. One by one, the faithful adherents of his family withdrew in disgrace or in despair; and he who professedly mocked at the existence of virtue and disinterested attachment, and classed all mankind into knaves and fools, died, as he deserved, without a friend.

On the King's death, Catherine made a very decent display of grief, and received the visits of condolence in a chamber lighted with tapers, and hung with funereal black from the ceiling to the floor.† She afterwards resided at Somerset-House, as Queen-dowager, and had a villa at Hammersmith, where she spent the summer months very privately. Her principal diversion during her widowhood was music, which she had always loved. She had

---

* See Burnet.

† Dryden, in his Monody on the death of Charles II., had the good taste to refrain from any mention of the Queen, "sensible that her grief would be an apocryphal, as well as delicate theme." Otway and others had not this forbearance. In one of these poetical "addresses of condolence," the grief of the Queen for the loss of her royal consort is compared to that of the Blessed Virgin!

concerts regularly, and on a splendid scale: in all other respects she lived with rigid economy. She was much respected by James II. and his court. In 1092 she returned to Lisbon, carrying with her (according to Walpole) some valuable pictures out of the royal collection, as part payment of a debt she asserted to be due to her from the crown; and died there December 30, 1705, at the age of sixty-three.

The picture at Windsor, from which the accompanying portrait is for the first time engraved, is by Sir Peter Lely. In every part, but more especially the drapery, it is admirably painted. She is represented as seated in a chair of state, and dressed in pearls and white satin, relieved by a dark olive curtain in the background. The attitude is rather unmeaning and undignified, but is probably characteristic. The face is round, the nose a little turned up; the eyes black and languishing; the mouth, though far from ugly, has an expression of pouting melancholy. This portrait appears to have been taken within the two first years after her marriage, while yet she loved her husband, and deeply resented those infidelities and negligences which she afterwards bore with such exemplary patience.

[To the foregoing elegant sketch of the life of the Queen of Charles the Second, we are tempted to append a somewhat long extract from Clarendon, which shows how much she lost in the esteem of her friends by the ease with which she yielded and reconciled herself to her husband's mistresses. We think we see a concealed sneer in the following extract from the "Chimney Scuffle," a satire printed in 1662, and therefore not long after the marriage, and soon after the first quarrel between the royal pair, and the subsequent condescensions of the Queen to Lady Castlemaine, on whose name it contains a rather poor pun:—

"Clear that Augean stable; let no stain
Darken the splendor of our Charlemain,

> Nor his court gate: may th' ladies of this time
> Be emulators of our Katherine,
> Late come, long wish'd:——
>
> The world's new moulded: she who t'other day
> Could chant and chirp like any bird in May,
> Stor'd with caresses of the dearest sort
> That art could purchase from a foreign court,
> Limn'd so by Nature's pencil, as no part
> But gave a wound, where'er it found an heart
> ' A fortress and *main castle* of defence
> Secur'd from all assailants saving Sense.'
>
> But she's a convert and a mirrour now,
> Both in her carriage and profession too;
> Divorc'd from strange embraces: as my pen
> May justly style her England's Magdalen.
> Wherein she's to be held of more esteem
> In being fam'd a convert of the Queen.
> And from relapse that she secur'd might be,
> She wisely daigns to keep her companie."

After relating the circumstance of Catherine's first introduction to Lady Castlemaine, the affronts and mortifications to which she was subjected by her opposition to the King's will, and particularly the abrupt dismissal of her Portuguese attendants, Lord Clarendon goes on to observe,—" At last, when it was least expected or suspected, the Queen, on a sudden, let herself fall first to conversation and then to familiarity, and, even in the same instant, to a confidence with the lady; was merry with her in publick, talked kindly of her, and in private nobody used more friendly. This excess of condescension, without any provocation or invitation, except by multiplication of injuries and neglect, and after all friendships were renewed, and indulgence yielded to new liberty, did the Queen less good than her former resoluteness had done. Very many looked upon her with much compassion; commended the greatness of her spirit, detested the barbarity of the affronts she underwent, and censured them as loudly as they durst, not without assuming the liberty, sometimes, of insinuating to the King himself, how much his own honour suffered in the neglect and disrespect of her own servants, who ought, at least in publick, to manifest some duty and reverence towards her majesty; and how much he lost in the general affections of his subjects: and that, besides the displeasure of God Almighty, he could not reasonably hope for children by the Queen, which was the great if not the only blessing of which he stood in need, whilst her heart was so full of grief, and whilst she was continually exercised with such insupportable afflictions. And many, who were not wholly unconversant with the King, nor strangers to his temper and constitution, did believe that he grew weary of the struggle, and even ready to avoid the scandal that was so notorious, by the lady's withdrawing from the verge of the court, and being no longer seen there, how firmly soever the friendship might be established. But this sudden downfall, and total abandoning her own greatness; this low demeanour, and even application to a person she had justly abhorred and worthily contemned, made all men conclude, that it was a hard matter to know her and, consequently, to serve her. And the King himself was so far from being reconciled by it, that the esteem which he could not hitherto but retain in heart for her, grew much less. He concluded that, all her former aversion, expressed in those lively passions which seemed not capable of dissimulation, was all fiction, and purely acted to the life, by a nature crafty, perverse and inconstant. He congratulated his own ill-natured perseverance; by which he discovered how he was to behave himself hereafter, and what remedies he was to apply to all future indispositions: nor had he, ever after, the same value of her wit, judgment, and her understanding, which he had formerly; and was well enough pleased to observe, that the reverence others had for all three was somewhat diminished."—ED.]

THE DUCHESS OF CLEVELAND.

> " Love is all gentleness and joy;
> Smooth are his looks, and soft his pace;
> *Her* Cupid is a blackguard boy,
> That rubs his link full in your face!"
>
> EARL OF DORSET.

IF any faith may be given to the scandalous chronicles of that period, the court of Cromwell, with its cant and cropped heads, its " weel spread looves, and lang wry faces," was not less licentious than that of Charles II.: the change was rather of manners than of morals; of costume, rather than of character. In the days of Oliver, Folly stalked about in solemn guise, and hid his bauble under a Geneva cloak; and in those of Charles, he flourished his coxcomb, and the " peal of his bells rang merrily out,"—and this was better at least than sanctified foolery and sober vice. " The *asinina stella*"* if not more predominant, was at all events more brilliant. It was not so much the supremacy of wickedness, as the magnanimous contempt of appearance—the brave defiance of decorum that distinguished the court and age of Charles II. from the solemnity of Cromwell's and the dulness of William's.

> " The sin was of our native growth, 'tis true;
> The *scandal* of the sin was wholly new."

The various causes which led to that general licence of manners which prevailed after the Restoration, are recorded by the historian,

> * " Che s'io non erro al calcolar de' punti,
> Par ch' asinina stella a noi predomini."
>
> *Salvator Rosa.*

and do not fall within the province of these light Memoirs: one of them was undoubtedly the personal character of that vain and profligate woman who, in the commencement of his reign, ruled the court and heart of Charles, and whose beauty and misconduct have doomed her to an infamous celebrity.

Sir William Villiers, descended from the eldest branch of the house of Villiers, (the younger branch becoming Dukes of Buckingham,) succeeded his uncle, Oliver St. John, in the title of Viscount Grandison, in the kingdom of Ireland. On the breaking out of the civil wars, he, with all his family, adhered to the King's party, and distinguished himself by his devoted loyalty and chivalrous bravery. At the siege of Bristol, in 1643, he was desperately wounded; and being carried to Oxford, died there a few days afterwards, at the age of thirty. Lord Clarendon, who relates the manner of his death, adds this captivating and well-drawn portrait:—" Lord Grandison was a young man of so virtuous a habit of mind, that no temptation or provocation could corrupt him; so great a lover of justice and integrity, that no example, necessity, or even the barbarities of this war, could make him swerve from the most precise rules of it; and of that rare piety and devotion, that the court, or camp, could not show a more faultless person, or to whose example young men might more reasonably conform themselves. His personal valour and courage of all kinds (for he had sometimes indulged so much to the corrupt opinion of honour as to venture himself in duels) were very eminent, insomuch as he was accused of being too prodigal of his person; his affection, zeal, and obedience to the King, was such as became a branch of that family." And he was wont to say, " that if he had not understanding enough to know the uprightness of the cause, nor loyalty enough to inform him of the duty of a subject, yet the very obligations of gratitude to the King, on the behalf of his house, were such as his life was but a due sacrifice; and therefore, he no sooner saw the war unavoidable, than he engaged all his brethren, as well as himself, in the service, and there were then three more of them in command in the army, where he was so unfortunately cut off." He married Mary, third daughter of Paul, Viscount Bayning, by whom he left an only daughter and heiress, Barbara Villiers, afterwards Duchess of Cleveland.

Of the early life and education of this too celebrated woman, I have not been able to collect any authentic information. She married, at the age of eighteen, Roger Palmer, Esq., a gentleman of fortune, and loyal adherent of the exiled King. Her first acquaintance with Charles probably commenced in Holland, whither she accompanied her husband in 1659, when he carried to the King a considerable sum of money to aid in his restoration, and assisted him also by his personal services. But her connexion with Charles cannot be traced with any certainty before the very day of his entrance into London: on the evening of that day, Charles, instead of sleeping in the palace of his ancestors, to which he had just been restored, skulked away privately to the house of Sir Samuel Morland, at Vauxhall, where he had an assignation with Mrs. Palmer.

That an accomplished prince, in the prime of life, skilled in all the arts that ensnare her sex,—the sovereign for whose sake her father had fought and bled; whom she had just seen restored— *miraculously* restored, as it was then believed,—to the throne of his fathers, welcomed to his capital with almost delirious joy, and who, in such a moment, threw himself and his new-found kingdom at her feet, should have conquered the heart and triumphed over the virtue of a woman so vain and volatile, is not marvellous: she was only nineteen, and thrown by the blind confidence or time-serving carelessness of her husband, into the very way of temptation. Thus far her frailty, if not excusable, might have been pardoned, if the end had not proved that personal affection for the King had little to do with her lapse from virtue, and that, in short, she was more of a Montespan that a La Vallière, more of an Alice Pierce than a Jane Shore.

In a few months after the Restoration, Palmer was created an

Irish peer, with the title of Earl of Castlemaine. He, meekest of men, was, or affected to be, a little sulky and restive at first under his new dignities, but means were soon found to pacify him; and he afterwards submitted to the coronet, and other honours which his beautiful wife showered on his head, with a spirit of philosophy and resignation which was quite edifying.*

The passion of the King for Lady Castlemaine, and her influence over him, were at their height at the time that his marriage with Catherine of Portugal was, from political motives, resolved on. When the Queen's arrival at Portsmouth was announced in London, Charles was supping at Lady Castlemaine's house in the Strand. Bonfires had been lighted, in token of respect and rejoicing, before every door in the street except hers— an omission which did not pass unobserved: nor did she attempt to conceal her despair, when the King left her to meet his bride. It was probably sincere; for she had as much reason to dread, as all good men had to hope from, the influence of a young and beloved Queen. Unhappily her fears and others' hopes proved groundless: the King could not break the fetters which her charms

* "But that which pleased me best was, that my Lady Castlemaine stood over against us upon a piece of White Hall. But methought it was strange to see her lord and her upon the same place, walking up and down, without taking notice one of another; only at first entry, he put off his hat, and she made him a very civil salute, but afterwards took no notice one of another; but both of them now and then would take their child, which the nurse held in her arms, and dandle it." This was on occasion of the Queen's triumphant entry into London, she being brought with great state by water from Hampton Court. Immediately after follows a trait of good-nature, which must not be suppressed, the rather because it is solitary: the worst, however, are not wholly bad. A scaffolding happened to fall at the moment, and Lady Castlemaine was the only one among the great ladies of court, who, from an impulse of humanity, ran down among the 'common rabble' to see what injury had been done, and took charge of a poor child which had been hurt in the crowd, "which methought was so noble. Anon came one booted and spurred, whom she talked with; and by and by, she being in her hair, she put on his hat, which was but an ordinary one, to keep the wind off: but it became her mightily, as every thing else do."—*Pepys' Diary*, vol. i. p. 161.

G

and her imperious temper had flung round him, and the Queen had not beauty and tact enough to win him from her rival.

Catherine had arrived in England with a fixed resolution not to admit Lady Castlemaine into her presence,—" her mother," she said, " had enjoined her not to do so:" but the King had determined otherwise; and the gay courtiers, who had the most influence over his mind, were precisely those who had every thing to hope from the misrule of Lady Castlemaine, and nothing to expect from the countenance of Catherine. Charles, like all weak men, had a dread of being governed by a *wife*; and they persuaded him that it was infinitely more magnanimous to be enslaved by a termagant mistress, than to comply with the reasonable demands of his Queen; and artfully represented the former, and not the latter, as the object of compassion. They observed, " that he had, by the charms of his person and of his professions, prevailed upon the affections and heart of a young and beautiful lady of a noble extraction, whose father had lost his life in the service of the crown; that she had provoked the jealousy and rage of her husband to that degree, that he had separated himself from her; and now the Queen's indignation had made the matter so notorious to the world, that the disconsolate lady had no place of retreat left, but must be made an object of infamy and contempt to all her sex, and to the whole world."*

To give colour to these insinuations, Lady Castlemaine had fled from the house of her husband,—not forgetting, however, to carry with her all her jewels, plate, and furniture,—and went over to Richmond, to be nearer Hampton Court, then the scene of battle.

---

* " Those discourses," continues Lord Clarendon, " together with a little book newly printed at Paris, according to the licence of that nation, of the amours of Henry IV., which was by them presented to him, and too concernedly read by him, made that impression upon his mind," &c.—*Clarendon's Continuation*, &c. It gratified the King to be compared to his grandfather, Henry IV. of France. In his fortunes and his failings there was some resemblance; in conduct and character, none whatever.

THE DUCHESS OF CLEVELAND.

The issue of this affair has been given in the Memoir of Queen Catherine. Lady Castlemaine was created one of the ladies of the bed-chamber, and soon after lodged in Whitehall, where she occupied apartments immediately over those of the King.*

From this time may be dated the absolute power which this haughty and abandoned woman exercised over the easy-tempered Charles,—an influence never exercised but for her own aggrandizement and his dishonour, or the ruin of his best friends and most faithful servants. In her chamber, and among the profligate crew who surrounded her, was prepared the plot against Lord Chancellor Clarendon, which ended in the disgrace and banishment of that great nobleman, the earliest and best friend of her father.† When he returned from Whitehall, after resigning the seals, she jumped out of bed in her night-dress to look down upon him as he passed, and stood upon her balcony, abusing him loudly, and in the coarsest terms her vulgar malice could suggest. When she quarrelled with the great Duke of Ormond, who had offended her in many ways, but chiefly by refusing to sanction her enormous drains upon the Irish treasury, she reviled him, swore at him, and finally told him "she hoped to see him hanged." To which the duke replied, with a grave humour becoming his character, that "far from wishing her ladyship's days shortened in return, his greatest desire was to see her grow old."

But her countenance was always extended to those who flattered

---

* See Pepys' Diary, vol. i. p. 212.—"My Lady Castlemaine is removed, as to her bed, from her own home to a chamber in Whitehall, next to the King's owne: which I am sorry to hear, though I love her much." Honest Mr. Pepys is oddly divided between his sense of right and his extravagant admiration for the beauty of Lady Castlemaine, whose very petticoats, trimmed with lace, "it did him good to look upon."

† The Lord Chancellor had refused to put the seal of office to some grant of a place which Lady Castlemaine had disposed of, saying he thought "the woman would sell every thing shortly;" which being repeated to her, she sent to tell him, "that she had disposed of this place, and did not doubt in a little time to dispose of *his*." She was as good as her word.

her passions, ministered to her avarice, or were subservient to her pleasures. She indeed gave encouragement to Dryden in the beginning of his literary career; but it seems to have been more through contradiction than any perception of merit, that she persisted in patronizing his first and worst play, after it had been summarily *executed*. He repaid her interference by a copy of verses, which is a signal instance of the prostitution of his muse, and in which he compares her to Cato. One would have thought, that even a poet's imagination, fired by admiration and gratitude, could scarcely find or make any comparison between the voluptuous vixen Castlemaine and the Roman Cato; but, as Steele observes, "there is no stretching a metaphor too far when a lady is in the case."

The sums which this harpy contrived to appropriate from the funds of the state almost exceed belief. She was, to use Burnet's coarse expression in speaking of her, "enormously ravenous:" it was, however, rather rapacity than avarice; for what was obtained unworthily, was lavished as extravagantly. Besides a grant of £5322 a-year out of the post-office, to her and her heirs, she had twenty thousand a-year out of the customs.* What sums were occasionally paid to her out of the revenues of Ireland cannot be ascertained; besides this income, immense in those days, she had at different times gifts in money, jewels, and plate, to an incredible amount; and this at the time when the King's household servants were cursing him because they had not bread to eat, and he himself wanted linen, and was stinted in writing-paper!†

---

* "Lord St. John, Sir R. Howard, Sir John Bennet, and Sir W. Bicknell, the brewer, have farmed the customs; they have signed and sealed ten thousand a-year *more* to the Duchess of Cleveland, who has likewise near ten thousand a-year out of the new farm of the Country Excise of beer and ale; £5000 a-year out of the post-office, and, they say, the reversion of all places in the Custom-house, the Green Wax, and indeed what not; all promotions, spiritual and temporal, pass under her cognizance." — *Andrew Marvel's Letters.* "Barclay (Berkeley) is still Lieutenant of Ireland: but he was forced to come over to pay ten thousand pounds rent to his landlady, Cleveland."—*Ib.*

† "This day I was told that my Lady Castlemaine hath all the King's Christ-

Berkshire-House was purchased for her by the King, in 1668; and as it was of great extent, she added to her income by converting part of it into separate houses and letting them;* but all was too little to supply her monstrous expenditure. Among her other extravagances was the vice of gaming, in one night she lost at Basset £25,000, and was accustomed to stake one thousand, and fifteen hundred pounds at a cast.

As the fair Castlemaine was one of those ladies who would " whisk the stars out of their spheres " rather than lose one iota of their will, it may be imagined that her connection with the King was not one long summer's day, all serenity and sunshine. In fact, not satisfied with " nodding him from the council-board" whenever the whim seized her, she gave way to such inexplicable caprices, and, upon the slightest cause, to such bursts of tempestuous passion, that she sometimes threw the whole court into an uproar, and drove the poor King half distracted. It is observable that as soon as she was well-assured of her power over Charles, and understood his character, she never attempted to carry any point by tenderness or cajolery; but, by absenting herself from court, or by direct violence, she hectored him, as Pepys says, out of his wits,—

> "And, with bent lowering brows, as she would threat,
> She scowl'd and frown'd with froward countenance
> Unworthy of fair lady's comely governance."
>
> *Spenser.*

Charles, wearied by the din of her vituperative tongue, and pained by the disagreeable sight of so beautiful a face deformed by demon passions, hastened to relieve his eyes and ears by granting

mas presents, made him by the peers, given to her, which is a most abominable thing: and that at the great ball she was much richer in jewels, than the Queene and Duchesse (of York) put both together."—*Pepys' Diary,* vol. i. p. 204.

* Berkshire-House was formerly the town mansion of the Howards, Earls of Berkshire, and afterwards of Lord Clarendon. It stood on the site of the Marquis of Stafford's princely residence, and the name of its former proprietor is still perpetuated in *Cleveland-row.*

her demands, however exorbitant. At times, however, being driven past the bounds of patience, he would make an attempt at resistance, which was sure to end in his discomfiture. Some instances on record of her coarse manners and termagant temper are ludicrous, and some disgusting.* Once, on some slighting words from the King, she called for her coach at a quarter of an hour's warning, and, taking with her her plate, jewels, and favourite servants, went off to Richmond; the King, under pretence of hunting, followed her there; and before he could prevail on her to return, he was forced to beg pardon on his knees, and, like a little boy that had been whipped, promised " to do so no more."

On another occasion it happened that the Queen, conversing in her drawing-room with the ladies in attendance, observed to Lady Castlemaine that she feared that the King took cold by staying so late abroad at her ladyship's house. Her ladyship answered, that the King did not stay late with her: on the contrary, he left her early; therefore she was not answerable for his taking cold: if he stayed late abroad, it must be *somewhere else*. The King, entering at that moment, overheard this insinuation, and sudden anger inspired him with unwonted spirit. He whispered in her ear that she was a bold impertinent woman, and commanded her to leave the court, and not appear again till he sent for her. The indignant fair one took him at his word, and retired to lodgings in Pall Mall. When she had remained there two days unnoticed, she began to be alarmed, and sent to ask permission to take her things from Whitehall. The King informed her she must come for them. To which, after a furious struggle between pride and policy, she condescended; and, the King meeting her there, was, after the usual submissions, forgiven, and harmony restored.

* On a certain occasion, the King being engaged to sup with her, "there being a chine of beef to roast, and the tide rising into their kitchen that it could not be roasted there, and the cook telling her of it, she answered, 'Zounds! she must set the house on fire, but it must be roasted!' So it was carried to Mrs. Sarah's husband's, and there it was roasted."—*Pepys' Diary*, vol. i. p. 253.

The Duke of Buckingham's disgrace, in 1667, was the occasion of a most bitter quarrel. The Duke was her kinsman, some say her lover, or at least her worthy coadjutor in all schemes of mischief and extravagance; and she took up his cause with all the determined violence of her temper and disposition. The consequence was a regular hurricane. The King told her she was "a jade that meddled with things she had nothing to do with at all;" and the lady retorted by calling his most sacred majesty a *fool*. In the end she prevailed, as usual, and Buckingham was restored to favour.

On another occasion, the King ventured to express his doubts as to her being the father of her youngest child. She was then near her confinement; and in a transport of rage she exclaimed, or rather swore, for her exclamations were usually oaths, that "whoever was the father, the King should own it; and she would have it christened in the chapel at Whitehall, and owned for the King's, or she would bring it into the Whitehall gallery, and dash the brains of it out before the King's face;" and forthwith she retired to the house of Sir Daniel Hervey, and shut herself up. The King was obliged to follow her, hearing that she threatened to print his letters, a threat she was very capable of executing. He there made concessions on his knees, and she was prevailed on to return to Whitehall,—"not as a mistress, for she scorned him, but as a tyrant to command him." The last and most tempestuous of these disgraceful scenes ended in her being raised to the dignity of Duchess. It is related by De Grammont in his happiest style of badinage. The King, it seems, had for some time shared her good graces with the accomplished Wycherly,* the handsome Churchill,† and a score of meaner rivals. But at length, though

---

* The commencement of her acquaintance with Wycherly is too *characteristic* to be given here. It may be found in Grainger, and in Dennis's Letters.

† Afterwards Duke of Marlborough. The five thousand pounds which the Duchess of Cleveland gave him, laid the foundation of his fortunes, by enabling him to purchase a commission. Yet he was afterwards known to refuse her twenty guineas, which she wanted to borrow from him at Basset.

not particularly nice in such matters, and averse to excite the storms he found it so difficult to allay, he began to be somewhat scandalized at the open infidelities of a woman whom he had so publicly distinguished, and ventured a little advice and raillery on the subject of one of her lovers (the "invincible Jermyn,") whom he considered a rival more contemptible and disreputable than Harte, Goodman, or Jacob Hall himself.* His imperious Sultana took fire instantly, and blazed away like a mine of gunpowder. Instead of defending herself, she attacked the King. She reproached him with the baseness of his *penchants*, his devotion to such idiots as Miss Stewart, Miss Wells, and that "*petite gueuse de comédienne*" (meaning Nell Gwynn): then followed floods of tears, and paroxysms of rage, in which she threatened, like another Medea, to tear her children in pieces, and fire his palace over his head. The King had never ventured to contend for peace without paying pretty largely for it; for, what was to be done with a fury, who on these occasions, all beautiful as she was, resembled Medea much less than one of her dragons? In the present instance, though his attachment to the lady was on the decline, and Miss Stewart reigned the goddess paramount of the day, he was obliged to buy a reconciliation at a dear rate. The Chevalier de Grammont was called in as mediator, and drew up articles of peace; in which it was agreed that Lady Castlemaine's new lover should be sent to make a little tour into the country: that she should raise no more disturbances on the subject of Miss Wells and Miss Stewart; and, in consideration of so much amiable condescension on the lady's part, she should be elevated to the rank of a Duchess, with all the honours and privileges pertaining to the title, and her pension doubled, to enable her to support her new dignity with becoming *éclat*. Soon afterwards, "in consideration of her noble descent, her father's death in the service of the crown, and by reason (as

---

* The two former were celebrated actors, and the latter a rope-dancer. Harte, of the King's company, had been a captain in the army, and was the finest actor of that day: he excelled in Othello. There is a picture of Harte in the Beauty-room at Windsor.

the letters patent set forth) of her own *personal virtues*," she was created Baroness of Nonsuch, Countess of Southampton, and Duchess of Cleveland. The title of Southampton must have doubly gratified her, as having been that of her old enemy, the excellent Lord Southampton, who had frequently excited her utmost displeasure, by refusing to put his seal as Treasurer to her exorbitant grants of money, &c.

After this last rupture, and her elevation of rank, the Duchess withdrew from the court, though she still occasionally appeared there: her influence over the King did not entirely cease till the reign of the Duchess of Portsmouth began, but she was no longer all-powerful: and gradually, as she debased herself more and more by her excesses, she sank into neglect and contempt. Pepys alludes in his Diary to a quarrel about this time between Lady Castlemaine and the Duchess of Richmond (the predecessor to the fair Stewart in that title), which threw the whole court into confusion; "wherein the Duchess of Richmond did call my Lady Castlemaine Jane Shore, and hoped she should live to see her come to the same end." There was, in truth, some poetical justice in the catastrophe of the Duchess of Cleveland, though the Duchess of Richmond had not the comfort of living to witness it. On the death of the Earl of Castlemaine, in 1703, she married a man of desperate fortune and profligate habits, well known by the name of Beau Fielding, and unequalled in those days for the beauty of his person.* Fielding had married her for the sake of her money; and when she either could not, or would not, any longer supply his extravagances, he so barbarously ill-treated her, that she was obliged to have recourse to a magistrate for protection against his outrages. Fortunately for her, it was discovered that he had a former wife living, a low woman, who had cheated him as he had cheated all the rest of her sex. He was prosecuted for bigamy, found guilty, but pardoned by Queen Anne. His conviction

---

* See "The Tatler," No. 50, for the "History of Orlando the Fair," *i.e.* the above-mentioned Beau Fielding: it is from the pen of Swift.

relieved the Duchess from his brutality, but she did not long survive it: she died of a dropsy at her house at Chiswick, October 9, 1709, miserable, contemned, and neglected; leaving a name more fitted to "point a moral," than to "adorn a tale."

The Duchess of Cleveland was the mother of six children, three sons and three daughters. Charles Fitzroy, her eldest son by the King, was born in 1662, and created, during the lifetime of his mother, Baron Newberry, Earl of Chichester, and Duke of Southampton. On her death he succeeded to the title of Duke of Cleveland, in which he was succeeded by his son William; after whose death, in 1774, the title became extinct, and has not since been revived.

Her second son, Henry Fitzroy, born in 1663, was created Baron of Sudbury, Viscount Ipswich, Earl of Euston, and Duke of Grafton. He was eminently handsome in his person, of a brave and martial spirit; but rough, illiterate, and rude in his manners. He married Isabella, only daughter and heiress of Harry Bennett, Earl of Arlington,* and was killed by a cannon ball at the siege

* This Duchess of Grafton was the most beautiful woman of her time; but it was in the court of William, and not in that of Charles that she reigned supreme "lady of hearts," and was celebrated by all the wits and poets of the day. Her picture is among the "Beauties" at Hampton Court. She bore to the end of her long life a most irreproachable character. I am tempted to add the following entries from Evelyn's Diary, which throw considerable interest round her premature union with the Duke of Grafton: she was then five and the Duke nine years old. "1672. Aug. 1. I was at the marriage of Lord Arlington's lovely daughter (a sweet child if ever there was any) to the Duke of Grafton, the King's natural son by the Duchess of Cleveland; the Archbishop of Canterbury officiated, the King and all the grandees of the court being present." The infant couple were married again in 1679, she being twelve years old and her husband sixteen. "I confess," says Evelyn, "I could give my Lady Arlington little joy, and so I plainly told her; but she said the King would have it so, and there was no going back. Thus this sweetest, hopefullest, most beautiful child, and most virtuous too, was sacrificed to a boy that has been rudely bred, without any thing to encourage them but his majesty's pleasure. I pray God the sweet child find it to her advantage; who, if my augury deceive me not, will in a few

of Cork, 1690, where he served under Marlborough as a volunteer. He was ancestor to the noble family of Fitzroy, in all its branches; the present Duke of Grafton being the fourth, and the present Lord Southampton the fifth, in descent from him.

George Fitzroy, her third son, was created by his father Earl and Duke of Northumberland. He was weak and dissipated, married meanly, and died without issue.

Anne Palmer Fitzroy, her eldest daughter, was born in 1661. The Earl of Castlemaine always considered this daughter as his offspring; but the King, by giving her the name of Fitzroy, assigning her the royal arms, and portioning her nobly at her marriage, seemed determined to claim a share of the parentage. She married Lennard Lord Dacre and Earl of Sussex, and left two daughters.

Charlotte Fitzroy, who rivalled her mother in beauty, but was far unlike her in every other respect, married the Earl of Lichfield, by whom she was the mother of eighteen children; one of her daughters, Lady Elizabeth Lee, married Young, the author of the *Night Thoughts.*

Barbara, her youngest daughter, whom the King acknowledged in public, but not in private, became a nun at Pontoise.

The beauty of the Duchess of Cleveland was of that splendid

---

years be such a paragon, as were fit to make a wife to the greatest prince in Europe.

"1683. I went to compliment the Duchess of Grafton, now laying-in of her first child, a son, which she called for, that I might see it. She was become more beautiful, if it were possible, than before, and full of virtue and sweetness. She discoursed with me of many particulars with great prudence and gravity beyond her years." This youthful and lovely mother was then just fifteen. She lived to walk at the Coronation of George II. as Countess of Arlington in her own right, and died in 1732.

and commanding character, that dazzles rather than interests; it was, however, perfect in its kind. At a time when she was most unpopular, and her charms and excesses were creating disturbances in the court and disaffection in the country, she went to Bartholomew Fair to view "the rare puppet-show of Patient Grizzle," (by which, it is to be hoped, she was greatly edified.) The rabble, recognizing her equipage, followed it with hisses and curses; but when she stepped out, and looked round in all the proud consciousness of irresistible beauty, the people, struck with admiration, changed their curses into blessings "on her handsome face," though it had helped to undo a nation. The picture at Windsor, (from which the portrait is engraved) represents her as Pallas, or Bellona: the last is certainly the more appropriate character; it is full of the imperious expression of the original. The face is perfectly beautiful; the rich red lips are curled with arrogance and "womanish disdain," and the eyes look from under their drooping lids with a certain fierceness of expression; the action, the attitude, the accompaniments, are all those of a virago; she grasps the spear with the air of an all-conquering beauty, and leans on her shield as if she disdained to use it; while the grand tempestuous sky in the background, with broken gleams of light flashing across it, is in admirable keeping with the whole.

[In the amusing entries of Pepys' Diary, we may trace the different vicissitudes of the Duchess of Cleveland's reign over the King; vicissitudes, indeed, which were not very great, for when the King's attachment to her was diminished, she still kept her place by her own effrontery. She was evidently much alarmed on the arrival of the Queen, fearing at once to lose her influence; and there is every reason for believing that her introduction at Hampton Court was a plan of her own, a resolution to make a desperate struggle for superiority at the outset. She succeeded, and the first years of the King's marriage were those of her greatest power. She still, however, showed outwardly, at least at times, something like attention to the Queen. Pepys, whose curiósity led him to see the ceremonies at the Queen's Catholic chapel when it was first opened, which was not long after the Duchess had been received a Maid of Honour, describes the Queen's devoutness, and adds, "but what pleased me best was to see my dear Lady Castlemaine, who, though a Protestant, did wait upon the Queene to Chapel." Pepys's admiration of the beauty of the royal mistress was now at its height, so as even to draw a rebuke from 'his lady,' "she calling her my lady, and the lady I admire." In the latter part of 1663, her influence seems to have been somewhat on the decline, and from this time till 1666, she was in part eclipsed by the beauty of Miss Stewart. It is singular how the admiration of Pepys changes with the King's love. In 1663, when he hears that Castlemaine is declining in the royal favour, he observes, "Saw my Lady Castlemaine, who, I fear, is not so handsome as I have taken her for, and now she begins to decay something. This is my wife's opinion also." Miss Stewart was now the object of his praise. "Mrs. Stewart is now the greatest beauty I ever saw, I think, in my life; and, if ever woman can, do exceed my Lady Castlemaine." In 1664 he observes, "My wife tells me the sad news of my Lady Castlemaine's being now become so decayed, that one would not know her; at least, far from a beauty, which I am sorry for." Again, in the early part of 1666, "I was sorry to see my Lady Castlemaine; for the mourning forcing all the ladies to go in black, with their hair plain, and without spots, I find her to be a much more ordinary woman than ever I durst have thought she was; and, indeed, is not so pretty as Mrs. Stewart." Poor Pepys! how many circumstances, independent of their own taste, influence people in judging of beauty and excellence.

It was not long after the period when the last of these observations was made, that occurred the anecdote above related by Mrs. Jameson, (at p. 88.) In the latter part of this year, though she seems still to have been out of favour, the King paid Lady Castlemaine's debts to the amount of thirty thousand pounds; and after the marriage of Miss Stewart to the Duke of Richmond, in 1667, she regained all her influence, and, to use the expression of the Diary, hectored the King to whatever she would. "My cousin Roger," says Pepys, "told us as a thing certain, that my Lady Castlemaine hath made a bishop lately; namely, her uncle, Dr. Glenham, who, I think they say, is Bishop of Carlisle; a drunken swearing raskal, and a scandal to the church; and do now pretend to be Bishop of Lincoln, in competition with Dr. Raynbow, who is reckoned as worthy a man as most in the church for piety and learning: which are things so scandalous to consider, that no man can doubt but we must be undone that hears of them." Her conduct now seems so far to have increased her unpopularity, and things appeared to be in so critical a posture, that in 1667 there was a serious design of getting rid of her for a time, in order to propitiate the parliament. It was rumoured that she would go to France with a pension; but her influence was too high, and she could not be brought to agree to the proposal. In the May of the following year, Pepys observes, "My Lady Castlemaine is, it seems, now mightily out of request, the King coming little to her, and then she mighty melancholy and discontented." The Duke of Buckingham, who now came into full power, was also suddenly opposed to her, as we learn from the same authority; and the design of sending her to France seems to have been again entertained towards the end of 1668. A letter preserved in the British Museum, (MS. Harl. No. 7001,) dated from London the 5th of December in that year, informs us that " a report is here also that my Lady Castlemaine intends to make a short journey into France; but I believe the resolution is not yet fixt, though to invite her my Lord Hawbry offers himselfe to attend her thither." Soon after this, in the January of 1668-9, we learn from Pepys "that my Lady Castlemaine is now in a higher command over the King than ever,—not as a mistress, for she scorns him, but as a tyrant to command him."

From this time we hear little more of Lady Castlemaine in Pepys. The project of sending her to France seems at a later period to have been put in practice, and she was residing there in

1678. The following letter, from the British Museum, shows that even there she was still intriguing:—

Ralph Duke of Mountague* to his Cousin.

"Paris, March 29, 1678. O.S.

"Sir,

"I am out of countenance at all the troubles you are pleased to give yourself in my concerns. I have heard something of what you tell me of the Queen's engagement to my Lady Arlington; but so many things come between the cup and the lip, especially at court, that till things are done, one must never despair, no more than I do of being Secretary of State, if my lord continues his favour to me, and can work off Sir William Temple. I know for certain that there is a great cabal to bring in Mr. Savile, who writ a letter last post to my Lady Cleveland, that his fortune depended upon her coming over, for that he had engaged his unkle, Secretary Coventry, for his place, but could not compass money to buy it, except she got him the King's leave to sell his bedchamber place, and some additional money to help. You may let my Lord Treasurer know this, but it must be kept very secret, for else it would hinder me knowing many things that may be for his service. It is not very well in Mr. Savile, who has those obligations to my Lord Treasurer, to manage such an affair underhand. For my part, I care not for the place, except I come in with his favour and kindness. I have tried no other ways to compass it, neither will I. Pray put my Lord Treasurer in mind of me, with the assurance that he has no servant truer to him than myself, nor more entirely.

Dear Cousin,
Your most faithful humble servant,
R. Mountague."

We find, indeed, that not long after this letter was written, the Duchess was in England, whether on the errand there alluded to

---

* He was at this time ambassador at the French court.

or not, we cannot venture to say. On her return to Paris, she addressed the following letter to the King. It is preserved among the Harleian manuscripts, in a volume of letters, numbered 7006, and affords us a singularly curious picture of her intriguing spirit, now smarting under the united stings of disappointment, humiliation, and anger.

"Paris, Tuesday the 28th, —78.

"I was never so surprized in my holle life-time as I was, at my coming hither, to find my Lady Sussex gone from my house and monastery where I left her, and this letter from her, which I here send you a copy of. I never saw in my holle life-time such government of herself as she has had, since I went into England. She has never been in the monastery two days together, but every day gone out with the ambassador;* and has often lain four days together at my house, and sent for her meat to the ambassador, he being always with her till five o'clock in the morning, they two shut up together alone, and would not let any maistre d'hôtel wait, nor any of my servants, only the ambassador's. This made so great a noise at Paris that she is now the holle discourse. I am so much afflicted that I can hardly write this for crying, to see a child that I doted on as I did on her, should make so ill return, and join with the worst of men to ruin me. For sure never malice was like the ambassador's, that only because I would not answer to his love, and the importunities he made to me, was resolved to ruin me. I hope your majesty will yet have that justice and consideration for me, that though I have done a foolish action, you will not let me be ruined by this most abominable man. I do confess to you that I did write a foolish letter to the Chevalier de Châtillon, which letter I sent inclosed to Madam de Pallas, and sent hers in a packet I sent to Lady Sussex by Sir Henry Tichborn; which letter she has either given to the ambassador, or else he had it by his man, to whom Sir Henry Tichborn gave it, not finding my Lady Sussex. But as yet I do not know which of

* Ralph Mountague, afterwards Duke of Mountague.

the ways he had it, but I shall know as soon as I have spoke with
Sir Henry Tichborn. But the letter he has, and I doubt not but
he has or will send it to you. Now all I have to say for myself
is, that you know as to love, one is not mistress of one's self, and
that you ought not to be offended at me, since all things of this
nature is at end with you and I, so that I could do you no
prejudice. Nor will you, I hope, follow the advice of this ill man,
who in his heart I know hates you, and were it not for his interest
would ruin you if he could. For he has neither conscience nor
honour, and has several times told me, that in his heart he despised
you and your brother: and that for his part, he wished with all
his heart that the parliament would send you both to travel, for
you were a dull governable fool, and the duke a wilful fool. So
that it were yet better to have you than him, but that you always
chose a greater beast than yourself to govern you. And when I
was to come over, he brought me two letters to bring to you,
which he read both to me before he sealed them. The one was a
man's, that he said you had great faith in; for that he had at
several times foretold things to you that were of consequence,[*] and
that you believed him in all things, like a changeling as you were.
And that now he had wrote you word, that in a few months the
King of France and his son were threatened with death, or at
least with a great fit of sickness, in which they would be in great
danger, if they did not die; and that therefore he counsell'd you
to defer any resolutions either of war or peace till some months
were past; for that if this happened, it would make a great change
in France. The ambassador, after he had read this to me, said,
'Now the good of this is,' said he, 'that I can do what I will with
this man; for he is poor, and a good sum of money will make him
write whatever I will.' So he proposed to me that he and I
should join together in the ruin of my Lord Treasurer and the
Duchess of Portsmouth, which might be done thus:—The man,
though he was infirm and ill, should go into England, and there,
after having been a little time, to sollicit you for money; for that

---

[*] See Burnet's History of his Own Times, vol. i. p. 422.

you were so base, that though you employed him, you let him starve; so that he was obliged to give him 50*l*., and that the man had writ several times to you for money. And, says he, when he is in England, he shall tell the King things that he foresees will infallible ruin him; and so wish those to be removed, as having an ill star, that would be unfortunate to you if they were not removed: but if that were done, he was confident you would have the most glorious reign that ever was. This, says he, I am sure I can order so as to bring to good effect, if you will. And in the mean time, I will try to get Secretary Coventry's place, which he has a mind to part with, but not to Sir William Temple; because he is the Treasurer's creature, and he hates the Treasurer; and I have already employed my sister to talk with Mr. Cook, and to mind him to engage Mr. Coventry not to part with it as yet, and he has assured my Lady Harvey he will not. And my Lord Treasurer's lady and Mr. Bertie are both of them desirous I should have it. And when I have it, I will be damn'd if I do not quickly get to be Lord Treasurer; and then you and your children shall find such a friend as never was. And for the King, I will find a way to furnish him so easily with money for his pocket and wenches, that we will quickly out Bab. May, and lead the King by the nose. So when I had heard him out, I told him I thank'd him, but that I would not meddle with any such thing: and that, for my part, I had no malice to my Lady Portsmouth, or to the Treasurer, and therefore would never be in any plot to destroy them. But that I found the character which the world gave him was true: which was, the Devil was not more designing than he was, and that I wondered at it; for sure all these things working in his brain must make him very uneasy, and would at last make him mad. 'Tis possible you may think I say this out of malice. 'Tis true he has urged me beyond all patience: but what I tell you here is most true: and I will take the sacrament on it whenever you please. 'Tis certain I would not have been so base as to have informed against him for what he had said before me had he not provoked to it in this violent way that he has. There is no ill thing which he has not done me, and that without any provocation of mine, but that I would not love him. Now, as to what relates to my daughter Sussex, and her behaviour to me, I must confess that afflicts me beyond expression, and will do much more, if what he has done be by your orders. For though I have an entire submission to your will, and will not complain whatever you inflict upon me; yet I cannot think you would have brought things to this extremity with me, and not have it in your nature ever to do cruel things to any thing living. I hope you will not therefore begin with me, and if the ambassador has not received his orders from you, that you will severely reprehend him for this inhuman proceeding. Besides, he has done what you ought to be very angry with him for. For he has been with the King of France, and told him that he had intercepted letters of mine by your order; by which he had been informed that there was a kindness between me and the Chevalier de Chatillon; and therefore you bad him take a course in it, and stop my letters; which accordingly he has done. And that upon this you order'd him to take my children from me, and to remove my Lady Sussex to another monastery; and that you was resolved to stop all my pensions, and never to have any regard to me in any thing. And that if he would oblige your majesty, he should forbid the Chevalier de Chatillon ever seeing me, upon the displeasure of losing his place, and being forbid the court, for he was sure you expected this from him. Upon which the King told him, that he could not do any thing of this nature: for that this was a private matter, and not for him to take notice of. And that he could not imagine that you ought to be so angry, or indeed be at all concerned; for that all the world knew, that now all things of gallantry were at an end with you and I. And that being so, and so publick, he did not see why you should be offended at my loving any body. That it was a thing so common nowadays to have a gallantry, that he did not wonder at any thing of this nature. And when he saw the King take the thing thus, he told him if he would not be severe with the Chevalier de Chatillon upon your account, he supposed he would be upon his own: for that in the letters he had discovered, he had found that the Chevalier had proposed to me the engaging of you in the marriage of the Dauphin and Mademoiselle :* and that was my greatest business into England.† That before I went over, I had spoke to him of the thing and would have engaged him in it; but that he refused it: for that he knew very well the indifference you had whether it was so or no, and how little you cared how Mademoiselle was married: that since I went into England it was possible I might engage somebody or other in this matter to press it to you; but that he knew very well, that in your heart you cared not whether it was so or no: that this business was set on foot by the Chevalier. Upon which the King told him, that if he would shew him any letters of the Chevalier de Chatillon to that purpose, he should then know what he had to say to him; but till he saw those letters he would not punish him without a proof for what he did. Upon which the ambassador shewed a letter, which he pretended one part of it was *double entendre*. The King said he could not see that there was any thing relating to it, and so left him, and said to a person there, 'Sure the ambassador was the worst man that ever was; for because my lady Cleveland will not love him, he strives to ruin her the basest in the world, and would have me to sacrifice the Chevalier de Chatillon to his revenge; which I shall not do, till I see better proofs of his having meddled in the marriage of the Dauphin and Mademoiselle than any yet the ambassador has shewed me.' This methinks is what you cannot but be offended at, and I hope you will be offended with him for his holle proceeding to me, and let the world see you will never countenance the actions of so base and ill a man. I had forgot to tell you that he told the King of France, that many people had reported that he had made love to me; but there was nothing of it; for that he had too much respect for you to think of any such thing. As for my Lady Sussex, I hope you will think fit to send for her over, for she is now mightily discoursed of for the ambassador. If you will not

* Mademoiselle was the daughter of Philip, Duke of Orleans, and Henriette, sister of King Charles II.

† This was Mountague's own proposal, made to the King in his letter to him of Jan. 10th, 1677-8, preserved in the Danby Papers, p. 48.

believe me in this, make inquiry into the thing, and you will find it to be true. I have desired Mr. Kemble to give you this letter, and to discourse with you at large upon this matter, to know your resolution, and whether I may expect that justice and goodness from you which all the world does. I promise you that for my conduct, it shall be such, as that you nor nobody shall have occasion to blame me. And I hope you will be just to what you said to me, which was at my house, when you told me you had letters of mine; you said, 'Madam, all that I ask of you for your own sake is, live so for the future as to make the least noise you can, and I care not who you love.' Oh! this noise that is had never been, had it not been for the ambassador's malice. I cannot forbear once again saying, I hope you will not gratify his malice in my ruin."

At the beginning of the year 1679, the Duchess of Cleveland was again in England, contrary it would seem to the King's will; for in the same volume which contains the preceding letter, is also preserved the following order from the King to the duchess, that she should immediately quit the country.

"WHITEHALL, FEB. ye 28, 78-9.

"I have already given you my reasones at large, why I think it fitt that you should absent yourself for some time beyond sea: as I am truely sorry for the occasion, so you may be sure I shall desire it no longer than it will be absolutely necessary both for your good and my service. In ye meantime I think it proper to give you notice under my hand, that I expect this compliance from you, and desire that you may believe with what trouble I write this to you, there being nothing I am more sensible off, than ye constant kindness you have ever had for me; and I hope you are so just as to think nothing can ever change me from being
      truely and kindly
       Yours,
        CHAS. REX."
         ED.]

THE COUNTESS DE GRAMMONT.

> "A woman of that rare behaviour,
> So qualified, that admiration
> Dwells round about her; of that perfect spirit,
> That admirable carriage,
> That sweetness in discourse—young as the morning,
> Her blushes staining his."
>
> FLETCHER.

THE COUNTESS DE GRAMMONT, or rather, to give her the fair and merited title by which she is better known, LA BELLE HAMILTON — young, beautiful, wise, and witty, and discreet withal, "even to detraction's desperation," seemed to have been placed in Charles's court purposely to redeem the credit of her sex. She moved, in that profligate sphere, in an orbit of her own: there were some, indeed, rash enough to reach at stars because they shone upon them, but she was beyond a mere coxcomb's flight; and on she passed, looking superior down in all the majesty of virtue, and all the light of loveliness.

> "Tal vagheggiata in ciel o luna, o stella,
> Che segue altiera il suo viaggio, et splende."

La Belle Hamilton!—the very name has a spell in it of power to carry us back a century and a half. What bright visions rise of flirtations at Summer Hill, and promenades at Tunbridge Wells! —of Maids of Honour, *coiffées à la négligence*, and gay gallants in perfumed periwigs!—what corantos, and galliards, and court

balls, and country frolics; and poor Lady Muskerry and her *bambino*, and her costume *à la Princesse de Babylon !*—But we must descend to grave biography, and take things in order. The advice of the giant Moulineau, "*Bélier, mon ami! commencez au commencement,*" is excellent; particularly when we are writing or reading the life of a celebrated beauty,—where the conclusion is to the beginning, like a musty moral out of Epictetus tacked to the end of a fairy tale.

Sir George Hamilton, fourth son of James first Earl of Abercorn, after distinguishing himself greatly in the civil wars, retired to France on the death of the King, his master. He resided abroad for several years, had a command in the French army, and in France several of his children were born and most of them educated; which accounts for the predilection they afterwards showed for that country.* At the Restoration, Sir George Hamilton returned to England with a numerous family of gallant sons and lovely daughters; among them ELIZABETH HAMILTON, his eldest daughter, who being then just at an age to be introduced at court, soon became one of its principal ornaments.

She appeared in that gay and splendid circle with many advantages. She was of noble descent, allied to the most illustrious families of England, Scotland and Ireland; she was the niece of the Duke of Ormond, her mother being the sister of that great nobleman; her eldest brother was groom to the bedchamber, and a special favourite of the King; her two younger brothers were distinguished among the brave and gay: she herself united to a most captivating person and manner, such accomplishments as few women of her time possessed, and which she had cultivated during her father's exile. It does not appear that Miss Hamilton accepted any ostensible office near the person of the Queen, or of the Duchess of York; but she was soon distinguished by the

---

* Two of Miss Hamilton's brothers died in the service of France, with the title of Count.

favour of both, more particularly by that of the duchess, and was habitually in their most select circles, as well as in all the balls, masques, banquets, and public festivities of the court.

It was at this time that De Grammont first met her; but it was long after his marriage that he dictated to her brother Anthony that enchanting description of her which appears in his Memoirs. The lover-like feeling which breathes through the whole—the beauty, delicacy, and individuality of the portrait, show that De Grammont, with all his frivolity and inconsistency, still remembered with tenderness, after a union of twenty years, the charms which had first touched and fixed his volatile heart.

She was then just arrived at that age, when the budding girl expands into the woman: her figure was tall, rather full, but elegantly formed: and to borrow Lord Herbert's beautiful expression, " varied itself into every grace that can belong either to rest or motion." She had the finest neck and the loveliest hand and arm in the world: her forehead was fair and open; her hair dark and luxuriant, always arranged with the most exquisite taste, but with an air of natural and picturesque simplicity, which meaner beauties in vain essayed to copy; her complexion, at a time when the use of paint was universal, owed nothing to art; her eyes were not large, but sparkling and full of expression; her mouth, though not a little haughtiness is implied in the curve of the under lip, was charming; and the contour of her face perfect.

The soul which Heaven had lodged in this fair person was worthy of its shrine. In those days, the very golden age of folly and affectation, the Beauties, by prescriptive right, might be divided into two factions, whom I shall call the *languishers* and *sparklers*. The languishers were those who, being dull by nature, or at least not bright, affected an extreme softness—lounged and lolled—simpered and sighed—lisped or drawled out their words— half shut their eyes—and moved as if "they were not born to carry their own weight:" the sparklers were those who, upon the strength of bright eyes and some natural vivacity and impertinence, set up for female wits; in conversation they attempted to dazzle by such sallies as would now be scarcely tolerated from the most abandoned of their sex; they were gay, airy, fluttering, fantastical, and talkative; they dealt in bon mots and repartees; they threw their glances right and left, *à tort et à travers;* and piqued themselves upon taking hearts by a *coup-de-main.* Miss Hamilton belonged to neither of these classes: though lively by nature, she had felt, perhaps, the necessity of maintaining a reserve of manner which should keep presumptuous fops at a distance. She wore her feminine dignity as an advanced guard,—her wit as a body of reserve. She did not speak much, but what she said was to the purpose,—just what the occasion demanded, and no more. *Fière à toute outrance* whenever she was called upon to stand on the defensive, she was less possessed with the idea of her own merit than might have been supposed; and, far from thinking her consequence increased by the number of her lovers, she was singularly fastidious with regard to the qualifications of those whom she admitted upon the list of aspirants.

De Grammont had hitherto received few repulses; but "*heureux sans être aimé,*" he began to be weary of pursuing conquests so little worth. Miss Hamilton was something new, something different from anything he had yet encountered in the form of woman. He soon perceived that the stratagems he had hitherto found all-prevailing,—flattery and *billets doux,* French fans and *gants de Martial,** —would be entirely misplaced in his present pursuit: he laid aside his usual methods of proceeding,† and, all

---

* Martial was a famous Parisian glove-maker of that time. "Est-ce que Martial fait les épigrammes aussi bien que les gants?" asks Molière's Comtesse d'Escarbagnas, in allusion to his Latin namesake. The English translator of the Mémoires de Grammont has rendered Miss Hamilton's "deux ou trois paires de gants de Martial" into "two or three pair of military gloves,"—a blunder only equalled by the translation of "Love's last Shift" into "La dernière chemise de l'amour."

† They were rather singular.—"Dès qu'une femme vous plait," says St. Evre-

his powers of captivating called forth by a real and deep attachment, he bent his whole soul to please; and he succeeded.

Meantime he had many rivals, but not such as were calculated to give him much uneasiness. Among them, the first, in rank at least, was the Duke of York, who became enamoured of Miss Hamilton's picture, which he saw at Sir Peter Lely's, and straight fell to ogling the fair original with all his might. The duke was extremely fond of hunting; and on his return from these expeditions, when he joined the circle in the duchess's drawing-room, he stationed himself near Miss Hamilton, and while he amused her with the exploits of himself, and his horses, and his dogs, his eyes expressed what his tongue left unsaid. It would sometimes happen, indeed, that those tender interpreters of his flame would wink and close "*au fort de leur lorgnerie;*" for princes, like other men, are subject to fatigue as well as love. The duchess, secure in the principles and character of her young favourite, never treated her with so much countenance and friendship as at this time. Miss Hamilton herself affected not to perceive the duke's passion; and when she was *obliged* to take notice of it, "elle prenait la peine de s'en divertir avec tout le respect du monde." Nor was she more easily pleased on the score of honourable proposals.

"So much the more as she refused to love,
So much the more she loved was and sought."

The Duke of Richmond was a gambler and a sot; but he stood nearest in blood to the throne after the Duke of York, and was considered the first match in the kingdom. Miss Hamilton thought otherwise. The duke, though much enamoured, demurred at making proposals, on the score of the lady's fortune; and she

mond to him, "vôtre prémier soin est d'apprendre si elle est aimée d'un autre, et le second de la faire enrager,—car de vous en faire aimer n'est que le dernier de vos soins."

never forgave him. In vain the King interfered and condescended to solicit her in his favour; in vain he offered to portion her nobly, in consideration of the services of her father and his own relationship to the duke,—he was rejected unequivocally. She could resist the invincible Jermyn, undazzled by the glare of that all-conquering reputation which found Lady Castlemaine an easy prey, and which even the fair Jennings could not withstand. She refused the Earl of Arundel, (afterwards Duke of Norfolk,) who laid himself, his expectant dukedom, and his thirty thousand a-year, at her feet; and disdained to be the first peeress of England at the expense of marrying a fool. The elder Russel tendered to her acceptance his "latter summer," and his vast possessions; the younger Russel, his nephew, did his best to supplant his uncle, with no better success; and Berkeley, Earl of Falmouth,* the personal friend and favourite both of the King and the Duke of York, whose rank, riches, and influence rendered him one of the greatest subjects in the kingdom; a man of pleasure by profession, vain, bold, and quick of wit,—even *he* confessed to St. Evremond, that "the possession of Miss Hamilton was alone wanting to crown all his desires; but that he had too much pride to owe her hand to the interference of her parents, and *dared* not hazard the refusal he anticipated from herself." De Grammont was not discouraged by the number, rank, and pretensions of his competitors: he was, in truth, but a younger brother, a banished man, under the displeasure of his own sovereign, deprived of his commission, and with no other resource but the gaming-table to supply his expensive habits; but he was handsome and brave, and possessed of unequalled powers of pleasing whenever he chose to exert them. He had the highest possible opinion of the understanding of his mistress, and his opinion of his own merit was not such as to induce him to despair.

* Lord Clarendon says, that Berkeley was " one upon whom the King had set his affection so much, that he had never denied any thing he asked for himself or any body else." He married the beautiful Miss Bagot, and was killed in the great sea-fight in 1665.

Meanwhile Miss Hamilton, though considerably occupied and interested by the assiduities of her captivating lover, found time and thoughts to give to other matters. She was wary and proud from the circumstances in which she was placed; but she had all the light-heartedness of youth, and was more than once seized with the whim of mingling a little innocent mischief, by way of variety, with the mischief of another sort with which she was surrounded. A fit subject for her mirthful humour presented itself in her cousin, Lady Muskerry.*

Lady Muskerry was not deficient in understanding, nor yet in good-nature; but she was to the last degree ridiculous and eccentric,—as mad as the Duchess of Newcastle, but after a less dignified fashion. She was excessively vain; extravagantly fond of dress, without a particle of taste; and a more indefatigable and enthusiastic dancer than her majesty the Queen, with even less capability of shining in that accomplishment; for she was deformed in her person, and Nature had shewn an undue partiality to one leg, by lengthening it at the expense of the other. It was the constant care of Lord Muskerry (a very good sort of man) to prevent his wife from rendering him supremely ridiculous by the exhibitions she was accustomed to make of herself before the whole court. But in vain; for the dancing mania was so strong upon her, that no restraint, short of durance under lock and key, could keep her in order.

The Queen, who could only please her husband by flattering his taste for pleasure,† announced her intention of giving a masked ball, which was to exceed in magnificence all the entertainments

---

* Margaret de Burgh, daughter of the Earl of Clanricarde, married to Lord Muskerry, eldest son of the Earl of Clancarty. Lady Muskerry was a great heiress, and, in spite of her deformity of person, was three times married.

† "La Reine avait de l'esprit, et mettait tous ses soins à plaire au Roi par les complaisances qui coutaient le moins à sa tendresse. Elle était attentive aux plaisirs et aux amusemens qu'elle pouvait fournir, surtout lorsqu' elle devait en être."

which had been given since her marriage. The guests were to represent bands from different nations, and each ticket contained the name of a lady and gentleman, who were considered as partners for the night: the costume in which they were to appear was also indicated. The King, who had much good-nature, and was perfectly *au fait* of all the intrigues which were going forward in his court, contrived that the guests should be paired as agreeably as possible to themselves, and assigned to the Chevalier de Grammont the delightful task of conducting Miss Hamilton. His majesty also left him the choice of the costume in which he would choose to appear. De Grammont, with the ready politeness of his nation, replied, "that as he had resided long enough in his majesty's court to become almost an Englishman, and even to be mistaken for one, he should enroll himself in the French corps, and disguise himself *à la Française;*" and he sent off his valet to Paris immediately, to order the most splendid dress that could be procured for this grand occasion.

Meantime, Lord Muskerry and his *chère moitié* were both in a fever of apprehension: he, lest his wife should be invited; and she, lest by any treasonable practices on his part she should be excluded. He took his measures so effectually, that she was passed over in the list of invitations, the Queen being well content to spare her *fête* the ridicule of such an exhibition. Lady Muskerry fretted with suspense and impatience; she was sure there was some mistake,—it was not possible that upon an occasion which gave her such an illustrious opportunity of shining in her favourite accomplishment, she should be excluded from court. She made Miss Hamilton the confidant of all her hopes and fears; and Miss Hamilton, possessed by the arch-spirit of mischief, determined to amuse herself and her brothers at the expense of her ridiculous cousin. A ticket was prepared with excellent device, in imitation of her own, which invited Lady Muskerry to the court ball, and bore the Queen's command that she should appear *en Babylonienne.* A page, disguised in the royal livery, delivered this to Lady Muskerry, with an apology for the mistake which had caused so long a delay. But Lady Muskerry was in too great a rapture to listen to apologies; thrice she kissed, upon her knees, the gracious billet which opened the door to paradise, and a treble gratuity was ordered to the fortunate page.

She then sat down to consider the important affair of her dress. The subject was embarrassing, and the time was short. She had never been in Babylon in her life; but others, she thought, might be better informed than herself: she therefore spent two days driving about to consult all her acquaintances upon the subject of her Babylonian attire,—among the rest Miss Hamilton. She took care, however, to keep her good fortune a profound secret from her husband; anticipating a degree of opposition in that quarter which she had not courage to brave: like many of her sex, she could rebel, but dared not disobey. Various were the tastes and opinions of those she consulted; and Lady Muskerry, that she might be assured of being in the right, adopted the suggestions of all; so that even Miss Hamilton herself could never have anticipated anything so marvellously absurd, or so extravagant, as the appearance her ladyship made *en Babylonienne*.

The night at length arrived; but, to the amazement of the whole court, De Grammont, hitherto renowned for his magnificence and gallantry, was not only one of the last to make his appearance, but when he did lead up Miss Hamilton, it was observed that though he wore a wig so vast, so powdered, and so essenced, that it eclipsed even that of Sir George Hewit*—the finest point-bands and ruffles, and the smallest hat that had ever appeared, yet his coat was merely an ordinary court-dress, rich indeed, but totally unbefitting the occasion. The count replied to the King's raillery by relating, with his unequalled spirit and pleasantry, the history of his hapless *costume à la Française;* which, according to his knavish valet, had been swallowed up in a quicksand near Calais. "But à-propos! sire," continued the count, when he had

---

* The beau *par excellence*, the original Sir Fopling Flutter of the day.

finished a story which threw the King and court into convulsions of laughter; "may I presume to ask your majesty who is that goblin *en masque*, whom I have encountered at the entrance? She had nearly laid violent hands upon me as I entered, insisting that I must be the cavalier appointed to lead her in the dance! May I perish, sire! if I do not think she has dropped from some planet, to lie in ambuscade at your palace gate and seize upon unwary cavaliers, for nothing beneath the moon was ever so monstrous or fantastic. She is enveloped in at least sixty yards of silver gauze, and carries a pyramid like that of Cheops on her head, *garnie de cent mille brimborions.*"

At this description the courtiers gazed at each other. The Queen looked round her wonder-struck, well assured that all whom she had invited were then present. "Odds-fish!" exclaimed the King laughing, "I have it! It is some new extravaganza of that crack-brained Duchess of Newcastle!"—and, to the consternation of those in the secret, and the delight of those who were not, he commanded that her Grace should be instantly admitted.

It was now Miss Hamilton's turn to be alarmed, and to blush and tremble behind her fan; for if Lady Muskerry had been introduced to the royal presence in her present grotesque garb, the jest would have gone much farther than she intended. Lord Muskerry, however, relieved her from her terrors. He had been standing in the circle while De Grammont was speaking, and whispered Miss Hamilton, "Now I, for my part, would lay a wager that it is another mad woman; and that no other than my own fantastic fool of a wife!" He immediately offered himself to execute the royal commission, and found her accordingly, still seated in her carriage at the gate, in a paroxysm of despair, and raving against the faithless cavalier who had been appointed to attend upon her. He conducted her home by main force, locked her up in her chamber, and placed a sentinel at her door. Miss Hamilton this time escaped undiscovered. For some other of her malicious frolics, played off at the expense of Miss Blague, "*aux blondes paupières,*" and that laughter-loving gipsy, Miss Price, who deserved the extremity of mischief, and the scene at Tunbridge Wells, in which poor Lady Muskerry was again made to play a principal part, the reader who has not read the *Mémoires de Grammont*, (if such there be,) is referred to that work. The grace, the spirit, the arch humour, which give to these "airy nothings" all their charm and importance, must, of necessity, evaporate in the best attempt at a translation.

While these festivities were going forward, the Chevalier de Grammont had every opportunity of paying the most assiduous court to his mistress; and the more difficult he found her of attainment, the stronger became his attachment. Even play, hitherto his ruling passion, could not detain him from Miss Hamilton's side; and his friends began to think the affair grew serious, when Lady Castlemaine's basset-table was forsaken for the Duchess of Ormond's drawing-room. St. Evremond undertook to give him some pertinent advice on the subject, representing the utter improbability of his prevailing with Miss Hamilton, and the utter impossibility of his marrying if he could; and ended by enumerating the suitors whom she had already refused, and whose pretensions were so far above those of an untitled, penniless, younger brother. "My good friend," replied the gay Chevalier, "thou art a philosopher; *tu connais la nature des étoiles du ciel; mais pour les astres de la terre, tu n'y connais rien.* I have just had a lecture from the King, of three hours' length, upon the same score. What do you tell me of those Ostrogoths, my rivals? Think you, if Miss Hamilton had deigned to listen to them, that I should have cared to obtain her? *Ecoutez, mon ami!* I will marry Miss Hamilton in spite of them and the world; I will have my banishment reversed; she shall be *Dame du Palais* to the Queen of France; my brother will be pleased to die some day or other for our particular gratification. Miss Hamilton shall be mistress of Sémeat* and Countess de Grammont, to make her

* The château of the De Grammont family.

amends for the loss of that oaf Norfolk, that sot Richmond, and that rake Falmouth. And what have you to say to this, *mon pauvre philosophe!*"

And so it proved; for Love in this instance was a better prophet than usual. De Grammont obtained the reward which his audacity and perseverance perhaps deserved, and carried off this paragon from all his competitors; but it was no sooner secured, than he seems, with his usual volatility, to have neglected his conquest. It has been said, with little probability, that one circumstance attending this marriage inspired Molière with the first idea of *Le Mariage Forcé*. Louis XIV. having been prevailed on at length to recall De Grammont, after a banishment of six or seven years,* he was in such haste to return to France, that he left London without performing his engagements to Miss Hamilton. Her two brothers, Anthony and George Hamilton, pursued him to Dover, and overtaking him at the inn, they exclaimed aloud, " Chevalier de Grammont, n'avez vous rien oublié à Londres ?" —" Pardonnez moi, messieurs," replied this ardent lover, "j'ai oublié d'épouser votre sœur." We may suppose that when his high-spirited mistress gave him her hand, she was unacquainted with this characteristic trait.

The Count de Grammont left England finally in 1669, about a year after his marriage. Charles, in a letter to his sister, the unfortunate Duchess of Orleans, dated in October that year, recommends the Countess de Grammont to his sister's friendship. " I writt to you," he says, " yesterday by the Compte de Grammont; but I beleeve this letter will come sooner to your handes, for he goes by Dieppe with his wife and family. And now that I have named her, I cannot chuse but againe desire you to be

---

* De Grammont, with his usual audacity and love of contradiction, had ventured to make himself particularly agreeable to a lady (Mademoiselle de Mothe-Houdancourt) whom his majesty as particularly admired : for this *crime* he was banished.

kind to her; for besides the merritt her family has on both sides, she is as good a creature as ever lived. I beleeve she will passe for a handsome woman in France, though she has not yett, since her lying-in, recovered that good shape she had before, and I am afraid never will."

It appears, from the slight manner in which Charles speaks of the Countess's beauty, that her charms were partly lost upon his gross taste: nor is it surprising that the man whose soul and senses were enslaved by the vulgar and vicious Castlemaine, should be dead to the intellectual graces and refined loveliness of Miss Hamilton.

The Countess de Grammont spent the rest of her life in the French court. Her beauty and elegance charmed the King, yet she did not universally please: Madame de Maintenon thought her "plus agréable qu'aimable," perhaps because, though she could amuse with her lively wit, she could not stoop to flatter. When Madame de Caylus called her "Anglaise insupportable," she probably spoke in the character of a French woman, and a rival wit and beauty.* Madame de Grammont, soon after her arrival in France, was appointed "Dame du Palais" at Versailles; and, in a few years afterwards, De Grammont became, by the death of his elder brother, one of the richest and most powerful of the *noblesse*.

It is pain to think that the man who had sufficient delicacy and discrimination to feel the accomplishments of such a woman as Miss Hamilton, and spirit enough to win and wear her, was so little worthy of his happiness. We look for something far beyond mere superficial talents and graces in him who was the husband of one so peerless. He was gay, gallant, polished in his address,

* [Madame de Sévigné, in her letters to Madame de Guignan, speaks generally of the Countess of Grammont as of a person by no means agreeable, somewhat affected, and much inclined to give herself haughty airs.—ED.]

and elegant in his person; his wit ready, pointed, yet perfectly
good-humoured: he told a story with inimitable grace—then, as
now, a true Parisian accomplishment. He appears to have been
a man of the most happy temperament, his vivacity and animal
spirits inexhaustible, and his invulnerable self-complacency beyond
the reach of a serious thought or a profound feeling of any kind.
But these are only the garnish and "outward flourishes," which
make a character, otherwise estimable, irresistible. Where was the
high honour, the chivalrous feeling, the refined sentiments, the
nobility of soul, the generous self-devotion, which should have
distinguished the husband of Miss Hamilton? Frivolous, worthless, heartless, inconstant, a selfish epicure, a gambler, a sharper,
a most malicious enemy, a negligent friend, and a faithless lover:
—such was De Grammont, such is the character which Bussy-
Rabutin,* and even his partial friend St. Evremond, have left of
him, and which he was well content to support in the "Mémoires"
which Hamilton wrote from his dictation, and published in his
lifetime.† Whether the lovely, noble-minded, and far-superior

* "Le Chevalier avait les yeux riants, le nez bien fait, la bouche belle, une
petite fossette au menton, qui faisait un agréable effet sur son visage; je ne sais
quoi de fin dans la physionomie, la taille assez belle s'il ne se fut point vouté,
l'esprit galant et délicat. Il écrivait le plus mal du monde.—Quoiqu'il soit
superflu de dire qu'un rival soit incommode, le Chevalier l'était au point qu'il eut
mieux valu pour une pauvre femme, en avoir quatre sur les bras que lui seul. Il
était liberal jusques à la profusion; et par là sa maitresse ni ses rivaux ne pouvait
avoir de valets fidèles. D'ailleurs le meilleur garçon du monde. Une chose qui
faisait qu'il lui était plus difficile de persuader qu'à un autre, était qu'il ne parlait
jamais sericusement, de sorte qu'il fallait qu'une femme se flattait beaucoup pour
croire qu'il fut amoureux d'elle."—*Histoire Amoureuse des Gaules.*

† Before the *Mémoires du Comte de Grammont* were published, they were of
course submitted to the censorship. Fontenelle was then Censeur Royal; and
he was so scandalized at the idea of a peer of France being represented as a
common sharper, or, in polite phrase, "one who used address to correct the errors
of Fortune," that he flatly refused his approbation. De Grammont, on hearing
this, hastened to wait upon the scrupulous censor, and demanded, with his usual
vivacity, what business he had to be more solicitous about a nobleman's reputation than he was himself? and desired that he would do him the favour instantly
to sign the licence, if the freedom with which his character was treated was the

woman, who had flung away herself upon his unworthiness, afterwards discovered how false was the foundation on which she had built her happiness, we have no means of knowing;—if not, she was more effectually blinded by love than many of her sex who have committed the same irreparable mistake.

They appear to have lived together on easy terms. Towards the latter part of her life, the Countess de Grammont became very devout, and was extremely scandalized by her husband's epicurism and infidelity. De Grammont, who had never known an hour's sickness, used to say he should *never* die. At last, however, in his seventy-fifth year, he fell dangerously ill, and the King (Louis XIV.) sent the Marquis Dangeau to him, to remind him that it was time to think of God. De Grammont listened to him with polite attention, and turning to his wife, said with a smile, " Comtesse, si vous n'y prenez garde, Dangeau vous escamotera ma conversion!" He recovered from this attack, and seemed more than ever convinced of his own immortality: but paid at length the forfeit of humanity, dying in 1707, at the age of eighty-six. From a letter of St. Evremond to Ninon de l'Enclos, it appears that his wife had the satisfaction of converting him at last, and that he died " très dévot."

The countess survived him but a short time: she left two daughters. Claude Charlotte, the eldest, inherited her mother's beauty, and her father's wit and vivacity. She married Henry Lord Stafford, and is the same Lady Stafford who was the friend and correspondent of Lady M. W. Montague. The youngest daughter died abbess of a convent in Lorraine.

---

only objection to the work. Fontenelle, as it may be supposed, made no more difficulties. He might have replied to De Grammont, as the latter did to Madame de Hérault. The Count had visited the lady to pay his compliments of condolence on the death of her husband: she received them with an air of extreme coldness; upon which, suddenly changing his tone, he exclaimed gaily, —" Le prenez-vous par là?—Ma foi, je ne m'en soucie pas plus que vous!"

The portrait annexed is from the picture by Sir Peter Lely, painted for the Duchess of York, and now at Windsor. We are told that, at the time, Lely was enchanted with his subject, and every one considered it as the finest effort of his pencil, both as a painting and a resemblance.* The dignified attitude and elegant turn of the head, are well befitting her who was "grande et gracieuse dans le moindre de ses movemens:" we have here " le petit nez delicat," the fine contour of face, the lovely bust, the open expansive brow, and the lips, ripe, rich, and breathing sweets, at least to the imagination. A few pearls are negligently interwoven among her luxuriant tresses, as if on purpose to recall Crashaw's beautiful compliment to his mistress:—

> " Tresses that wear
> Jewels but to declare
> How much themselves more precious are.
>
> Each ruby there,
> Or pearl, that dare appear,
> Be its own *blush*,—be its own *tear*.

The countenance has infinitely more spirit and intellect than Sir Peter Lely's beauties in general exhibit; and though, perhaps, a little too proud and elevated in its present expression, in must have been, when brightened into smiles, or softened with affection, exquisitely bewitching. The neck and throat are beautifully painted, the drapery is grand and well-disposed, and the background has a rich and deep tone of colour, finely relieving the figure.

There is a slight defect in the drawing of the right arm. Lely, did not, like Vandyke, paint his hands and arms from nature; they are in general all alike, pretty and delicate, but destitute of individual character, and often ill drawn. In the present instance this is the more to be regretted, because Miss Hamilton, among her other perfections, was celebrated for the matchless beauty of her hand and arm.

* Chaque portrait parut un chef-d'œuvre ; et celui de Mademoiselle Hamilton parut le plus achevé. Lely avoua qu'il y avait prit plaisir, &c.

ÉPÎTRE DE ST. EVREMOND À M. LE CHEVALIER DE GRAMMONT,

À l'occasion de son amour pour Mademoiselle Hamilton.

Il n'est qu'un Chevalier au monde !
Et que ceux de la table ronde,
Que les plus fameux aux tournois,
Aux avantures, aux exploits,
Me pardonnent si je les quitte
Pour chanter un nouveau mérite ;
C'est celui qu'on vit à la cour,
Jadis si galant sans amour,
La même qui sût à Bruxelles
Comme ici plaire aux demoiselles ;
Gagner tout l'argent des maris,
Et puis revenir à Paris,
Ayant couru toute la terre
Dans le jeu, l'amour, et la guerre.
Insolent en prospérité,
Fort courtois en nécessité,
L' ame eu fortune liberale,
Aux créanciers pas trop loyale :
Qui n'a changé, ni changera,
Et seul au monde qu'on verra
Soutenir la blanche vieillesse
Comme il a passé la jeunesse ;
Rare merveille de nos jours !
N'étaient vos trop longues amours,
N'était la sincère tendresse
Dont vous aimez votre princesse,
N'était qu' ici les beaux désirs
Vous font pousser de vrais soupirs,
Et qu' enfin vous quittez pour elle
Votre mérite d' infidelle—
Cher et parfait original !
Vous n'auriez jamais eu d'égal.
Il est des heros pour la guerre,
Mille grands hommes sur la terre,
Mais au sens de Saint Evremond
Rien qu'un Chevalier de Grammont ;
Et jamais ne sera de vie,
Plus admiré et moins suivie !

THE COUNTESS OF OSSORY.

"Her person was a paradise, and her soul the cherub to guard it."
DRYDEN.

EMILIE DE NASSAU, Countess of Ossory, was the eldest daughter of Louis de Nassau, Lord of Beverweert, of Odyke, and Auverquerque, in Holland, the acknowledged, but not legitimate, son of Maurice Prince of Orange. He was a man of tried virtue, talents, and courage, and the intimate friend of De Witt.

Lady Ossory is interesting from her extreme beauty, her tenderness, and her feminine virtues. But her alliance with the house of Ormond, which connected her at the same time with all the noblest families of England and Ireland,* and made her the daughter, wife, and mother of heroes, has rendered her something more than merely interesting; has shed around her person and memory that lustre which best becomes a woman,—the lustre reflected from the glory and the virtues of her husband.

* And more immediately with those of Butler, Hamilton, Stewart, Beaufort, Chesterfield, Devonshire, Derby, Clancarty, and Clanricarde, &c. Lady Ossory's marriage was partly the means of raising others of her family to English alliances and English honours; her youngest sister, Charlotte de Nassau, married the Earl of Arlington, and was mother to the first Duchess of Grafton; her youngest brother, Henry de Nassau d'Auverquerque, was created Earl of Grantham.

The father of the Earl of Ossory was James, the GREAT Duke of Ormond; and never, upon conqueror or potentate, was that epithet more justly bestowed. He was, without exception, the most illustrious character of the times in which he lived; without reproach as a man, a subject, a patriot, and a soldier. He had attached himself, from principle, to the cause of Charles the First; and through the whole of the civil wars had maintained his cause with the most unshaken constancy, and the most generous self-devotion. After having expended his patrimony in the service of that monarch and his successor, and finding that all was lost, except honour, he refused the conditions offered by Cromwell, and, making his escape in a small boat, joined the fortunes of the exiled monarch; and was afterwards in his prosperity, as in his adversity, his ablest counsellor, and truest friend,—never his flatterer, or his favourite.*

The Duchess of Ormond his wife, and the mother of Lord Ossory, was a woman of great beauty, and of an undaunted spirit. She was the heiress of the Earl of Desmond, and her union with the duke, then Lord Thurles, put an end to the feuds and lawsuits which had for years divided the houses of Desmond and Ormond, and threatened the ruin of both. Their marriage, however, was not only a marriage of policy, but of passion; their early attachment was attended by various difficulties and romantic distresses, and in particular by one circumstance, which throws so deep an interest round the character of the duchess, that I venture to relate it.

She was a ward of the King (Charles I.) who bestowed the

---

* As the loyalty of Ormond was that of principle, the favour or displeasure of his capricious master never made the slightest alteration in his demeanour; so that his courteous equanimity sometimes abashed the King. The Duke of Buckingham on one occasion whispered, "I wish your majesty would resolve me one question; whether it be the Duke of Ormond who is out of favour with your majesty, or your majesty with the Duke of Ormond? for you appear the most out of countenance of the two!"

guardianship of her person and her vast estates on the Earl of
Holland. While the lawsuit was pending between her and Lord
Thurles, she happened to meet her young adversary at court, and
struck with his noble qualities and fine person, fell in love with him;
she was young, inexperienced, and as self-willed as a conscious
beauty and a great heiress may be supposed to have been; and
took so little care to conceal the partiality she felt, that not only
the object of her affection, but the whole court, was aware of it.
The King sent to Lord Thurles, desiring that he would desist from
any pretensions to the hand of the young lady, as his majesty
designed her for another. To this the lover replied, with a spirit
which justified the lady's choice, that he should be sorry to displease
his majesty, but that he considered he had even a better title than
any other nobleman about the court to pay the Lady Elizabeth
those attentions which were due to her beauty and merits, being
himself her " poor cousin and kinsman." The Lady Elizabeth, on
her part, was not slow to declare her abhorrence of the match
proposed by the King, and her determination to marry Lord
Thurles, and none other. The union was in all respects the most
eligible for both; no other means could be found to put an end to
their family dissensions, and Lady Elizabeth strongly felt, and as
eloquently pleaded, that reason and interest were on the side of
her girlish passion. But the King was resolute; her guardian,
according to the fashion of obdurate guardians from time imme-
morial, placed the young lady in durance vile, and not only those
consequences ensued which are *de rigueur* in such cases, but others
which certainly were not anticipated by any of the parties concerned.

The young lovers kept up a constant correspondence of letters
and tokens, by means of Lady Isabella Rich, the daughter of the
Earl of Holland, who not being so strictly secluded as her father's
ward, contrived to meet Lord Thurles secretly. Lady Isabella
was handsome, lively, good-natured, and attached to Lady Elizabeth, with whom she had been educated; but she was not of an
age or a disposition to carry on this clandestine intercourse with

safety to herself. In short—not to be too circumstantial—Lady Isabella found her friend's lover only too agreeable; she fell a victim to passion and opportunity, but certainly not to any preconcerted villany on the part of Lord Thurles, who was then only nineteen; the whole tenour of his life, before and after, belies such an imputation. The consequences were, that Lady Isabella became the mother of an infant, which was immediately sent abroad and carefully educated at Paris, without any knowledge of his parents. The secret was so faithfully kept, that not even a breath of suspicion rested upon Lady Isabella; and soon afterwards, Lord Thurles, by bribing the avarice of Lord Holland,* obtained his consent and his interest with the King, and married Lady Elizabeth.

Several years afterwards, when the Duke visited Paris, his first care was to inquire for this son, whom he found a blooming and hopeful youth, accomplished in all the exercises which became his age: the father could not deny himself the pleasure of sending the unhappy mother some tidings of her child; but having occasion to write to his wife the same day, he made a fatal mistake in the direction of the two letters, and that which was intended for Lady Isabella fell into the hands of the Duchess of Ormond.

The duchess passionately loved her husband; and notwithstanding the lapse of years, she must have felt, on this occasion, as a woman would naturally feel on discovering that she had been betrayed in the tenderest point by her lover and her friend. She was still sitting with the letter open in her hand, lost in painful astonishment, when Lady Isabella was announced; an exchange of letters and a mutual explanation took place, and the scene which must have ensued may be imagined. Lady Isabella standing before her injured friend, bowed down to the earth with "penetrative shame," while that generous friend, unable to bear the sight of her humiliation, threw her arms round her neck, and

* He bought the earl's consent with 15,000*l.*

with tears and a thousand fond caresses, endeavoured to reconcile her with herself, assured her of her perfect forgiveness, and promised that the past should be to her as if it had never been.

And she kept her word; for it is even said, and, if true, it is a rare instance of female discretion, that not even the duke ever suspected his wife's knowledge of this transaction.

It happened, after the time of which we speak, that Lady Isabella and her family being obliged to fly from England, the Duchess of Ormond offered her an asylum in her house at Caen; and Lady Isabella, worthy in this instance of such a friend, accepted the offer as frankly as it was made. She resided for two years under the roof of the Duke and Duchess of Ormond, in all honour and confidence. The duchess never condescended to doubt either the truth and love of her husband, or the honour and gratitude of her friend; her domestic peace was never disturbed by petty jealousy, nor her noble confidence wronged by those she had trusted. It is justice to Lady Isabella to add, that she preserved to the end of her life an unblemished reputation, and died unmarried.*

To return to the Earl of Ossory. When the Duke of Ormond withdrew to France, in 1655, he found himself obliged to leave his wife and family behind; and soon afterwards Cromwell caused the Earl of Ossory to be arrested, upon no specific charge, and committed to the Tower.† His mother waited upon the Protector

* Her son died young before the Restoration. These particulars, which were not known till after the death of the duke, may be found in Carte's Life of Ormond, vol. iii. folio.

† [The Earl of Ossory had, previously to this, been himself residing at the French court. It was there that the excellent and amiable Evelyn became acquainted with him, and their friendship continued until the Earl of Ossory's death, when he took his last farewell of Evelyn as of the " oldest friend " he had. In his Diary, Jan. 13, 1649-50, Evelyn, at Paris, commemorates the "exercises on horseback" of Ossory and his brother Richard; and soon after he relates the following anecdote. "May 7. I went with Sir Richard Browne's lady and my

to remonstrate, and to solicit his enlargement, pleading the quiet and inoffensive life which she led with her children in London. Cromwell told her plainly, that he had more reason to fear her than any body else. She replied with dignity and spirit, and in the presence of a numerous drawing-room, that "she desired no favour at his hands, but merely justice to her innocent son;" and that "she thought it strange that she, who had never been concerned in a plot in her life, nor opened her mouth against his person and government, should be represented as so terrible a person."—"No, madam," replied Cromwell, "that is not the case; but your worth has gained you so great an influence over all the commanders of our party, and we know so well your power over your own party, that it is in your ladyship's breast to

wife, together with the Earle of Chesterfield, Lord Ossorie, and his brother, to Vamber, a place neere the citty famous for butter; when coming homewards, being on foote, a quarrel arose between Lord Ossorie and a man in a garden, who thrust Lord Ossorie from the gate with uncivil language; on which our young gallant struck the fellow on the pate, and bid him aske pardon, which he did with much submission, and so we parted: but we were not gon far, before we heard a noise behind us, and saw people coming with gunns, swords, staves, and forks, and who followed flinging stones; on which we turn'd and were forc'd to engage, and with our swords, stones, and the help of our servants, (one of whom had a pistol,) made our retreate for neare a quarter of a mile, when we took shelter in a house where we were besieg'd, and at length forc'd to submit to be prisoners. Lord Hatton, with some others, were taken prisoners in the flight, and his lordship was confin'd under three locks and as many doores in this rude fellow's master's house, who pretended to be steward to Monsr. St. Germain, one of the presidents of the Grand Chambre du Parliament, and a canon of Nôtre Dame. Severall of us were much hurt. One of our lacquies escaping to Paris, caused the bailiff of St. Germain to come with his guard and rescue us. Immediately afterwards came Mous^r. St. Germain himselfe in greate wrath, on hearing that his housekeeper was assaulted; but when he saw the king's officers, the gentlemen and noblemen, with his majesty's resident, and understood the occasion, he was ashamed of the accident, requesting the fellow's pardon, and desiring the ladys to accept their submission and a supper at his house." "I have often heard that gallant gentleman my Lord Ossorie affirme solemnly, that in all the conflicts he ever was in, at sea or on land, (in the most desperate of both which he had often been,) he believ'd he was never in so much danger as when these people rose against us. He us'd to call it the *battaill de Vambre*, and remember it with a greate deale of mirth as an adventure *en cavalier*."—ED.]

act what you please." She answered, "that she must needs construe this speech into a civil compliment:" but a compliment and a shrug were all she could get from the politic Protector, till Ossory fell dangerously ill. She then solicited for him with such vehemence, that Cromwell at length set him at liberty; and the earl, attended by his brother, Lord Richard, disguised as his servant, escaped to the Hague. He was received there with high honour by his father's friends, and in particular by M. de Beverweert, who entertained the English royalists with great hospitality. In her father's house, Lord Ossory had frequent and almost daily opportunities of seeing and conversing with the Lady Emilie: the more he saw and knew of her the more he admired, and at length loved, with all the enthusiasm of his character; and he assured his father that "the happiness of his life depended on passing it with her."

At this time the Earl of Ossory was about four-and-twenty, he was tall, well-made, and handsome, with an open expressive countenance, and fine teeth and hair; he rode, fenced, and danced, remarkably well; played on the lute and guitar; spoke French eloquently, and Italian fluently; was a good historian; and seems to have had a taste for light and elegant literature; for Sir Robert Southwell represents him as so well read in poetry and romance, that "in a gallery full of pictures and hangings, he could tell the stories of all that were there described." These, however, were the mere superficial graces which enabled him to please in a drawing-room; and to these he added all the rare and noble qualities which can distinguish a man in the cabinet and in the field. He was wise in council, quick and decided in action, as brave in battle as an Amadis of Gaul,—gallant "beyond the fiction of romance," humane, courteous, affable, temperate, generous to profusion, and open almost to a fault. "In a word," says the historian, "his virtue was unspotted in the centre of a luxurious court; his integrity unblemished amid all the vices of the times; his honour untainted through the course of his whole life;" and it is most worthy of remark, that in those days, when the spirits of men were heated with party rage, when profligate pens were wielded by profligate and obscure individuals, and satire " unbated and envenomed," was levelled at whatever was noble, or beautiful, or good in the land, not a single expression can any where be traced to contradict or invalidate this universal testimony. " No writer," (I quote again from history,) " ever appeared, then or since, so regardless of truth and of his own character, as to venture one stroke of censure on that of the Earl of Ossory."*

Such a man might have pretended to the hand of any woman upon earth ; and no woman—though she had been a throned and sceptred queen, in beauties, virtues, graces, friends, exceeding all account, and dowered with kingdoms—but would have been honoured in his choice. If, therefore, some difficulties attended his marriage, it will easily be believed that they arose not on the part of the lady of his love.

The Duke of Ormond had commenced a treaty of marriage for his son with a daughter of Lord Southampton,† which he broke off with regret, for her portion was double that of the Lady Emilie: and fortune was at this time an object in the Ormond family, reduced as they were by exile, confiscation, and losses of every kind. M. de Beverweert would give his daughter no more than £10,000; and he insisted on his future son-in-law being put into immediate possession of £1200 a-year; a large income in those days, but which would have been a mere trifle when the family were in power and prosperity. The Duchess of Ormond was put to great difficulties, the condition of her estate in Ireland scarce allowing her to part with so large a portion of it, "but she could deny

---

* Kippis' Biog. Brit. vol. iii. p. 84; Collins ; Carte's Life of Ormond, vol. iii. ; and Sir Robert Southwell's Ireland.

† Afterwards Lady Russel,—the LADY RUSSEL, whose very name sanctifies the paper upon which it is written. It is, however, no imputation upon Lord Ossory's taste that he preferred the lady he knew and loved to the lady he had never seen, and whose character had not yet been developed by those trials, out of which she arose an angel upon earth.

nothing to her beloved son."* The duke, who looked upon this alliance as a means of strengthening his interest with De Witt, gave his consent, and the marriage was celebrated at the Hague, November 17, 1659. The following year the King's restoration took place, and Ossory brought his young and beautiful bride in triumph to England.

It does not appear that Lady Ossory was remarkable for her wit; but she had excellent sense, an affectionate heart, and the sweetest temper in nature.† Her husband might have said of her, as Shakspeare so beautifully says of his mistress:

> "Fair, kind, and true is all my argument;
> Kind is my love to-day, to-morrow kind,
> Still constant in a wondrous excellence."‡

The power she obtained and preserved in her husband's noble heart, is no slight argument of her superior understanding; in that age of universal gallantry, Lord Ossory *dared* to be faithful to his wife; and there lived not the man who would have dared to banter him upon the subject. The only fashionable folly he was known to indulge in, was gaming; he sometimes played high,— an imprudence into which his habits, as a courtier, necessarily led him. After having lost deeply, he would return home, thoughtful and moody; and when his wife tenderly inquired the cause, and he would tell her that he was "vexed with himself for playing the fool, and gaming, and had lost, perhaps, a thousand pounds;" she would still desire him "not to be troubled, for she would find means to save it at home."—"She was, indeed," adds the grave historian of the family, "an admirable economist, always cheerful, and never known to be out of humour; so that they lived together in the most perfect harmony imaginable. Lord Ossory never found any place or company more agreeable than he found at home; and when he returned thither from court, they constantly met with

---

* Verbatim from Carte, vol. iii.
† Carte, vol. iii.   ‡ Sonnet 105.

open arms, with kind embraces, and the most moving expressions of mutual tenderness."*

But this picture, bright and beautiful as it is, had its shades. In this world of ours, "where but to think, is to be full of sorrow," Lady Ossory was so far most happy, that though she suffered *through* those she loved, (as all must do who embark their happiness in their affections,) she never suffered *by* them: but she lost several of her numerous family at an early age, and the frequent absence of Lord Ossory, whilst engaged in the highest civil and military employments, must have doomed her to many widowed hours. The reckless valour, too, with which he exposed his life, and which was such as even to call down a rebuke from his brave father, must have filled the gentle bosom of his wife with a thousand fond anxieties: yet might not those partings and meetings, those alternations of hope and fear, those trembling terrors for his safety, those rapturous tears which greeted his return, have assisted to keep freshly alive, through a long series of years, all the romance of early passion? And was not this much? Did Lady Ossory buy too dearly the proud happiness of belonging to that man, upon whom the eyes of all Europe were fixed to gaze and to admire? who from every new triumph brought her home a faith and love unchanged,—depositing his honours at her feet, and his cares in her gentle arms? Let the woman who reads this question, answer it to her own heart.

An idea may be formed of Lady Ossory's life and feelings, by a rapid glance over her husband's brilliant career. He was twice Lord-Deputy in Ireland; twice an ambassador: there was no considerable action fought by sea or land, during the reign of Charles II., in which he did not distinguish himself: he was at the same time a general in the army, and rear-admiral of the Red; and in 1673, he hoisted the Union flag as Commander-in-Chief of the whole fleet, in the absence of Prince Rupert. During the

* Carte's Life of Ormond, vol. iii.

Dutch war, the principle and policy of which he entirely disapproved,* he nevertheless served with heroic valour, if not with enthusiasm; and he would have destroyed the whole fleet of Holland, if the timidity of the King's council had not defeated his scheme.† He was Commander-in-Chief in Ireland, a Knight of the Garter, and a privy-councillor, lord of the King's bed-chamber, and lord-chamberlain to the Queen. He lived, when in London, with such munificent hospitality, that it must have required all Lady Ossory's skill, as an economist, to manage their household. He was remarkable for seeking out all the foreigners of any distinction or merit who visited England, and was fond of entertaining them at his table.‡ To this, perhaps, he partly owed his widely extended reputation on the Continent. When he was Envoy-Extraordinary in France, in 1667, Louis XIV. endeavoured to prevail upon him to enter into his service. He offered him personally, and through his ministers, the most magnificent appointments; and when these were refused, he was desired only to name what would content him for himself and his friends.

* See his famous speech in defence of his father against Lord Shaftesbury. [Evelyn has this entry in his Diary, 12th March, 1671-2;—" Now was the first blow given by us to the Dutch convoy of the Smyrna fleete, by Sir Robert Holmes and Lord Ossorie, in which we received little save blows, and a worthy reproch for attacking our neighbours 'ere any war was proclaim'd, and then pretending the occasion to be, that some time before, the Merlin yacht chanceing to saile thro' the whole Dutch fleete, their admiral did not strike to that trifling vessel. Surely this was a quarrel slenderly grounded, and not becoming Christian neighbours. We are like to thrive accordingly. Lord Ossorie several times deplor'd to me his being engaged in it; he had more justice and honour than in the least to approve of it, tho' he had ben over persuaded to the expedition."—ED.]

† It is not now understood why this plan, which was allowed to be simple and feasible, though requiring great courage to execute, was not acceded to; when some of the council objected, Ossory told the King, "that he would blow up the whole Dutch fleet with a farthing candle, or have his head set upon Westminster Hall beside Cromwell's."

‡ Dryden describes the house of Ormond as one " open as that of Publicola, where all were equally admitted, where nothing that was reasonable was denied, where misfortune was a powerful recommendation, and where want itself was a powerful mediator, and stood next to merit."

K

Finding all in vain, the King, at his departure, loaded him with favours, and presented him with a jewel worth £2000.

It was not alone the dangers of battle that Lady Ossory had to fear for her husband; his chivalrous honour and the vehemence of his character sometimes perilled his life in more private encounters. His memorable quarrel with the Duke of Buckingham is well known. The duke had asserted in the House of Lords, that "whoever opposed the Bill then under discussion," (the Irish cattle Bill), "had either an Irish interest, or an Irish understanding." Ossory called on the duke to retract his words, which he considered as an insolent reflection on his country, or meet him with his sword in his hand to maintain them. The whole affair, in which Ossory behaved with so much frankness and gallantry, and in which the duke cut such a pitiful, or rather such an infamous figure, may be found at length in Clarendon.

In 1671, occurred that extraordinary attempt on the life of the Duke of Ormond by the ruffian Blood, of notorious memory; it is supposed at the instigation of Buckingham. There was, in fact, something so audacious and so theatrical in the idea of hanging the duke upon the gallows at Tyburn, that it could only have originated with that "fanfaron de crimes." Such, at least, was the general opinion at the time. A few days after this event, Lord Ossory meeting the Duke of Buckingham in the King's chamber, the colour flushed to his temples with passion, and his eyes sparkled with such ire, that the duke took refuge behind the King's chair. "My lord," said Ossory, stepping up to him, "I know well that you are at the bottom of this late attempt of Blood's upon my father; and therefore I give you fair warning, if my father comes to a violent end by sword or pistol,—if he dies by the hand of a ruffian, or the more secret way of poison, I shall not be at a loss to know the first author of it. I shall consider *you* as the assassin; I shall treat you as such, and I shall pistol you, though you stood beside the King's chair; and I tell it you in his majesty's presence, that you may be sure I shall keep my word." So saying, he turned upon his heel, leaving the duke so completely overawed, that he had not even spirit to utter a denial.*

But it is time to stop; the imagination lingers over the subject, unwilling to approach the catastrophe. To complete the glorious picture, such a spirit should have passed away from the earth, as unstained by grief as by fear—unembittered, unbroken to the last; and it was far otherwise. In 1080, the Earl, leaving Lady Ossory at the seat of her daughter, Lady Derby, came to London to prepare for his departure on a new expedition. He had been appointed governor of Tangier, but with forces so inadequate that he considered himself cast away, " not only on a hazardous adventure, but an impossibility."† "This," says Evelyn, "touched my lord deeply, that he should be so little consider'd as to put him on a business in which he should probably not only lose his reputation, but be charged with all the miscarriages and ill-successe. My lord being an exceeding brave and valiant person, and who had so approved

* I believe no writer has remarked the singular coincidence between the characters and fortunes of the Duke of Ormond, and his ancestor, the Earl of Ormond, of Elizabeth's time. Both were brave, popular, enthusiastically loyal, and inflexibly honest; both were accomplished courtiers, and lived to experience the ingratitude and injustice of the princes they had served; both experienced many changes of fortune, and lived to an extreme old age, so as to behold their heirs in the third generation; both were opposed to the reigning favourites, for the enmity of the Duke of Ormond and Buckingham was at least equal to that of the Earl of Ormond and Lord Leicester. As Buckingham was believed to have instigated Blood in his attempt on the Duke of Ormond, so Leicester was known to have attempted the assassination of Ormond by means of a hired cutthroat, who was afterwards, like Blood, forgiven and rewarded. The following anecdote is very characteristic:—The Earl of Ormond coming one day to court, met Lord Leicester in the ante-chamber. After the usual salutations, " My lord," said Leicester, insolently; " I dreamed of you last night !"—" Indeed," replied Ormond, " what could your lordship dream of me ?"—" I dreamed that I gave you a box on the ear."—" Dreams are interpreted by contraries," replied the high-spirited Irishman, and instantly lent him a cuff on the ear, which made the favourite stagger. For this he was committed to the Tower by Elizabeth.

† Lord Sunderland said in council, that "Tangier must necessarily be lost; but that it was fit Lord Ossory should be sent, that they might give some account of it to the world."—*Evelyn's Memoirs.*

himself in divers signal batailes, both at sea and land; so beloved and so esteem'd by the people, as one they depended upon in all occasions worthy of such a captain; he looked on this as too great an indifference in his majesty, after all his services and the merits of his father, the Duke of Ormond, and a designe of some who envied his virtue. It certainly took so deep roote in his mind, that he who was the most voide of feare in the world, (and assur'd me he would go to Tangier with ten men, if his majesty commanded him,) could not beare up against this unkindness."

The extreme heat of the weather, the fatigue he underwent in making his preparations, and the deep sense of the injury he had received, which seems to have struck upon his heart, threw him into a delirious fever: the last coherent words he spoke, were to name his wife, and recommend her and her children to his father's care.* He died at the house of his brother-in-law, Lord Arlington, four days afterwards, in his forty-sixth year: leaving behind him a character which poetry cannot embellish, nor flattery exaggerate. Even the muse of Dryden cowered when he approached the theme: after reading the life of Lord Ossory in plain and not very elegant prose, his poetical panegyric appears cold and strained.† The reply of the Duke of Ormond to some

* "My son's kindness to his wife, and his care of her, increases my value for him, and my sorrow for him, and I am glad he expressed it so frequently, when he thought of that sad hour which is come upon us; but there was no other need of it than the manifestation of his good-nature, for I am ready to do for her, whatever she or her friends can wish."—Letter of the Duke of Ormond to Lord Arlington.

† Dryden was a practised hand at an elegy and a panegyric, and in the present instance he was more in earnest than usual; but turn from his tuneful couplets to the simple entry which Evelyn has made in his Diary, of the "death of his noble and illustrious friend, the Lord Ossorie."—" His majesty never lost a worthier subject, nor father a better or more dutiful son; a loving, generous, good-natured, and perfectly obliging friend; one who had done innumerable kindnesses to several before they knew it, nor did he ever advance any that were not worthy: no one more brave, more modest; none more humble, sober, and every way virtuous. Unhappy England in this illustrious person's loss! Universal was the mourning for him, and the eulogies on him: I staid night and day by his bed side

impertinent comforter is well known, and is the most comprehensive and affecting eulogy ever pronounced:—" I would not exchange my dead son for any living son in Christendom!"*

Lord Ossory died before his unhappy wife could even hear of his illness. She did not, upon her bereavement, break out into any tumultuous sorrow; she bowed her head to the stroke with apparent resignation, and never raised it again. She survived her husband little more than three years, and dying in January, 1684, was buried in Christ Church.

The Countess of Ossory was the mother of twelve children, of whom, two sons and three daughters survived her.

Her eldest son, James, succeeded his grandfather as Duke of Ormond, in 1688. He inherited the virtues, talents, and splendid fortunes of his princely race. He was twice Lord-Lieutenant of Ireland, which he governed with more affection from the people, and kept his court in greater splendour than ever was known in that kingdom. He was twice Captain-General and Commander-in Chief of the land forces of Great Britain, a knight of the Garter, and Lord-Constable of England at the coronation of William the Third. But in 1715, he was impeached in the House of Commons by a factious party; and in a moment of pique and disdain he refused to wait his trial, retired to France, and joined the party of the Pretender: he was of course attainted, his estate declared forfeit, and his honours extinguished. Having thus rashly decided, he did not, like his friend Bolingbroke, restore himself to favour

---

to his last gasp, to close his dear eyes! O sad father, mother, wife, and children! What shall I add? he deserved all that a sincere friend, a brave soldier, a virtuous courtier, a loyal subject, an honest man, a bountiful master, and a good Christian could deserve of his prince and country."—*Evelyn's Memoirs*, vol. i. p. 490.

* In the private desk of the duke was found a Prayer upon the occasion of his son's death, in which the old man implores that "this dispensation might melt, not break his heart."

by betraying the cause he had embraced: he died at Avignon (where he had for some time subsisted on a pension from the King of Spain,) leaving no issue. To this Duke of Ormond, Dryden has dedicated his *Fables;* and to his duchess (a daughter of the Duke of Beaufort,) is addressed the beautiful introduction to the Tale of *Palamon and Arcite.*

Lady Ossory's second son, Lord Charles Butler, was created Earl of Arran on the death of his uncle Richard. He married a daughter of Lord Crewe, and dying in 1758, the title became extinct: he was the last male representative of this branch of the family.

Of the three daughters, the eldest, Lady Elizabeth, married William ninth Earl of Derby. Lady Emelia died unmarried, at the age of one hundred, having lived through six reigns; and Lady Henrietta was united to her cousin, Henry de Nassau, Earl of Grantham.

The portrait, never before engraved, is after the picture by Wissing, in the Beauty-room at Windsor; the dress is a crimson boddice, not very becoming, with a veil shading the hair; the arms and hands are ill drawn, but the face is beautiful, the features small and delicate, with just that charming expression of modesty and innocence, which the fancy would love to ascribe to the wife of Ossory.

[The following letter was written by the Duke of Ormond to the Countess of Clancarty, on Lord Ossory's death.

"KILKENNY, Aug. 11, 1680.

"Since I may claim a part in your letter to my wife, having so great a share in the sad subject of it; and since she is not in composure enough to write herself, she desires you would receive from me her and my thanks for the consolation you intend us, and which really your pious reflections and advices do afford. I confess we have need of all the assistances of reason and religion to support us; for though there be nothing in this life more natural or more visible than the frailty of it, and that we know whoever comes into this world must, a little sooner or a little later, as certainly go out of it, and that a grave is as sure a receptacle as the womb; yet either too much value of ourselves, or rather too little regard to the God of life and death, makes us bear afflictions of this kind, when they come home to ourselves, with less submission and resignation than we ought. You have, like us, lost an eldest son, dear to you, and valuable in the world; and we were in the same degree of relation to yours, that you were to ours. That God that gave you strength and patience, and an holy acquiescence, continue his comforts to you, and confer them on us."

The Queen, on this truly melancholy occasion, wrote with her own hand the following letter to the duke.

Indorsed, "Received 3rd September, 1680."

"My Lord Duke of Ormond,

"I do not think any thing I can say will lessen your trouble for the death of my Lord Ossory, who is so great a loss to the King and the publicke, as well as to my own particular service, that I know not how to express it: but every day will teach me, by shewing me the want I shall find of so true a friend. But I must have so much pity upon you, as to say but little on so sad a subject; conjuring you to believe that I am,

My Lord Duke of Ormond,
Your very affectionate friend,
CATHERINA REGINA."

The following brief character of Lady Ossory's two sons, and of her son-in-law, are taken from Spring Macky's Memoirs, 1733, 8vo., p. 10.

"JAMES, DUKE OF ORMOND.— On Queen Anne's accession to the throne he had the command given him of the expedition to Cadiz; which miscarried, not by his fault, as it appeared plainly in the examination of that affair in the House of Peers; and he had the good luck in his return to burn the French fleet at Vigo, and to assist at the solemn *Te Deum*, sung by the Queen at St. Paul's for that expedition; when it appeared how much he was the darling of the people, who neglected their sovereign, and applauded him more, perhaps, than ever any subject was on any occasion. He was sent soon after Lord-Lieutenant of Ireland, where he governed with more affection from the people, and his court was in greater splendour, than ever was known in that kingdom.

"He certainly was one of the most brave, generous, princely men that ever was, but good-natured to a fault; loved glory, and consequently was crowded with flatterers: never knew how to refuse any body, which was the reason why he obtained so little from King William, asking for every body. He had all the qualities of a great man, except that one of a statesman, hating business; loved, and was beloved by the ladies; of a low stature, but well shaped; a good mien and address; a fair complexion, and very beautiful face."

Dean Swift, in his Manuscript Notes, observes of the foregoing, that it is "fairly enough writ."

"LORD BUTLER OF WESTON.—Is Earl of Arran in Ireland, and brother to the Duke of Ormond: he commanded a troop of Horse-Guards; was gentleman of the bed-chamber to King William; of very good sense, though he seldom shewed it; of a fair complexion, middle stature."

Dean Swift observes on this paragraph: "This is right, but he is the most negligent of his own affairs."

"HENRY D'AUVERQUERQUE, EARL OF GRANTHAM.—He married the Duke of Ormond's sister; he is a very pretty gentleman, and fair complexioned."

"A good for nothing," saith Dean Swift.—ED.]

LADY DENHAM.

"For sweetest things turn sourest by their deeds—
Lilies that fester, smell far worse than weeds!"

SHAKSPEARE.

THIS beautiful woman is interesting from the poetical fame of her husband, and her own tragical and mysterious fate; but she presents, in all respects, a lamentable contrast to the gentle and blameless Lady Ossory.

Lady Denham was the eldest of two sisters, daughters of Sir William Brooke, K.B., and nieces of Digby, Earl of Bristol.* Both were beautiful and lively; or, as De Grammont expresses it, "*faites pour donner de l'amour, et pour en prendre;*" and their profligate uncle, who was at this time intriguing against the influence of Lady Castlemaine, introduced them at court, in the hope that one or both would captivate the heart of the versatile Charles. How far these young girls, and both were then very young, lent themselves to this project, or were acquainted with his purposes, is not clear; but Lady Castlemaine interfered in good time to prevent the accomplishment of the earl's hopes: and the King, who had just purchased a peace at the usual hard price, was not inclined to endanger it for the sake of Miss Brooke. She next attracted the notice of the Duke of York; but in the midst of this flirtation, she was married by the interposition of her

---

* Frances Brooke, the younger sister of Lady Denham, married Sir Thomas Whitmore, K.B., ancestor of the Whitmores of Shropshire.

friends, at the age of eighteen, to Sir John Denham,* then a widower, and old enough to be her father, or her grandfather; and who seemed determined to avenge, in his own person, all the satirical tirades and the poignant ridicule with which he had formerly visited faithless wives and betrayed husbands. Denham had led a dissipated life, and his age was neither pleasing nor respectable: although hardly more than fifty, he is described, at the period of his marriage, as " ancient and limping,"† and was ill calculated either to captivate or to rule a young and wilful beauty. This disproportioned union covered him with ridicule: his beautiful wife became at once the object of open assiduities, and himself almost frantic with jealousy. The Duke of York, who had rather neglected Miss Brooke before her marriage, renewed his attentions. The lady was not disposed to be absolutely cruel, but she was in disposition haughty, and inclined to coquetry; she gave herself airs accordingly, and the duke, who was the most stupid and ungainly of lovers, contrived to render himself on the present occasion, supereminently ridiculous: Pepys describes him as following her up and down the presence-chamber, " like a dog." It is consistent with the character of James and his family, historically branded with the reproach of systematic ingratitude, that no remorseful or generous feeling seems to have restrained him in this pursuit, although he was under particular personal obligations to Denham, which nothing could cancel: during the civil wars, when the prince was a mere boy, and in imminent danger of his liberty or his life, Denham had conveyed him out of England at

* Sir John Denham was born in Dublin, (where his father held the high office of Chief Baron of the Exchequer in Ireland,) in 1615. He attached himself devotedly to the royal cause, and was on the Restoration knighted, and appointed Surveyor of the Buildings to the King,—Sir Christopher Wren as his deputy. This was the more necessary, as, according to Evelyn, Sir John was a better poet than an architect. A great part of the family estates, situated at Egham and its neighbourhood, were wasted by Denham at the gaming-table; the rest were confiscated during the civil wars. His reputation as a poet rests upon his " Cooper's Hill." Sir John left three children by his first wife, who was a Miss Cotton.

† Aubrey's Letters. De Grammont says he was seventy-nine when he married Miss Brooke; he probably looked much older than he really was.

his own personal risk, and placed him in the hands of the Queen at Paris. As for Lady Denham, she had declared, with an effrontery worthy of the education she had received in the house of her uncle, that she would not be a " mistress to go up and down the privy stairs, but would be owned publicly;" and the duke accordingly visited her publicly and in state, attended by all the gentlemen of his household.

This, however, was not enough to satisfy our perverse and arrogant beauty. Brounker, whose name is handed down to us as the most famous chess-player of his time, filled in the household of the duke the same honourable office which Tom Chiffinch held in that of the King, his brother; and he made himself extremely useful in this negociation. Lady Castlemaine, who had lost the power of blushing for any thing, did not blush to be his coadjutor. Thus surrounded by tempters, and the worst of tempters, those of her own sex, Lady Denham was determined, that since the fates had decreed her fall, it should at least be surrounded with all possible éclat.

The place of lady of the bedchamber to the Duchess of York being vacant, Lady Denham demanded it of the duke: the duke had the assurance to insist that it should be given to her. The duchess, though in general submissive to his will, and accustomed to his infidelities, resisted on this occasion, well knowing that the high spirit and uncommon talents of Lady Denham exposed her to the chance of playing a very secondary personage in her own court: she had the example of Queen Catherine before her as a warning; and the duke had that of his brother as an encouragement, and he was equally peremptory. Everywhere Sir John Denham was beset by malicious congratulations on his wife's elevation, so that he would have hung himself in despite and despair, but that he had too much wit and too little courage.

The matter was still in discussion, when Lady Denham was seized with sudden indisposition, of which, after languishing some days, she expired, January 7th, 1667, in the full bloom of her youth and beauty, and before she had completed her twenty-first year. It was believed at the time that she had been poisoned in a cup of chocolate,* and her death was so sudden, it took place so critically, and was accompanied by such agonizing symptoms, that there was some ground for the belief: Lady Denham herself ceased not to aver, with tears, that she had been poisoned. Her husband was so strongly suspected, that for some days afterwards his house in Scotland-Yard was surrounded by an enraged populace, who threatened to stone him on his appearance. Others did not scruple to accuse the Duchess of York of being privy to this horrible affair, and an infamous libel to that effect was posted on her door; but there is not the slightest ground for believing in the accusation. Sir John Denham is not so easily acquitted: it is remarkable that he became insane immediately after his wife's death, and continued so for several months.† This insanity, might, however, have been

* Aubrey, who lived at the time, asserts the fact without any circumlocution. Pepys says that the universal belief was, that Lady Denham was poisoned, and that the physicians would assemble the day after her death, to examine into the symptoms and causes of her decease; which examination never took place.

[We think that the very entries of Pepys are sufficient to shew the improbability of her death by poison. On the 10th November, 1666, "I hear that my Lady Denham is exceedingly sick, even to death, and that she says, and every body else discourses, that she is poisoned; and Creed tells me, that it is said that there hath been a design to poison the King." On the 12th, "Creed tells me of my Lady Denham, whom every body says is poisoned, and she hath said it to the Duke of York; but is upon the mending hand, though the town says she is dead this morning." The poisoning story is here connected with a rumoured attempt on the King, and it is evident, as was then the case on every such rumour, the town was full of different reports about it. We hear nothing more of her in Pepys till the second of the following January, when she died, so that her death was by no means "sudden," or her illness very short: "Lord Brouncker tells me that my Lady Denham is at last dead. Some suspect her poisoned, but it will be best known when her body is opened to-day, she dying yesterday morning." It may also be remarked that, in Pepys, in the space of less than two months, 'every body's discourses' are reduced to the suspicion of some.—ED.]

† In justice to Denham it should be observed, that Butler, in his bitter and outrageous satire, entitled "Verses on the Recovery of Sir John Denham from his late Madness," makes no allusion to the death of Lady Denham.

caused by terror, or by indignation and grief, and not by remorse, as it was insinuated. The matter was at the time hushed up with all convenient speed, and the horrible fate by which this unhappy woman expiated her errors remains a mystery.

Sir John Denham died in 1668, about a year after his wife; he had completely recovered from his insanity some months before his death; and, in the interval, wrote his poem on the death of Cowley.

Except the portraits of Miss Hamilton and Lady Bellasys, there is not one among the Beauties at Windsor that can be compared to this picture of Lady Denham, either for delicacy of execution, or splendour of colouring. She is represented seated on a bank, with flowers in her lap, dressed in rich amber-coloured satin: the neck, bosom, hands, and arms, are beautiful; the face is not generally considered as attractive, yet the features, which are too large and striking for a delicate beauty, have a singular expression which rivets the attention,—blending capacity, pride, and the capability of strong passions. Her complexion is fair, but glowing and fresh like a full-blown flower: her hair of a lovely brown. The whole disposition of the picture, and the magnificent colouring of the drapery and the background, have never been surpassed by Lely, even in his most celebrated works. It is now engraved for the first time.

———

[The curious sketch of the Life of Sir John Denham, given by the antiquarian Aubrey in his entertaining Letters and Lives of Eminent Persons, seems to us by no means an improper supplement to the life of his lady. Aubrey was a great collector of gossiping stories, which, from their nature, are not absolutely to be depended upon.

"I have heard Mr. James Howe say, that he was the dreamingest young fellow; he never expected such things from him as he hath left the world. When he was there, he would game extremely; when he had played away all his money, he would play away his father's cappes wrought with gold. His father was Sir John Denham, one of the Barons of the Exchequer; he had been one of the Lords Justices in Ireland; he married Ellenor,* one of the daughters of Sir Garret Moore, knight, Lord Baron of Mellifont, in ye kingdome of Ireland, whom he married during his service in Ireland, in ye place of Chief Justice there.

"Sir John was not supposed to be a witt. At last, viz. 1640, his play of "*The Sophy*" came out, which did take extremely. Mr. Edmund Waller sayd then of him, that he broke out like the Irish Rebellion,—threescore thousand strong, when nobody suspected it. He was much rooked by gamesters, and fell acquainted with that unsanctified crew to his ruine. His father had some suspicion of it, and chid him severely; whereupon his son John (only child) wrot a little Essay in 8vo, pointed *against gaming*, and to shew the vanities and inconveniences of it, which he presented to his father, to let him know his detestation of it: but shortly after his father's death (1638,) (who left 2000 or 1500 lib. in ready money, two houses well furnished, and much plate,) the money was played away first, and next the plate was sold. *I* remember, about 1646, he lost 200 lib. one night at Newcutt.

* * * * *

"In 1646-7 he conveyed or stole away the two Dukes of Yorke and Gloucester from St. James's (from the tuition of the Earle of Northumberland,) and conveyed them into France to the Prince of Wales and Queen-mother. It was at Wilton, the seat of the Earl of Pembroke, in 1652, that he translated the —— book of Virgil's *Æneis*, and also burlesqu't it.† He married for his first wife the

---

* She was a beautiful woman, as appears by her monument. Sir John, they say, did much resemble his father.

† "He burlesqued Virgil, and burnt it, saying, that 'twas not fitt that the first poet should be so abused." From Mr. Chr. Ware, tutor to William Lord Herbert.

daughter and heire of —— Cotton, of Glocestershire, by whom he had 500 lib. per annum, one son and two daughters.

"He was much beloved by King Charles the First, who much valued him for his integrity. He granted him the reversion of the Surveyor of his Buildings, after the decease of Mr. Inigo Jones; which place after the restoration of King Charles II., he enjoyed to his death, and gott seaven thousand pounds as Sir Christopher Wren told me of, to his owne knowledge. Sir Christopher Wren was his deputy.

"An. Dom. 166- he married his second wife, — Brooke, a very beautiful young lady; Sir John was ancient and limping.

"The Duke of Yorke fell deeply in love with her. This occasioned Sir John's distemper of madnesse in 166-, which first appeared when he went from London to see the famous free-stone quarries at Portland, in Dorset. When he came within a mile of it, turned back to London againe, and would not see it. He went to Hounslowe, and demanded rents of lands he had sold many yeares before; went to the King, and told him he was the Holy Ghost; but it pleased God that he was cured of this distemper, and wrott excellent verses, particularly on the death of Abraham Cowley, afterwards. His second lady had no child, and was poysoned by the hands of the Co. of Roc. with chocolatte. At the coronation of King Charles II. he was made knight of the Bath.

"He died in 1668-9, March the 23rd; was buried in Westminster Abbey, near Sr Jeffrey Chaucer's monument.

"He delighted much in bowles, and did bowle very well. He was of the tallest, but a little uncurvetting at his shoulders, not very robust. His haire was but thin and flaxen, with a moist curle. His gate was slow, and was rather a stalking, (he had long legges.) His eie was a kind of light goose gray, not big; but it had a strange pierciugness, not as to shining and glory, but (like a Momus) when he conversed with you, he look't into your very thoughts.

"In the time of the civill warres, Geo. Withers, the poet, begged S⁻· Jo. Denham's estate of the Parliament, in whose cause he was a captaine of horse. It (happened) that G. W. was taken prisoner, and was in danger of his life, having written severely against the King. S⁻· John Denham went to the King, and desired his ma^tie not to hang him; for that whilest G. W. lived, he should not be the worst poet in England. Sir John was satyricall when he had a mind to it."—Ed.]

NELL GWYNN.

> "How sweet and lovely dost thou make the shame
>   Which, like the canker in a fragrant rose,
> Doth spot the beauty of thy budding name!
>   Oh, in what sweets dost thou thy sins enclose,
> That tongue that tells the story of thy days,
>   Making licentious comments on thy sport,
> Cannot dispraise but in a kind of praise:
>   Naming *thy* name, blesses an ill report.
> Oh, what a mansion have those vices got
>   Which for their habitation chose out thee!
> Where Beauty's veil doth cover every blot,
>   And all things turn to fair that eyes can see!"
>
> SHAKSPEARE. *Sonnet* 95.

NELL GWYNN,—pretty, witty, merry, open-hearted Nelly,—has much more than her own frailties to answer for; and they (alas, that we must needs say it!) are enough, in all conscience. Her very virtues have proved mischievous, inasmuch as they have given occasion to certain scoffers to blaspheme "the sun-clad power of chastity." Wicked arguers against that law of society which comprises all female virtues in one, have set up the name of Nell Gwynn as a rallying point; and under that name, with all its gay associations of wreathed smiles, arch sayings, sweet looks, kind feelings, and benevolent deeds, they fight their battles, without considering that she, and one or two others, are but exceptions to a general rule, harsh in particular applications, but on the whole, just and friendly to our sex.

It is, at least in *one* sense, rather a delicate point to touch on the Life of Nell Gwynn: one would fain be properly shocked, decorously grave, and becomingly moral; but, as the lady says in *Comus*, "to what end?" It were rather superfluous to set about proving that Nell Gwynn was, in her day, a good-for-nothing sort of person; in short, as wild a piece of frailty, as ever wore a petticoat. In spite of such demonstrations, and Bishop Burnet's objurgations to boot, she will not the less continue to be the idol of popular tradition, her very name provocative of a smile, and of power to disarm the austerity of virtue, and discountenance the gravity of wisdom. It is worth while to inquire in what consists that strange fascination, which, after the lapse of a century and a half, still hangs round the memory of this singular woman. Why is her name still familiar and dear in the mouths of the people?* why hath no man condemned her? why has satire spared her? why is there in her remembrance a charm so far beyond, and so different from mere celebrity? Other women have become famous and interesting in spite of their lapses from virtue, and some from that cause. Rosamond Clifford is the heroine of romance; Agnes Sorel, of history and chivalry; Jane Shore, of tragedy; La Vallière, of sentiment and poetry; and Gabrielle d'Estrées has been immortalized by the love of a hero, to whom she was most faithless, and of whom she was most unworthy. But Nell Gwynn—Heaven knows—had little to do with romance, or tragedy,† or chivalry, or sentiment: and her connexion with the King, with all the scandal it gave rise to, would have made her, as in other cases, a mark for popular hatred and scurrility,

---

* The head of Nell Gwynn was a popular sign in her own days, and long after; and is still to be seen over an old ale-house in Chelsea. Signs are seldom other than acknowledgments of a general good-will in the public for the thing or person signified.—C. L.

† Except on the stage,—and then she was "out of her calling."

but for those redeeming qualities which "turned dispraise to praise," and made

> "Both faults and graces loved of more and less."

A sprinkling of hypocrisy, or a few cooling drops of discretion, had rendered Nell Gwynn either far better or far worse, and placed her on a par with the women around her; as it was, she resembled nothing but herself. She may, perhaps, be compared, in some few points, with her fair and famed contemporary, Ninon de l'Enclos. Both had talents, wit, vivacity, and much goodness of heart; both were distinguished for the sincerity and permanency of their friendships, their extensive charity and munificence to literary men: what Ninon was to Racine and Molière, Nell was to Dryden and Lee. But there is this difference,—that Ninon, with all her advantages of birth, talents, independent fortune, and an education, not only *soigné*, but learned, became from choice, or perverted principle, what Nell, poor, uneducated, and unprotected, became from necessity or accident.

A woman, when she has once stepped astray, seldom pauses in her downward career till "guilt grows fate, that was but choice before," and far more seldom rises out of that debasement of person and mind, except by some violent transition of feeling, some revulsion of passion leading to the opposite extreme. In the case of Nell Gwynn the contrary was remarkable. As years passed on, as habit grew, and temptation and opportunity increased, her conduct became more circumspect, and her character more elevated. The course of her life, which had begun in the puddle and sink of obscurity and profligacy, as it flowed, refined. For the humorous and scandalous stories of which she is the subject, some excuse may be found in her plebeian education, and the coarseness of the age in which she lived: when ladies of quality gambled and swore, what could be expected from the orange-girl? But though her language and manners bore to the last the taint of the tavern and the stage, hers was one of those fine natures which *could* not be corrupted; the contaminating influence of the atmosphere around her had stained the surface, but never reached the core.

These observations, which irresistibly suggested themselves, may seem misplaced, and should rather have followed than preceded her life: but it is the *character* of Nell Gwynn which lends an interest to her memoirs, though the reverse be more commonly the case. The events of her life may be related in a few words. It was marked by no romantic incidents, no signal reverses of fortune, no tragic expiation of error. It is quite impossible to make a heroine of her, in prose or in verse.

The family of Nell Gwynn was of Welsh extraction, as may be inferred from the name: her parents were natives of Hereford, of which city one of her noble descendants was afterwards bishop,* and where, according to a local tradition, she was herself born. Other authorities state that she first saw the light in a garret in Coal-yard, Drury-lane. However this may be, it is certain that her earliest years were spent in London, and in the very lowest haunts of vulgar profligacy. While yet a mere child, she was an attendant in a tavern, where the sweetness of her voice and her sprightly address recommended her to notice. She was afterwards, still in extreme youth, a servant to a fruiterer, and in this capacity employed to sell oranges at the theatres. Here her beauty and vivacity attracted the notice of Lacy the comedian, her first lover, who was soon rivalled in her good graces by Hart, the handsomest man and most accomplished actor of that day.†

* Lord James Beauclerk died Bishop of Hereford, in 1782.

† Charles Hart was the great-nephew of Shakspeare, his father William being the eldest son of the poet's sister Joan. Contemporary authors are full of eulogiums of this great actor, and allusions to his various excellencies.—See Dryden, Cibber, the *Spectator*, Fuller, and the *Roscius Anglicanus*.

Rymer says, "What Mr. Hart delivers, every one takes upon content; their eyes are prepossessed and charmed by his action, before aught of the poet's can approach their ears; and to the most wretched of characters he gives a lustre and brilliance which so dazzles the sight, that the deformities in the poetry cannot be perceived."—*Tragedies of the Last Age Considered.*

Under the successive tuition of these two admirers, both of whom were masters of their art, Nell Gwynn was prepared for the stage, for which she had a natural *penchant;* and, in 1667, we find her enrolled in the King's company of comedians, who were then acting under Killigrew's patent, at the new theatre in Drury-lane.* Before the Restoration, no woman had appeared on the English stage, the female parts being all acted by men.† The novelty and attraction of seeing beautiful women in such characters as Desdemona, Ophelia, Aspasia, &c., was undoubtedly one cause of that mania for theatrical amusements, which was one of the characteristics of the time. Nell Gwynn at once became popular in her new vocation. She was so great a favourite, that the public endured and even applauded her in characters for which her talents were altogether unfitted; as Valeria in the *Royal*

---

* There are the following entries in Pepys' Diary, under the year 1667, relative to Nell Gwynn:—

"To the King's house; Knipp took us all in, and brought to us Nelly, a most pretty woman, who acted the great part of Cœlia to-day, very fine, and did it pretty well: I kissed her, and so did my wife; and a mighty pretty soul she is."—Vol. ii. p. 8.

"To the King's house; and there going in, met with Knipp, and she took us up into the tiring-rooms; and to the woman's shift, where Nell was dressing herself, and was all unready, and is very pretty, prettier than I thought. But, Lord! to see how they are both painted, would make a man mad."—Vol. ii. p. 135.

"With my wife to the King's playhouse; and there saw *The Surprizall;* which did not please me to-day, the actors not pleasing me; especially Nell's acting of a serious part, which she spoils."—Vol. ii. p. 171.

† The name of the first female actress is a disputed point: it is only certain that the first part played by a woman was Desdemona; the apologetic prologue delivered upon the occasion may be found in Malone's *History of the English Stage.* Before this time, it once happened that Charles II. being in the theatre, and expressing some impatience because the play did not immediately begin, Sir William Davenant came forward, and apologized in these words:—"Please your majesty, they are shaving the queen." This oft-told jest does not seem to have been well understood by those who have repeated it. It had a double allusion, which made it doubly *piquant;* for it was just at the time that Queen Catherine's *barber* had arrived from Portugal, whose office caused much wonder and amusement among the courtiers.

Martyr, Alicia in the *Black Prince*, and Cidaria in the *Indian Emperor*, which her admirer Pepys allows that she played "most basely;"* she also appeared as Queen Elizabeth in the *Earl of Essex*. Nell Gwynn in Queen Elizabeth must have been rare,— something like Polonius "enacting Julius Cæsar in the Capitol." But, on the other hand, she excelled in comedy, and in all parts in which dancing and singing were requisite. The character of Florimel in the *Maiden Queen* appears to have been her *chef-d'œuvre* in this style. Her easy gracefulness of address, arch expression, and musical voice, rendered her unrivalled as a speaker of prologues and epilogues: several of Dryden's best, and it is well known that he excelled in these productions, were written expressly for her. For instance, the prologue to *Aurengzebe*, and the ludicrous epilogue to *Tyrannic Love*, in which, after stabbing herself most heroically in the part of Valeria, and the mutes appear in conclusion to carry off the dead, she gives the bearer a box on the ear and jumps up, exclaiming,—

> "Hold! are you mad? you d—d confounded dog!
> I am to rise and speak the epilogue!"

In this epilogue, Dryden, who, with all his admiration for Nell Gwynn, was aware of her unfitness for the part she acted, puts into her mouth a kind of confession of her own deficiencies:—

> "I am the ghost of poor departed Nelly;
> *   *   *
> To tell you truth, I walk because I die
> Out *of my calling*—in a tragedy!"

And the concluding lines contain an allusion to one of her personal characteristics,—the extreme negligence of her dress:—

* "To the King's house, and there saw *The Mad Couple*, which is but an ordinary play; but only Nell's and Hart's mad parts are most excellent done, but especially hers: which makes it a miracle to me to think how ill she do any serious part, as the other day, just like a fool or changeling: and, in a mad part, do beyond all imitation almost."—Vol. ii. p. 171.

> "As for my epitaph, when I am gone,
> I'll trust no poet, but will write my own:
> 'Here Nelly lies, who, though she lived a slattern,
> Yet died a princess, acting in St. Catherine!'"

The same year that Nell Gwynn first appeared on the stage, she attracted the notice of the witty Lord Buckhurst, (afterwards the Earl of Dorset,) who took her from the theatre, and allowed her £100. a-year.*

The absence, however, was not long: she returned to the stage in 1668, and appeared in her great character of Almahide, in Dryden's *Conquest of Granada*. In spite of what Pepys says of her acting serious parts vilely, (which was true, in general,) she produced a great effect in this character, as is evident from the extraordinary success of the play, and the allusion to her, long afterwards, by Lord Lansdown, in his *Progress of Beauty*:—

> "And Almahide, once more by kings adored."

The prologue to this tragedy was written for her by Dryden.†

---

* Pepys, vol. ii. p. 92, 4to. edit.—"Mr. Pierce tells us, what troubles me, that my Lord Buckhurst has got Nell away from the King's house, and gives her £100. a-year, so as she hath sent her parts to the house, and will act no more." And the following entry a few days after. "To Epsum, and hear that my Lord Buckhurst and Nelly are lodged at the next house, and Sir Charles Sedley with them; and keep a merry house. Poor girl! I pity her; but more the loss of her at the King's house."

"To the King's playhouse, and there saw *The Indian Emperour*: where I find Nell come again, which I am glad of; but was most infinitely displeased with her being put to act the Emperour's daughter, which is a great and serious part, which she does most basely."—Vol. ii. p. 112.

"Nelly and Beck Marshall falling out the other day, the latter called the other my Lord Buckhurst's mistress. Nell answered her, 'I am but one man's mistress, though I was brought up in a tavern to fill strong waters to gentlemen; and you are mistress to three or four, though a Presbyter's praying daughter!'" —Vol. ii. p. 140.

† See his works for this Prologue, "To be spoken by Mistress Ellen Gwynn, in a broad-brimmed hat and waist belt."—*Scott's Edition of Dryden*, vol. iii.

It seems that Nokes, the favourite buffoon of the rival theatre (the duke's house,) had lately drawn crowds, by appearing in a huge broad-brimmed hat, though where the jest lay it is impossible to guess. Dryden ridiculed this extravagance, by causing Nell to appear in a hat double the size, with brims as wide as a cart-wheel; her slight short figure, just visible under this vast overhanging circumference, and the archness with which she delivered the satirical address, were irresistibly droll, and produced all the effect expected; and much more, if the tradition be true, that it was in this grotesque costume Nell first captivated her royal lover: but there is reason to doubt it.* All that can be ascertained is, that from this time the King openly distinguished her; and after the first performance went behind the scenes, and took her away in his carriage to sup with him. Soon after, Lord Buckhurst resigned her for the consideration of an earldom and a pension.†

After this elevation (as the contemporary writers express it, and, no doubt, very sincerely thought it,) we find Nelly dignified in the play-bills with the title of "Madam Ellen," by which name she was popularly known. She appeared on the stage once or twice after the birth of her eldest son, but retired from it altogether in 1671. About this time she was created one of the ladies of the Queen's privy-chamber, under which title she was lodged in Whitehall.‡ Madam Ellen lost none of her popularity by her

* See Pepys' Diary, vol. ii. p. 179.

† Others say that Dorset himself introduced her at court, to shake the influence of the Duchess of Cleveland.

‡ Pegge's Curialia, p. 58. This was too disgraceful, but the disgrace rests with Charles who offered, and the Queen who endured the outrage, rather than upon Nell Gwynn, who certainly never sought the dignity. It is illustrative of the morals of the time, that a female writer, in the Dedication of a Comedy to Mistress Ellen Gwynn, chooses her principal topic of compliment from the connexion of that lady with majesty; and congratulates her upon the children born from that union, as peculiar blessings sent down from Heaven upon the mother and the kingdom. "Nor can Heaven give you more, who has expressed a particular care of you in every way, and above all in the bestowing on the world and you two noble branches, who have all the greatness and sweetness of their

"elevation." She carried with her into the court the careless assurance of her stage manners; and, as Burnet says, continued " to *hang on* her clothes with the same slovenly negligence;" but she likewise carried there qualities even more rare in a court than coarse manners and negligent attire,—the same frolic gaiety, the same ingenuous nature, and the same kind and cordial benevolence, which had rendered her adored among her comrades. Her wit was as natural, and as peculiar to herself, as the perfume to the flower. She seems to have been, as the Duchess de Chaulnes expressed it, " femme d'esprit, par la grace de Dieu." Her bonmots, fell from her lips with such an unpremeditated felicity of expression, and her turn of humour was so perfectly original, that though it occasionally verged upon extravagance and vulgarity, even her maddest flights became her; "as if," says one of her cotemporaries, " she alone had the patent from heaven to engross all hearts." Burnet calls her " the wildest and indiscreetest creature that ever was in a court;" and speaking of the King's constant attachment to her, he adds, " but, after all, he never treated her with the *decencies* of a mistress." This last observation of the good bishop is certainly " twisted into a phrase of some obscurity:" the truth is, that Nell had a natural turn for goodness, which survived all her excesses; she was wild and extravagant, but not rapacious or selfish,—frail, not vicious; she never meddled with politics, nor made herself the tool of ambitious

royal and beautiful stock," &c. &c. Indeed, some passages in this extraordinary address come so near to blasphemy, that a mind, not overtinctured with piety, must recoil from the repetition of them. " So excellent and perfect a creature as yourself, differs only from the Divine Powers in this," &c.; and again, " When you [that is Nelly!!] speak, men crowd to listen with that awful reverence as to holy oracles, or divine prophecies." It is charitable to hope, that by ' Divine Powers,' the authoress insinuated nothing beyond the Paphian deities; and by ' oracles and prophecies,' meant only the responses of the Priestess of Cytherea. We turn with pleasure to the social qualities of this divinity, which have never been disputed, and are prettily touched upon in another part of this dedication. " You never appear, but you glad the hearts of all that have the happy fortune to see you, as if you were made on purpose to put the whole world into good-humour."

courtiers. At the time that the King's mistresses were everywhere execrated for their avarice and arrogance, it was remarked that Nell Gwynn never asked anything for herself, never gave herself unbecoming airs, as if she deemed her unhappy situation a subject of pride : there is not a single instance of her using her influence over Charles for any unworthy purpose; but, on the contrary, the presents which the King's love or bounty lavished upon her, she gave and spent freely; and misfortune, deserved, or undeserved, never approached her in vain. Once, as she was driving up Ludgate-Hill, she saw a poor clergyman in the hands of the sheriff's officers, and struck with compassion, she alighted from her carriage, inquired into the circumstances of his arrest, and paid his debt on the spot; and finding, on application to the vouchers he had named, that his character was as unexceptionable as his misfortunes were real, she generously befriended him and his family. The plan of that fine institution, Chelsea Hospital, would probably never have been completed, at least in the reign of Charles, but for the persevering and benevolent enthusiasm of this woman, who never let the King rest till it was carried into execution.

These, and many other instances of her kind nature, endeared her to the populace. On one occasion, a superb service of plate, which had been ordered for the Duchess of Portsmouth, was exhibited in the shop of a certain goldsmith, and the common people crowded round the window to gaze. On learning for whom it was intended, they broke out into execrations and abuse, wishing the silver melted and poured down her throat, and loudly exclaiming, that " it had been much better bestowed upon Madam Ellen."

Strange as it may seem, Nell piqued herself upon her orthodox principles and her reverence for the clergy, partly from a sincere religious feeling which had been early and unaccountably impressed on her mind, and never left her; and partly, perhaps, out of opposition to the Papist favourite, the Duchess of Portsmouth. Madame de Sévigné gives in one of her letters so piquant a description of Nell Gwynn and her merry impertinence to her rival, that instead of referring to the volume, I give the passage at length.

"Kéroualle" (the Duchess of Portsmouth) " n'a été trompée sur rien. Elle avoit envie d'être la maîtresse du roi; elle l'est...... Elle a un fils qui vient d'être reconnu, et à qui on a donné deux duchés. Elle amasse des trésors, et se fait aimer et réspecter de qui elle peut; mais elle n'avoit pas prévu trouver en chemin, une jeune comédienne, dont le roi est ensorcelé. Elle n'a pas le pouvoir de l'en détacher un moment. La comédienne est aussi fière que la Duchesse de Portsmouth : elle la morgue, lui dérobe souvent le roi, et se vante de ses préférences. Elle est jeune, folle, hardie, débauchée, et plaisante : elle chante, elle danse, et fait son métier de bonne foi : elle a un fils ; elle veut qu'il soit reconnu. Voici son raisonnement : 'Cette demoiselle,' dit elle, 'fait la personne de qualité. Elle dit, que tout est son parent en France. Dès qu'il meurt quelque grand, elle prend le deuil. Hé bien ! puisqu'elle est de si grande qualité, pourquoi s'est elle faite......? Elle devroit mourir de honte. Pour moi, c'est mon métier ; je ne me pique pas d'autre chose. Le roi m'entretient ; je ne suis qu'à lui présentement. J'en ai un fils, je prétends qu'il doit être reconnu ; et il le reconnoîtra, car il m'aime autant que sa Portsmouth.' "—" Cette créature," continues Madame de Sévigné, " tient le haut du pavé, et décontenance et embarrasse extraordinairement la duchesse."

Besides her apartment in Whitehall, in quality of lady of the Queen's privy-chamber, Nell Gwynn had lodgings in Pall Mall,* where she frequently entertained the King and a few of his chosen companions with *petits soupers* and select concerts. On one of these occasions she had collected together some new and excellent

---

* At the left hand corner of St. James's-square: the walls of the back room on the ground-floor were (within memory) entirely of looking-glass, as was said to have been the ceiling.—*Pennant's London*, p. 90.

performers, and the King was so much enchanted, that he expressed his approbation in strong terms. "Then, sir," said Nell, holding out her hand, "to shew that you do not speak merely as a courtier, let me have the pleasure of presenting these poor people with a gratuity from your majesty!" The King, feeling in his pocket, declared he had no money, and turning to the Duke of York, asked him if he had any? The duke replied, "No, sir, I believe not above a guinea or two." Nell, shaking her head, with her *petit air malin*, and drolly mimicking the King's tone and habitual expression, exclaimed, "Odds fish! what company have I got into here!"

Cibber, who relates this anecdote, and lived about the same time, tells us that Nell was never known to have been unfaithful to the King, from the moment he first noticed her, and that she was "as much distinguished for her personal attachment to him, as her rivals were by their titles and grandeur." Her disinterested affection, her sprightly humour, her inexhaustible powers of entertainment, and constant desire to please, must have formed an agreeable contrast to the rapacity, ill temper, affectation, and arrogant caprices of the other court ladies. Charles, in spite of every attempt made to detach him from her, loved her to the last, and his last thought was for her :—"Let not poor Nelly starve!" Burnet, who records this dying speech, is piously scandalized that the King should have thought of such "a creature" in such a moment; but some will consider it with more mercy, as one among the few traits which redeem the sensual and worthless Charles from utter contempt.

After the King's death, Nell Gwynn continued to reside in Pall Mall, where she lived on a small pension and some presents the King had made her. She survived him about seven years, conducting herself with the strictest decorum, and spending her time in devotion, and her small allowance in acts of beneficence: she died in 1691. Dr. Tennison, then Vicar of St. Martins, and afterwards Archbishop of Canterbury, preached her funeral sermon, in which he enlarged upon her benevolent qualities, her sincere penitence, and exemplary end. When this was afterwards mentioned to Queen Mary, in the hope that it would injure him in her estimation, and be a bar to his preferment, "And what then?" answered she hastily; "I have heard as much: it is a sign that the poor unfortunate woman died penitent; for if I can read a man's heart through his looks, had she not made a pious and Christian end, the doctor could never have been induced to speak well of her!"

Nell Gwynn was possessed of little at her death, and that little was by her will distributed in charity. She left, among other bequests, a small sum yearly to the ringers of the church of St. Martin, where she was buried, which donation they still enjoy.

She bore the King two sons, Charles and James Beauclerc. Charles Beauclerc, her eldest son, was born in Lincoln's Inn Fields, in 1670, a short time before his mother quitted the stage. The occasion of his being titled and acknowledged, is too characteristic to be omitted. When the children of the Duchesses of Cleveland and Portsmouth had been dignified with titles, orders, and offices, Nell Gwynn naturally felt piqued that *her* sons, whose filial claims upon his majesty, as the fountain of honour, were *at least* as well founded, should be passed over, and she took her own whimsical method of hinting her wishes to the King. One day, when his majesty was present, and her eldest son was playing in the room, she called to him aloud, in a petulant tone, "Come here, you little bastard!" The King, much shocked, reproved her: she replied meekly, and with the most demure simplicity, that "indeed she was very sorry, but had no better name to give him, poor boy!"

A few days afterwards, this nameless young gentleman was created Baron of Heddington and Earl of Burford; and in 1683, DUKE OF ST. ALBANS, Registrar of the High Court of Chancery, and Grand Falconer of England. He inherited his mother's per-

sonal beauty, and served with great bravery under King William.*
This first Duke of St. Albans married Lady Diana Vere, sole
daughter of Aubrey de Vere, twentieth and last Earl of Oxford,
and the greatest heiress in rank and descent in the three kingdoms.† She was very young at the period of her marriage, and
as amiable and as innocent as lovely. She was the mother of
eight sons, of whom Lord Vere Beauclerc, (ancestor of the present
duke,) was distinguished as a naval commander; and Lord Sidney
Beauclerc was the father of that Topham Beauclerc, who was the
friend of Dr. Johnson, and one of the worthies of Boswell. The
present Duke of St. Albans is the fifth in descent from Nell
Gwynn.

Her younger son, Lord James Beauclerc, died in his childhood
at Paris.

The secret of Nell Gwynn's popularity seems to have consisted
in what is generally called *heart*, in a kindness and candour of disposition which the errors and abject miseries of her youth could not
harden, nor her acquaintance with a corrupt court entirely vitiate.
On comparing and combining the scattered traits and personal allusions found in contemporary writers, it appears that she was in
person considerably below the middle size, but formed with perfect
elegance; the contour of her face was round, her features delicate,
her eyes bright and intelligent, but so small as to be almost concealed when she laughed; her cheek was usually dimpled with
smiles, and her countenance radiant with hilarity, but when at rest
it was soft and even pensive in its expression; her voice was
sweet and well modulated; her hair glossy, abundant, and of a
light auburn; her hands were singularly small and beautiful, and

---

* ["He is a gentleman every way *de bon naturel*, well-bred, doth not love
business; is well affected to the constitution of this country. He is of a black
complexion, not so tall as the Duke of Northumberland, yet very like King
Charles."—*Spring Macky.*—Ed.]

† Her picture, by Kneller, is among the Beauties at Hampton Court.

her pretty foot so very diminutive, as to afford occasion for mirth as well as admiration.

The engraved portrait is after a picture by Sir Peter Lely, in the possession of General Grosvenor: it agrees perfectly with the foregoing description, and there can exist no doubt of its authenticity. The dress is certainly in the extreme of that negligence for which the lady was remarkable;

"Robes loosely flowing—hair as free."

Her left hand rests upon a lamb which she crowns with flowers. The turn of the neck and the air of the head are full of grace and character; and the whole picture, though a little injured by time, is exquisitely painted.

[Mrs. Jameson has said enough to make her readers suppose that there were versions of the youthful history of Nell Gwynn which differed much from the one she has given. It would, indeed, have been strange had not the love of scandal, and even curiosity and less culpable feelings, been employed, not only in raking up, but in inventing, anecdotes relating to the obscure beginnings of one who had gained so great a notoriety. As far as regards Nelly, or her contemporaries in the same class, the bad feelings are long ago laid asleep and forgotten; but with many of our readers one at least, that of curiosity, may still live, and for its gratification we will trace briefly one of the stories that were sent afloat of her birth and first introduction to the world. It will easily be seen, that the object of the person who wrote it was to make her birth appear as respectable as possible.

She was the daughter, (this story tells us,) of a tradesman in mean circumstances, who early implanted in her mind a great sense of virtue and delicacy, the former of which she was not long in parting with, and yet without the misfortune of losing the latter. She no sooner became conscious of her own charms, than she solicited her father to permit her to go into the world under the protection of a lady, where she imagined that her beauty would soon raise admirers; and by having an opportunity of a more unrestrained manner, she was not without hopes of making her fortune at the expense of some visitor of the lady in whose house she was to live as a companion. She soon attracted the admiration of a celebrated lawyer, " from whom a family now flourishing in the world is descended ;" and he began to conceive a violent passion for her, and his hopes of success were inflamed from the frequent opportunities he had of conversing with, and the degree of her station, which he imagined would expose her to the temptation of accepting presents and money as the price of her virtue. We are told that the lady had a penchant for this handsome lawyer; and that when she perceived his attentions to Nell Gwynn, she from that moment conceived an aversion to Nell, and in a few days turned her out of her house.

Nell Gwynn, thus reduced, was coldly received by her father, who had already been prejudiced against her by her mistress. He threatened to abandon her for ever, if she did not consent to go into Yorkshire and live with her aunt, who was the wife of a parish-clerk in the little village of ——. Nell would not listen to this proposal, and cast her eye upon the stage. She left her father's house, took a private lodging, and as her appearance was elegant, she passed for a young lady just come up from the country. In this retirement she applied herself to reading plays, and having a little money which her mistress had given her, and ten guineas which the lawyer had made her a present of, she went very often to the theatre, to study the acting of the different performers then in vogue. After living a month or two in this manner, she wrote a letter to Betterton, inviting him to her lodgings, and there disclosed her scheme of coming on the stage, and desired he would give his opinion of her powers in recitation. He told her plainly that she was not then fit for the stage, though she seemed to have a genius that way, and advised her to seek some other mode of livelihood. Her scheme being so far defeated, and her money diminishing apace, she began to be alarmed lest poverty should overtake her; and resolved to quit her apartments, and to try and introduce herself at the theatre by dressing herself in the garb of an orange-girl.

Her plan, it seems, answered better than might have been expected. No sooner had she appeared in the pit and behind the scenes with her oranges, than the eyes of the actors, and the young wits and men of fashion who frequented the theatres, were fixed upon her, all anxious to know the story and birth of the handsome orange-girl. Betterton, who soon knew her in her disguise, seemed astonished at her resolution, and began to form great expectations from one, whose propensity to the stage was so violent as to induce her to appear in so low a character for the sake of acquiring instruction.

An actor prevailed upon her to quit her profession of orange-selling, and offered to share his salary with her; and she accepted his proposal, and lived with him in easy tranquillity, for some time. She afterwards left him, and lived with her former acquaintance, the lawyer.

According to the story we are now following, Nell passed through several hands before she attracted the attention of the King; but the history of all her intrigues has no claim to a place in our pages. Suffice it to say, that one of her possessors is said to have been the notorious Rochester; and that when kept by him she is said to have made her first attempt to patronise the poet, Dryden, who, as a writer, was the object of Rochester's peculiar jealousy. "She had heard one day at the play, that Dryden was in distress, on account of a tragedy he had offered to the stage being, from some capricious consideration of the Lord Chamberlain, rejected. She mentioned this circumstance to Rochester, and begged him to interpose his interest to have the objection removed, and the play brought upon the stage; but in this suit she was unsuccessful. So far from complying with it, he stirred himself to have Dryden discarded at court, and recommended an obscure individual of the name of Crown, to write a masque to be represented before their majesties."

A long story is told of the manner in which Nell Gwynn left Rochester, and of the revenge taken by the latter in his writings. She was now the mistress, if we believe this story, of a brother of the " Duchess of Cleveland," who enjoyed some share of the King's favour, but from whose eyes he studiously concealed Nell Gwynn.

" One day however, in spite of his caution, his majesty saw her, and that very night possessed her. Her lover carried her to the play, at a time when he had not the least suspicion of his majesty's being there; but as that monarch had an aversion to his robes of royalty, and was incumbered with the dignity of his state, he chose frequently to throw off the load of kingship, and consider himself as a private gentleman.

" Upon this occasion he came to the play, *incog.*, and sat in the next box to Nell and her lover. As soon as the play was finished, his majesty, with the Duke of York, the young nobleman and Nell, retired to a tavern together, where they regaled themselves over a bottle; and the King showed such civilities to Nell, that she began to understand the meaning of his gallantry.

" The tavern-keeper was entirely ignorant of the quality of the company; and it was remarkable, that when the reckoning came to be paid, his majesty, upon searching his pockets, found that he had not money enough about him to discharge it, and asked the sum of his brother, who was in the same situation: upon which Nell observed, that she had got into the poorest company that ever she was in at a tavern. The reckoning was paid by the young nobleman, who that night parted both with his money and mistress. Such were the gradations by which this celebrated courtesan rose to the eminence of an imperial mistress: and in that situation it must be owned, of all this prince's favourites, she was both the most prolific and the least offensive to the jarring interests of the 'court or country. She observed an evenness of conduct, and behaved with so much mildness, that none were her enemies who were friends to the King, and none ever libelled her, but the malevolent Lord Rochester."

Many stories are told of Nell Gwynn's charity and goodness of heart. Her benevolent exertions in behalf of the neglected author of *Hudibras*, were equally unsuccessful with the King, as with his minister Buckingham. She was not always, however, disappointed in her charitable intentions. One day, when she was "rolling about town in her coach," a poor wretch solicited charity at her coach-door, representing himself as an old soldier who had been disabled in the civil wars, while fighting in the royal cause. The heart of Nell Gwynn was touched by his distress; she hurried to lay his griefs before the King, and from this circumstance, we are told, arose her zeal for the establishment of Chelsea Hospital.

One day, when he had been struggling in the council, and torn to pieces by the multiplicity of petitions presented to him for redress, the outrageous behaviour of the ministers, and the fierce contentions of parliament, he retired into Nell's apartment very pensive, and seemed quite broken under the influence of grief: she took the liberty to ask his majesty the cause of his disorder. "O Nell!" says he, "what shall I do to please the people of England? I am torn to pieces by their clamours."—"If it please your majesty," says she, "there is but one way left, which expedient I am afraid it will be difficult to persuade you to embrace."—"What is that?" says his majesty, in a tone that denoted curiosity.—"Dismiss your ladies, may it please your majesty, and mind your business: the people of England will soon be pleased."

We are tempted to add, from the same source which has furnished us with the foregoing version of her history, another anecdote of Nell's mode of drawing the King's attention to his own affairs. That she often exerted herself to effect this object, seems certain; though she might be partly influenced by opposition to the other royal mistresses, whose exertions had quite another aim.

"One day, when the council had met and waited long for his majesty's appearance, one of the lords came to the apartment of the King, but was refused admittance. He complained to Nell of this insufferable dilatoriness; upon which she laid a wager with the nobleman, of a hundred pounds, that, that very evening, she would fall upon a scheme that would bring him to the council. She sent for Killigrew, a character so well known in those times, that none of our readers can be ignorant of his station; and desired him to dress himself in boots, and in every respect as if he was going a journey, and enter the King's apartment without ceremony. Killigrew immediately engaged in her scheme, equipped himself, and entered the apartment. As soon as his majesty saw him, 'What, Killigrew! are you mad? Why, where are you going? Did I not order that nobody should disturb me?'—'I don't mind your orders, not I,' says Killigrew; 'and I am going as fast as I can.'—'Why, where,' says his majesty, 'where are you going?'—'Going? why to hell,' says Killigrew. 'To hell? and what to do there?' says his majesty. 'To fetch up Oliver Cromwell from thence,' says he, 'to take some care of the national concerns; for I am sure your majesty takes none.'

"This expedient, concerted by Nell Gwynn and executed by Killigrew, had the desired effect; for he immediately went to the council, and, as long as he could bear the badges of royalty, continued with them."

Another story, given by the same writer, is highly characteristic of our heroine. One day she was driving in her coach to Whitehall. Her coachman refused to give way to another coach, in which was a lady of quality. High words soon arose between the two coachmen, and the other refused to give way, because, he said, he had himself the honour to be driving a countess, whilst his lady was neither more nor less than a ——, applying to his mistress a very offensive term. The indignant coachman jumped from his seat, and administered to the offender a severe beating. When Nell Gwynn inquired the cause of the quarrel, and her coachman repeated to her the offensive expression which had stirred up his choler, "Go, you blockhead!" said she, "never fight again in such a cause, nor risk your carcass but in defence of truth." The King laughed heartily, when he heard the story, and complied with the lady's request, when she desired a place for her coachman.—ED.]

THE DUCHESS OF SOMERSET.

> " Chaste was she, to detraction's desperation,
> And wedded unto one she had loved well—
> A man known in the councils of the nation,
> Cool and quite English—imperturbable,
> Though apt to act with fire upon occasion,
> Proud of himself and her;—the world could tell
> Nought against either, and both seemed secure—
> She in her virtue, he in his hauteur."
>
> LORD BYRON.

IN the reign of Charles the Second, there were three Duchesses of Somerset: it has therefore been a matter of some difficulty to appropriate the beautiful picture in the gallery at Windsor to its true original.

The first of these ladies was Frances, widow of William second Duke of Somerset; more celebrated by the title of the Marquis of Hertford—he who eloped with Lady Arabella Stuart in the reign of James the First. She died, very old, in 1679.

The second was Sarah, wife of John fourth Duke of Somerset; the daughter of a physician, and the widow of George Grimstone, Esq. The prints and pictures of this Duchess bear no resemblance to the picture known at Windsor as the Duchess of Somerset, neither is she mentioned in the Court Chronicles of the day: her fame rests upon a far different basis,—that of a foundress of almshouses and a benefactress of colleges. She died, at a very advanced age, in 1692.

The third duchess (Lady Elizabeth Percy) did not bear that title till 1682, and the picture in question must have been painted before that time. This, however, is not a conclusive argument. According to Horace Walpole, and others, Sir Peter Lely died suddenly, in 1680, while painting a portrait of the *"beautiful Duchess of Somerset:"* now there could have been no other *beautiful* Duchess of Somerset alluded to, except the Lady Elizabeth, who so soon afterwards bore that title. There is, I must confess, a maturity of beauty about this portrait, which scarce agrees with the youthful age of the lady. It is difficult to reconcile all these circumstances, and it is not without diffidence, and some feeling of uncertainty, that the accompanying portrait has been adjudged to the Lady Elizabeth Percy.

This beautiful woman, who united in her own person the long-descended honours and vast possessions of the House of Percy, was the sole daughter of Josceline, eleventh and last Earl of Northumberland, in the direct line, and Lady Elizabeth Wriothesley, youngest daughter of the Earl of Southampton.

Her father, dying abroad, left her, an infant of four years old, heiress of all the immense estates of her family, and holding in her own right six of the oldest baronies in the kingdom: those of PERCY, LUCY, POYNINGS, FITZ-PAYNE, BRYAN, and LATIMER.

The Lady Elizabeth Percy was early consigned to the care of her grandmother, the old Countess of Northumberland,[*] who gave her a strict and excellent education. But so great an heiress could not be long kept in retirement, or in ignorance of her own rights and importance; even in her infancy she was surrounded

---

[*] Lady Elizabeth Howard, second wife of Algernon tenth Earl of Northumberland.

by suitors, who sighed,—not for her immature charms, but her broad lands and proud titles; and it was her peculiar fate to be three times a wife, and twice a widow, before she was sixteen.

She was first married, at the age of thirteen, to Henry Cavendish, Earl of Ogle, (only son of the Duke of Newcastle,) who assumed immediately the name and arms of Percy. The young earl was about the same age as his bride, and a boy of great promise; but he unfortunately died within a few months after his marriage, in 1680.

Upon his death, lovers, or rather suitors, again crowded round the youthful countess, then in her fourteenth year. Among them were Thomas Thynne, of Longleate Hall; and the celebrated adventurer, Count Koningsmark. The personal advantages of Koningsmark possibly attracted the notice of the inexperienced girl; but her relations hastened to prevent the effects of his captivating assiduities, by contracting her to Mr. Thynne; but before the marriage could be actually solemnized, Thynne was murdered in his carriage, while driving through Pall Mall, by three assassins hired by Koningsmark for the purpose. The count himself escaped abroad; but the three wretched instruments of his crime were apprehended, and suffered on the very spot on which it was committed.

Thynne seems to have been a weak man, and a heartless libertine to boot; and Lady Elizabeth may be pardoned for the little regret she bestowed on his tragical fate. As her affections had never been engaged, or even her inclinations consulted in this union, she was, after the first shock, easily consoled; and in three months afterwards, (May 20th, 1682,) she married Charles Seymour, sixth Duke of Somerset.

The duke was then in his twentieth year, possessed of a fine commanding person, dark complexioned, and regularly handsome; he was generous, brave, and magnificent, with a cultivated mind, and a taste for the fine arts; but so inordinately arrogant in his manners, and vain of his illustrious rank, that in his own time, and since, he has always been distinguished as the "PROUD DUKE OF SOMERSET."* This ruling foible, which in its excess almost bordered on insanity, threw a shade of ridicule over his character in public; but in private, it was supported by such high qualities of heart and mind, that no man, perhaps, was ever so much adored, and at the same time beheld with such awful reverence by his family and dependents. His wife gave a strong proof of her love for him, when, in spite of her own pride of ancestry, and it was not inconsiderable,— for she had been educated with a high idea of all the importance which attached to her as the heiress and representative of the Percies,—she sacrificed her pride to her affection. Her first act, when she came of age, was to release her husband from the disagreeable obligation imposed by her marriage articles, of changing the name of Seymour for that of Percy; while she dropped her own family name, illustrious and dear as it must have been in her eyes, to take that of her husband, —dearer to her because it was *his:* and this was just as it should be, in the right and true feeling of an affectionate woman.

The duchess was subsequently one of the greatest ornaments of the court of William the Third and Queen Anne; and on the disgrace of the Duchess of Marlborough, succeeded her as Groom of the Stole to the Queen. She died in 1722, after having presented her husband with thirteen children, of whom two only survived her.

Her eldest son Algernon, Earl of Hertford, distinguished himself in the Duke of Marlborough's wars, and was in every respect

* His children were not allowed to sit in his presence; his servants obeyed by signs; and when he travelled, the roads were cleared before him by his outriders. "Get out of the way!" cried one of these to a countryman who was driving a pig, "my lord duke is coming, and does not choose to be looked upon." The fellow, a true John Bull, snatched up his pig in a rage, and holding him up at the carriage window, exclaimed, "But I will see him! and *my pig shall see him too!*"

one of the most accomplished noblemen of his time. His wife (who, by an odd fatality, was one of the family of Thynne) was that amiable Duchess of Somerset, many of whose letters have been published in Shenstone's correspondence. Through their only daughter, who became the representative of the Percies and Seymours, the title of the former family, and the possessions of both, descended to the present Duke of Northumberland.*

This portrait of the Duchess of Somerset was engraved, many years ago, under the mistaken title of the Countess of Ossory. With the exception of the right hand, the position and drawing of which are really inexcusable, this is one of the loveliest pictures in the Gallery of Beauties. She is represented leaning on a pedestal; the head is a little inclined, the complexion fair, and the features beautiful. The drapery, which is of a pale blue, is rather too negligently put on;—I am at a loss to tell for what it is intended, as it is so arranged that, on the least movement, it must inevitably fall from the lovely form it conceals. The bust is much exposed; but nothing can exceed the delicacy of the tints and pencilling in the neck and bosom, and the sweet and tender manner in which the whole picture is executed. The back-ground is equal to the rest.

[Spring Macky gives the following account of Charles Duke of Somerset, descended of the ancient family of *Seymour*, which made so great a figure in the reign of Edward the Sixth.

"The duke, in the reign of King Charles the Second had the Garter, and married the heiress of Piercy of Northumberland,

---

* After the death of the Duchess Elizabeth, the duke married, in 1725, Lady Charlotte Finch. A short time after their union, his young bride wishing to command his attention, playfully tapped him on the shoulder with her fan: her husband, startled at such a freedom, turned upon her frowningly,—"Madam," said he, "my first wife was a Percy, and *she* never took such a liberty!"

which much increased his estate; but he made no considerable figure till the reign of King James, when, being in waiting as bed-chamberman, and at the arrival of the Pope's Nuncio in England, and refusing to assist at the ceremony of the introduction, he was dismissed from all his employments. He, notwithstanding, did not enter into the measures of the Revolution, but for some years warmly opposed the designs of King William's ministers; joined in impeaching the Partition; and protested against acquitting those who advised it. Yet upon the French King's sending the Duke of Anjou to Spain, he came over to the service of his country, and was made President of the Council, and joined with a great deal of zeal in the measures concerted for preventing the growing power of France. On the Queen's accession to the throne, he was made Master of the Horse; and appears at court, with a great deal of warmth, for a party that seems to suffer by King William's death.

" He is of a middle stature, well shaped, a very black complexion, a lover of music and poetry; of *good judgment,* but by reason of great hesitation in his speech, wants expression."

Dean Swift says, that " he had not a grain of good judgment, hardly common sense."—ED.]

THE DUCHESS OF RICHMOND.

> "Lost in a labyrinth of doubts and joys,
> Whom now her smiles revived, her scorn destroys;
> She will, and she will not—she grants, denies,
> Consents, retracts, advances, and then flies."
>
> GRANVILLE.

AMONG the beautiful women of Charles's court, none were more conspicuous during their life, or have been more celebrated since their death, than Frances Stewart—"La Belle Stewart" of De Grammont's Memoirs, and afterwards Duchess of Richmond: yet her character as a woman is neither elevated nor interesting; and the passion which the King long entertained for her, and the liberties in which she indulged him, either through weakness or a spirit of coquetry, exposed her, at one period, to very disgraceful imputations. On a review of her whole conduct, as far as it can now be known and judged from the information of contemporary writers, the testimonies in favour of her virtue appear to preponderate; yet it must be confessed that we are left to choose between two alternatives, and it is hard to tell which is the worst: if "La Belle Stewart" was not the most cold and most artful coquette that ever perplexed the wits of man, she was certainly the most cunning piece of frailty that ever wore the form of woman.

Frances Theresa Stewart was the daughter of Walter Stewart, Esq., third son of Lord Blantyre. The family had been distinguished for loyalty, and had suffered much in the civil wars.

Walter Stewart took refuge in France, where, as it appears, either himself or his wife was attached to the household of the widowed Queen Henrietta Maria. Miss Stewart was thus brought up under the eye of royalty; and such was the admiration which even her budding and immature loveliness attracted in the French capital, that Lewis the Fourteenth wished to have detained her, merely as an ornament to his court, and offered her mother to portion and marry her nobly; but on the restoration of the royal family, the Queen-dowager refused to leave her young favourite behind, and brought her, with her mother and her sister Sophia, in her train to England. I have not been able to ascertain the date of Miss Stewart's birth, but she must have been so extremely young at the period of her arrival, as not to have reached her full growth.* Partly through the influence of the Queen-mother, and partly owing to her father's claims on the royal protection, she was appointed one of the Maids of Honour to Catherine of Braganza in 1663; but some months elapsed before her beauty, expanding into all the graces of womanhood, produced that sensation which it afterwards caused in the court.

Soon after her arrival, Miss Stewart formed a kind of friendship with Lady Castlemaine; which, considering her duty to the Queen, and the character of the favourite, was not very reputable, and is scarcely excused by her youth and inexperience. Lady Castlemaine, either confiding in her own charms, or contemning the childish character and trusting in the coldness of the young beauty, affected to patronise her, had her constantly at her side, and almost forced her upon the King's notice. She was the last to perceive what a formidable rival she had raised up for herself; and then, as was natural in her vain, vindictive mind, all her fondness turned to measureless hatred. This enmity extended itself even to the waiting-maids of the rival beauties, and the court was sometimes so disturbed by the squabbles of these abigails, that the King

* Pepys.—He observes, in one passage, that Miss Stewart had grown considerably since he last saw her: this was in 1664.

exposed himself to ridicule by interfering to restore peace between them.

There seems to have been but one opinion as to the consummate loveliness of Miss Stewart. Her features were faultless and regular, her complexion dazzling, her hair fair and luxuriant. Her figure, which rose above the common height, was well proportioned, though slender; she danced, walked, dressed with perfect elegance, and sat her horse with peculiar grace. To her Parisian education she owed that *air de parure* which excited De Grammont's admiration, as being so " truly French." She was polished and gentle in her deportment, and does not appear to have been infected by the coarseness of her friend Lady Castlemaine, either in mind or manners. Lord Clarendon adds one trait, which ought not, in justice, to be omitted,—" that she was never known to speak ill of any one." This constitutional good-nature, her childish disposition, her dislike to all serious pursuits or conversation, and her perfect indifference to state intrigues, must have captivated Charles even more than the transcendant beauty of her face and figure. He had a just aversion for all learned and political ladies: with less reason, though a wit himself, he hated wit in a woman, and any thing like sentiment or refinement appeared to him absolutely superfluous, and merely synonymous with prudery and hypocrisy.

Charms such as Miss Stewart possessed, would certainly have dealt destruction round the whole court, but for two powerful reasons. In the first place, the King's admiration was so early and so ardently displayed, that no well-bred courtier dared openly to interfere with his homage, or obstruct his views; and secondly, Miss Stewart's understanding was not equal to her beauty. The frivolity of her mind, the shallowness of her character, and the coldness of her temper, must have diminished the power of mere external grace, in a court adorned by such women as Miss Hamilton and Lady Chesterfield.

She seems to have possessed just wit enough to feel her power, and use it "for the convenience of her own fortune."* Fond of adoration, yet armed with indifference; weak, yet cunning; and taught by the lessons of an intriguing mother, she was able to turn the arts of men against themselves: she could grant small favours, hold out alluring hopes, descend, in fact, far beneath a woman's dignity, and strangely compromise a maiden's modesty. But what then? she preserved a sort of negative reputation; and this, I am afraid, is all that can be granted to Miss Stewart. Perhaps, if we consider the situation in which she was placed, even this is much: she was pursued for years by a gay, enamoured, captivating monarch; and not only kept him at bay, and trifled with his passion, but drew within the vortex of her destructive charms some of the courtiers, whose youth or vanity forgot the greatness of the risk in the greatness of the temptation.

Among the most distinguished of these was the Duke of Buckingham,—he who, at once "chemist, fiddler, statesman, and buffoon," could adapt himself to all women as well as to all men. Miss Stewart's amusements were so childish, that Count Hamilton assures us, "tout y était, hors les poupées;"† blindman's-buff, and hunt the slipper, were among her favourite diversions. In the presence-chamber she used to employ herself in building houses of cards: while those who wished to secure the good graces of the beautiful favourite, forsook the basset-table to supply her with materials, or affected eagerly to partake her amusement. Among

---

* Clarendon, p. 338, folio edit.

† Miss Stewart was not absolutely singular in her penchant for romping or childish diversions. For instance, we find the following memorandum in Pepys: "I did find the Duke and Duchess of York, and all the great ladies, sitting upon a carpet on the ground, there being no chairs, playing at ' I love my love with an A, because he is so and so;' and, 'I hate him with an A, because of this and that;' and some of them, but particularly the duchess herself and my Lady Castlemaine, were very witty."—*Pepys' Diary*, vol. ii. p. 311.

these, Buckingham, that universal genius, was conspicuous for his skill in this frail species of architecture: he sang well; he was an excellent mimic, he composed impromptu fairy tales to admiration, and couplets more remarkable for their wit than their delicacy. These accomplishments, and his gay impertinence, made him so agreeable to Miss Stewart, that with the King's permission, or at least in his presence, she used to send for the duke to amuse her whenever she felt *ennuyée*. Buckingham's original design had been to secure an influence over her mind, which should enable him, by governing her, to rule his master; but he was caught in his own device: he was unable to resist the charms and flattering smiles of this young Armida; and at length exchanged the character of an amusing companion, to assume that of a sighing Damon. The metamorphosis was so little pleasing to Miss Stewart, that he received a repulse, from which he did not soon recover; and which, as it compromised him with the King, left him completely at her mercy. Instead of making her subservient to his purpose, he was obliged to content himself with being subservient to hers.

The younger Hamilton was another of her lovers: it does not appear that he was distinguished for his skill in card-houses, and by his own confession, he did not pique himself on his ready invention of fairy tales and scandalous stories for her amusement. The manner in which he first attracted the particular notice of Miss Stewart, gives us a strange idea of the coarse manners which prevailed in Charles's court. A brilliant circle had assembled one evening in Miss Stewart's apartments at Whitehall, and Lord Carlingford, an old Irish peer, undertook to amuse the young beauty by making what is vulgarly called a "lantern of his jaws;" that is, holding a lighted taper in his mouth for a certain time. Hamilton would not be outdone in this noble accomplishment, and he confounded his competitor by holding at once two tapers in his capacious mouth. Killigrew humorously complimented him, and offered to back him against a lantern, while Miss Stewart was thrown into ecstasies.

N

From this time Hamilton was more particularly graced by her favour, and made one of her select *coterie;* he presented her with a beautiful little horse, on which she had an opportunity of displaying her inimitable elegance as an equestrian, and was always at her side to teach her how to manage her spirited steed. In short, the lady became every day more gracious, and the gentleman more enamoured; and if De Grammont, then in love with Miss Hamilton, had not interfered, with a kind of fraternal interest, and roused Hamilton from his inconsiderate dream, this affair would probably have ended in his disgrace, and consequent ruin, as his fortunes depended wholly on the King's favour. De Grammont represented to him that Miss Stewart had in reality no other view than that of making him her "esclave de parade;" that Charles, though in general the most easy and peaceable of men and monarchs, was not to be trifled with on certain points. "Point de raillerie avec le maître, c'est à dire, point de lorgnerie avec la maîtresse." Hamilton had just so much sense, or so little love, as to take this friendly advice, and withdrew his pretensions in time to escape banishment from the court, which assuredly would have been the consequence of his temerity.

Miss Stewart had also the honour of inspiring with a more serious and fervent passion Francis Digby, one of the sons of the Earl of Bristol, and a brave and accomplished young man. This attachment is not alluded to in the Memoirs of De Grammont, being of a later date than the events recorded there; nor can we guess at the degree of encouragement she may have given him, except by remembering her character. It was sufficient to turn his head, and to make him rush upon danger and death as a relief; he was killed in the sea-fight between the English and the Dutch in the year 1672. His devoted love for Miss Stewart was so well and so publicly known, that Dryden made his fate and her cruelty the subject of his song, "Farewell, fair Armida."*

* This song is more common-place, and deserved the ridicule thrown on it in the *Rehearsal*, where it is ludicrously parodied in "A song made by Tom Thimble's first wife after she was dead."

To these distinguished admirers we may add two others, not unknown to fame. Philippe Rotier, the celebrated medallist, who was called over to England to cut the die for the new coinage, exhibited her head on the reverse for Britannia. This man became so passionately enamoured of Miss Stewart while she sat to him, as nearly to lose his senses. Walpole says, that the profile which the same artist afterwards engraved for a medal, displays the most perfect face ever seen.*

Nat Lee, the poet, has addressed a dedication to her, which is perfect "Midsummer madness;"† but as he was already on the high road to Bedlam, that is not very surprising. The Duke of Richmond‡ also sighed for her, but he contented himself for some

---

* In Waller's poems is an epigram on this medal, beginning—

"Our guard upon the royal side,
On the reverse our beauty's pride," &c.

It contains a compliment to Miss Stewart, which implies that her resistance to the King received its full credit at court; the verses are common-place, and if there be any point in the last line,

"Virtue's a stronger guard than brass!"

it can only mean that the virtue of Miss Stewart, such as it was, stood her in more stead than the brass of Lady Castlemaine!

† For instance:—"Something there is in your mien so much above what we vulgarly call charming, that to me it seems adorable, and your presence almost divine, whose dazzling and majestic form is a proper mansion for the most elevated soul; and let me tell the world, nay sighing speak to a barbarous age, (I cannot help calling it so, when I think of Rome and Greece,) your extraordinary love for heroic poetry is not the least argument to show the greatness of your mind and fulness of perfection. To hear you speak, with that infinite sweetness and cheerfulness of spirit that is natural to your grace, is, methinks, to hear our tutelar angels; 'tis to bemoan the present malicious times, and remember the Golden Age; but to behold you, too, is to make prophets quite forget their heaven, and blind a poet with eternal rapture!" &c. &c.

‡ Charles Stewart, Duke of Richmond and Lennox: he was the last Duke of Richmond of his family. After his death, Charles II. conferred the title on the son of the Duchess of Portsmouth. The present head of that branch of the Stewarts, from which the Duke of Richmond and Lord Blantyre (Miss Stewart's grandfather) were both descended, is, I believe, the Earl of Galloway.

time with distant homage, and with drinking pint bumpers in honour of her beauty, till he had almost lost the little intellect nature had bestowed on him; but what he lost in wit he seems to have gained in audacity, for he made the fair lady understand, that though reduced for the present to drown his love in wine, he was ready to make her a duchess whenever she was willing to elope with him. In the mean time, though the King had the power of keeping all competitors at a distance, he was not himself more *avancé*. Miss Stewart retained her power by standing most pertinaciously on the defensive, without actually driving him to despair. When the Queen fell dangerously ill, she was immediately surrounded by the obsequious and rapacious courtiers, and regarded as her probable successor: the atrocious advice of the Duke of Buckingham on this occasion, has been related in the memoir of Queen Catherine. Miss Stewart, on her quarrel with Lady Castlemaine, had made a great display of duty to the Queen, who treated her with kindness, and seems to have placed some confidence in her discretion. While the King pursued her with the most undisguised and insulting attention, Miss Stewart certainly avenged some of the wrongs of her mistress, and her whole sex, by the dexterity with which she contrived to torment her accomplished but profligate lover. She stooped at times to very equivocal compliances when afraid to lose him; at another moment she would talk of throwing herself into a French convent: and her airs and caprices, her alternate fits of hauteur and tenderness, so agitated the King, that he sometimes appeared at the council-board like a man distracted. He offered titles which were refused, and presents—which were accepted; he set about reforming his *ménage d'amour* in compliance with her affected scruples and pretended jealousy; he promised to give up Lady Castlemaine, and to discard his singers and actresses, and other superfluous ladies then on his establishment;—in vain! till at a critical moment the Chevalier De Grammont stepped in to his majesty's assistance. De Grammont had just received from Paris a certain calèche, which he presented to the King. Such a calèche, so light, so elegant in its form, so finished in all its appointments, had never before been seen in England: it excited the admiration of the whole court. The Queen, Lady Castlemaine, and Miss Stewart, were each eager to be the first to exhibit themselves in this wonderful calèche. The preference was given to Miss Stewart, —a preference which, it was scandalously insinuated, cost the fair lady some diminution of that immaculate purity upon which she had hitherto piqued herself.

It may be said, in excuse for Miss Stewart, that her situation was peculiar and difficult; the King was armed with a power, which, in those days, few thought of resisting; and either to free herself from his pursuit; or anxious to be made a duchess on reputable terms, she listened to the addresses of the Duke of Richmond. Love (even by her own confession) had little to do with this choice; the duke was merely a good-natured fool, addicted to habitual intoxication; and with no one recommendation to a lady's grace but his high rank, and his near relationship to the royal family.

One evening, Lady Castlemaine, who kept paid spies to watch all the movements of her dangerous rival, discovered that she had an appointment with the Duke of Richmond, and instantly informed the King, with the most insulting expressions, to whom, and for whom, he was sacrificed. Driven by this female fury, the King rushed to the apartment of Miss Stewart: her women looked terrified, and denied him access, assuring him that their lady had retired to rest, much indisposed, and unable to see him. He pushed them aside, and forced his way rudely to her chamber. On entering abruptly, he found the fair lady reclining on a couch, and certainly neither indisposed nor asleep. The Duke of Richmond was seated at her side. The inexpressible confusion of the lovers, thus surprised, can only be imagined; and the King, unable to restrain his rage, burst into a torrent of threats and reproaches, which seemed to terrify the Duke much more than they discomposed Miss Stewart. The room in which this scene took place overlooked the river; he cast a glance at the window, then at the King, whose eyes sparkled, and whose frame trembled with unwonted passion; and judging it best not to trust his safety within reach of the lion's paw, he made no reply, but with a profound bow, backed out of the apartment, leaving the lady to make her peace as best she might. She, who well knew the character of Charles, assumed a high tone on the occasion, insisted on her right to receive the addresses of the duke in what manner and what time she pleased, complained of insult and tyranny, and threatened to throw herself into a nunnery abroad. The King left her in anger, and in the utmost agitation. The following day the Duke of Richmond was ordered to quit the court; but, not being gifted with the assurance or magnanimity of his mistress, or through that best part of wisdom, which some call cowardice and some discretion, he had anticipated the royal commands, and retired the night before.

A few days afterwards, Miss Stewart took an opportunity of throwing herself at the feet of the Queen her mistress, and very pathetically entreated her protection and forgiveness; the good-natured Catherine, now subdued to "the quality of her lord," forgave her. She considered, that since she must needs suffer a rival, it would be better to trust the gentleness of Miss Stewart, than to be outbraved by the insolent termagant, Castlemaine; and that by preventing the flight or marriage of a woman whom her husband loved to distraction, she was giving herself a claim to his eternal gratitude; in consequence, she charitably exerted herself to bring about a reconciliation between the King and his coy, perverse mistress, and succeeded so well, that for awhile all was peace and smiles—a hollow peace and most deceitful smiles. One cold dark night, in the month of March, 1667, Miss Stewart found means to steal from her lodging in Whitehall; and joined the Duke of Richmond at a tavern in Westminster, where he had horses waiting, she eloped with him into Surrey, and they were privately married the next morning by the duke's chaplain.

"What dire events from amorous causes spring," we are not

now to learn from tale or history. A catastrophe, which hung upon the caprice of a giddy woman, influenced the destiny of three kingdoms.

The King was transported with rage at a step which seemed to set his love and power at defiance: all who were suspected of having been privy to the marriage of Miss Stewart with the Duke of Richmond (among whom were some of the King's best friends and wisest counsellors,) fell under his extreme displeasure. The great Lord Clarendon was deprived of the Seals and banished,* and his dismissal was followed by those consequences, which paved the way for the Revolution.

Pepys, in his Diary, records a conversation which took place soon after her marriage, between the Duchess of Richmond and one of the lords of the court, which is very consistent with her character and conduct throughout. She said, that "when the Duke of Richmond first made love to her, she did ask the King, and the duke did so likewise; and that the King did not at first refuse his consent." She confessed, "that she was come to that pass, as to resolve to have married any gentleman of 1500*l.* a-year, who would have had her in honour, for she could not longer continue in the court without submitting to the wishes of the King, whom she had so long kept off, though he had liberty more than any other had, and more than he ought to have had;" she said that "she had reflected on the occasion she had given the world to think her a bad woman, and that she had no way but to marry,

---

* "The Earl of Clarendon's son, the Lord Cornbury, was going to her (Miss Stewart's) lodgings, upon some assignation that she had given him about her affairs, knowing nothing of her intentions. He met the King in the door, coming out, full of fury. And he, suspecting that Lord Cornbury was in the design, spoke to him as one in a rage that forgot all decency, and for some time would not hear Lord Cornbury speak in his own defence. In the afternoon he heard him with more temper, as he himself told me. Yet this made so deep an impression, that he resolved to take the Seals from his father."—*Burnet's History of his own Time,* vol. i. p. 354.

and leave the court rather in this way of discontent than otherwise, that the world might see she sought not any thing but her honour."—"She hopes, though she hath little reason to hope, she can please her lord so as to reclaim him, that they may yet live comfortably in the country on his estate."* Evelyn believed her to be worth about 6000*l.* in jewels: among these was a pearl necklace, then valued at 1100*l.*, the King's first present to her: he had allowed her, while in the court, 700*l.* a-year for her clothes; but these were trifles, compared to the sums lavished on Lady Castlemaine and Lady Portsmouth. There is reason to believe, that had Miss Stewart been more complying, she might have commanded any thing which it was in the power of the weak monarch to bestow.

But little is known of the Duchess of Richmond after her marriage: she resisted for some time all temptations and entreaties to return to the court; but in 1668, she was appointed one of the ladies of the Queen's bedchamber, and was lodged in Somerset House, where Catherine then resided. Pepys says, "that the apartments allotted to her and the duke were sumptuous, and that the King frequently visited her, but merely in courtesy." About two years after her marriage she was attacked by the small-pox, from which she recovered with great difficulty. The King paid her much attention during her illness, and even afterwards, when the ravages of that cruel disease had so impaired her matchless beauty, that she was scarcely to be recognised: one of her brilliant eyes was nearly quenched for ever.†

In 1672, the Duke of Richmond was appointed ambassador to the court of Denmark, and died at Elsinore the same year. His duchess did not accompany him abroad; and after his death she continued to reside in the court near the person of the Queen, with whom she continued a favourite; and Charles having attached him-

* Pepys, vol. ii. p. 46.
† Vide Letters from Rouvigny to Louis XIV., in Dalrymple's Memoirs.

self to the Duchess of Portsmouth, La Belle Stewart was no longer honoured or dishonoured by his assiduities. She never married again after the loss of her husband, nor do we hear any thing more of her till her death, which took place in 1702. During the latter part of her life, her time seems to have been divided between cards and cats; and in her last will she bequeathed several of her favourite cats to different female friends, with legacies for their support. The well-known line in Pope's Moral Essays,—

" Die, and endow a college—or a cat!"

alludes to the will of the Duchess of Richmond.

Warton, with more good nature than probability, supposes this to have been a delicate way of providing for poor, and probably proud gentlewomen, without making them feel that they owed their livelihood to her mere liberality: if this were the only scruple, methinks it would have been more generous to have left the annuities unburthened with the cats. The bulk of her property was left to her nephew, Walter Stewart, commonly called the Master of Blantyre, for the purchase of certain estates, to be attached to the name and family, and called, in memory of the donor, " Lennox's love to Blantyre."

Miss Stewart had a younger sister, Sophia Stewart, married to William, third son of the Lord Bulkeley; she too was celebrated for her beauty.

The engraved portrait is from the Gallery of Beauties at Windsor, and represents the Duchess of Richmond as Diana. She holds a bow in one hand, and with the other supports her dress, as if tripping over the dew. The drapery is of a pale yellow. The features are regular, but deficient in expression; and the nose is not sufficiently aquiline to agree with other portraits of Miss Stewart, and with the minute descriptions of her person which have been handed down to us. The landscape in this picture is most beautifully painted.

MRS. LAWSON.

"Condamnée à la celebrité, sans pouvoir être connue."
DE STAEL.

BY this title the portrait in the Beauty-room at Windsor has always been traditionally known; but, according to the present style, Mrs. Lawson should properly be Miss Lawson, as the lady here represented was certainly unmarried.*

Horace Walpole, Granger, and others, have supposed this picture to be that of Miss Lawson, one of the daughters of the brave and celebrated Admiral Sir John Lawson, who died in consequence of the wounds he received in the sea-fight of 1665, and of whom Lord Clarendon has left us a noble character.

This opinion, which is unsupported by any proof except the name, appears, on examination, very improbable. Sir John Lawson was a man of very low extraction, who had formerly been a ship-boy of Hull, and rose, under Cromwell, to be admiral of the fleet. Himself and his whole family had been Puritans and Republicans; and, although upon the Restoration he declared for the King, saying it was his duty to defend and fight for his country, no matter who governed it, it is not very likely that his family should be distinguished at court, where he himself seldom came.

* In the reign of Charles II., and long afterwards, Mrs. or Mistress was the usual appellation of a young unmarried woman. Married women were entitled *Madam*. The word *Miss* was seldom used but in a very disreputable sense.

His eldest daughter married Richard Norton, Esq., of Southwick, which was considered so great a match, that to bestow on her a portion worthy of it, Sir John impoverished himself and the rest of his family.* There is not the slightest reason to suppose that this young lady had any claims to be included in a series of Court Beauties.

The Mrs. Lawson of the Windsor Gallery, must have been one of the five daughters of Sir John Lawson, a Roman Catholic baronet, of Brough, in Yorkshire. He married Catherine Howard, a daughter of the Earl of Carlisle, whose younger brother, Thomas Howard,† became the second husband of Mary Villiers, Duchess of Richmond, and sister of the Duke of Buckingham. Thus, a woman of high rank and intriguing spirit, connected by her first marriage with the blood royal, and the sister of the reigning favourite, became the aunt of the five Miss Lawsons.

There is reason to believe, from various scattered notices, that this Duchess of Richmond introduced one of her nieces at court, with a view of captivating the easy affections of Charles, and counteracting, through her influence, the ascendancy of the Duchess of Portsmouth. One part of this plan appears to have succeeded, for Miss Lawson became the object of the King's admiration, whose attentions to her were so public, that they are frequently alluded to, and the Portsmouth faction was thrown into some consternation.

But it also appears, that on this occasion Charles met with very unusual resistance, and that Miss Lawson was not easily won,—if, indeed, she was won at all, of which there is no existing proof. There is a coarse political satire of that time, (about 1674) quoted by Sir William Musgrave, in which all the celebrated beauties of the court are represented as contending for the post of *Maîtresse*

---

* See Clarendon's History, and Campbell's Lives of the Admirals.

† He fought a duel with the invincible Jermyn, on account of that "angel-devil" Lady Shrewsbury.

en titre. Miss Lawson is mentioned among the rest; but she is rejected, by reason of her "too great modesty." There are other contemporary songs, epigrams, satires, worthless in themselves, where Miss Lawson's name occurs. She is never alluded to but as one hitherto innocent, and exposed to danger from the intrigues of her aunt, and the profligate pursuit of the King. The following passage will serve as a specimen:

> "Yet, Lawson, thou whose arbitrary sway,
> Our King must, more than we do him, obey,
> Who shortly shall of easy Charles's breast,
> And of his empire, be at once possest;
> Though it indeed appear a glorious thing
> To command power and to enslave a King;
> Yet, ere the false appearance has betray'd
> A soft, believing, unexperienced maid,
> Ah! yet consider, ere it be too late,
> How near you stand upon the brink of fate."*

Sir William Musgrave adds, "that the five sisters became nuns at York," and this is all that can be discovered concerning the original of this portrait. If we may believe in the existence of innocence, which even slander appears to have respected, and satire itself to have compassionated; and if we can suppose it possible that such innocence could be maintained in a corrupt court, surrounded not only by temptations, but by the most villanous snares, we ought to deem Miss Lawson acquitted, notwithstanding the evil society in which she appears.

The picture, which is by Wissing, is not in itself eminently lovely or interesting; but, as one of the Windsor Beauties, it could not well have been omitted in this collection. It is very beautifully painted; and in the face there is an expression of mildness and goodness, which agrees with the few particulars which have been collected relative to that Mrs. Lawson, whom I suppose to have been the subject of the portrait.

* Musgrave's Biographical Adversaria, MS. No. 5723, British Museum.

THE COUNTESS OF CHESTERFIELD.

"Extremely mad the man I surely deem,
That weens with watch and hard restraint to stay
A woman's will, that is disposed to go astray.
It is not iron bands, nor hundred eyes,
Nor brazen walls, nor many wakeful spies,
That can withhold her wilful, wandering feet;
But fast good will and gentle courtesies."

SPENSER.

LADY ELIZABETH BUTLER, eldest daughter of the Duke and Duchess of Ormond, and sister of the gallant and accomplished Lord Ossory, was born at Kilkenny, on the 29th of June, 1640. Her birth had nearly cost the life of her excellent mother, who had scarcely recovered from the effects of a long and dangerous confinement, when the civil wars broke out: the events which followed, and which so deeply involved in their consequences the happiness and fortunes of the Ormond family, need not be related here. The childhood of Lady Elizabeth was passed in scenes of tumult and constant vicissitude, but always under the care and protection of her mother; at length, her parents were driven from their country and obliged to seek a refuge upon the Continent, where the duchess resided for some time with her young family, principally at Caen in Normandy. The marriage between Lady Elizabeth Butler and the young Earl of Chesterfield was arranged at the Hague in 1659, and was to have taken place at the same time with that of her brother, Lord Ossory; but it appears that the duchess just at that time was obliged to give up the portion intended for her daughter, to aid the King in his necessities: the exact date of the marriage is uncertain, but it was probably solemnized at the Hague in the beginning of the year 1660.

Lady Elizabeth was then about nineteen, and the young earl in his twenty-fifth year: a marriage so suitable in age, in rank, and in personal accomplishments, was rendered miserable, by circumstances over which neither had any control.

Lord Chesterfield had previously married Lady Anne Percy, the daughter of Algernon, Earl of Northumberland: she died very young in 1654, leaving him a widower at the age of twenty. He afterwards travelled, and spent two years in the various courts of Italy; whence he returned in 1659, and received the hand of Lady Elizabeth, according to a family compact between his mother, the Countess of Chesterfield, and the Duke of Ormond. He is described by Hamilton as a handsome man, without any advantages of figure, as he was neither tall nor graceful; but the beauty of his head and features compensated for other deficiencies. He was accomplished and intelligent, skilled in riding, fencing, dancing, and in all the exercises then thought necessary to form a complete gentleman; he was courteous to his inferiors, but haughty and ceremonious in the society of his equals. A temper, naturally inclined to jealousy and suspicion, had not been amended by a long residence in Italy: the profligacy which there prevailed universally, had subverted his own principles, and implanted in his mind certain prejudices and opinions, very derogatory to women in general. His young bride, on the contrary, had been educated in the bosom of domestic happiness; she came to him fresh from the tuition and example of an amiable and dignified mother, and she appears at first to have regarded her husband with a timid and fond admiration, which a little attention and devotion on his part, would have converted into an attachment for life. Whether he had left some Italian love beyond the Alps, or had already begun to devote himself to Lady Castlemaine, whose first and most favoured lover he is said to have been, cannot now be known. It is only certain, that he met the affection of his young and charming wife with a negligent, frigid indifference, which astonished, pained, and humiliated her: finding, however, that all her tenderness was lavished in vain, and that her attempts to win him from a rival rather increased than diminished his aversion, mingled pique and disgust seem to have succeeded to her first affection and admiration, and their conjugal arrangements were in this melancholy and unsettled state when the Restoration took place, and Lady Chesterfield accompanied her husband and her family to England.

The Duchess of Ormond was not an indifferent spectator of her daughter's domestic misery. It appears, from a very respectful and submissive letter from the earl to his mother-in-law, that she had interfered kindly but discreetly, with a hope of healing all disquiet. To reconcile himself with his wife's parents, Lord Chesterfield took her to Ireland in 1662; they spent three months at Kilkenny Castle, and there Lady Chesterfield witnessed the marriage of her sister, Lady Mary Butler, with Lord Cavendish afterwards the first Duke of Devonshire.

The King hated Chesterfield, on account of the favour with which Lady Castlemaine had regarded him; but the earl had claims on the royal attention which could not be overlooked. On the arrival of Catherine of Braganza, he was created chamberlain of her household, and in virtue of his office was lodged in Whitehall. Thus thrown into the very midst of a gay court, Lady Chesterfield, from a neglected wife, living in privacy, and even poverty, became suddenly a reigning beauty: captivating and piquante, rather than regularly handsome, there was something in the archness and brilliance of her wit, in the elegance of her small, but perfect figure, and in the exquisite neatness of her person and dress, which distinguished her from the half-attired, languishing, flaunting beauties around her. Only Miss Hamilton rivalled her in vivacity and mental acquirements, and only Miss Stewart surpassed her in charms.

She was immediately surrounded with professed adorers; and strange to tell, one of the first who sighed for her in vain was her own husband.

Lord Chesterfield found his charming wife universally admired, while the vulgarity and arrogance of Lady Castlemaine became every day more apparent and more intolerable from the force of contrast: he began to wonder, and with reason, at his own blindness and indifference to so many charms, and his passion at length rose to such a height, that, casting aside the fear of ridicule, he endeavoured to convince her, by the most public attentions, that his feelings towards her were entirely changed. Unfortunately, it was now too late: the heart he had wounded, chilled, and rejected, either could not, or would not be recalled; he found himself slighted in his turn, and treated with the most provoking and the most determined coldness. A spirit of coquetry, a dangerous love of general admiration, and all the intoxication of gratified vanity, now filled that bosom which had come to him pure, warm, and innocent, and which he had once occupied to exclusion of almost every other thought and feeling: the punishment was cruel, but scarce more than he deserved. Finding that all his advances were repelled, he was seized with jealousy and rage; he felt assured that a transition so complete, from extreme tenderness and trembling solicitude to the most perfect indifference, could only be caused by some favoured lover, and his suspicions fixed at once on the Duke of York,—not without apparent reason, for the duke's admiration of his wife had been very unequivocally displayed. But a more dangerous rival, wholly unsuspected, existed in George Hamilton, the younger brother of Miss Hamilton, and first-cousin to Lady Chesterfield.

Hamilton, either out of contradiction, or *étourderie*, had been amusing himself and alarming all his friends, by offering his assiduities to Lady Castlemaine, then in the height of her favour and her power. But Lady Chesterfield, having in a manner opposed herself with peculiar and feminine spite to the woman who had withdrawn her husband's affections from her in the first year of her marriage, and whom she every way detested, was not content with the legitimate triumph of winning back her husband from her trammels, she resolved to deprive Lady Castlemaine of her new admirer, and to add George Hamilton to her own train of adorers. This laudable resolve was not very difficult to execute, for Hamilton was the most inflammable of men; he was only "le petit cousin," and she had constant opportunities of meeting him, either in the society of his sister, or at the apartments of his aunt, the Duchess of Ormond. He could not see with impunity one of the loveliest women of the time: he began to waver in his allegiance to Lady Castlemaine, and while he yet hesitated, one or two encouraging glances from the blue eyes of Lady Chesterfield brought him at once to her feet.

We should not forget, while reading De Grammont's Memoirs, that they were written by the brother of George Hamilton, who considered himself as a betrayed and injured lover, and whose account of Lady Chesterfield's conduct was likely to be coloured by his own exasperated feelings: notwithstanding the conspicuous figure she makes in those Memoirs, and the malicious gaiety with which her coquetry and her indiscretion are exposed, I can find no direct accusation against her virtue either there or elsewhere. Pepys, who was likely to hear all the scandal of the court, mentions her ever with respect, as "that most virtuous lady;"* yet he never speaks of her husband without some slighting expression or discreditable allusion. In the present case, Lord Chesterfield had placed himself beyond the pale of sympathy; his former treatment of his wife was so well known at court, that his jealous airs exposed him to universal ridicule.

At this time it happened that the guitar-player Francisco, (mentioned in the Introduction,) had rendered that instrument so much the fashion, that all the beauties and courtiers affected to

* Pepys' Diary, vol. i. p. 177—194.

cultivate it with enthusiasm; and in the midst of this universal *raclerie,* Lady Chesterfield was as proud of possessing the finest guitar in England, as her brother, Lord Arran, of being confessedly the best player next to Francisco himself. The Guitarist had composed a certain sarabande, which the King greatly admired and patronised; and very soon nothing but this sarabande was heard at court. The Duke of York wished to learn it from Lord Arran; and he, being resolved to give the sarabande every possible advantage, invited the duke to accompany him to his sister's apartments, that he might hear it performed on this wonderful guitar, which was the envy of all the fair amateur players in the court.

In all this there was nothing extraordinary; but Lord Chesterfield, possessed by jealousy and suspicion, saw in this rendezvous nothing less than a scheme to accomplish his dishonour. While the two musicians were practising the sarabande, and Lady Chesterfield did the honours of her celebrated guitar, her husband sat watching the trio with "jealous leer malign," and internally resolving that nothing should induce him to leave the room; but in the midst of these agreeable reflections, an order arrived from the Queen to attend her majesty immediately in his quality of Lord Chamberlain, for the purpose of introducing the Muscovite ambassadors to her presence. The unhappy earl, execrating in his secret soul all guitars, ambassadors and officious brothers-in-law, was under the necessity of obeying the royal commands, and had not been ten minutes in the Queen's presence-chamber, when, to his confusion and dismay, he beheld the Earl of Arran standing opposite to him, and unaccompanied by the Duke of York. The moment he was released, he hastened home, and without waiting for any explanation, gave way at once to all the transports of jealous rage. The poor guitar was the first victim of his fury; it was broken into ten thousand pieces. After this exploit the first person he met on leaving his house was George Hamilton, upon whom his suspicions had never rested for a moment; in fact, it had been Hamilton's study to persuade him that all his assiduities were directed to Lady Castlemaine. To him, therefore, he confided his griefs; exaggerating the coquetry of his wife, the attentions of the duke, and the intermeddling of Lord Arran. He related at length the curious scene of the *bas verts*, when the fair Stewart, in presence of the whole court, suffered her beautiful ankle to be produced, in emulation of that of Lady Chesterfield: while the Duke of York stood aloof, refusing to admire, and declaring, with many a gallant oath, that there was "point de salut sans les bas verts." Now, as Lady Chesterfield had introduced this fashion, her husband conceived that the duke's speech could admit of but one interpretation:—Othello's handkerchief was not more conclusive. Hamilton began to think so too, and to take a more than friendly interest in the subject; and Chesterfield, imputing his indignation to a disinterested sympathy with his own wrongs, continued to pour his complaints into his ear, till Hamilton was driven to desperation. He began to suspect that Lady Chesterfield was merely trifling with him,—a supposition which, considering her character, was not improbable; and he was convinced that the Duke of York was a preferred lover, which assuredly was not a necessary consequence. In a fit of angry impatience, he advised Lord Chesterfield to carry his wife off to his country-seat. The poor countess was immediately conveyed down to Bretby by her infuriated husband, and Hamilton for awhile triumphed in his vengeance.*

* This story, which is related at length in the Memoirs of De Grammont with infinite grace and liveliness, but in a tone very unfavourable to Lady Chesterfield, is thus, with more brevity, and probably with more truth, narrated by honest Mr. Pepys, in his Diary. "This day, by Dr. Clarke, I was told the occasion of my Lord Chesterfield's going and taking his lady (my Lord Ormond's daughter) from court. It seems he not only hath been jealous of the Duke of York, but did find them two talking together, though there were others in the room, and the lady, by all opinions, a most good, virtuous woman. He the next day (of which the duke was warned by somebody that saw the passion my Lord Chesterfield was in the night before) went and told the duke how much he did apprehend himself wronged, in his picking out his lady in the whole court to be the subject of his dishonour; which the duke did answer with great calmness, not seeming to understand the reason of complaint; and that was all that passed: but my lord did presently pack his lady into the country in Derbyshire, near the Peake;

The whole of the circumstances soon became public; the lady was generally pitied, and none believed that her husband had any just cause for the tyranny he had exercised on this occasion. Dorset, Etheredge, Rochester, and all the rhyming wits of the court, pursued Lord Chesterfield with showers of epigrams. The famous sarabande, which had been the first occasion of this terrible fracas, was set by the Chevalier de Grammont to new words, bitterly reflecting on the conduct of this " mari loup-garou," and soon the whole court had them by heart; they were sung universally, and, (as Count Hamilton gravely adds,) " toutes les dames les voulurent avoir pour les apprendre à leurs enfants."

Lady Chesterfield never again appeared at court; and learning to whom she was really indebted for the severity exercised towards her (the justice of which she was far from admitting,) she vowed vengeance against George Hamilton, and forthwith proceeded to execute her purpose with all the cunning of an *intriguante*, and all a woman's wit and wilfulness. She penned a long and artful letter to Hamilton, gave him a most eloquent and heart-rending description of her miserable state, of the melancholy prison, surrounded by rocks, precipices, and morasses, in which she was confined; of the ruthless tyranny of her husband, now her gaoler, and of her own repentance. She informed him that the earl was under the necessity of leaving home for a week, and conjured him to seize that opportunity to visit her, and listen to her justification. Hamilton, already devoured by regrets for her absence, and remorse for his own share in causing it, received this insidious letter with transport, and fell at once into the snare. He immediately mounted his horse, and rode post down to Bretby. It was towards the close of a severe winter, and a hard frost prevailed. He passed a whole night under the windows of Bretby Hall, almost congealed with cold, without receiving the least sign of recognition or compassion. On returning to the little village inn where he was

which is become a proverb at court, to send a man's wife to the Peake when she vexes him."—p. 194.

lodged incognito, he learned that Lord Chesterfield was not absent
— nor likely to be so; and on looking round him he beheld, instead
of a prison a splendid palace; and instead of a horrible solitude,
a magnificent and cultivated domain, which, till a recent possessor
levelled its fine woods, was considered one of the most beautiful
seats in England. He perceived how grossly he had been beguiled,
and soon discovered that he was only the propitiatory victim in the
reconciliation which had just taken place between the countess and
her husband. On his return to London he would willingly have
suppressed the story of this luckless expedition; but Lady Chesterfield was not inclined to make a mystery of the revenge she had
taken on her rash and too officious lover: the story reached the
King's ears, and he insisted upon learning the details from Hamilton himself, who was called upon to relate his own ridiculous
adventure in presence of the whole court; so that the lady's
vengeance was in every respect complete, and, perhaps, not
unmerited.

Lady Chesterfield's retirement (or banishment) took place in
1662; about a year afterwards she gave birth to a daughter, and
thenceforward her time was spent entirely at Bretby, if not happily,
at least irreproachably. She died in 1665, before she had
completed her twenty-fifth year. Her infant daughter, Lady
Elizabeth Stanhope, was educated by her grandmother, the excellent Duchess of Ormond, and afterwards married John Lyon,
fourth Earl of Strathmore.

After the premature death of his beautiful and unhappy wife,
Lord Chesterfield married Lady Elizabeth Dormer, and died in
1713, at the age of eighty.

There is a tradition relating to the death of Lady Chesterfield,
which cannot be passed without remark, as it is to be met with in
many works, and is even alluded to by Horace Walpole. It is
said that her husband, having caused her to take the sacrament
upon her innocence respecting any intimacy with the Duke of

York, bribed his chaplain to put poison into the sacramental cup, and that she died in consequence. This horrible accusation rests upon no proof whatever; it is only certain that it was current during the life of the earl, and even believed by some of his own family. Lord Chesterfield's son by his third wife, married Lady Gertrude Saville, daughter of the Marquis of Halifax. The marquis and the old Earl of Chesterfield quarrelled, and the latter obliged Lord Stanhope to bring his wife to Lichfield, breaking off all intercourse between the families. Lady Stanhope had always on her toilette her father's work, "Advice to a Daughter." Her father-in-law took it up one day, and wrote on the title-page, "Labour in vain." On her side the lady, not to be outdone in impertinence, made her servant, out of livery, carry in his pocket a bottle of wine, another of water, and a gold cup; and whenever she dined or supped in company with her father-in-law, either at home or abroad, she never would drink but of those liquors from her servant's hand. It was a hint to the earl and the company present, that the crime which his lordship was suspected of having perpetrated by a sacred beverage, was full in the recollection of his daughter-in-law. The most surprising part of the story is, that the old earl endured this.

In the correspondence of this Earl of Chesterfield recently published, there are two letters to the countess in a tone more polite and sententious than affectionate. It appears certain that he never succeeded in winning back her tenderness; and he has recorded her death in his memorandum-book, without a single remark or expression of regret.

The portrait is engraved, for the first time, after the beautiful picture by Lely, in the possession of Mr. Fountaine, of Narford. It is the same which is mentioned by Granger, and which was copied in crayons for Horace Walpole. Its authenticity is beyond a doubt.

[The following letter was written by the Duke of Ormond to his sister the Countess of Clancarty, on occasion of the death of his daughter Lady Chesterfield.

"Moore Park, July 22, 1665.

" My dear Sister,
"Nothing could give me greater assistance against the increase of misfortune by the death of my daughter Chesterfield, than to find you bear your affliction with so much constancy. It is certain that as we are born to die, that the longer we live, the more of these trials we must be subject to. The separation of friends and relations has been, and must be so frequent, that the expressions of consolating and compassionating are a road as much beaten as that of death, in which all mankind are appointed to travel. And as on other ways, so on that, some go faster than others; but he that goes slowest is sure to come to his journey's end. God of his mercy prepare us for, and prepare for us, a good reception.

"The letters which should have been sent, I now send you; if there be any thing else that may add comfort to you within my power, it will as certainly arrive to you, when it is known to,
My dearest Sister,
Your most affectionate Brother and Servant,
Ormonde."

The following letter from Elizabeth Lady Chesterfield, which may be either the earl's second or third wife, preserved in the British Museum, contains an allusion to the banishment of our heroine to the Peake. It is addressed to "Mrs. Coollpeper, at her house next dore to the Arche in Lincons inne feilds, London."

"Nov. 9.

"Deare Mrs. Coollpeper,
"My women, as allsoe your letters, doe me the favour to tell me I am so happie to be in your thoughts, which I am extreme proud of, and I must still beg the continuence of it, and

that I may sometimes at your best leasure heare from you, you will be obliging if you please to descant me with a little news from your world. You know Darbysher is a dull place, and needs some thing to make it pleasint. I will assure you I know nothing will please me better than hearing from you, writ whatever you will. I suppose my Lady Dencell's discretion will lett her be a little decent this winter. Pray God she be not condemnd to Darbysher at last for ever, as sume body was about ten or twelf yeare agoe,* for that pockie gallant's mistress have that ill for them if they doe not behave themselves wisely, they are packed out of their heaven London. I am glad to heare my Lady Freschwell is coming to towne, because pore Moll may have somebody to hang upon besids ye weake La. Northumberland. I am obliged to you for wishing me at London this winter, though I shall be more desirous of it next, for now theare are none of being theare except your good selfe. I know not whether the Grand Passer is a lover of me or noe now, haveing not sine him a long time, I thinke it is no greate mater whether he be or noe, if I am not hated by you, I will be soe contented with that good fortten, that noe other things shall trouble

Your affect. humble servant,
E. CHESTERFIELD.

" Pray pardon a thoussand blotts here, for I am so neare my time that I am ill at case, and cannot mend my faults now."

Macky observes of Philip Stanhope, Earl of Chesterfield, that " he was very subtle and cunning, never entered into the measures of King William, nor ever did make any great appearance in any other reign." On which Dean Swift says, " If it be old Chesterfield, I have heard he was the greatest knave in England."—ED.]

* There is no date to this letter, and by the words *ten or twelf yeare agoe*, it may probably be written by the Earl of Chesterfield's third wife, Lady Elizabeth Dormer, eldest daughter and co-heiress to Charles Earl of Caernarvon. She died in 1679.

THE COUNTESS OF ROCHESTER.

"Such her beauty, as no arts
  Have enrich'd with borrow'd grace;
Her high birth no pride imparts,
  For she blushes in her place.
Folly boasts a glorious blood ;—
  She is noblest, being good."

HABINGTON.

LADY HENRIETTA BOYLE, Countess of Rochester, was the youngest daughter of Richard second Earl of Cork, and first Earl of Burlington. Her mother was the Lady Elizabeth, sole daughter and heiress of Henry Clifford, Earl of Cumberland. Thus she was the grand-daughter of that extraordinary man known in history as the GREAT Earl of Cork, who went to Ireland a needy adventurer in the reign of Elizabeth, and lived to see himself and five of his sons peers of England or of Ireland: by the mother's side she was descended from one of the proudest, most illustrious, and most powerful families among the old feudal aristocracy of England,—the Cliffords of Cumberland.

The Earl of Burlington, (for he was generally distinguished by his English title,) had been a firm Loyalist; and at the Restoration, to which he mainly contributed, he found himself high in favour at court, to which his four daughters were immediately introduced. The eldest became Countess of Thanet, the second married the celebrated Earl of Roscommon, the third became the wife of Lord Hinchinbroke, afterwards Earl of Sandwich. The youngest, who was also the most beautiful, was sought in marriage by Laurence Hyde, the second son of Lord Chancellor Clarendon.

The marriage of Anne Hyde with the Duke of York, the power and talents of the great Chancellor, then at the height of favour, gave to the whole family of the Hydes a degree of importance and influence at court, which was increased by the connexions they formed with the first and oldest nobility; for who would have rejected an alliance which had not been disdained by the first prince of the blood? Henry Hyde, the eldest son of the Chancellor, and afterwards Lord Cornbury, had fixed his affections on Theodosia Capel, the daughter of Arthur Lord Capel, and she became the "Madame Hyde" of De Grammont's Memoirs. Mrs. Hyde was naturally witty and lively, but from a strange sort of affectation, she fancied she should succeed better as a languishing than as a sparkling beauty: accordingly she changed her airy and swimming grace into a mincing gait, modulated her voice to the most approved drawl, and veiled her brilliant eyes so successfully, that the sleepy elongated eyelid thenceforth became the fashion of the court. Her sister-in-law, Lady Henrietta Hyde, was by nature what Mrs. Hyde became by fashion and affectation; she was a blonde of the most delicate description, with a profusion of fair hair, and a complexion transparently pink and white, like the Alpine berry shining through the new-fallen snow: her manners were as gentle and blameless as her face was beautiful. She was married to Laurence Hyde about the year 1663, and the utter dissimilarity between herself and her husband in character and temper, was, perhaps, the foundation of their domestic happiness.

Laurence Hyde was a man of great natural talent, improved by a careful education under the eye of his father, who had early initiated him into business, and intended him for the diplomatic service. He was handsome, with a good figure, and a dark complexion: his temper was naturally violent, but while he governed his family imperiously, he seems to have possessed the power of inspiring those around him with love as well as fear. "I never knew a man," says Lord Dartmouth,* "who was so soon put into a passion, that was so long before he could bring himself out of it, in which he would say things that were never forgot by any body but himself. He therefore had always more enemies than he thought, though he had as many professedly so as any man of his time." It might have been supposed that this warmth of temper, in which there was too much heat to be false,† and the incumbrance of a beautiful wife, who was simple enough to be content with the admiration of her husband, and to nurse her own children, were ill calculated to raise the fortunes of a man in such a court as that of Charles the Second; but polished manners, great sagacity in affairs, and his near relationship to the throne during three successive reigns, served Lord Rochester in lieu of more complying virtues, and a more accommodating wife. Notwithstanding the impeachment, disgrace, and exile of his illustrious father, which followed within a few years after his marriage with Lady Henrietta, we find Laurence Hyde, supported by his own talents and the friendship of the Duke of York, running a prosperous career. He was ambassador to John Sobieski, King of Poland in 1676, and afterwards envoy to Holland; he was First Lord of the Treasury in 1679, and in 1681 he was created a peer by the title of Viscount Hyde of Kenilworth; and in 1683, the earldom of Rochester, becoming extinct in the Wilmot family,‡ was conferred upon him. On the accession of James the Second he received the staff of High Treasurer, and was for some time considered as the chief favourite of the King, and at the head of all affairs.

It is perhaps the highest eulogium that could be pronounced on the character and conduct of his fair, gentle-looking, and really amiable wife, that while her husband was treading the steep and tortuous paths of court diplomacy, rising to rank and honours, and

* In a note upon Burnet's History. † Burnet's History.
‡ By the death of John Wilmot, only son of the famous, or rather notorious, Earl of Rochester.

filling the highest offices in the state, we do not even hear of her, except in her domestic relations. In the recent publication of the Clarendon Papers,* Lady Rochester is seldom mentioned: but from the manner in which she is alluded to, we may infer, without danger of being mistaken, that she was the excellent and submissive wife of an impatient and despotic husband; that she lived in the utmost harmony with her children and her relatives; that she frequented the court but little; that, without possessing any striking qualities, she inspired those who were allied to her with equal respect and affection; and that her health was so delicate and precarious, as to be a subject of constant solicitude to those who loved her.†

This is all we can gather from contemporary authorities. It should seem that her days flowed along in one even course of unpretending duties and blameless pleasures; duties such as her sex and station prescribed, pleasures such as her rank and fortune permitted,—interrupted and clouded by such cares and infirmities as are the common lot of mortality. This description of Lady Rochester may appear a little insipid after the piquante adventures of a Cleveland and a Chesterfield, and others of her more brilliant and interesting contemporaries; yet there is in its repose and innocence something that not only refreshes, but sweetens the imagination. As in a garden, where peonies, and pinks, and carnations, and tall lilies,

> "And canker blooms, with full as deep a die,
> As the perfumed tincture of the roses,"

flaunt to the eye and allure the sense, should we suddenly find a

---

* The Correspondence of Henry Hyde, Earl of Clarendon, and his brother Laurence Hyde, Earl of Rochester, edited from the original MSS.

† Thus, to give one instance from a letter of Lord Clarendon to his brother Lord Rochester: "God Almighty preserve you and my sister, and all yours. I am very much afraid lest this change should make impression on my sister's tender health; but she has seen such variety of changes in our poor family, that I doubt not her wisdom and resolution, if her strength do not fail her."—Vol. ii. p. 133.

jasmine trailing its light tendrils and luxuriant foliage round a lordly elm, with what delight should we appropriate its starry, unsullied blossoms, and place them in our bosom!

During the first years of her marriage, Lady Rochester became the mother of two sons and four daughters; of these, her eldest daughter, Lady Anne Hyde, was by far the most interesting, and appears to have been the favourite of her father and mother. In 1682, they married her to the young Earl of Ossory, the grandson of the great Duke of Ormond. Very early marriages were then customary: Lord Ossory was not more than nineteen, his bride not quite fifteen, when they were united. She was beautiful, innocent, and affectionate,* but unhappily inherited her mother's delicacy of constitution; we find her praised and admired for her early wit, sense, and vivacity, nor is it any argument against the truth of this praise, that she should be subject to superstitious terrors, and a believer in dreams and divinations, in days when philosophers studied alchymy and astrology. Lady Ossory was married too young, and her sensitive, imaginative disposition seems to have preyed on her health. She died from the consequences of a second and premature confinement, at the age of eighteen.†

* In the Clarendon Correspondence are two short letters, which Lady Ossory addressed to her father, about two years after her marriage. Her father, it seems, had written to her with some asperity,—perhaps under the influence of one of those moods of temper to which he was subject; and the earnest tenderness and humility with which she deprecates his anger, and professes her entire obedience, are very touching: they give us a high idea of the parental power as it was exercised in those days.

† Her death took place at Dublin Castle, January 25, 1685. Some fancies might possibly contribute to this calamity; for the young lady was impressed with the common superstitious notion, as to thirteen people sitting at table. A short time previous to her death, Dr. John Hough, (afterwards Bishop of Worcester,) was going to sit down, when, perceiving that he made the thirteenth, he stopped short and declined taking his place. She immediately guessed at his reason, and said, "Sit down, Doctor, it is now too late; it is the same thing, if you sit or go away." He believed that the circumstance affected her, as she was in very indifferent health, and had been subject for some time to hysterical fainting

To die young, innocent, and beloved, is not a misfortune; it is to die half an angel:—

> "Our great good parts put wings unto our souls
> That waft them up to Heaven."

The old Duke of Ormond lamented her honestly and feelingly;[*] her young husband more acutely, but *he* was soon consoled.[†] The blow fell heaviest upon her parents;—it seems to have struck her poor mother to the earth. Among the papers of Lord Rochester, one was found containing meditations on the anniversary of his daughter's death: on recalling his own sensations, he dwells with a kind of painful astonishment on the remembrance, that during a whole week which elapsed between the death of Lady Ossory and the arrival, "by reports, by messengers, by condoling friends, of the dreadful sound of that shot, which was fired a week before;"— during this interval he had been occupied in the cares, business, and pleasures of life, *and no internal voice* had whispered to him or to the mother, that she, the beloved one, who had derived her

---

fits. The poor lady's imagination seems to have been peculiarly susceptible of such impressions, for another story is related, that may perhaps have accelerated the fatal event. Upon the death of the Countess of Kildare, Lady Ossory, being then only seventeen, dreamed that some one came and knocked at her chamber-door; and that calling to her servant to see who was there, and nobody answering, she went to the door herself, and opening it, saw a lady muffled up in a hood, who drawing it aside, she saw it was the Lady Kildare. Upon this she cried out, "Sister, is it you? what makes you come in this manner?"—"Don't be frightened," replied she, "for I come on a very serious affair; and it is to tell you that you will die very soon." Such was her dream as she related it herself to Dr. Hough.

[*] The Duke of Ormond, in a letter to Sir R. Southwell, says, "I was in great perplexity for the sickness of the young lady I brought a stranger with me into this country, which it hath pleased God to put an end to in her death. I am not courtier, that is dissembler enough, to equal hers with other losses I have sustained of the like kind; but I assure you, her kindness and observance of me, and her conduct in general, hath gained very much upon my affections, and promised so much satisfaction in her, that I am extremely sensible of her loss."

[†] Lord Ossory, about a year after the death of his first wife, married Lady Mary Somerset.—*Vide* Memoir of Lady Ossory, p. 134.

being from them, who was, as it were, a part of their very existence, lay senseless and dead, and the life that was the joy of their's had departed from the world in which they breathed, insensible, unconscious of the stroke. How many have felt this before and since! "It pleased God," says the bereaved father, "to take her away, as it might be on this day, and I lived on, almost a week longer, deceived in my vain expectations that I should hear better of her, and that the worst was past; till here comes the dismal news, a week after the blow was given! a week's time I had spent, after her lying cold and breathless, in the ordinary exercises of my life;—nay, I think I had wrote from hence to her after the time she was dead, with the hopes that my letter should find her better; with expressions of tenderness for the sickness she had endured; of wishes for her recovery; of hopes of being in a short time happy in her company; of joy and comfort to myself, in being designed to go to live again in the same place with her:—I say I had written all this:—to whom? to my poor dead child! Oh, sad and senseless condition of human life!" This speaks to the heart, for it is the language of the heart.

He goes on to express his grief when the calamity was made known to him, and adds, "In the midst of this I had my wife lying weak and worn with long and continual sickness, and now, as it were, knocked quite on the head with this cruel blow;—a wife for whom I had all the tenderness imaginable; with whom I had lived long and happily, and had reason to be well pleased; whose fainting heart and weak spirits I was to comfort and keep up when I had none myself!"

This tender allusion to Lady Rochester shows how much she must have suffered on this occasion; and the simple and unobtrusive testimony to her merit, still existing in the hand-writing of her husband, is worth more than twenty sonnets in her praise, though Waller himself had penned them.

But Lord Rochester had little time for the indulgence of his own feelings, or for the consolation of others; while yet, as he expresses it, drowned in sorrow for the loss of his best child, he was hurried to attend on the spectacle of a dying monarch,—Charles the Second. Soon afterwards he was raised, by the friendship of his successor, to a more eminent and splendid station than he had yet enjoyed, and plunged into all the turmoil of politics. Lady Rochester was amongst those most distinguished by the new Queen,—the beautiful and amiable Maria of Modena. Burnet mentions a visit which the Queen paid to Lady Rochester when confined to a sick room: at the time of this visit rumours were afloat that James had tampered with Lord Rochester on the subject of religion; and it was said, that as the earl was found contumacious (that is, conscientious) upon this point, the staff of Lord High Treasurer would be taken from him. Lady Rochester, it is said, attempted to deprecate this intention, and the Queen said, "that all the Protestants were turning against them, so that they knew not how they could trust any of them." To which Lady Rochester replied, "that her lord was not so wedded to any opinion, as not to be ready to be better instructed." Lady Rochester had never before meddled with politics, and this first attempt was not successful; nor, it must be owned, much to her credit: it is right to add, that it rests on very suspicious evidence—that of an enemy.

Towards the end of the year 1686, Lady Rochester, after a long interval, gave birth to a fifth daughter, and survived her confinement only a few months: she died at Bath, whither her husband had taken her for the benefit of her health, on the 12th of April, 1687: she was in her forty-second year.

The Earl of Rochester, after acting a conspicuous part in the great events of the Revolution, and the angry politics of Queen Anne's reign, died in the year 1712.

Lady Rochester left five children. Her eldest son, Henry Lord

Hyde, succeeded to his father's title, and eventually to that of Clarendon.* He married the daughter of Sir William Leveson Gower, herself a celebrated beauty, and the mother of a beauty far more celebrated,—of Lady Catherine Hyde, afterwards that Duchess of Queensbury upon whom Pope and Prior have conferred an immortality, more lasting than the pencil of Lely or of Kneller could bestow on her mother and grandmother. Richard Hyde, the second son of Lady Rochester, died young on his passage to the West Indies.

Her eldest surviving daughter, Lady Henrietta, married James Earl of Dalkeith, son of the unfortunate Duke of Monmouth, and ancestor of the Duke of Buccleugh.

Lady Mary Hyde married Lord Conway, ancestor of the Marquess of Hertford.

Lady Catherine, who was Maid of Honour to Queen Anne, died unmarried.

The picture from which the portrait is engraved, hangs in the Beauty Room at Windsor. It was traditionally supposed to represent the wife of Wilmot, the witty and profligate Earl of Rochester,—who, though an heiress,† was no beauty; *au contraire,* —till Horace Walpole and Granger set the matter right. It is a delicate and pleasing, but not a striking picture; the face is soft and beautiful, without any expression, and accords with the gentle and lady-like character of the original: the back-ground is well painted. The drapery, which is of the palest blue, harmonizing with the extreme delicacy of the complexion, is rather more decorous, and not less inexplicable, than Lely's draperies usually are.

---

* The present Earl of Clarendon is descended from Lady Rochester in the female line.

† *La triste Héritière* of De Grammont; she was Miss Mallet of Enmere.

P

[Laurence Hyde, Earl of Rochester, was second son to the Lord Chancellor Clarendon, and was a nobleman that had had all the improvement of education and experience, with a good capacity. He was, when very young, employed by King Charles the Second in foreign negotiations; and was, by King James the Second, made Lord High Treasurer of England, knight of the Garter, and created Earl of Rochester. He opposed King William's coming to the throne, and generally thwarted the measures of the court; till the King, to gain him and his party in opposition to France, upon the breach of the Partition treaty, made him Lord-Lieutenant of Ireland, and a member of the cabinet; but, contrary to all expectations, he was thrown out again, yet had always a very considerable pension during that King's reign.

On Queen Anne's accession he was again made Lord-Lieutenant of Ireland, which he soon quitted; and not being made Lord High Treasurer, which he expected, he was so disgusted, as to come no more to court.

He was easily wound up to a passion, which is the reason why he so often lost himself in the debates of the House of Peers; and the opposite party knew so well how to attack him, as to make his great stock of knowledge fail him. He was, notwithstanding, one of the finest men in England for interest, especially the church party, and was very zealous for his friends. He was of a middle stature, well shaped, and of a brown complexion.

In the year 1684, the Earl of Rochester was nominated Lord-Lieutenant of Ireland in the room of the Duke of Ormond; but that appointment determining with the death of his majesty, the white staff was again put into the Earl of Rochester's hands by King James II.

When he was Lord Treasurer in the reign of James the Second, he checked as much as possible the lavish expenditure of the court; and it is said that he complained to the King of the extravagance of the Princess of Denmark, (afterwards Queen Anne); and that when James recommended her to be in future more economical, her friend Lady Churchill, afterwards the celebrated Sarah Duchess of Marlborough, exclaimed, " Ah, Madame, this is the advice of your uncle, old Rochester!" This is an anecdote which speaks much in his praise. He was never popular with any party, and by his own he appears to have been a nobleman more respected and feared than loved.

Among the original correspondence of the great Duke of Ormond, now in the possession of Mr. Colburn, are two letters from the Earl of Rochester; one to the Duke of Ormond, the other to the Duke of Beaufort, on the second marriage of the young Earl of Ossory, which seems to have followed the death of his first wife much sooner than Mrs. Jameson has stated. As neither have been printed, we are tempted to give the first.

To the Duke of Ormond, then at Bodminton.

"WHITEHALL, JULY 31, 1685.

" Though it be not long since I waited on your Grace, and that I hope wee shall meet again very soone, I cannot omitt till then to tell you the part I take in the satisfaction I know your Grace must have, on seeing my Lord of Ossory soe well disposed off, and setled in the allyence of soe good and great a family. How tender soever this subject may be to me, you know my thoughts very early upon it, and I doe as heartily wish you and your family all happyness in this marryage as any man liveing can doe. I pray God make the continuance of it long, and give you health and strength to the same proportion you now enjoy, to make your grand-children the more happy. It is what I always wished for, and what I shall always endeavour to contribute to, and will ever be, with the greatest truth and sincerity,

Your Grace's most faithfull,

and most obedient servant,

ROCHESTER."—ED.]

ELIZABETH BAGOT,

AFTERWARDS

COUNTESS OF FALMOUTH, AND COUNTESS OF DORSET.

> "So far as doth the daughter of the day
> All other lesser lights in light excel,
> So far doth she in beautiful array
> Above all other maidens bear the bell;
> No less in virtue that beseems her well,
> Doth she exceed the rest of all her race."
>
> SPENSER.

WE know far too little of Miss Bagot, since all that can be known of her only excites a wish to know more. The lovely sketch of her in De Grammont's Memoirs, the yet more beautiful and finished portrait which the pencil of Lely has bequeathed to us, are just sufficient to awaken a degree of admiration and interest, which the few particulars we can collect from other sources serve rather to increase than to gratify.

When, upon the restoration of the royal family, the clandestine union of the Duke of York and Anne Hyde was formally acknowledged by himself and sanctioned by the King, she was of course admitted to all the privileges and honours which belonged to her

as first Princess of the Bood, and wife of the heir-presumptive.* She was allowed a truly royal establishment; consisting of a Chamberlain, Master of Horse, the usual retinue of lords in waiting and pages; and, though last not least, four Maids of Honour: the choice of the latter being left entirely to herself.

Her first selection, it should seem, was not either brilliant or fortunate. The four young ladies who formed her retinue were soon dispersed different ways; some married, and some—as the Scotch say—" did *worse*."

For example; there was that laughter-loving, frolic-seeking gipsy Miss Price, who was suspected, even before her appointment, of having forfeited all claims to the title, if not to the office, of Maid of Honour. She was soon dismissed: the very *mal-à-propos* death of a lover having brought to light a certain casket of *billets doux*, all in the hand-writing of the fair Price, and the duchess having unluckily and inadvertently read aloud the two first before witnesses, found herself under the necessity of burning the remainder; and for the sake of example, and as a warning to all young ladies in the same predicament not to be found out in future, Miss Price was ordered to go and weep her lover elsewhere than in the royal ante-chamber. In spite of this dismissal, Miss Price appears to have maintained her ground in society, since we fre-

---

* Anne Hyde was married in 1659. Without the slightest pretensions to beauty, she had a presence so noble, and an air at once so gracious and so commanding, that Nature seems to have intended her for the rank she afterwards attained. On her elevation to the second dignity of the kingdom, she "took state upon her" as if accustomed to it from her cradle; and, as Grammont observes, held out her hand to be kissed " avec autant de grandeur et de majesté, que si de sa vie elle n'eut fait autre chose."

By her spirited conduct she obliged the Duke of York to acknowledge his marriage with her, contrary to his own intentions and the wishes of the King, and in defiance of the Queen-mother, who vowed in a rage, that whenever " that woman was brought into Whitehall by one door, she would go out of it by the other." Yet she was afterwards reconciled to the match, and acknowledged the duchess as her daughter.

quently hear of her afterwards; and her unscrupulous good-nature, vivacity, and knowledge of the world, rendered her a favourite at court.

The next was Miss Hobart, with whose name scandal was more malignantly busy, though not so loud. She was not handsome, but she had talents, and a turn for mischievous intrigue, which raised her up some bitter enemies. The duchess, who esteemed her, and was far too reasonable and good-natured to listen to the slanders she could not silence, removed Miss Hobart from her post of Maid of Honour, and placed her immediately about her own person, and under her own protection, as her woman of the bed-chamber.

The third of these damsels was Henrietta Maria Blagg;* "*La Blague aux blonde paupières*" of De Grammont's Memoirs. She was the same to whom Miss Hamilton, in the spirit of mischievous frolic, sent the *gants de Martial* and the lemon-coloured ribbons, in order to set off to more advantage the flaxen ringlets and *fade* complexion of this most fair, most insipid, and silly of coquettes. After figuring in her lemon-coloured coiffure at that famous court-ball which has already been described in the Memoirs of Miss Hamilton, and making two or three attempts to rival Miss Price,—who carried off one of her lovers, and, at the wicked instigation of Miss Hamilton, did her best to carry off another,—Miss Blagg resigned her maiden office in the duchess's court, and it is to be hoped her coquetry also, and married Sir Thomas Yarborough, a Yorkshire baronet, as singularly fair as herself; to show the world, says Hamilton, "Ce que produirait une union si blafarde."

The fourth was Miss Bagot, the subject of the present Memoir, and the only one of the number who had any real pretensions to sense and beauty.

* She was the daughter of Colonel Blagg, or Blague, of the county of Suffolk. Her sister, so often mentioned in Evelyn's Memoirs, was a most amiable and accomplished woman, and afterwards the wife of the first Lord Godolphin.

MISS BAGOT.

Elizabeth Bagot was the daughter of Colonel Hervey Bagot, third son of Sir Hervey Bagot, Baronet, one of the ancestors of the present Lord Bagot. Her mother, Dorothea Arden, of the Ardens of Park Hall, in Warwickshire, died in 1649, leaving an only daughter, an infant. Colonel Bagot, soon after the death of his first wife, married Elizabeth Rotheram, who made an affectionate and careful step-mother.

The whole family of the Bagots had adhered to the party of Charles the First, and had suffered more or less in the royal cause. Colonel Hervey Bagot had particularly distinguished himself by his chivalrous loyalty, and his defence of Lichfield: these claims were not overlooked like those of many others. On the Restoration, he became one of the Gentlemen-pensioners of Charles the Second, and his daughter Elizabeth was appointed Maid of Honour to the Duchess of York.

She had hitherto been brought up in retirement, but we have no particulars of her life or education before she first appeared at court in 1661, and immediately fixed attention. Her beauty was the more striking, because it was of a style and character very unusual in England. She was a brunette, with fine regular features, black eyes, rather soft than sparkling, and a well-proportioned figure on a large scale : her dark but clear complexion was, upon the slightest emotion, suffused with crimson ; so that, as Hamilton says so gracefully, " Elle rougissait de tout sans rien faire dont elle eût à rougir."

So lovely a creature must have moved among her companions like a being of another sphere, and hardly required the *fadeur* of Miss Blagg, or the vulgarity of Miss Price, as foils to her superior charms. Charles Berkeley, Earl of Falmouth, after sighing awhile in vain for Miss Hamilton, turned to Miss Bagot, as the only one who could compete with her in beauty,—who was not so highly gifted in mind as to have a right to be fastidious,—who had not wit enough to make her lovers her jest,—and, with her soft dark eyes and varying blushes, did not look like one who could reduce a suitor to despair.

Falmouth was young, brave, and handsome; he had been one of the faithful companions of the Duke of York in his exile, and by him introduced to the King: he soon became the declared favourite of both, and a sharer in all their profligate adventures. He had done everything in his power to prevent the acknowledgment of the duke's marriage with Anne Hyde, which he regarded as disgraceful to his patron: he even went so far as to traduce her infamously, but was afterwards obliged to retract the unmanly slander. This offence the duchess magnanimously forgave, but her father, Lord Clarendon, as bitterly avenged, by leaving us in his history a most odious picture of Berkeley, whom he describes as a "young man of a dissolute life, and prone to all wickedness in the judgment of all sober men . . . . One in whom few men had ever seen any virtue or quality which they did not wish their best friends without."*

But whatever might have been Lord Falmonth's vices and follies in the opinion of all sober men, it is not likely that he would be judged with severity in a court where he was all-powerful,—where profligacy, so far from being a fault, was a proof of loyalty if not of wit, and the received distinction of a real cavalier,—where neither by the King nor any one else apparently, except Miss Hamilton, "had he ever been denied what he asked, either for himself or others." It is no great imputation on Miss Bagot's sense or taste that she should be dazzled by the personal advantages of Lord Falmouth, and excuse or disbelieve many faults in one who was bent to please her, and who possessed so many powers of pleasing. We find, therefore, without surprise, that she soon exchanged the title of Maid of Honour for that of Countess of Falmouth. This marriage, which must have taken place about 1663, did not remove Lady Falmouth from the court she had

* Clarendon's Life.

previously adorned, but merely placed her in a more conspicuous and exalted rank; and for a year and a half she shone in that gay sphere, an object of admiration and envy. We have also reason to believe that she was, at this period of her life, a beloved and happy wife as well as a worshipped beauty; for whatever might be the faults of Lord Falmouth, his attachment to her must have been passionate and disinterested, since she had no portion, and there was scarce an unmarried woman of any rank or fortune that would have rejected his suit. Perpetual constancy, perhaps, had been too much to expect from a man of his temperament and morals; but he was not long enough her husband to forget to be her lover. Rich in all the gifts of nature and fortune, young and thoughtless in the gayest of courts, "round like the ring that made them one, the golden pleasures circled without end"—that is, for a few short months, for so long did this eternity of happiness endure, and no longer. In 1665, Lord Falmouth, partly from a wish to distinguish himself, and partly from an attachment to the Duke of York, volunteered, with many other young noblemen and gentlemen, to serve on board the fleet in the first Dutch war. The engagement off Harwich, called in history the *great* sea-fight, being one of the most memorable of our naval victories, took place on the 3rd of June, 1665. The Earl of Falmouth, who was on board the Royal Charles, the duke's ship, and standing close to his royal highness in the thick of the fight, was struck dead by a cannon-ball. The same shot killed Lord Muskerry and young Boyle, the son of the Earl of Burlington. The duke escaped, but was covered with the blood of his devoted friends. This great victory, like many others, had no permanent results, and was most dearly bought. It threw many of the first families in the kingdom into mourning: "But no sorrow," says Clarendon, "was equal—at least no sorrow so remarkable, as the King's was for the Earl of Falmouth. They who knew his majesty best, and had seen how unshaken he had stood in other very terrible assaults, were amazed at the floods of tears he shed upon this occasion;"* and it is said

* "The King, it seems, is much troubled at the fate of Lord Falmouth: but I do not meet with any man else that so much as wishes him alive again, tho

that the Duke of York deemed the glory he had gained in this action, and even his own safety, dearly purchased by the loss of his young favourite.

When princes mourn, they mourn in public; when widows mourn,—they sometimes mourn in public too; but Lady Falmouth does not appear to have done so, for we hear nothing of *her* grief. The best proof we have of the reality of her sorrow is, that her name does not appear in any of the contemporary memoranda for two or three years: during this time she seems to have lived retired from the court, or at least to have taken but little share in its amusements. Towards the end of the year 1667, there was a report that she was engaged to marry young Henry Jermyn, one of the heroes of De Grammont's Memoirs; but she escaped a union with this notorious coxcomb, and the next we hear of her is her marriage with the celebrated Earl of Dorset.

The Earl, when only Lord Buckhurst, had passed a youth even more dissolute and extravagant than that of Lord Falmouth. Like him, he had volunteered in the sea-fight of 1665, and like him had distinguished himself by his light-hearted bravery; but in one respect more fortunate than his predecessor, he lived long enough to redeem his youthful extravagances, and instead of being remembered as a mere man of wit and pleasure, he has left a brilliant reputation as an accomplished gentleman, a patron of letters, the most honest and disinterested courtier, and most consistent statesman of that day. His marriage with the widow of Lord Falmouth could not have been one of interest, since she had no fortune but her pension from the King; and to have been the choice of such a man as the Earl of Dorset, when he must have been nearly forty and she herself upwards of thirty, is a fair argu-

---

world conceiving him a man of too much pleasure to do the King any good, or offer any good advice to him. But I hear of all hands he is confessed to have been a man of great honour, that did show it in this his going with the duke, the most that ever man did."—*Pepys' Diary*, vol. i. page 344.

ment that neither the beauty nor the reputation of the lady had been impaired during her long widowhood.

The Countess of Dorset died in 1684, leaving no children by either of her husbands. After her death, Lord Dorset married Lady Mary Compton, daughter of the Earl of Northampton, a woman celebrated in her time for her virtue, beauty, and accomplishments.

This portrait of Miss Bagot, which is now engraved for the first time, is from a picture by Lely, in the possession of Earl Spencer. It is one of the chief ornaments of the splendid gallery at Althorpe, and certainly one of the finest of all Lely's female portraits. It is so full of expression and character, and coloured with such uncommon power and richness of effect, as to remind us of Vandyke. The landscape in the back-ground is particularly fine: the cannon-ball which she poises in her lap as though it were a feather, we must suppose to be merely metaphorical, and allusive to the death of her first husband. From the introduction of this emblem, the pensive air of the head, and the shade of sorrow which is thrown over the features, we may suppose this fine picture to have been painted in the interval between her first and second marriage.

MRS. NOTT.

WOULD that this fair, sentimental, Madonna-like creature could speak, and tell us who and what she was! The pencil has immortalized a lovely face, tradition has preserved a name; and must we be satisfied with these? Is there no power in conjuration to make those ruby lips unclose and reveal all we long to know? Are they for ever silent? The soul that once inhabited there, that looked through these mild eyes, the heart that beat beneath that modest vest,—are they fled and cold? and of all the thoughts, the feelings, the hopes, the joys, the fears, the "hoard of unsunn'd griefs" that once had their dwelling there, is this—this surface—where beauty yet lives " clothed in the rainbow tints of heaven," but mute, cold, impassive—all that remains? Why should the vices of a Castlemaine, the frailties of a Nell Gwynn be remembered, and their evil manners live in brass, while the virtues which might have been opposed to them have been "written in water?" Is it not a pity that Fame, that daughter of the skies, should, in the profligate times of Charles, have caught something of the contagion around her, and, like other fair ladies, have laid aside her celestial attributes, to sink into the veriest scandal-loving gossip that ever haunted a card-table? When she put her trumpet to her mouth, at every blast a reputation fell; and the malignant echoes, instead of dying away in whispers, have been repeated from generation to generation. They who were a shame to their sex have been chronicled to all time; but she who was chaste as ice,

"Or the white down of heaven, whose feathers play
Upon the wings of a cold winter gale,
Trembling with fear to touch th' impurer earth,"

she whom Calumny spared, Fame neglected; a species of injustice, for which the said *Dame renommée* deserves to have her trumpet broken, and her wings stripped from her shoulders.

But then, it may be asked, is not the praise that waits on feminine virtue far too delicate to be trusted to such a brazen vehicle? more fitted to the poet's lyre than the trumpet of fame? And is it not better, while gazing on that beautiful face, which looks all innocence, to lose ourselves in delightful fancies and possibilities which none can disprove, rather than trace the brand of vulgar scandal on that brow,—scandal which we cannot refute,—nor those soft, sealed lips repel? Is it not better to admire we know not who, than turn away with disgust, as we do from the portraits of a Shrewsbury or a Southesk, whose beauty shocks us like the colours of an adder? This fair creature, with her veil, and her book and her flowers, and the little village church in the back-ground, looks far too good and demure for a Maid of Honour, —I mean for a Maid of Honour of Charles's court: for Heaven forbid that we should reflect on the honourable virginity of our own days! and yet the whole of the information which has been obtained amounts to this; that Mrs. Nott was one of the Maids of Honour to Queen Catherine, and nothing more can be known of the original. As for the picture, it is some satisfaction to know, while we gaze upon it, that slander has never breathed upon those features to sully them to our fancy; that sorrow, which comes to all, can never come there; that she shall keep her lustrous eyes, while those which now look upon her are closed for ever; and smile, still smile on, for other ages—"in midst of other woes than ours;" and this is something to dwell upon with pleasure, when all the rest is silence.

The portrait has always been one of the most admired of all the Windsor Beauties, and is painted with great sweetness and truth of colouring. The drapery is crimson, relieved with a white veil. The vase of flowers in the back-ground is finished with a delicacy worthy of Verelst.

[This "Madonna-like creature" was a Stanley of Kent, the wife of a gentleman of the name of Notts, whose family had been of gentilitial rank for a generation or two in the city of Canterbury.

Her history appears not to be much known. She was a distant cousin of the famous and lovely Lády Venetia Stanley, the mistress of the Earl of Dorset, and the incomparable wife of that character "great in all numbers," Sir Kenelm Digby. Probably Mrs. Nott was introduced at court by George Digby, Earl of Bristol; and she might have been an early and youthful friend of his daughter, Lady Anne Digby, Countess of Sunderland. Her name has had the good fortune to escape being recorded in the *Chroniques scandaleuses* of the day, and therefore we are bound to think that she was a pure and virtuous lady.—ED.]

THE COUNTESS OF SOUTHESK.

"How should woman tell
Of woman's shame, and not with tears?—She fell!"
MRS. HEMANS.

WHEN the accompanying portrait was first copied and engraved for publication, it was supposed to represent Frances Brooke, Lady Whitmore, the younger sister of Lady Denham; by which name the portrait has been traditionally known in the gallery at Windsor. But on examining the duplicate which exists at Narford, in the possession of Mr. Fountaine, and referring to the authority of Horace Walpole and Granger, there can be little doubt that it represents a woman much more notorious, Anne, Countess of Southesk. By this title the picture has always been distinguished at Narford since the days of Sir Andrew Fountaine, the first possessor, and the contemporary of the original; and by this name it was recognised as an original by Horace Walpole. The copy made in crayons by his order, is now at Strawberry Hill, and noted in his catalogue as that Lady Southesk, who figures so disgracefully in De Grammont's Memoirs.

To take up the history of this woman seriously, would be a waste of indignation: the little that is known of her we could wish to be less—and it shall be told as gently as possible.

Lady Anne Hamilton was the eldest daughter of William second Duke of Hamilton, who, like all his family, was distinguished in the civil wars for his devoted and chivalrous loyalty. He lost his life at the battle of Worcester, fighting for an ungrateful and worthless King; and his wife, Lady Elizabeth Maxwell (the daughter of the Earl of Dirletown,) whom he had married very young in 1638, was left a widow, with four daughters,—the eldest, Lady Anne, being then about eleven years old.

Where she spent her younger years,—how and by whom she was educated, cannot now be ascertained. The early loss of her noble father seems to have been her first misfortune, and the cause of all the faults, follies, and miseries which succeeded. The Duke of Hamilton had been distinguished in the court of Charles the First for his accomplishments and integrity; he was so remarkable for his love of truth, that it was said "that candour seemed in him not so much the effect of virtue as of nature, since from his infancy upwards he had never been known to lie on any temptation whatever." Burnet, who gives this testimony to the noblest and first of virtues, adds, that he was "handsome, witty, considerate, brave, and generous." He married young, against his own inclinations, and merely in obedience to the wishes and views of his brother, whom he idolized;† but being married he became an exemplary husband and father, and the gentle virtues of Lady Elizabeth appear to have won at length his entire confidence and affection. In a letter addressed to his wife on the eve of the battle of Worcester, he gives her the most endearing appellations that tenderness and sorrow could dictate in such a moment: "I recommend to you," he says, "the care and education of our poor children; let your great work be to make them early acquainted with God and their duty, and keep all light and idle company from

---

* History of the Dukes of Hamilton.

† His brother was James first Duke of Hamilton, beheaded by the Parliament during the civil wars. There is a portrait and memoir of William Duke of Hamilton, the father of Lady Southesk, in Lodge's Portraits of Illustrious Persons.

them." After his death this letter was found in his pocket-book, stained with his blood. How far his last and most affecting adjuration was attended to by his widow, we do not know; but we know that in the case of one of his children it proved fruitless.

The death of her father was not only an irreparable misfortune to Lady Anne, as it deprived her of a guardian and monitor, but it made an essential difference in her worldly prospects: although the titles and estates of the Hamilton family were transmitted in the female line, she was passed over, and the honours devolved on her cousin, the eldest daughter of James the first Duke of Hamilton, who became Duchess of Hamilton in her own right, while Lady Anne was destined to comparative insignificance. Still the high rank and virtues of her father, and the irreproachable conduct of her mother, render it difficult to account for the unguarded situation in which she was early placed, and her degenerate lapse from the virtues of her family. The very first notice we have of Lady Anne Hamilton, when she could not be more than eighteen, exhibits her as the friend and companion of Lady Castlemaine (then Mrs. Palmer,) and not only involved, as her confidante, in her intrigue with Lord Chesterfield, but most probably at the same time the object of his attentions.* She was then apparently a beautiful giddy flirt, prepared by the lessons and example of Lady Castlemaine for every species of mischief; and there is too much reason to believe, that when she attracted the notice of Lord Carnegie, the eldest son of the Earl of Southesk, she had ceased to be worthy of the hand or name of any man delicate on the score of female propriety, or jealous of his own honour.

The family of Carnegie (or Kerneguy,) is now, I believe, extinct in all its branches. It was then one of the oldest in Scotland, and traced its origin to a noble Hungarian, who was naturalized in the country in the reign of Malcolm Canmore. James Carnegie,

---

* Vide Correspondence of Philip second Earl of Chesterfield.

second Earl of Southesk, was a loyal and devoted adherent to the fortunes of Charles the First, and is also honourably mentioned for his general worth and integrity; his son Robert, Lord Carnegie, spent several years on the Continent, and during the government of Cromwell resided at Paris, where he was much distinguished by Louis XIV., who gave him a commission in the Scots Guards. He is described as a man of fine natural parts and graceful manners, improved by travelling;* but under these superficial advantages, he concealed deep, dark, malignant passions, and a temper at once dissembling and vindictive: he had, besides, a predilection for bull-baiting, for the bear-garden, and the cock-pit, which we cannot reconcile with our ideas of an accomplished gentleman, even of that day. His marriage with Lady Anne Hamilton was celebrated soon after the Restoration; but the date is not mentioned in any of the old peerages.

After her appearance at court, Lady Carnegie plunged at once into every species of dissipation; nor did the birth of two sons in the first years of her marriage check the career of thoughtless levity, and worse than levity, to which she abandoned herself. Her husband, meantime, was not gifted with the patience of a martyr; and though jealousy was not the fashion in Charles the Second's time, Lord Carnegie, the courtier, the travelled man of the world, after having committed the folly of marrying a wild, vain, unprincipled girl, had the still greater folly to be jealous of his wife, and to betray it to the scoffing court. While he was smarting under a thousand agonies,—not indeed doubting his dishonour, but only uncertain which of his wife's numerous admirers he should select for the especial object of his hatred and vengeance,—he was summoned down to Scotland to attend the death-bed of his father; and while he was thus engaged, Lady Carnegie seized the opportunity to add the Duke of York to the list of her lovers.

During her husband's absence, she appears to have so far

* Vide Douglas's Scottish Peerage.

braved opinion, as to exhibit her royal captive every where in open triumph; but in a few weeks Lord Carnegie re-appeared with the title of Earl of Southesk, an accession of dignity which his fairer half would most willingly have dispensed with, if she could also have dispensed with his very incommodious return. It now became necessary to keep some measures of decency, and the duke never visited her without being accompanied by some of the gentlemen of his retinue, by way of form. On one of these occasions he was attended by his Irish friend, Dick Talbot,* then only distinguished for his loyalty, his love of pleasure, his reckless good-nature, and hair-brained precipitancy.

While the duke was conversing with Lady Southesk, Talbot was placed at a window, as sentinel. He had not been there many minutes, before a carriage drew up at the door, and out stepped the husband. Talbot knew him well as Lord Carnegie; but having just returned from abroad, he had no idea that his former companion had lately changed his name—no recollection of his hereditary title; and it never occurred to him that the Lady Southesk, whom his patron was entertaining, was the wife of his old friend Carnegie. On seeing him alight he flew to prevent his entrance, telling him with a significant laugh, and a warm shake of the hand, that if he too was come to visit the beautiful Lady Southesk, he had only to go seek amusement elsewhere; for that the Duke of York was just then engaged in paying his compliments to the lady, and had placed him there expressly to prevent any *mal-à-propos* interruption.

Southesk, instead of forcing his way into his own house, and avenging on the spot his injured honour, was so utterly confounded by the cool impudence and obvious blunder of the unlucky Talbot, that he suffered himself to be fairly turned out by the shoulders, and sneaked off with a submission, partly the effect of surprise, partly of policy; for he had not courage to brave openly the heir-

* Afterwards Duke of Tyrconnel.

presumptive to the crown. The history of this ludicrous adventure was speedily spread through the whole court; it became the subject of ballads, lampoons, and epigrams innumerable, and covered the unfortunate earl with a degree of contempt and ridicule, which added to his shame and despair.

Yet even this public exposure and its consequences did not banish Lady Southesk from society: she continued for some years to haunt the court: she sought at the gaming table a relief from ennui, and endeavoured to conceal by art the ravages which dissipation, rather than time, had made in her once lovely face. Pepys mentions her, among the beauties of the day, as parading her charms in the park and the theatre; and to use his own coarse, but forcible expression, "*devilishly* painted." Her latter years were embittered by sorrows, against which a woman's heart, however depraved, is seldom entirely hardened. In her days of triumphant beauty, she had neglected her children; and in age they became her torment. Her eldest son, Lord Carnegie, treated her with coldness, and seemed to enter into his father's wrongs and feelings towards her; her youngest and favourite son, William Carnegie, a youth of great beauty of person and splendid talents, was killed in a duel at the age of nineteen. He had been sent to Paris to complete his education, and there meeting with young Tallemache, the son of the Duchess of Lauderdale,[*] they quarrelled about a profligate actress; and in this unworthy cause William Carnegie perished, in the spring and blossom of his years.

Lady Southesk died before her husband, and did not long survive the loss of her son, which occurred in 1681; but the date of her death is not mentioned. Lord Southesk died in 1688, and was succeeded by his son Charles, Lord Carnegie, who, like all his family, was devotedly attached to the house of Stuart. After the Revolution he never visited the English court, but continued to reside in Scotland, either at Kinnaird in Forfar, or at the Castle

---

[*] She was Countess of Dysart in her own right.

of Leuchars, the ancient seats of his family. He died in 1699, and left a son, the fifth and last Earl of Southesk.

Lady Southesk had three sisters, who all married in Scotland, and apparently passed their lives there. The eldest, Lady Elizabeth Hamilton, became Countess of Glencairn; Lady Mary married Lord Calendar; and Lady Margaret became the wife of William Blair, of Blair.

This picture is not very brilliantly or powerfully painted; the girlish and almost rustic simplicity of the face, and the demure colour of the drapery, which is of a dark lavender tint, strangely belie the character of the woman to whom it is here attributed; but for reasons already stated, I have little doubt that it is really the portrait of the Countess of Southesk.

Granger, and Sir William Musgrave, all three well versed in the biography of our peerage, as well as in pictorial and domestic antiquities, it is generally supposed to represent Susan Armine, "the widow of Sir Henry Bellasys, and mistress of the Duke of York."*

Methinks, if this magnificent-looking creature could speak, she would certainly exclaim against this last disreputable and unmerited title, or insist that it should be understood with a reservation in her favour: but since those lips, though stained with no "Stygian hue," are silenced by death, and can only *look* their scorn, we must plead, in defence of Lady Bellasys, that if the circumstances of her life gave some colour to the slander which has been unadvisedly stamped on her fair, open brow, she estimated, as a woman ought to estimate, her own and her sex's honour.

Susan Armine was the daughter of Sir William Armine, of Osgodby, in Lincolnshire. Her mother, Mary Talbot, was a niece of the Earl of Shrewsbury, and a lady distinguished in her time for her various learning, as well as for her gentle and feminine virtues and extensive charities.† It appears that Susan Armine was their only child and heiress, and that she was married very young, according to the fashion of those times, to Henry Bellasys, the son and heir of Lord Bellasys, and nephew of Lord Fauconberg.‡ Lord Bellasys, who had greatly signalized himself

or after the Restoration, both circumstances equally improbable. Among the family pictures at Tabley, (the seat of the Leycesters,) there is a very fine full-length portrait, nearly resembling this at Windsor: it is there entitled Lady Byron, and attributed to Lely. On the whole it is quite impossible to reconcile the very contradictory evidence relative to the person and the picture, but by attributing the portrait at once to Lady Bellasys, on the most probable grounds and the most credible testimony.

* Horace Walpole, Anecdotes of Painting; Granger's Biographical History of England; and Musgrave's MS. notes to Granger, British Museum.

† Lady Armine died in 1674. It is said that she founded three hospitals for the sick and the poor, one of which (at Burton Grange, Yorkshire,) still exists.

‡ In the reign of Charles II. the name was spelt indifferently Bellasses and

in the royal cause, became, after the Restoration, the friend and favourite of the Duke of York; and his son Henry was created a knight of the Bath, in recompense for his own gallantry and his father's loyalty.

From the few particulars which have been preserved relating to Sir Henry Bellasys, we may pronounce him to have been eminently brave and generous, but of a rash and fiery disposition. His headlong impetuosity first involved him in a luckless mistake, which led to the murder of an innocent man,* and afterwards occasioned his own death, in the prime of life, and within a few years after his marriage. The circumstances, which form, perhaps, the severest satire against duelling that ever was penned, and might well excite a smile but for the tragical result, are thus related:—Sir Henry, after a late revel, was conversing apart with his dear and sworn friend Tom Porter, then Groom of the Chamber to the King. As they spoke with animation, and rather loud, some one standing by asked if they were quarrelling? "Quarrelling?" exclaimed Sir Henry, turning round; "no! I would have you to know that I never quarrel but I strike!"—"How!" said Porter, "strike! I would I could see the man that dare give me a blow!" Sir Henry, flushed with recent intemperance, and only sensible to the defiance implied in these words, instantly struck him. They drew, of course, but were immediately separated by their friends. Porter left the house, and meeting Dryden, told him, in a wild manner, what had just passed, and that he must fight Sir Henry Bellasys presently; for if he waited till the morrow, he "knew they would be friends again, and the disgrace of the blow would rest upon him." He borrowed Dryden's servant, whom he ordered to watch for Sir Henry, and give him notice which way he went. He then followed his carriage, stopped it in Covent-Garden, and called on his friend to alight.

Bellasys, but more recently Belasyse. The title of Fauconberg became extinct within the last few years.

* See Pepys, vol. i. p. 133.

They drew their swords and fought on the spot, some of their acquaintance and others looking on; till Sir Henry Bellasys, finding himself severely wounded, staggered, and had nearly fallen, but sustaining himself by an effort, he called to Tom Porter, and desired him to fly. "Tom," said he affectionately, "thou hast hurt me; but I will make a shift to stand on my legs till thou mayst withdraw, for I would not have thee troubled for what thou hast done!" He then kissed and embraced him: but Porter, unable to speak, could only shew him that he too was wounded, and bleeding. In this state they were carried home. Sir Henry Bellasys died of his wounds within four days after the encounter; and thus, in consequence of a foolish and drunken outrage, perished a young man of high hopes, noble birth, generous feeling, and approved gallantry, by the hand of the man he most loved, and for whom he would willingly have shed his blood. This extraordinary duel, which even then excited more ridicule than sympathy,* occurred in 1667.

Of Lady Bellasys, married so young, and so early left a widow, we do not hear at this time. She was the mother of one son, an infant; and it appears that she lived in retirement for some years after the death of her husband. It was about the year 1670 that she was first distinguished at court,—not so much for her beauty, as for her wit, her vivacity, her high spirit and uncommon powers of mind. These qualities fascinated the Duke of York. It was said of him, that he was as indifferent to beauty as Charles was to virtue and intellect in woman. Some of the ladies whom the duke most admired were so homely, that the King used to aver, that the priests had inflicted his brother's mistresses on him by way of penance. It is, however, certain that those women whom the duke selected as the peculiar objects of his homage, do rather more honour to his taste, than the favourites of Charles do to his: Lady Denham, Arabella Churchill, Miss Sedley, Lady Bellasys,

* "It is pretty to hear how all the world doth talk of them, and call them a couple of fools, who killed each other for pure love."—*Pepys.*

to say nothing of Miss Hamilton and Miss Jennings, whom he also passionately admired and vainly pursued, are proofs that something like education and refinement were necessary to attract his attention, and something like wit and understanding to keep him awake. Lady Bellasys, who had virtue and spirit as well as wit and bright eyes, gained a strong influence over his mind without compromising her own honour; and after the death of the first duchess of York, in 1672, he actually placed in her hands a written contract of marriage, only requiring secrecy, at least for a time. This affair coming to the knowledge of the King some months afterwards, he sent for his brother, and rebuked him very severely, telling him that "at his age it was intolerable that he should think to play the fool over again," alluding to his former marriage with Anne Hyde. But neither the threats of the King, nor the arguments and persuasions of Lord Bellasys, her father-in-law, who thought himself obliged, in honour and duty, to interfere, could, for a long time, induce Lady Bellasys to give up this contract of marriage, and brand herself with dishonour. She yielded, at length, when the safety and welfare of the duke and the peace of the nation were urged as depending on her compliance; but even then, only on condition that she should be allowed to keep an attested copy in her own possession; to which they were obliged, though most reluctantly, to consent. In return for this concession, Lady Bellasys was created, in 1674, a peeress for life, by the title of Baroness Bellasys of Osgodby, having succeeded, on the death of her father and mother, to the family estates.

It is said that the Duke of York, who seems to have loved Lady Bellasys as well as he could love any thing, made many attempts to convert her to his own religion, but in vain. It was even supposed that there was some danger of the lady converting her royal lover; a suspicion which raised a strong party against her among the duke's Roman Catholic dependants, and led to much of the slander from which her name and fame have suffered.

About ten years after these events, Lady Bellasys married a

gentleman of fortune, whose name was Fortrey, of whom we know nothing but that she survived him. Her son, Henry Bellasys, succeeded in 1684 to the title and estates of his grandfather, as Lord Bellasys of Worlaby, and died about the year 1690: he married Anne Brudenell, a beautiful woman, and sister of the celebrated Countess of Newburgh, Lord Lansdowne's *Mira*. She afterwards married Charles Lennox, Duke of Richmond; and from her the present duke is descended.

It is to be inferred, from a letter of Swift to Mrs. Dingley, (or rather to *Stella*,) that Lady Bellasys appeared again at court in the reign of Queen Anne, and from this daughter of her former lover she received every mark of distinction and respect. She died on the 6th of January, 1713, bequeathing her rich inheritance among her nearest kinsmen: Lord Berkeley of Stratton was appointed the executor of her will, with a legacy of ten thousand pounds.

Horace Walpole, in allusion to this portrait, thinks it probable that Charles, by admitting Lady Bellasys into the gallery at Windsor, meant to insinuate the superiority of his own taste over that of his brother; if so, he has not assuredly taken the best means of proving it, since every other face, however regular and beautiful, appears insipid when placed in contrast with this noble creature,—Miss Hamilton's, perhaps, alone excepted.

Lady Bellasys is here represented as St. Catherine. Her left hand rests on the wheel, and supports the palm branch; her right hand is pressed to her bosom. The drapery, which is dark blue and crimson, falls round her in grand and ample folds, and is coloured with exceeding richness. In the back-ground two cherubs are descending to crown her with myrtle, and she turns her large dark eyes towards them with an expression of rapturous devotion. Her jet black hair, falling from beneath a coronet of gems, flows in ringlets upon her neck; and this peculiarity, as well as the uncovered amplitude of the bosom and shoulders, seems to refer the portrait to the time of Charles II. On a critical examination of the features, we are obliged to allow the absence of beauty; the contour of the face is not perfect, and the nose and mouth are rather irregular in form; but then, as a certain French cardinal said of his mistress, " *c'est au moins, la plus belle irrégularité du monde,*"—and the eyes and brow are splendid. They have all the life and vivacity which Burnet attributes to this *intractable* lady, as he styles her.* There is so much of poetry and feeling in the composition of this picture; so much of intellectual grandeur in the turn of the head; such a freedom and spirit in the mechanical execution; and such a rich tone of colour pervading the whole, that the portrait might be assigned at once to Vandyke, if other circumstances did not render it improbable. It bears no traces of the style of Sir Peter Lely, and I am inclined to agree with Horace Walpole, who attributes it decidedly to Huysman. Huysman was the pupil of Vandyke, and he may have painted this picture in the early period of his residence in England, and before he quitted the powerful and spirited style of his former master, to imitate the effeminate graces of Lely. There is at Gorhambury, in the possession of Lord Verulam, a portrait of Queen Catherine, indisputably by Huysman, so nearly resembling this picture in the composition and style of execution, that it adds strength to this persuasion;—but I am far from presuming to decide where abler judges cannot agree.

* See Burnet, History of his Own Times, vol. i. p. 393.

THE COUNTESS OF SUNDERLAND.

"Gracious to all, but where her love was due
So fast, so faithful, loyal, just, and true;
That a bold hand as soon might hope to force
The rolling lights of heaven, as change her course."

WALLER.

ANNE DIGBY, Countess of Sunderland, succeeded to a title which had already been distinguished in the person of her mother-in-law, Dorothy Sidney, the first Countess of Sunderland, Waller's celebrated *Sacharissa*. The second Countess of Sunderland wore her honours with equal grace; she was equally beautiful and blameless, and she played a much more interesting and important part in the real game of life: but she had no poet to hymn her into fame, to immortalize her girdle, and even her waiting-maid,*—to render her name, like that of Sacharissa, a sweet and familiar sound to the fancy and the ear. The celebrity of the second Lady Sunderland is of a very different kind; it has been dimmed by the breath of malice, and mixed up with the discord of faction; part of the obloquy which attended the political career of her husband fell on her, and party rancour added other imputations; but all evidence deserving of the slightest credit is in favour of the character and conduct of this accomplished woman,—the friend of the angelic Lady Russell and of the excellent Evelyn.

* Waller's Poems. See his address to Sacharissa's waiting-maid, Mrs. Braughton, beginning, "Fair fellow-servant!" &c.

Lady Anne Digby was the second daughter of George Digby, Earl of Bristol; her mother was Lady Anne Russell, daughter of Francis second Earl of Bedford, a woman of the most amiable character and unblemished life. Lord Bristol, who played a most conspicuous part in the civil wars, after the Restoration was one of the most remarkable characters of that time; a compound of great virtues and great vices, splendid talents and extravagant passions: such was his inconsistency of principle and conduct, that Walpole describes him as "one contradiction." He appears, in fact, to have been deeply tinged with that eccentricity (to give it no stronger name) which characterized so many of his noble family in the seventeenth century. His property having been confiscated in the time of Cromwell, he resided abroad for several years, following the various fortunes of his royal master. Clarendon tells us, that at this time he entered deeply into the libertine excesses of Charles's vagabond court; " that he left no way unattempted to render himself gracious to the King, by saying and doing all that might be acceptable to him, and contriving such meetings and jollities as he was pleased with," although he was at this time married, and the father of two daughters. His poor wife lived as well as she might, occasionally residing at Paris, but generally at the Hague or at Amsterdam; and while abroad, she married her eldest daughter, Lady Diana Digby, to a Flemish nobleman, the Baron Von Mall, of whom we know nothing farther.

At the Restoration, Digby recovered his estates; he became a favourite at court, where his youngest daughter appeared with all the advantages which her father's rank, her mother's virtues, and her own beauty and vivacity could lend her. Lady Anne was at this time not quite seventeen, exceedingly fair, with a profusion of light brown tresses, tinged with a golden hue; she had a complexion of the most dazzling transparency, small regular features, and a slight delicate figure, yet with a certain dignity of presence which is said to have particularly distinguished the Digbys of that age. About the same time Robert Spencer, the young Earl of Sunderland, returned from his travels and appeared at court. He was the only son of Henry, the first Earl of Sunderland,* and Dorothy Sidney, and was now about one-and-twenty, eminently handsome in person and full of talents and spirit. He fixed his affections on Lady Anne Digby, and to a match so suitable in years, rank, and in merit, there could be no objection; but even here, when all the preliminaries were settled between the two great families with due pomp and ceremony, the course of true love was not destined to run smooth. The deeds were prepared, the wedding-clothes were bought,—even the day was fixed, yet the marriage had nearly been broken off. The Earl of Bristol, in consequence of some extravagance of language, was called up before the House of Commons to justify himself; he made a most eloquent speech, but with so much heat and gesticulation, that he was compared to a stage-player; and what was worse his rhetoric did not appear to have much effect upon the Commons, while the Lords were incensed at his appearing before the other house without their express permission: in short, his disgrace or ruin was impending, and Lady Anne had nearly been the innocent victim of her father's misconduct or indiscretion.

In this state of things, those who envied her beauty and her good fortune, or hated her family, reported every where that the marriage was broken off,—that Lord Sunderland had gone out of town, after sending her "a release of all claim and title to her, and advice to his own friends not to inquire into the reasons for his conduct, for he had reason enough for it." All this scandalous exaggeration, which Pepys gives us at full length, was merely " a weak invention of the enemy." It is possible that Lord Sunderland's mother and his uncle, the Earl of Leicester, began to look coldly on the connexion; for the former entertained some jealousy of her daughter-in-law, and the latter disliked and opposed Lord Bristol: but Lord Sunderland did not leave London, nor did he remit his attentions to his chosen bride. After a little delay, the

* Killed in the battle of Newbury at the age of twenty-three. See a most interesting memoir of this brave and accomplished nobleman in Lodge's "Portraits and Memoirs."

preparations and the courtship went forward as before; and in the month of July, 1663, the marriage was celebrated with more than usual magnificence. The four or five years which immediately followed her marriage, were probably the happiest of Lady Sunderland's life. Her husband was young, of a gay, magnificent spirit, full of talent and sensibility; and though he entered into the dissipation of the time, and unhappily contracted a passion for deep play, still his early love of literature, a natural elegance of mind, and above all, the affection of a beautiful and accomplished wife, whom he esteemed as well as loved, kept him for some time clear from the open profligacy and crooked politics of a court, where he was always well received, and where his countess took the place due to her rank and loveliness without entering into its follies. Most of their time was spent at Althorpe, and there, within the first four years of her marriage, Lady Sunderland became the mother of three children; Robert Lord Spencer, born in 1664, and two daughters.

They lived at this time with considerable magnificence, so regulated by the excellent sense and domestic habits of Lady Sunderland, that they might long have continued to do so without injury to their splendid income, had not the earl's unhappy predilection for gambling diminished his property, preyed on his spirits, and at length led him to play a more deep and ruinous game of political intrigue, in which he made shipwreck, not only of fortune and domestic happiness, but virtue, honour, fame, and all that man ought to cherish beyond life itself.

He was appointed Ambassador to Spain in 1671; and the countess was preparing to follow him, when the ill success of the earl's embassy, and his recall within a few months, prevented this intended journey. Lord Sunderland, on his return, being appointed Ambassador Extraordinary to the French court,* Lady Sunderland

* "October 8th, 1674. I took leave of Lady Sunderland, who was going to Paris to my lord, now ambassador there. She made me stay dinner, and afterwards sent for Richardson, the famous fire-eater," &c.—*Evelyn's Diary.*

joined him at Paris; they remained there together for about a year. From this time there was an end of Lady Sunderland's domestic peace; her restless and ambitious husband became deeply involved in all those dark, disgraceful schemes of court policy which threatened the very foundation of English freedom. She had not even the consolation which belongs to many a wife whose husband treads the giddy path of ambition,—that of seeing her lord honoured and useful in his generation, and thus, in the gratification of her pride, finding some amends for disappointed love. Endued with splendid abilities of every kind, cultivated by study; with an intellect to comprehend the universe, to weigh the destinies and wield the resources of great nations; with the most consummate address, the most insinuating graces of manner, and with a knowledge of human nature, or rather of the world, allowed to be unrivalled,—with all these advantages Lord Sunderland united no generous feeling or patriotic principle, no elevated or enlarged views of policy. To obtain wealth, office, power for himself,—to baffle or betray his rivals,—to govern one king through his mistresses and his vices, and dupe another through his friendship and his virtues,—such were the objects he pursued. After being twice Prime Minister of England and at the summit of power; alternately the leader, the tool, and the victim of a party, this really accomplished but most miserable man sank into the grave, leaving behind a reputation for political profligacy, which happily has been more than redeemed by later statesmen of his family.*

In the midst of many trials and anxieties, Lady Sunderland appears ever superior to her husband in sense, in virtue, and in feeling. All the notices of her scattered through Evelyn's Diary, exhibit her uniformly in the most amiable and respectable light; he appears to have been the confidant of her secret charities, as well as of her domestic afflictions: on one occasion he notes in his

* The history of Lord Sunderland's political career, from 1671 to 1695, and of the double and treacherous part he played in the Revolution, may be found in all the records of that period:—as a tissue of venality, inconsistency, and falsehood, it is perhaps unexampled.

Diary, that Lady Sunderland "gave him ten guineas to bestow in private charities," (equal to thirty pounds at the present time.)

In 1686, when Lord Sunderland was Lord President of the Council, and principal Secretary of State, Evelyn writes to her in these terms: "I am not unmindful of the late command you laid upon me, to give you a catalogue of such books as I believed might be fit to entertain your more devout and serious hours; and I look upon it as a peculiar grace and favour of God to your ladyship, that amidst so many temptations and grandeur of courts, the attendance, visits, diversions, and other circumstances of the palace, and the way you are engaged in, you are resolved that nothing of all this shall interrupt your duty to God and the religion you profess, wherever it comes into competition with the things of this world, how splendid soever they may appear for a little and (God knows!) uncertain time. Madame, it is the best and most grateful return you can make to heaven for all the blessings you enjoy; amongst which is none you are more happy in than in the virtue, early and solid piety of my Lady Anne, and progress of your little son. Madame, the foundation you have laid in these two blessings will not only build, but establish your illustrious family, beyond all you can make of gallant and great in the estimation of the world," &c.

This letter does more honour to Lady Sunderland than to Evelyn. The sentiments are rather uncouthly expressed, but *such* sentiments never would have been addressed by Evelyn to a woman suspected of levity and hypocrisy. The little son he alludes to was her son Charles, the common ancestor of the Duke of Marlborough and Earl Spencer. Her eldest son, early emancipated from her control, and unchecked by his father, plunged into every species of dissipation; she endeavoured to reform him by an early marriage, and proposed to unite him with the daughter of Sir Stephen Fox. She used Evelyn's intervention in this affair; but Sir Stephen was not well inclined to the match: he evidently disliked the character of the young lord, but excused himself by pleading the extreme youth of his daughter. The countess was deeply mortified and disappointed, but soon afterwards received a deeper blow in the death of her son, who died at Paris in his twenty-fourth year. In her second son Charles, afterwards Lord Spencer, Lady Sunderland sought and found consolation; he was in every respect a contrast to his brother, and, at the early age of fifteen, Evelyn alludes to him as a youth of extraordinary hopes, and of singular maturity of intellect. But it was Lady Sunderland's fate to suffer through the virtues as well as the vices of her nearest and dearest connexions; the trial and execution of her cousin, the excellent Lord Russell, and her husband's cousin, Algernon Sidney, in 1683, overwhelmed her with affliction. In one of her letters to Evelyn, she describes her own and her mother's grief in strong and affecting terms. Her tenderness for her mother, Lady Bristol, was at all times truly filial: she now devoted herself to her comfort, and from this time the old lady spent most of her time in the society of her daughter, either at Althorpe or in London.

Evelyn, in his Diary, gives an account of a visit which he paid to Lady Sunderland in 1688. Having invited him to Althorpe, she with true aristocratic magnificence provided a carriage and four to convey him from London, and all his expenses going and returning were defrayed by her command, although Evelyn was himself a man of large and independent fortune. He describes Althorpe, its beautiful park, its tasteful gardens, and noble gallery of pictures, in language which would serve for the present time,— "and all this," he adds, "is governed by a lady who, without any show of solicitude, keeps every thing in such admirable order, both within and without, from the garret to the cellar, that I do not believe there is any in this nation, or in any other, that exceeds her in such exact order, without ostentation, but substantially great and noble. The meanest servant is lodged so neat and cleanly; the service at the several tables; the good order and decency,—in a word, the entire economy is perfectly becoming a wise and noble person. She is one who, for her distinguished esteem of me, from a long and worthy friendship, I must ever honour and celebrate. I wish from my soul the lord her husband, whose parts and abilities are otherwise conspicuous, was as worthy of her, as by a fatal apostacy and court ambition, he has made himself unworthy! This is what she deplores, and it renders her as much affliction as a lady of great soul and much prudence is capable of. The Countess of Bristol, her mother, a grave and honourable lady, has the comfort of seeing her daughter and grandchildren under the same economy."*

Lady Sunderland was the mother of seven children; three of them, a son and two daughters, had died in their childhood. The others, except Lord Spencer, appear to have been under the same roof with her at the period of Evelyn's visit. Charles Spencer was pursuing his studies under an excellent and learned tutor. Her two eldest daughters, Lady Anne and Lady Elizabeth, were lately married, and are described as "admirable for their accomplishments and virtue." Lady Anne, now in her twenty-first year, was the wife of James Lord Arran, son of the Duke of Hamilton; Lady Elizabeth, who was scarcely seventeen, had just married Donogh Macarty, Earl of Clancarty, a handsome, dissipated, wrong-headed Irishman, of whom Evelyn remarks, "that he gave as yet no great presage of worth." He does not tell us what induced Lord and Lady Sunderland to bestow on him their youthful and lovely daughter, unless it was the earl's "great and faire estate in Ireland."

In 1689, Lady Sunderland quitted her family to accompany her husband abroad; at the Revolution, he was excepted from pardon both by William and James, and went to hide his head in Holland; there, after suffering the extremity of misery, he was arrested by order of the States, but soon afterwards liberated by the inter-

---

* Evelyn's Diary, vol. i. p. 613.

position of King William. On this occasion Lady Sunderland addressed to the King the following letter, partly the expression of gratitude, and partly of supplication.

Lady Sunderland to King William III.

"AMSTERDAM, March 11th, 1689.

"The relief I had by your majesty's justice and grace from the sharpest apprehensions that ever I lay under, may, I hope, be allowed a sufficient plea for the liberty I now take to present you my most humble acknowledgments for that great charity of yours; I dare not impute it to any other motive: but, however unfortunate my present circumstances are, I have this to support me, that my thoughts, as well as actions, have been and are, and I dare to say ever will be, what they ought to be to your majesty; and not only upon the account of the duty I now owe you, but long before your glorious undertaking, I can't but hope you remember how devoted I was to your service, which was founded upon so many great and estimable qualities in you, that I can never change my opinion, whatever my fortune may be in this world; and may I but hope for so much of your majesty's favour as to live quietly in a country where you have so much power, till it shall please God to let me end my days at my own home, I shall ever be most truly and humbly thankful."

Whatever may be thought of the humble tone and petitionary vehemence of this letter, the style is dignity itself compared to the utter prostration of mind which is exhibited in those of Lord Sunderland. The above letter I presume to have been enclosed in the following, addressed to Evelyn, and which I am enabled to give at length from the original autograph.* It is not the best specimen which might have been selected of Lady Sunderland's epistolary style, but the circumstance under which it was written, and the sentiments contained in it, render it particularly interesting.

* In the Collection of Mr. Upcott.

"AMSTERDAM, March 12th, 1689.

"Under all the misfortunes I have gone through of late, I cannot but be sensible of that of not having heard a word from you. Indeed, I have sometimes need of your letters, as well for to help me as pleas me: and indeed, my good friend, they do both; wherefore, pray make amends. I am sure you have heard of the unusual proceeding my lord met with in this country; but, by the King's grace and justice, he is releast. I heer inclosed, send you a paper which was writ by your advice and another very good friend. If it be not what you like, I hope the sinceritye will make amends; for, indeed, it is exactly true, every tittle, I dare say. I thank God, my lord is come to a most comfortable frame of mind, and a serious consideration of his past life, which is so great a comfort to me, that I must call upon you, my good frend, to thanke God for it, and to pray that I too may be truly thankfull. As to what relates to this world, we desire nothing but to live quietly in Holland, till it shall pleas God we may end our days at Althorpe: that were a great blessing to us; but it will not be thought of such an inestimable price by others as we esteem it; and therefore, I hope in God 'twill not be envyed us. I am sure nothing else in our fortune deserves envy; and yet, having reduced my lord to the thoughts he has, it is for ever to be acknowledged by me to Almighty God, as the greatest of mercies. Pray for me, and love me, and let me hear from you. Do inclose your letters to this merchant. God send us a happy meeting! Farewell!

"Yours,

"A. S."

"Pray remember to urge, that, desiring to live in Holand, till wee can be allowed to live at Althorpe, is neither a sign of a Frenchman nor a Papist; and I thanke God my lord is neither. He has no pretensions, and will have none; and therefore interest cannot make him say it; but he never did anything but suffer it to be said, besides going to chapel, as hundreds did, who now value themselves for good Protestants. God knows that was so much to my soul's grief; but more had been wrong; and I dare say he is most heartyly and most Cristianly sorry for what he has done."

In a postscript to this letter, she tells Evelyn that she has sent him some rare plants. Thus, in the midst of her own distresses, she could bear in mind the peculiar tastes and occupations of her friend: and when we recollect his character, and that he was a friend of thirty years' standing, we cannot suppose this trifling, but delicate present, was intended to quicken Evelyn's zeal in their behalf, or that it could have weighed for a moment with such a man. However this may be, Lord Sunderland's contrition, his wife's supplications, and the intercession of his friends, proved effectual. He was suffered to reside unmolested at Utrecht for some months, and obtained permission to return to England the following year: but they were scarcely settled again at Althorpe, when the death of her favourite daughter, the young Countess of Arran, (in 1690,) overwhelmed Lady Sunderland with affliction. Evelyn wrote her on this occasion a long letter of condolence, which may be found in his works.*

Evelyn's simple yet cordial testimony to the exemplary conduct and domestic virtues of Lady Sunderland, may well be placed against the malicious scandal of a party. The letters of the Princess Anne to her sister the Princess of Orange, written at this period, allude to Lady Sunderland and her lord in terms of the most vulgar and virulent abuse;† but we must remember that,

---

* Vol. ii. p. 290.

† "I cannot end my letter without telling you, that Lady Sunderland plays the hypocrite more than ever; for she goes to St. Martin's morning and afternoon, because there are not people enough to see her at Whitehall chapel, and is half an hour before other people come, and half an hour after everybody is gone at her private devotions. She runs from church to church after the famousest preachers, and keeps such a clatter with her devotions, that it really turns one's stomach. Sure there never was a couple so well matched as she and her good husband; for as she is the greatest jade that ever was, so is he the subtillest workingest villain that is on the face of the earth." Lord Sunderland had lately declared himself a Roman Catholic, which probably made Lady Sunderland more

besides her hatred and fear of Lord Sunderland, Anne had a private and personal reason for detesting his wife. An intimate friendship existed between Lady Sunderland and Lady Churchill, afterwards the celebrated Duchess of Marlborough; and Anne, whose romantic attachment for Lady Churchill, was now at its height, beheld in Lady Sunderland a rival in the affections of her favourite. Her letters have been quoted as authority against Lady Sunderland; but besides that Anne was a weak fool, and a fond jealous friend, her evidence, suspicious under any circumstances, is absolutely contradicted by the testimony of Evelyn, of Lady Russell, and Lady Sunderland's own letters.* In one of

frequent and attentive in her public devotions; a little malignity would easily turn this against her, and a little exaggeration render it remarkable or ridiculous.

* Of these there are about thirty in the collection of Mr. Upcott, through whose kindness I had an opportunity of looking over them. They extend through a period of about twenty years, and convey, on the whole, a most delightful impression of her character, of the strength of her domestic affections, and the sincerity of her attachments.

In the very beautiful Life of Lady Russell, prefixed to the late edition of her letters, there is the following passage, (page 101.) "Lady Sunderland's letters to Lady Russell are not extant; but the following expressions in her answer to one of them, ought to have forcibly struck Lady Sunderland from the pen of Lady Russell:—' So unhappy a solicitor as I was once for my poor self and family, my heart misgives me when I aim at anything of that kind any more.' The rest of the letter proves, in the least offensive manner, that she was perfectly aware of the flattering and insincere character of her correspondent."

On this passage I must remark, that the opinion against Lady Sunderland's sincerity has no foundation but in the letters of Queen Anne, (quoted in the preceding note,) and, as Lady Sunderland's historian, I must, in justice to her, place one or two passages from Lady Russell's letters in contrast with the one above quoted. In 1689 she thus writes: "I think I understand almost less than any body, yet I knew better things than to be weary of receiving what is so good as my Lady Sunderland's letters; or not to have a due regard of what is so valuable as her esteem and kindness, with her promises to enjoy it my whole life." And again, in a letter written about 1692, she says, "You have taken a resolution to be all goodness and favour to me: and, indeed, what greater mark can you almost give than remembering me so often, and letting me receive the exceeding advantage of your doing so, by reading your letters, which are all so edifying?—when I know you are continually engaged in so great and necessary employments as you are, and have but too imperfect health, which, to any other

these, addressed to Evelyn, she begs his prayers, his sympathy for her lord, who writhing under conscious self-abasement, rejected by all parties, disgraced by the court, despised by the people, was in truth a pitiable object. " Forget not," she says, " forget not my lord in your prayers for his conversion, which if I could see, I could with comfort live in any part of the world on very little." She speaks of his penitence—his humiliation; and expresses a hope that he will be content to live with her in retirement: his latter years were indeed passed in retirement, but not in content. Before he left the court for the last time, he was heard to say, that "there was no rack like what he had suffered." This admission, coming from him in an agony, ought to be recorded as a legacy to those who view " the seals of office glitter in their eyes, and pant to grasp them !"

Besides the friendship existing between Lady Sunderland and Lady Marlborough, there had been a constant interchange of kindness and good offices between the Earl of Sunderland and Lord Marlborough; and in the year 1701 the two families were united by the marriage of Lord Spencer with Lady Anne Churchill, the second and favourite daughter of Marlborough. She was particularly endeared to her parents—not by beauty alone, but by the extreme sweetness of her disposition, and a maturity of judgment above her years: and Lady Sunderland, who was her godmother, appears to have regarded her with exceeding tenderness and admiration long before the idea of uniting her to her son could possibly have entered into her imagination. Lord

in the world but Lady Sunderland, would unfit for at least so great dispatches as you are charged with. These are most visible tokens of Providence, that every one that aims to do their duty shall be enabled to do it." (Lady Russell to Lady Sunderland, Letters, pp. 252—302.) If Lady Russell believed her correspondent to be an *insincere* and *flattering* woman, what shall we say of the sentiments here expressed?—that Lady Sunderland could not go beyond them in flattery and insincerity. There is a long letter from Lady Sunderland to the Prince of Orange, a masterpiece of diplomatic obscurity and affectation, inserted in Dalrymple's Memoirs, and there said to have been written under the dictation of her husband; it cannot therefore be brought in evidence against her.

Spencer was at this time in his thirtieth year; he had a fine person and an admirable understanding, improved by early and assiduous study. "He was remarkable," says the historian of Marlborough, "for a sedateness above his years; but in him a bold and impetuous spirit was concealed under a cold and reserved exterior." Fresh from the study of Greek and Roman lore, he was almost a republican in politics, and had distinguished himself in the House of Commons as an animated speaker in behalf of liberty in its best and largest sense. His deportment in private life was not winning, his father's errors had thrown him into an opposite extreme, in manners as in principles; instead of the bland elegance of address which distinguished the earl, Lord Spencer, wishing to avoid even the shadow of adulation, was either haughty and unbending, or blunt and frank to a degree almost offensive. He had been married young to Lady Arabella Cavendish, daughter of the Duke of Newcastle, and had lost her in childbirth after a short but happy union; her death had thrown a gloom over his mind, adding to the habitual coldness and harshness of his manners. In spite of all these drawbacks, he interested Lady Anne Churchill; but his violent politics displeased her father, and Lady Marlborough, who, termagant as she was, doated on her children even while she tormented them, feared lest her daughter's happiness should be sacrificed to a man of Lord Spencer's cold, unaccommodating temper. All these difficulties, in time, gave way before the zealous, indefatigable exertions of Lady Sunderland, who knew what were the feelings of her son, and sympathized in them with a mother's heart. She first won over Lady Marlborough, who prevailed on her husband to listen to the promise of the Earl of Sunderland, that his son should be guided in his public conduct by Lord Marlborough. The earl overrated his son's docility, as it afterwards appeared; but for the present he prevailed, and the marriage was solemnized in January 1701, when Lady Anne was not quite sixteen.

Thus Lady Sunderland had the satisfaction of ensuring the domestic happiness of her son in his union with a most amiable and lovely woman, whose charms and tenderness soothed down his asperities, and she was spared the pain of witnessing its early termination. This young and adored wife and mother died in 1716, in her twenty-ninth year: a most affecting proof of her angelic disposition and her devotion to her husband is preserved in the letter she wrote to be delivered to him after her death.* As her person was of a small size, as well as very beautiful, she became a favourite and fashionable toast with her husband's party, under the title of THE LITTLE WHIG. Her son Charles became afterwards Duke of Marlborough; and her son John, commonly called Jack Spencer, was the father of the first Earl Spencer.

The second Earl of Sunderland died a broken-hearted man in 1702; but his widow, the Dowager Lady Sunderland, survived him for several years, living respected and beloved in the bosom of her family. At length she sank under the accumulated infirmities of age, and expired at Althorpe, April 16, 1715. She had lived to see her accomplished son, the third Earl of Sunderland, Lord-Lieutenant of Ireland, Privy Seal, and Secretary of State; and as distinguished by his patriotism and integrity, as by his talents, activity, and ambition.

The picture, from which the portrait is engraved, is by Lely, and one of the "Beauties," in the Windsor Gallery: it is remarkable for the exceeding delicacy and tenderness of the execution, and the lady-like sweetness and elegance of the turn and expression. It has never before been engraved.

* Coxe's History of the Duke of Marlborough, vol. iii. p. 616.

MRS. MIDDLETON.

"Pictures like these, dear Madam, to design,
Asks no firm hand and no unerring line;
Some wandering touches, some reflected light,
Some flying touch, alone can hit them right."

POPE.

It is evident, from the number of portraits which exist of this "Beauty" *par excellence,* and the frequent allusions to her in contemporary memoirs, that she must have been a very admired and distinguished personage in her day; yet of her family and life but little is ascertained, and that little is not interesting. She is one of the equivocal heroines of De Grammont, and her brief history, as far as it is known, can hardly serve "to point a moral." And yet what is to be done?—to treat it seriously, were indeed to "break a butterfly upon a wheel;" she fluttered through her day "with insect pinions opening to the sun;" and, apparently, whatever was most admirable and interesting about her, has been preserved in the lovely pictures of her at Windsor and Althorpe. It is impossible to look on *them* without wishing to know who and what was the fair original. Yet if there had been no Lely, there would have been no Mrs. Middleton;—at least, we could have spared all that the pencil has not perpetuated.

She was the daughter of Sir Roger Needham, a relation of the excellent and celebrated Evelyn; and married to Mr. Middleton, a man of good family but small fortune, of whom nothing is known but that he gave his name to a very beautiful coquette, who, under the shelter of that name, is said to have played some fantastic tricks.

Mrs. Middleton was never attached to the court, nor had she rank or fortune to enable her to take any distinguished place there, but her charms, the admiration she inspired, her love of pleasure and her love of splendour, drew her within that brilliant but dangerous vortex. We find her associating habitually with many well known characters of her own sex, those who were distinguished for correctness of conduct, as well as those who were notorious for the reverse; and surrounded by admirers, the gayest and noblest cavaliers of that dissipated court.

Among these was the Chevalier de Grammont: she appears to have been the first who attracted his notice after his arrival in England. "Then," says his gay historiographer, "lettres et présens trottèrent:"—the first were answered, the last not rejected. But the lover *en restait là*: the lady was not quite so facile as the gentleman expected. "Il s'apperçut que la belle prenait volontiers, mais qu'elle ne donnait que peu;" and, in his usual style, he seems to have taken pains to make himself hated where he failed in making himself loved.

It appears, that in addition to her pretensions as a beauty, Mrs. Middleton affected the airs of a *précieuse*. She talked as if she had just arrived from that fantastic land the *pays du tendre*, so minutely described with all its districts, its river *d'inclination*, and its various villages of *jolis-vers*, and *petits soins*, &c. in the most famous romance of the time;[*] but though she sometimes put her lovers to sleep by discoursing in a strain of the most refined senti-

---

[*] The Clélie of Mademoiselle de Scuderi. "There will be no talking to your sister when she has read Clelia, for the wise folks say it is the most improving book that can be read."—See Lady Russell's Life, p. 91.

mentalism, and discussing *mal-à-propos* the most high-flown maxims of Platonic gallantry, " the fair Madam Middleton," as Pepys calls her, is not accused of suffering her adorers to perish through an excess of cruelty. How the lively De Grammont could possibly have been captivated by a woman " qui ennuyait en voulant briller," we are not told : perhaps her indolent, languid beauty charmed him by force of contrast with the beauties he had left behind in France. However this may be, her trifling appears to have at length exasperated him ; and finding, after awhile, that he had more than one competitor,—that young Ralph Montagu (afterwards Duke of Montagu) and Dick Jones (the celebrated Lord Ranelagh) were not only rivals, but, as he had reason to suspect, successful rivals, he was preparing for his faithless, or rather his ungrateful mistress, the most signal vengeance which his ingenious, indefatigable, and malicious nature could devise; when, happily for poor Mrs. Middleton, he encountered a more powerful charmer, and both his love and his despite were driven out of his eddying brain by the all-conquering attractions of La Belle Hamilton.

It is said that the Duke of York also admired Mrs. Middleton (which may account for her picture being at Windsor ;) and William Russell, brother to the Earl of Bedford, was another of her adorers: but he too transferred his allegiance from this indolent, alluring coquette, to the lively, graceful, elegant Miss Hamilton.

De Grammont says of his *ci-devant* flame, that the ambition of appearing a wit, " ne lui a donné que la reputation d'ennuyeuse, qui subsistait longtemps après sa beauté." It must, then, have existed a long while, for nearly twenty years after this period, in 1683, she paid Evelyn a visit, in company with her old admirer Colonel Russell ; and Evelyn mentions her as that " famous and indeed incomparable beauty Mrs. Middleton." Neither, as I think, should we entirely trust to the fidelity of De Grammont's portrait of her: he was a malicious disappointed lover, and Hamil-

ton, who records it, a satirist by profession. Pepys says, that Evelyn described Mrs. Middleton to him as fond of painting, and excelling in it; a pursuit which speaks her not quite the indolent, inane creature which others represent her.

In one of the letters of Dorothy Lady Sunderland,* (Waller's Sacharissa,) she thus alludes incidentally to Mrs. Middleton, "Mrs. Middleton and I have lost old Waller; he is gone away frightened:" from which it appears that the poet, in his old age, had enlisted himself in the train of her admirers.

With this "famous beauty," as with others of her class, a youth of folly was succeeded by an old age of cards. She became one of the society of the Duchess of Mazarin,† whose house at Chelsea was maintained on the footing of one of the modern gambling-houses, with this exception, that it was the resort of the dissipated and extravagant of *both sexes*. Many of the women who were occasionally seen in this society, were women of amiable character and spotless reputation, led thither by fashion, and the lax opinions and habits of the time; and probably more attracted by the fascinating manners of the duchess, and the wit and gaiety of St. Evremond, and by the "petits soupers ou régnait la plus grande

---

* Letters from the Countess of Sunderland to the Earl of Halifax, published at the end of Lady Russell's Life and Letters.

† The too celebrated Hortense Mancini, whose story is well known. She arrived in England in 1676, and lived on a pension of 4000*l.* a-year, granted her by Charles II. This sum was inadequate to supply her capricious extravagance, and her propensity to gambling; and after a life of strange vicissitudes and wanderings over half Europe, she died at Chelsea in 1699, and her body was immediately seized and detained by her creditors. In her youth she had amused herself with throwing handfuls of gold out of her window into the court-yard below, merely for the diversion of seeing the valets and grooms scramble for it; in her old age she was reduced frequently to want the means of subsistence, and to be indebted to her devoted friend St. Evremond for a few hundreds, (which he could ill spare,) to meet the necessities and distresses of the moment. The best account of this extraordinary woman, "this famous beauty and errant lady," as Evelyn styles her, may be found in Miss Berry's delightful book, "The Comparative View of Society in England and France," p. 227.

liberté du monde et un égale discretion," (if we may trust St. Evremond,) than by the bassette-table. It appears, for instance, that Lady Rochester, Lady Arlington, the Duchess of Grafton, Lady Derby, were visitors, if not *habituées*; but Mrs. Middleton was one of the latter. Among the occasional poems of St. Evremond there is a little piece which he entitles, "Une Scéne de Bassette," in which the interlocutors are Mrs. Middleton, Madame Mazarin, and Mr. Villiers. La Middleton is discussing with Villiers the charms of some rival beauties:—

MRS. MIDDLETON.

"Dites nous qui des deux vous semble la plus belle
De Mesdames Grafton et Litchfield?*—laquelle?

MR. VILLIERS.

Commencez: dites nous, Madame Middleton,
Votre vrai sentiment sur Madame Grafton.

MRS. MIDDLETON.

De deux doigts seulement faites-la moi plus grande,
Il faut qu'à sa beauté toute beauté se rende.

MR. VILLIERS.

L'autre n'a pas besoin de cette faveur-là.

MRS. MIDDLETON.

Elle est grande, elle est droite—

MR. VILLIERS.

Après cela?

MRS. MIDDLETON.

Madame Litchfield un peu plus animée
De tout ceux qu'elle voit se verrait fort aimée," &c.

After some farther discourse, equally pointless, Madame Mazarin, enraged at her ill-luck at the bassette-table, and the interruption which this silly conversation causes to the more serious business of the evening, angrily attacks Mrs. Middleton:

* Lady Isabella Bennet, Duchess of Grafton; and Charlotte Fitzroy, Countess of Litchfield, natural daughter of Charles II. by the Duchess of Cleveland.—See pp. 90, 91, of this work.

> "Vos beaux discours d'appas, de grace, de beauté,
> Nous content notre argent—il ne m'est rien resté," &c.

And Mrs. Middleton replies in a pique;

> "Nous n'avons pas appris à garder le silence
> Comme vous avez fait dans vos couvens de France,
> Monsieur, Monsieur Villiers, allons nous consoler;
> Il est d'autres maisons, où l'on pourra parler."

The exact date of Mrs. Middleton's death is unknown, but it probably took place between 1685 and 1690; and while she could still eclipse younger beauties by her mature but unrivalled attractions. St. Evremond lamented her in a monody,* not worth transcribing:—but his epitaph on her is rather graceful: it is as follows:

> "Ici gît Middleton, illustre entre les belles,
> Qui de notre commerce a fait les agrémens.
> Elle avait des vertus pour les amis fidèles,
> Et des charmes pour les amants.
>   Malade sans inquiétude,
> Resolue à mourir sans peine, sans effort,
>   Elle aurait pû faire l'étude
>   D'un philosophe sur la mort.
> Le plus indifferent, le plus dur, le plus sage
> Prennent part au malheur qui nous afflige tous
> Passant, interromps ton voyage,
> Et te fais un mérite à pleurer avec nous."

There are many pictures of Mrs. Middleton, but the two most beautiful are those at Windsor and at Althorpe, both by Sir Peter Lely; the first represents her with the insignia of bounty or abundance, and the latter as Pandora opening her casket of evils. Whether the artist intended in either case to be significant or satirical, is uncertain. At Elvastone, in Derbyshire, the seat of the Earl of Harrington, there is another exquisite picture of Mrs. Middleton. The portrait which has been engraved for this collec-

---

* "Stances irréguliers sur la Mort de Madame Middleton."—*Œuvres de St. Evremond*, tom. i. p. 92.

tion, is in the Windsor Gallery. It is distinguished by exceeding brilliance and harmony of colour; the face is beautiful, but not of a high order of beauty; it has that fulness of form and very sweet but somewhat heavy expression, which belonged to the character of the woman; the complexion is fair but richly blooming, and painted with transparent delicacy of touch. The drapery is of a pale amber-colour relieved with white.

The picture has been engraved in mezzotinto, with the erroneous title of Lady Middleton. There is also a fine print of her, a full-length, after Lely, properly designated as Madam Jane Middleton: and the beautiful picture at Althorpe has been engraved for Dr. Dibdin's *Ædes Althorpianæ*.

THE COUNTESS OF NORTHUMBERLAND.

> "Court virtues bear, like gems, the highest rate,
> Born where Heaven's influence scarce can penetrate.
> In life's low vale (the soil the virtues like)
> They please as beauties,—here, as wonders strike;
> Though the same sun, with all-diffusive rays,
> Blush in the rose and in the diamond blaze,
> We prize the stronger effort of his power,
> And justly set the gem above the flower."
>
> Pope.

This Countess of Northumberland, the wife of the last male heir of the Percies, and afterwards of an ambassador and minister of state, did not, from accidental circumstances, mingle much in the court of Charles II.; nor, from her mild unpresuming nature, was she personally influential in any of the private state intrigues of that time; but she was distinguished for her uncommon grace and beauty and her blameless life, no less than by her high rank and her descent from one of the most illustrious characters in our history; above all, she was the sister of Lady Russell. The frequent allusions to her in the memoirs and letters of that admirable woman, are sufficient to throw a peculiar interest round Lady Northumberland, and give her an importance in our eyes beyond what her own rank and beauty could have lent her.

Elizabeth Wriothesley was the youngest daughter of the Lord

Treasurer Southampton,* by his second wife Lady Elizabeth Leigh,† daughter and sole heiress of the Earl of Chichester. She was born about the year 1647. The eldest sister, Lady Audrey, was betrothed to Josceline Lord Percy, son of Algernon tenth Earl of Northumberland; but before the arrangements were completed, the bride elect died in her fourteenth year.‡ Lady Elizabeth thus remained sole heiress to the estates of her maternal grandfather Lord Chichester, and her name was substituted for that of Lady Audrey in the marriage contract with Lord Percy, apparently without any reference to the wishes or feelings of either party. In the year 1662, when she was about fifteen, and Lord Percy not quite eighteen, the marriage was duly solemnized: such early marriages were usual in those times, but as Lady Russell observes, it was acceptance rather than choice, on either side. Yet being generally arranged by the parents, with a reference to fitness of rank, age, temper, education, and a regard for the future happiness of their children, many of these conventional unions might be mentioned as examples of conjugal felicity: that of Lady Elizabeth appears to have been almost without alloy during its short duration.

For about two years after their marriage, the young bride and bridegroom did not live much together. Lord Percy pursued his studies and exercises under the care of a tutor, and Lady Percy resided with her own family at Titchfield, in Hampshire; but in 1664 and 1665, we find her residing at Petworth with her husband, and hence her affectionate letters to her sister Lady

---

* Thomas fourth Earl of Southampton, so celebrated for his talents, his loyalty, and his unimpeachable integrity. He was the grandson of that Earl of Southampton who was the friend of Essex, and, what is more, the friend and patron of Shakspeare.

† Lord Southampton's eldest daughter by his first wife, (Rachel de Rouvigny,) had also been christened Elizabeth. She married Edward Noel, eldest son of Baptist Lord Campden, and afterwards the first Earl of Gainsborough.

‡ The Earl of Northumberland, in a letter to Lord Leicester, dated Nov. 2, expresses his deep regret for the death of Lady Audrey, " because she was of a nature, temper, and humour likely to make an excellent wife."

Rachel are dated.* Her eldest daughter, Lady Elizabeth, was born in 1666; in 1668 she gave birth to a son and heir, Henry Lord Percy, and in the year following she had another daughter, Lady Henrietta, who died an infant.

Her husband succeeded to his father's titles and possessions in 1668, and became the eleventh Earl of Northumberland, but he did not long enjoy these honours. In the following year he lost his infant son, and the death of this boy, which occurred soon after her confinement, made so deep and painful an impression on the mind of his mother, that the earl determined on making a tour to the Continent as the best means of diverting her grief; and accordingly they set off for Paris, attended by the philosopher Locke as their physician. For reasons which do not appear, but probably from the delicate state of the countess, her husband left her at Paris under the care of Locke, and proceeded alone to Italy: having reached Turin, he was seized with a fever which terminated fatally. He died May 21, 1670, in his twenty-seventh year,—"in the midst of the brightest hopes which this promising young nobleman had excited in the breasts of all good men, that he would prove a shining ornament of his noble house, and an honour to his country," &c.

So far the peerage; we are not told of the grief of his widow, but we may believe it to have been poignant and sincere, since it for some time totally changed her appearance, and so dimmed the native beauty of her cheek, as to give her, at the age of four-and-twenty, a look of faded and premature age.

Not that she was absolutely inconsolable; grief in the young heart either kills at once or is quickly cured, and eternal sorrow is at least as rare as everlasting love. She continued to reside at Paris, where Ralph Montagu, the English ambassador, paid her every attention that could be offered in her afflicted state: these attentions, after a while, awakened a corresponding gratitude in

* See the Life of Lady Russell, p. 8.

the bosom of the lady, and Montagu began to cherish hopes that attentions of different kinds, and with different views, might some time or other prove acceptable.*

Ralph Lord Montagu, afterwards Earl and Duke of Montagu, had been appointed ambassador to the French court in 1669. He was a man of splendid habits, eager and insatiable in acquiring wealth, and not very scrupulous, it is said, with regard to the means; but liberal to others, magnificent and even lavish in his expenditure.† He had transcendent abilities as a statesman, and possessed a cultivated and refined taste in the arts, particularly painting and architecture. De Grammont describes him as " peu dangereux pour sa figure," but almost irresistible from his fascinating manners, his assiduity, and his vivacity. About two years after her first lord's death, Montagu began to pay Lady Northumberland marked devotion. He followed her to Aix in the winter of the year 1672. Madame de Sévigné was then in Provence on a visit to her daughter, and Madame de la Fayette thus writes to her from Paris: " Voilà un paquet que je vous envoie pour Madame de Northumberland. On dit ici que si M. de Montagu n'a pas un heureux succès de son voyage, il passera en Italie, pour faire voir que ce n'est pas pour les beaux yeux de Madame de Northumberland qu'il court le pays : mandez nous un peu ce que vous verrez de cette affaire, et comme il sera traité." This is an amusing instance of that excessive vanity which characterized Montagu. It would have been interesting to learn what Madame de Sévigné

* In the Life of James II. occurs the following entry, which I am unable farther to elucidate. " July 13, 1672. Buckingham proposed to the King to get Lady Percy (the infant heiress of Earl Josceline) for Lord Harry, (the king's natural son, afterwards Duke of Grafton). Buckingham at the same time offered to the Countess of Northumberland, to get the King to consent that he should command the Duke of York to marry her."

† His want of principle in money matters, (and also in other matters,) was contrasted with exceeding generosity and high feeling in particular cases: for instance, when he regained by a law process an estate which had been illegally wrested from his family, he remitted to the defendant, Lord Preston, the arrears and costs of suit, thinking the loss of the estate sufficient.—See Granger.

thought of the fair lady, and of the treatment the lover met with, but unhappily her reply is not extant. We may presume that he was not driven to despair; as we find that he followed the countess back to Paris, and was there with her in April 1673. She is again mentioned in a letter from Madame de la Fayette to Madame de Sévigné, from which it appears that her beauty, withered by recent sorrow and self-neglect, did not dazzle the lively Frenchwoman, and that her quiet but amiable disposition, joined to a want of command of the French language, prevented her from producing much effect in society.

"Madame de Northumberland me vint voir hier; j'avais été la chercher avec Madame de Coulanges: elle me parut une femme qui a été fort belle, mais qui n'a plus un seul trait de visage qui se soutienne, ni où il soit resté le moindre air de jeunesse: j'en fus surprise; elle est avec cela mal habillée, point de grâce, enfin je n'en fus point de tout éblouie. Elle me parut entendre fort bien tout ce qu'on dit, ou pour mieux dire tout ce que je dis, car j'étais seule. M. de la Rochefoucauld et M. de Thianges, qui avaient envie de la voir, ne vinrent que comme elle sortait. Montagu m'avait mandé qu'elle viendrait me voir, je lui ai fort parlé d'elle; il ne fait aucune façon d'être embarqué à son service, et parait très rempli d'esperance."

This letter is dated from Paris, April 15, 1673. It is a pity we have not on record the whole course of a wooing which, notwithstanding the gentle temper of the lady, and the tact and assiduity of the lover, seems to have been diversified in the usual style. Lady Northumberland was jealous of the Duchesse de Brissac, to whom Montagu was formerly attached; and Madame de la Fayette thus writes to her friend about a month after the date of her last letter. "Montagu s'en va; on dit que ses espérances seront renversées: je crois qu'il y a quelque chose de travers dans l'esprit de la nymphe."

It happened, however, that just at this time Montagu was so

far from being a dismissed or despairing lover, that he was on the eve of success: he won the heart of the young countess, and, in the same year, (1673,) they came to England privately, and were married at Titchfield in Hampshire, the family seat of the Wriothesleys. It appears that she afterwards recovered those attractions for which she had been distinguished in early youth; for Evelyn alludes to her, eight or ten years afterwards, as "the most beautiful Countess of Northumberland."

In 1675 she was in England, and for some years afterwards she was involved in troubles relative to the disposal of her only daughter by the Earl of Northumberland.* The dowager-countess, who appears to have been a meddling, jealous old woman, demanded to have the entire charge and disposal of the young heiress on her mother's second marriage. Lady Russell, ever right in judgment as kind in heart, alludes to this affair in one of her letters to her husband. "The two Lady Northumberlands have met at Northumberland-House, after some propositions offered by my sister to the other, which were discoursed first yesterday before my Lord Chancellor, between the elder lady and Mr. Montagu: Lord Suffolk, by my sister, offers to deliver up the child, upon condition he will promise she shall have her on a visit for ten days or a month sometimes, and that she will enter bonds not to marry the child without her mother's consent, nor till she is of years to consent; and on her part, Mr. Montagu and she will enter into the same bonds, that when she is with them, at no time they will marry or contract any marriage for her without the grandmother's consent: but she was stout yesterday and would not hear patiently, yet went to Northumberland-House and gave my sister a visit: I hope for an accommodation. My sister urges, it is hard that her child (that if she has no other children must be her heir) should be disposed of without her consent, and in my judgment it is hard; yet I fancy I am not very apt to be partial."

* See the preceding memoir of this celebrated heiress, afterwards Duchess of Somerset, p. 168.

It was in truth a hardship, and Lady Northumberland felt it and resisted it as such; but the old dowager contrived at length to get Lady Elizabeth completely into her hands, and made her the subject of constant intrigues with men of power who wished for wealth, and rich men who wished for rank and power. The premature marriage of Lady Elizabeth with the famous Tom Thynne, of Longleat, is known to have taken place through the manœuvres of her grandmother, and against the consent of her mother.

Between 1675 and 1678, Lady Northumberland and Lord Montagu were in England, and Montagu commenced the building of Montagu-House, on the decoration of which he lavished immense sums. Their married life was not all sunshine; for Montagu, besides being deeply and disgracefully involved in the state intrigues of that period, was a dissipated man of pleasure. Lady Northumberland, who had endowed him with her wealth, appears to have derived no pride nor pleasure from his political exaltation: and, left to herself in his frequent absences, she pined in the midst of her splendour for calmer and more domestic happiness. In the year 1678, Charles (the habitual scoffer at all religion) ordered Montagu to find out and consult, in his name, a certain astrologer at Paris, in whom he put great faith. Montagu found the man, and saw that he was capable of being corrupted by money. He therefore prompted him to give such hints to the King as should serve his own ends. At the same time he was carrying on an intrigue with that mischievous and abandoned woman the Duchess of Cleveland, and had the folly and weakness to trust her with this affair of the astrologer. She afterwards, in a fit of ill humour and jealousy, vowed his ruin; and although she had long been dismissed from the court and from the King's affections, she had still sufficient art and power to accomplish this object. She sent over to Charles a detailed and exaggerated account of Montagu's transactions with the astro-

---

* It was burnt down in 1685, and Montagu immediately began to rebuild it with more cost and splendour than before. It is now the British Museum.

loger; in consequence of which he was disgraced, and Lord Sunderland succeeded him in his embassy. Montagu then revenged himself, by entering into a secret intrigue with Louis XIV. for the removal of the Lord Treasurer Danby, who was exceedingly obnoxious to the French government, and opposed the Roman Catholic interest. For the ruin of Lord Danby, (to be accomplished within a given time,) Montagu asked the sum of one hundred thousand crowns, or an annuity of forty thousand livres for life. This infamous bargain was duly fulfilled, on one side at least; Danby was disgraced, and sent to the Tower, but Montagu only received half the stipulated sum from the French government.* He was afterwards in opposition to the court, and voted for the Exclusion Bill, which gave unpardonable offence; and in 1680 he retired to France, whither Lady Northumberland followed him. She was not of a temper or character to be a participator in these transactions; but she had an ample share in the distress and degradation to which they led, and their effect on the haughty, restless, and excitable temper of her husband, necessarily re-acted on her and her happiness. From several slight allusions to her in the letters of Lady Russell and Lady Sunderland, she appears to have suffered much from ill health; to have passively, or at least patiently, endured her husband's infidelities, and never to have interfered with his political intrigues.

They resided unmolested at Paris for several years, and were there during the trial and execution of Lord Russell. So that Lady Northumberland was not near her sister in the hour of affliction; neither had she, though tenderly devoted to her, a mind

---

* He was, moreover, reduced to the necessity of making repeated and humiliating applications for the money, at the risk of a discovery, which would have endangered his head. See the letter from the Duchess of Cleveland to Charles II., which ruined Montagu with the King, given at full length in the "Comparative View of Society in England and France;" and the history of Montagu's subsequent intrigues with the French court, in Barillon's despatches to Louis XIV: See also Burnet's History, vol. ii. p. 25.

sufficiently strong to afford support and consolation to one who, in feeling and in intellect, was so much her superior.

In Lady Russell's Letters from 1685 to 1690, the following notices of Lady Northumberland occur. The first alludes to the revocation of the edict of Nantes by Louis XIV.:—

"I read a letter last night from my sister at Paris; she writes, as every body who has humane affections must, and says that, of 1,800,000, there is not more than ten thousand (Protestants) esteemed to be left in France; and they, I guess, will soon be converted by the dragoons, or perish."

11th July, 1686. "I hear by my sister Montagu, she found a sickly family at Paris; her daughter in a languishing condition, worn to nothing with a fever, which has hung about her for the last six weeks. The doctors apprehend a hectic, but youth, I hope, will overcome it." The allusion is to her only daughter by Montagu, who is afterwards frequently mentioned in Lady Russell's letters, and seems to have been often on a visit with her.

Within a year afterwards, Lady Northumberland lost her eldest son at the age of twelve. "I believe she takes it heavily," writes Lady Russell, "for truly I have not seen her since the child died on Sunday morning."—"Now my own sad trials making me know what a mean comforter I can be, I think the best service is to take some care of her two children, who are both well now; and I hope God will be pleased to keep them so, and teach her to be content."*

After this affliction, Lady Northumberland retired to Windsor, and continued to reside there for some time. The delicate health of her children seems to have been a constant source of uneasiness to her. She had now (1687) one "fine *lovely* boy," (for so Lady

* Letter xlii.

Russell designates him,) and of her two daughters, the eldest, Lady Percy, was Duchess of Somerset;* the youngest, Anne Montagu, who was about fourteen, was a slight, fair girl, whose health caused her much anxiety; hence the frequent allusions to these children, and prayers for their preservation, which occur in Lady Russell's letters. In 1688, Montagu, who had always been a zealous friend of liberty,† was one of the chief promoters of the Revolution; and being created an earl by King William, Lady Northumberland dropped her first husband's title, and is thenceforth styled Countess of Montagu.

In the following year, the attainder of Lord Russell being reversed, his execution was formally denounced as *murder* by the House of Commons, and a committee appointed to discover and examine those who were the advisers and promoters of it. The proceedings on this occasion appear to have deeply agitated his widow, and renewed all the bitterness of those regrets which the lapse of six years had in some respect softened. Having given so many passages of Lady Russell's letters expressive of her affection for her sister, it is pleasing to see how truly that affection was returned: a melancholy letter from Lady Russell to the countess drew from her this tender reply:

Lady Montagu to Lady Russell.

"BOUGHTON, DEC. 23, 1689.

"I am very sorry, my dear sister, to find by yours, which I received by the last post, that your thoughts have been so much disturbed with what I thought ought to have some contrary effect. It is very true, what is once taken from us in that nature can never be returned; all that remains of comfort, (according to my temper,) is the bringing to punishment those who were so wickedly and unjustly the cause of it. I confess it was a great satisfaction

* See p. 169, of this work.
† So the biographies,—perhaps we should rather say a zealous enemy of the court in which he had been disgraced.

to me to hear that was the public care; it being so much to the honour, as well as what in justice was due to your dead lord, that I do not doubt, when your sad thoughts will give you leave to recollect, you will find comfort. I heartily pray God you may, and that you may never have the addition of any other loss, which is, and ever shall be, the prayers of

Your entirely affectionate,
E. Montagu."

Boughton, in Northamptonshire, whence this letter is dated, was the family seat of the Montagu's; and Lord Montagu was now engaged in enlarging and embellishing the house, and planting and decorating the grounds with his characteristic taste and enthusiasm, and indifference to expense. After the Revolution much of their time was spent there.* In the beginning of 1690, the health of the Countess of Montagu visibly declined, and in September following she died at Boughton, in her forty-fourth year.

Lady Russell thus feelingly alludes to her death: "She was my last sister, and I ever loved her tenderly. It pleases me to think that she deserves to be remembered by all those who knew her: and after forty years acquaintance with so amiable a creature, one must needs, in reflecting, bring to remembrance so many engaging endearments as are at present embittering and painful."†

To this simple eulogium nothing need be added. Lady Montagu had four children by her second husband; her two eldest sons, Ralph and Winwood, died young, one son and one daughter survived her: her son John Montagu, Lord Monthermer, became second Duke of Montagu after the death of his father in 1709; he

---

* Boughton is the property of the present Lord Montagu. When the Duke of Marlborough visited Boughton, he expressed great admiration of the waterworks. "But they are not comparable to your Grace's *fire-works!*" replied Montagu with a bow and a smile.

† Letter to the Bishop of Salisbury, dated Oct. 16, 1690.

married the youngest daughter of the great Duke of Marlborough. Lady Anne Montagu married Alexander Popham, Esq. of Littlecotes, Wiltshire; and secondly, Lieutenant-General Hervey.

After the death of the Countess of Montagu, the earl, whose splendid tastes and extravagant habits had brought him into some difficulties, determined to repair his fortunes by marrying another heiress. Elizabeth Cavendish, daughter of Henry Duke of Newcastle, and widow of the last Duke of Albemarle, possessed immense riches by marriage and inheritance. The pride of wealth, rank, and grandeur, seems to have disordered intellects naturally weak, and she declared she would give her hand only to a sovereign prince. It is a fact that Montagu wooed her and won her in the character of the Emperor of China. He afterwards kept her in a sort of confinement in Montagu-House, still without undeceiving her; and she was always served on the knee as Empress of China. She died of mere old age in 1738.

The portrait of the Countess of Northumberland is engraved after the picture at Windsor. I suppose it to have been painted after her second marriage, for it does not represent her in the bloom of youth, and has more of elegance and dignity than of beauty; the complexion is fair, and the expression all sweetness. The position of the right arm is rather stiff; yet Lely appears to have been fond of this attitude, for he has repeated it in other pictures: the drapery is of a rich brown. The back-ground, which is a fine bit of woodland landscape, with a waterfall in the distance, is admirably painted.

THE DUCHESS OF PORTSMOUTH.

"Her birth, her beauty, crowds and courts confess,
Chaste matrons praise her, and grave bishops bless;
In golden chains the willing world she draws,
And hers the Gospel is—and hers the laws;
Mounts the tribunal, lifts her scarlet head,
And sees pale Virtue carted in her stead!
Lo! at the wheels of her triumphant car
Old England's genius, rough with many a scar,
Dragg'd in the dust!"
POPE.

THIS is a name disgracefully celebrated, but only a small portion of that disgrace can justly rest upon her who bore it. The period of her reign, for so it may be called, is historically infamous, but the least part of that infamy rests upon the woman herself. If we could tear from the chronicles of our country that leaf which bears the name of Louise de Quéroualle, it were well; but since this cannot be, we ought not to close our eyes to its import, for it conveys a deep lesson. It is impossible to study history without admitting, that the political influence of women has been great in all ages; it has been modified by the difference of manner and the degree of intelligence,—it has been more or less ostensible, more or less mischievous,—but at all times it has been great, and it increases with the progress of civilization and the diffusion of knowledge. It is not in these days that we are to listen to commonplaces out of the *Spectator* and the *Ecole des Femmes*. Let it be granted, that " women are formed for private life alone ;" but in that privacy—in our nurseries and boudoirs, are inculcated and directed the principles and opinions of those men who are to legislate for the happiness and welfare of nations. This species of indirect influence increases with the spread of civilization and intelligence ; it cannot be denied—it cannot be suppressed : is not the next alternative to render it beneficial to society ? If a woman could once be taught to feel, to appreciate the grand stake she has in the political institutions of her country, and to understand the interests of humanity at large, she would no longer mix up with these considerations the petty passions, errors, and prejudices, and personal feelings which have rendered at all times the political interference and influence of the sex a fertile source of evil, and a never-failing topic of reproach and regret; for evil has been almost constantly the result. The gallantry of men and the vanity of women may here suggest instances of the contrary ; but for one Volumnia, how many Cleopatras ! for one Agnes Sorel, how many Pompadours and Portsmouths ! One thing, however, is certain, that, thanks to the progressive diffusion of freedom and knowledge, we are not likely to behold again in civilized Europe the common decencies of life braved by the insolent triumph of a *maîtresse en titre:* nor " sin in state, majestically drunk," trampling over the destinies of great nations and the interests of millions of men. A Maintenon will never more half depopulate France, nor a Portsmouth bargain with a foreign despot for the sale of English liberty.

Louise Renée de Penencovet de Quérouaille,* of a noble but impoverished family in Brittany, was appointed Maid of Honour to the Duchess of Orleans in the year 1669 ; she was not more than nineteen, when, by the interest of some relations in power, she was taken from the convent to which the poverty of her house

---

* The name is spelt variously, Keroual, Kerouaille, and Quérouailles. In England she was Anglicised into Madam Carwell.

had at first consigned her, apparently for life, and at once introduced to all the pleasures and temptations of a magnificent and dissipated court : her introduction took place at a critical moment, and in deciding her future fate, has made her destiny and character matter of history.

The conquest, or the ruin of Holland, had long been one of the favourite projects of Louis XIV. The Dutch, however, resisted his overgrown power, as their ancestors had formerly defied that of Philip II. of Spain. In order to carry his plans into execution, Louis found it necessary to detach England from the interests of Holland. This was matter of some difficulty, for an alliance with France against Holland was so odious to all parties in England, so contrary to the national prejudices and interests, that though Louis did not despair of cajoling or bribing Charles into such a treaty, the utmost caution and secrecy were necessary in conducting it.

The only person who was at first trusted with this negotiation, was Henrietta Duchess of Orleans, the sister of Charles, and sister-in-law of Louis, fatally celebrated in French history as MADAME d'Angleterre. She was at this time about five-and-twenty, a singular mixture of discretion, or rather dissimulation, with rashness and petulance; of exceeding haughtiness, with a winning sweetness of manner and disposition, which gained all hearts. She had inherited some of the noble qualities of her grandfather Henri Quatre, and all the graces and intriguing spirit of her mother Henrietta Maria. Early banished from England by the misfortunes of her family, she regarded the country of her birth with indifference, if not abhorrence. A French woman in education, manners, mind, and heart, she was an English woman only in the peculiar style of her beauty, uniting the utmost majesty of form with a profusion of light hair, eyes as blue and bright as those of Pallas, and a complexion "petri de lis et de roses." On her husband, the worthless, stupid, profligate Duke of Orleans, her wit and charms were equally thrown away. Louis was well aware of her unbounded power over the mind of Charles II., whose affection for her was said to exceed that of a brother for a sister: he had never been known to refuse her anything she had asked for herself or others, and Louis trusted that her fascinations would gain from the King of England, what reason, and principle, and patriotism would have denied.

To cover the interview between the brother and sister with some kind of pretext, which should give it the appearance of an accidental or friendly meeting, Louis undertook a progress to his new Flemish provinces; and until Catherine of Russia astonished Europe by her pompous triumphal voyage down the Bosphorus, nothing had equalled in lavish and luxurious ostentation this famous journey. An army of thirty thousand men preceded and followed the royal party; in one spacious and superb equipage, all glass and gilding, travelled the King, the Queen, Henrietta, and Madame de Montespan; then followed their repective retinues; then the Princesses; the Dauphin and his court, Mademoiselle de Montpensier (la grande Mademoiselle) and her court. This was just before the fatal affair of her marriage with Lauzun, who on this occasion rode at the head of the royal guards. It was a perpetual series of fêtes, banquets, and triumphs; the apparent honours were principally for Madame de Montespan; the real object of this splendid journey was known only to Henrietta of Orleans, who enjoyed in secret her own importance, which gave a new zest to the pleasures with which she was surrounded. When arrived at Dunkirk, she embarked for England, with a small but chosen retinue, and met her brother at Dover, where this celebrated conference took place. The event showed that Louis had not reckoned too much on her power; she gained from the facile and unprincipled Charles all that she asked, and the shameful treaty which rendered the King of England the pensioned tool of France, was arranged at Dover in the beginning of June 1670.*

---

* France agreed to give two millions of livres (150,000*l.*) for the King's conversion to Popery; and three millions a-year for the Dutch war. Large sums of money were distributed to Buckingham, Arlington, Clifford.—See the documents in Dalrymple, vol. i., Appendix.

Henrietta brought in her train Mademoiselle de Quérouälle, and during her short stay, the exceeding beauty and almost childish graces of this young girl captivated Charles, who was observed to pay her much attention; she, however, returned to Versailles with her royal mistress, and there, within a few days afterwards, witnessed her dreadful death. Voltaire doubts, or affects to doubt, that Henrietta was poisoned, because of the odium which such a suspicion must have thrown on the father of his patron, the Regent-duke of Orleans; but the recent publication of some private memoirs of that time has cleared up the shocking mystery. The intrigues which led to the murder of this unhappy woman, present such a scene of accumulated horrors and iniquity, that, for the honour of human nature, one could wish that the curtain had never been raised which hid them from our knowledge.

On the occasion of her death, the Duke of Buckingham was sent over to France as Envoy Extraordinary; he had been the first to observe the impression which Mademoiselle de Quérouälle had made on the King's excitable fancy, and he resolved to turn it to his own advantage. He had quarrelled with the Duchess of Cleveland—had sworn hatred and vengeance against her; and now to raise her up a rival, who should be wholly governed by himself, seemed to this Proteus of gallantry and harlequin of politics, a very master-stroke of art—worthy of Machiavel himself. He persuaded Louis seriously, that the only way to bind Charles to the French interest, was to give him a French mistress: and he told Charles, jestingly, that he ought to take charge of his sister's favourite attendant, if only out of "decent tenderness" for her memory. As to Mademoiselle de Quérouälle, a convent was all she could look to in France, and she was not found impracticable. Matters, in short, were soon arranged; an invitation so decorously worded as to spare the lady's blushes, was sent from the English court, and she was immediately despatched to Dieppe with part of the Duke of Buckingham's suite, and his Grace's promise to join her with all convenient speed. But what did that most careless and inconsistent of human beings? His admirable scheme of policy, by which he was to build up his own fortunes and power, and ruin all his enemies, was but "one of the thousand freaks that died in thinking;" he totally forgot both the lady and his promise, and leaving the disconsolate nymph at Dieppe to manage as she could, passed over to England by way of Calais. Montagu, then our ambassador at Paris, hearing of the duke's egregious blunder, immediately sent over for a yacht, and ordered some of his own people to convey her with all honour to Whitehall, where she was received by Lord Arlington with the utmost respect, and immediately appointed Maid of Honour to the Queen. "Thus," says Burnet, "the Duke of Buckingham lost all the merit he might have pretended to, and brought over a mistress, whom his own strange conduct threw into the hands of his enemies."

Though the lady carried it at first very demurely, the purpose of her visit was pretty well understood.* Dryden, the court poet of the time, hailed her arrival in some complimentary stanzas, entitled the "Fair Stranger," not worth quoting here;† and St. Evremond addressed to her an epistle, which, for different reasons, I shall refrain from quoting; it is sufficient, that the elegance of the diction was worthy of his pen; the sentiments worthy of his epicurean philosophy; and the morality—worthy of the occasion.‡

The next we hear of Mademoiselle de Quérouaille is from Evelyn, who notes in his diary that he had seen "that famous beauty, the new French Maid of Honour;" but adds, "in my opinion, she is of a childish, simple, and baby face." We may judge, from all the pictures of La Quérouaille, that when young, her beauty, though exquisite, must have had the character, or rather the want of cha-

---

* It had been foretold, apparently; for Madame de Sévigné thus writes to her daughter: "Ne trouverez-vous pas bon de savoir que Kéroual dont l'étoile avait été devinée avant qu'elle partit, l'a suivie très-fidèlement? Le Roi d'Angleterre l'a aimée, elle s'est trouvé avec une légère disposition à ne le pas haïr; enfin," &c.—Lettre 190.

† See Dryden's Works. Scott's edit. vol. xi. p. 103.

‡ Œuvres de St. Evremond, vol. iii. p. 280.

racter, thus described by Evelyn.* Within a year afterwards he met her on a visit at Euston, the seat of Lord Arlington, where she was obviously invited for the gratification of Charles. The French ambassador, Colbert,† and a number of ladies of high rank, nobles, and courtiers, were there at the time. Charles came over every other day from Newmarket, and made no secret of his attentions to the young beauty.‡

In the year 1672 she bore the King a son, (who was created, in 1675, Duke of Richmond and Earl of March in England, and Duke of Lennox and Earl of Darnley in Scotland.)§ In the following year Mademoiselle de Quéroualle was created by letters patent, (August 19, 1673,) Baroness Petersfield, Countess of Farneham, and Duchess of Portsmouth. Yet further to exalt and blazon a shame which sought neither disguise nor concealment, Louis XIV. conferred on her the duchy of Aubigny, in the province of Berri, in France,‖ as a mark of his friendship for his good brother the King of England, and of his respect for the lady, whose progenitors, as the preamble sets forth, "had always held a considerable rank in Brittany, and had done good service to the throne," &c. Finding that she was likely to prove a staunch supporter of his interests in England, Louis added to the title and dignity of duchess and peeress of France the revenues of the territories of Aubigny, and a considerable pension.

The unbounded power which this woman acquired over the easy disposition of her royal lover, was not owing to any superiority of wit or intellect, nor did she attempt to govern him, like the Duchess

---

* Evelyn's Diary. This note is dated November 1670, about a month after her arrival in England.

† Brother to the great minister Colbert: he had signed the treaty at Dover.

‡ See Evelyn, vol. i. p. 419.

§ These titles had lately reverted to the Crown by the death of the last Duke of Richmond of the Stewart family, the husband of La Belle Stewart.—See p. 170.

‖ By virtue of this grant, the present Duke of Richmond is Duc d'Aubigny, and a peer of France.

of Cleveland, by violence and caprices; though imperious and wilful, she was more artful and flexible; she studied to please and observe the King till she had fixed him, then, if he refused or delayed her wishes, she had tears and sullens, and fits of sickness at command. Her rapacity and prodigality were quite equal to those of her predecessor. "This day," says Evelyn, " I was casually shewn the Duchess of Portsmouth's splendid apartment at Whitehall, luxuriously furnished, and with ten times the richness and glory of the Queen's; such massy pieces of plate, whole tables, stands, &c. of incredible value!" And yet at this time Charles was reduced to the basest expedients for money: shuffling with his ministers, duping his friends, exasperating his people, and absolutely begging like a mendicant of Louis XIV., and using the intercession of the duchess to obtain from him occasional supplies.*

The following note in Evelyn, also relating to the extravagance of the Duchess of Portsmouth, is very characteristic. " Following his majesty this morning through the gallery, I went with the few who attended him into the Duchess of Portsmouth's dressing-room within her bed-chamber, where she was in her morning loose garment, her maids combing her, newly out of her bed, his majesty and the gallants standing about her; but that which engaged my curiosity was, the rich and splendid furniture of this woman's apartment, now twice or thrice pulled down and rebuilt to satisfy her prodigality and expensive pleasures, while her majesty's does not exceed some gentlemen's wives in furniture and accommodation. Here I saw the new fabric of French tapestry, for design, tenderness of work, and incomparable imitation of the best paintings, beyond any thing I had ever beheld. Some pieces had Versailles, St. Germains, and other palaces of the French king, with huntings, figures, and landscapes, exotic fowls, and all to the life, rarely

---

* The Whig party, at one of their meetings, proposed to impeach some of his mistresses, upon account of the poverty in which their extravagance had involved him. On which old Lord Mordaunt said, "that they ought rather to erect statues to the ladies who made their lover dependent on Parliament for his subsistence."—*Vide* King James's Memoirs, and Dalrymple.

done. Then for Japan cabinets, screens, pendule clocks, great vases of wrought plate, tables, stands, chimney furniture, sconces, branches, braseras, &c. all of massive silver, and out of number; besides some of his majesty's best paintings. Surfeiting of this, I dined at Sir Stephen Fox's, and went contented home to my poor, but quiet villa. What contentment can there be in the riches and splendour of this world, purchased with vice and dishonour!"

There was, in truth, but little of contentment within those splendid walls. It may be, that there was not much repentance for the sin—nor much sense of dishonour; but fears, and jealousies, and perplexities, and heart-aches, disgraceful and malicious intrigues, public and private conspiracies, and all the demons that wait on pride, avarice, perfidy, ambition, haunted the precincts of this temple of luxury; the new peeress, in her gems and ermine, was laughed at by Nell Gwynn,* hated by the Queen, despised in private, and lampooned in public.

In 1675, the arrival of the Duchess of Mazarin in England had nearly overturned the empire of the Duchess of Portsmouth. That "Ladye errant," after many and notable adventures, came over with the professed intention of captivating the King; that very King to whom the short-sighted policy of her uncle had once refused her as a bride!† Hortense concealed, under a languid air and a careless manner, as much arrogance and ambition as a Cleveland or a Portsmouth, with more natural wit than either of them. But born to beauty, rank, power, wealth, she was the complete spoiled child of nature and fortune,—a sort of female Buckingham in her uncontroulable passions, her extravagant whims, and instability of purpose. She had scarcely arrived in London, where she was received with distinction, when a sudden passion

* See p. 156 of this work.
† It is true that Charles in his exile had offered to marry this niece of Cardinal Mazarin, and it is true that the offer was refused; it was then Mazarin's interest to keep well with Cromwell, and the return of Charles to his throne was deemed impossible.

for the Prince de Monaco put to flight all her ambitious views on the heart of Charles; for with her the last caprice was ever paramount. The court was thus spared the delectable amusement of a combat of daggers or bodkins between the rival duchesses; but St. Evremond was in despair, and Charles in a fury. The vagrant heart of this royal Squire of Dames had been captivated in the first moment by the attractions of Mazarin; she was now dismissed from Whitehall, and he withdrew her pension. After awhile his wrath subsided; he restored her pension at the earnest intercession of some of her friends at court, but returned to La Portsmouth, whose power over him was increased by this short estrangement: she could not however, by all her arts, detach him from Nell Gwynn, whose genuine wit, unfailing animal spirits, and careless humour, were a relief from the vapours, caprices, and political cabals which often annoyed him in the duchess's boudoir.*

As years passed on, her power grew by habit, and with it her arrogance. The ladies of the court tossed their heads at poor Nell, the untitled mistress; but the most immaculate in character, the most illustrious in rank, thought themselves happy in the notice and intimacy of the ennobled courtesan. Now and then she had to endure mortifications: it is true the Arlingtons, the Sunderlands, the Arundels, the Cliffords, the Lauderdales— even the lovely young Duchess of York, combined to surround the favourite with a glory which kept her in countenance, and served to gild over her shame; but the Russells, the Cavendishes, the Butlers, stood aloof. She

---

* One of Andrew Marvel's satires thus alludes to the indolent Charles and his insolent mistresses:

> "In loyal libels we have often told him
> How one has jilted him, the other sold him;
> How that affects to laugh, how this to weep,
> But who can rail so long as he can sleep!
> Was ever Prince by two at once misled,
> False, foolish, old, ill-natured, and ill-bred?"

At all times the licence of personal satire has kept pace with the licence of manners and morals; but the remedy is sometimes as bad as the disease,—or rather is itself a disease.

once sent word to the excellent and venerable Duchess of Ormond, that she would dine with her on such a day. The duchess did not decline the *honour*, but she sent her two granddaughters, Lady Betty Stanhope and Lady Emily Butler, out of the house on this occasion, and received the Duchess of Portsmouth alone. They sat down to dinner, with only her chaplain *en tiers* ; and we may easily suppose that the Duchess of Portsmouth did not again invite herself to the table of the Duchess of Ormond.*

Carte, who gives us this characteristic trait, has also related an almost incredible instance of the impertinence, rapacity, and influence of the favourite. When the daughter of the ill-fated Henrietta of Orleans became Queen of Spain,† Charles ordered the famous jeweller Laguse to prepare an ornament of gems of the value of fifteen thousand pounds, as a present to his niece; and Lord Ossory was appointed envoy extraordinary to convey it to her, with the usual compliment of congratulation; but the duchess having in the interim cast her eyes on the jewel, it so pleased her fancy that she insisted on appropriating it. The King had every art but the art of saying *no*, and Ossory's journey was stopped on the plea that economy was the order of the day, and that it was too expensive; on the same economical principle the jewel was presented to the Duchess of Portsmouth. What became of it afterwards I do not know.

On another occasion, the Duke of York took it into his head to descant in her presence on the virtue and piety of Louis XIV., who, at the command of a new confessor, had sent Montespan into a convent during Lent, in order that he might be contrite with a better grace. The duke related all the circumstances, and dwelt upon them with much eloquence and solemnity, to the infinite impatience and embarrassment of the duchess: she was however *quitte pour la frayeur.*

* Carte's Life of Ormond.
† She was sent into Spain at the age of fourteen, and perished, like her mother, in the bloom of youth, and by a similar death.

The Queen detested her; but the little spirit which poor Catherine had at first exhibited, as well as her affection for the King, had long subsided,—the first into passive endurance, the latter into absolute indifference. When the Act was passed in 1678, obliging all persons to take a test against Popery, and a proviso was inserted in favour of the Queen and nine ladies about her person, she required all her attendants to cast lots, but named the Duchess of Portsmouth with herself as excepted, and not to be exposed to the uncertainty of a lot. The excuse made for this piece of complacency to her rival was her own perilous situation, which made it necessary to display an extreme alacrity in anticipating the wishes of the King. This conduct, the effect of fear only, excited so little gratitude, that not long afterwards we have an instance of the abject and heartless slavery of Charles, and of the unfeeling insolence of his sultana, which cannot be recorded without indignation. The duchess was Lady of the Bed-chamber to the Queen, as Lady Castlemaine had been before her,—not so much to preserve appearances, as to give her, by virtue of her office, a right to lodgings in Whitehall. It may easily be imagined that the duties of her place were dispensed with; but, on one occasion, contrary to her usual custom and the Queen's wishes, she chose to attend on her majesty at dinner, and behaved with so much effrontery, that the Queen, who had little command of temper, was thrown into extreme disorder, and at last burst into tears.* The duchess laughed behind her fan, and uttered some words of derision almost aloud; this audacity excited so much disgust and indignation, that the King interposed. Catherine's spirit was, however, a mere flash of excited temper; and the next time we hear of her, she is the Duchess of Portsmouth's partner at loo.†

Many intrigues were carried on against the imperious favourite; many attempts were made to remove her, or introduce a rival, or a substitute, in the heart of the indolent, inconstant Charles,—but without effect. She had numerous enemies, and not one friend;

---

* Sir John Reresby's Memoirs.   † Lady Sunderland's Letters.

but she had so many spies and dependants around her, she was so well served through fear or interest, that she contrived to anticipate or defeat all the plots against her, and keep old Rowley chained to her footstool while he lived.*

Nor did she reign merely through the influence of her beauty and her feminine arts. If this woman had confined herself to securing her personal influence in the heart of Charles,—if she had been satisfied with amassing wealth and appropriating diamonds, the world had wanted one signal instance of mischievous, misplaced power in our sex. We find the Duchess of Portsmouth, almost from her first arrival in England, engaged in the deepest and most dangerous state intrigues; and so completely did she fulfil the intentions and instructions of Louis in binding her lover to the French interests, that England, to use the strong expression of one historian, "was, in her time, little better than a province of France." As far as the government was concerned, this was true; but, fortunately, the tide of national feeling had set in a contrary direction, and though repressed for awhile, it was afterwards nobly asserted.

In the boudoir of the Duchess of Portsmouth was concerted that treaty, or rather that conspiracy, between Charles II. and Louis XIV., a principal article of which was, that Charles should not call a Parliament for a certain number of years; and that during that time, he should have money from the court of France to enable him to govern independently, and carry his measures

---

* The interest of the story of "Peveril of the Peak" turns on a plot of this kind,—fictitious of course, but resembling in its outline the story of Miss Lawson, (see p. 186)). The King obtained the nick-name of Old Rowley from that of an ugly old horse in the royal stud, which was celebrated for the number and beauty of its offspring. He was ignorant of this satirical cognomen, till one day happening to visit one of the Maids of Honour, he found her singing a most libellous song on "Old Rowley the King." After listening a few minutes at the door, he tapped gently: "Who's there?" said Miss Howard from within; "Old Rowley himself, madam," replied the King, opening the door.

without the consent of his people. The amount of this pension caused much dispute. The plea used by Charles to persuade Louis to come in to his terms was "that it would render England for ever dependent on him, and put it out of the power of the English to oppose him." These were the King's own words,—may they stick like plague-spots to his memory! The Duchess of Portsmouth promised for her lover, that if Louis would give four millions of livres, he should enter into all the engagements the King of France could desire. The terms were at last arranged between Bouillon, the French envoy, and Lord Sunderland.

During this secret negotiation, French money was lavished on all sides à *pleines mains*: not only the ministers, courtiers, and their dependants, but some of the women of the highest rank in the court accepted presents and *gratifications* from France, on conditions pretty well understood: and "*not* to be corrupted was the shame."* Many of these transactions were well known to the King, who treated them with profligate indifference, and even raillery. While Charles and his confidants were bribed into compliance with the wishes of Louis, the French ambassador and the

---

* The French minister thus writes to his master:—"Lady Arlington having offered in her husband's presence to accept of the present intended for her husband, he reproached her, but very obligingly." About a year afterwards, he says:—" My Lord Arlington made me a visit on purpose to let me know how much he is penetrated with the marks of esteem and distinction which your majesty has given by the magnificent present made to Lady Arlington." Again, "Lady Shrewsbury, on receiving her French pension, said, 'She would make Buckingham comply with the King in all things.'" Again, "If your majesty thinks I ought again to press Lord Hollis to accept the box of diamonds, I may, by means of Lady Hollis, make him accept of it. I don't presume she will be so difficult as he has been." (Lord Hollis died before the box could be again offered to him, and it was given to Lord St. Albans.) Montagu was promised 100,000 livres for contriving the disgrace and fall of Lord Danby, (but received only half the sum ;) "Lord Sunderland and the Duchess of Portsmouth hinted that they expected *gratifications* from France." (They received 10,000 and 5000 pistoles with a very good grace.) See the original despatches quoted in Dalrymple's Appendix.

Duchess of Portsmouth were intriguing with the popular, or Whig party, in order to embarrass the government, and prevent the King from becoming too independent; and Charles was duping, or trying to dupe, all parties in turn. In the midst of this scene of perfidy and meanness, and moral and political debasement,—while the traitor nobles, and their more traitorous king, were licking the dust like reptiles round the footstool of a French courtesan, was she, on whom so much of the odium has been thrown, the most culpable or the most contemptible figure in the vile group? Like Circe, who retained her human and feminine attributes in the midst of the herd of wretches around her, transformed and degraded by the taste of her enchanted cup, *she* had still some womanly feelings left,—and for *her*, Justice might find some excuse; for the others none. She was introduced to the French court just in time to witness the *elevation* and triumph of Madame de Montespan: to see her the object of envy to the women, and of obsequious homage to the men; to see her carriage surrounded by a troop of horse, and her levee crowded by obsequious nobles: —was it to be expected that she alone was to look beyond this illusion, and turn from a temptation which she had learned to regard as an object of ambition? She was a foreigner: treachery to England was truth and good service to her own country; perfidy on one side was patriotism on the other, - at least it has been accounted so in other heroines; only this French Judith was satisfied with turning the head of her lover, and had no wish to cut it off. Farther—she was a woman, with the feelings and affections of a woman. She was attached to Charles, was true to him—to him who believed her the only friend he had in the world, yet did not hesitate to dupe her whenever he wished,—through her, to dupe others. She doated on her son, and by these two feelings, superior even to her fears and her avarice, she was frequently governed by the intriguing ministers around her. For instance, when the Bill to exclude the Duke of York from the throne was agitated with such factious clamour, the nation beheld the strange spectacle of the French mistress leagued with the Whig and Protestant faction, and intriguing with the popular leaders of the House of Commons against the court; because that Machiavel, Shaftesbury, had represented to her, that if the usual law of succession was once set aside, her son the Duke of Richmond would become of more importance, and even have some chance of succeeding to the throne : and such was her ignorance or her imbecility, that she fell at once into the snare. They also worked on her fears, by threatening to vote her a public grievance. It is said, that on this occasion, she threw herself at the feet of the King and shed a flood of tears, beseeching him not to sacrifice her and himself to his affection for his brother: but this time she kneeled and wept in vain.

It is curious, that during that grotesque and sanguinary farce, the Popish plot, which threatened even the person of the Queen, the Duchess of Portsmouth not only escaped its ill-devouring snares, but enjoyed a kind of popularity; so that when a member of the House of Commons rose up to move an address, "That she should be sent out of the kingdom," the purport of his speech was no sooner guessed, than it was drowned in a tumult of dissentient voices. One part of this pretended plot being the murder of the King, she had an excuse for being on the opposite side. It is even said, that at the trial of poor old Lord Stafford, she was in the court dealing out smiles and *bon-bons* to the witnesses against him.

It is said, in the Life of Lord Russell, that the old Earl of Bedford offered the Duchess of Portsmouth one hundred thousand pounds to procure the pardon of his son, and that she refused it. As she was never known to resist a bribe, it is more probable that she did make the attempt, and failed. In this instance, as in some others, the Duke of York's influence outweighed hers.

In the year 1681, her son, the Duke of Richmond, then about nine years of age, was installed a knight of the Garter. At this period, and previously, the knights of the Garter wore the blue ribbon round the neck, with the George appendant on the breast;

but the duke's mother having some time after his installation introduced him to the King with his ribbon over his left shoulder, and the George appendant on the right side, his majesty was so much pleased with the alteration, that he commanded it in future to be adopted. Thus the Duchess of Portsmouth has some claim to be considered as joint patroness of the most noble order of the Garter with the Countess of Salisbury, of chivalrous memory, whose face could not have been more fair, and whose fame, by all accounts, was not much fairer.

About the same time, another secret treaty with France was arranged in the boudoir of Madame la Duchesse. The principal article of this treaty was, that Charles should never more call a Parliament, and should receive on that condition two millions of livres for one year, and a million and a half for two years more. Lord Hyde, Lord St. Albans, and the Duchess of Portsmouth, were only privy to this infamous bargain, which was managed verbally, but the proofs of which remain in Barillon's despatches. It is well known that after this treaty, or rather *treason*, had been consummated, Charles dissolved his Parliament, and never assembled another. It was a little later, about 1082, that Louis, being resolved to seize on Luxembourg, the key to the Netherlands and Germany, prevailed on Charles, through the influence and caresses of the Duchess of Portsmouth, to look on quietly while this piece of arbitrary injustice was perpetrated against the faith of treaties, and against the interest of England. Charles received 300,000*l.* for his passive treachery. The amount of the *gratification* which rewarded the duchess is not ascertained; but she ever afterwards piqued herself on this affair of Luxembourg, and boasted of it as the last and best piece of service she had rendered the court of France.* In the midst of these vile state intrigues, the interior of Whitehall is described by contemporaries as a scene "of inexpressible luxury and profaneness, gaming and all dissoluteness;"

---

* Burnet, vol. ii. p. 181.　Dalrymple, vol. i. Appendix to book i.　Evelyn, vol. i. p. 537.

but the under current was bitterness, terror, and gloom. Charles, who had been so remarkable for his easy gaiety, had latterly sunk into a kind of melancholy apathy; the duchess became alarmed by his illness and her own unpopularity. She changed her conduct after the dissolution of the last Parliament, turned against the popular party, connected her interests with those of the Duke of York, and brought Lord Sunderland again into the administration: in fact, Sunderland, whose insinuating arts few could withstand, found means to work on her feelings and her fears. He began by proving to her, that her son could never hope to succeed to the crown; but that, through his (Lord Sunderland's) interest and that of the Duke of York, she might gain an immense hereditary settlement for him. The Duke was not wanting in promises on his part, so that on one occasion, in 1684, when the duchess was seized with a sudden indisposition, (the consequence of that habitual *gourmandise* in which she indulged,) she called the King to her, and made him swear, in case of her death, to stand by his brother. On her recovery, the Duke of York sent to thank her for a proof of interest, which appeared at least sincere; yet he contrived to delay, and at length to evade the promised settlement on her son. Meantime the King's spirits declined; nothing, as it was commonly said, went near his heart, for in truth he had no heart; but the inextricable web of difficulties in which his duplicity and extravagance had involved him began to prey on his mind. He had been false to all, he was mistrusted by all; insignificant abroad, contemptible at home: while Louis XIV., sick of his vacillating, and tired of his complaints and his mean importunities, not only withheld his pension and intrigued with his subjects against him, but actually threatened to publish through Europe the articles of their secret treaties, which would not only have rendered him detestable in the eyes of all men, but might have proved fatal to his crown and life;*—his father had lost his head for much less cause. Charles was struck at once with terror and

* Barillon, the French envoy, confesses that he had a discretionary power to threaten Charles with this discovery, but was to keep it in reserve *as a stroke of thunder.*

rage to be thus over-reached; his gaiety forsook him, and with it his good-breeding and good-nature, which were mere manner and temperament. To his natural laziness was added extreme depression of spirits, and a sudden and unusual fit of jealousy increased his ill-humour. In 1684, the Grand-Prieur de Vendome,* brother to the Duke of Vendome, came over from France on some secret mission, and had particular orders to ingratiate himself with the Duchess of Portsmouth. This Grand-Prieur appears to have possessed in himself a rare union of qualifications; he was prelate, statesman, soldier, courtier, and a man of gallantry;—very handsome, and very slovenly. He began by losing his money to the duchess; and then, under pretence of state affairs, was so frequently closeted with her, that the King, roused from his usual indolence and indifference, ordered the Grand-Prieur to quit England. Yet his behaviour to the duchess at this very time displayed an increase of fondness and confidence, and whether there were any real grounds for this suspicion remains doubtful.

Such was, at this period, the alteration in Charles's spirits and deportment, that the Duchess of Portsmouth began to tremble for him and for herself. When she was about to make a journey to Bath, whither Sir Charles Scarborough (the court physician) had ordered her, Lord Sunderland stopped her departure, by asking her if she could be such a fool as to let the King feel he could do without her? And taking advantage of her fondness for her lover,† his fertile brain and restless spirit, which seem to have "toiled in frame of villanies," conceived a new plot: he persuaded the duchess that the only means of restoring the King to health and spirits, was to prevail on him to change his measures entirely, reconcile himself to the Parliament and people, banish the Duke of York,

* He was the grandson of Henri Quatre, consequently cousin to the King. He came over first in 1680.

† The expressions used by Dalrymple.

and recall Monmouth.* The duchess listened; always impotent in mind, facile as she was headstrong, and without any fixed principle of conduct, except that of securing the King's affections and her own power over him, she readily lent herself to Sunderland's projects; but in the very commencement of this new intrigue, Charles was seized with apoplexy.

It must be allowed that the deportment of the Duchess of Portsmouth, in his last moments, considering her situation and her tenets of belief, did her some honour. She had often been compared to Alice Pierce in the lampoons of the day, but her conduct was very different. It was made a subject of reproach to her, that she was found seated by the King's pillow and supporting his head, where the Queen ought to have been (but where the Queen *was not*); and it was considered "a piece of indecency," that she had desired Bishop Kenn to take the Duke of Richmond to his father to receive his last blessing;† but her solicitude on these points does not surely deserve so hard a construction. On the second day of the King's seizure, Barillon writes that he found the duchess in her apartment overwhelmed with affliction; but that instead of speaking of her own grief or her own affairs, she appeared extremely anxious for the state of the King's soul. "Nobody," said she, "tells him of his condition, or speaks to him of God. I cannot with decency enter the room; the Duke of York thinks only of his affairs. Go to him, I conjure you, and warn him to think of what can be done to save the King's soul; lose no time, for if it be deferred ever so little, it will be too late!"

She had all along been in the secret of Charles's real sentiments

---

* Lord Sunderland's aim was to ingratiate himself with the Prince of Orange, whose party was becoming every day stronger in England.

† The good bishop was much blamed for his compliance.—*Vide* Burnet. This was the same bishop who, when Charles II. lodged at his house at Winchester, refused to admit Nell Gwynn into it. The King put himself into a passion; but Nell defended the bishop, observed that he only did his duty, and retired voluntarily to another lodging.

with regard to religion, and a priest being brought, he died in the profession of the Catholic faith. He frequently recommended the Duchess of Portsmouth and her son to his successor, "in terms," says Burnet, "as melting as he could fetch out;" and after his death, the first visit of condolence which James the Second paid was to the Duchess of Portsmouth; the second to the Queen-dowager, whose grief, in truth, was the more apocryphal of the two.

Soon after the death of Charles the Second, the Duchess of Portsmouth retired to France, carrying with her a large sum in money and jewels;* and from this time, though her life was prolonged beyond the usual term of humanity, very few particulars are known concerning her. She lived at first with considerable splendour, but lost immense sums at play; and her pension from England being stopped, it appears that she was reduced to great difficulties. She came over to England in 1699, and found her son the Duke of Richmond married to Lady Anne Brudenell, widow of Lord Bellasys, and the father of three children. She returned to Paris, but came over again in 1715, and was presented to the Princess of Wales, afterwards Queen Caroline.† Her object, it is said, was to obtain a pension from the English govern-

* [She seems at this time to have been involved in debt. The following curious entry occurs in the interesting memoirs of the Marquis de Sourches, lately discovered and published at Paris by M. Bernier. March, 1685. "On assuroit encore que ce prince (James II.) étoit allé rendre deux visites fort honnêtes à Madame la Duchesse de Portsmouth, l'une des maîtresses du feu roi son frère; mais qu'à la dernière visite, il lui avoit conseillé que, si elle vouloit se retirer d'Angleterre, comme elle sembloit en avoir envie, elle eût le soin de payer toutes ses dettes, ne pouvant pas se faire fort auprès d'elle, si elle en usoit autrement, d'empêcher que les Anglois ne lui firent quelqu' insulte."—ED.]

† At the first drawing-room held by George I., the Duchess of Portsmouth, the Countess of Dorchester, ci-devant mistress of James II., and the Countess of Orkney, mistress of William III., found themselves standing together in the royal presence. "Good Lord!" exclaimed Lady Dorchester, whose impudence equalled her wit, "who would have thought that we three —— should have met here!" They had all been raised to the peerage on the same terms.

ment; if she had the assurance to ask it, apparently the government had not the assurance to grant it. In 1718 she was a poor pensioner on the French court, and was living on an allowance of eight hundred a-year. In the Memoirs of the Duc de Saint Simon she is thus incidentally mentioned :

" Le Régent accorda à la Duchesse de Portsmouthe 8,000 liv. d'augmentation de pension à 12,000 liv. qu'elle en avait déjà: elle était fort vieille, très convertie et pénitente, très mal dans ses affaires, reduite à vivre dans sa campagne. Il était juste et de bon exemple de se souvenir des services importants et continuels qu'elle avait rendus de très bonne grâce à la France, du temps qu'elle était en Angleterre, maîtresse très-puissante de Charles II."

Voltaire, who saw her about this time at the age of seventy, describes her as still surprisingly beautiful, "avec une figure encore noble et agréable, que les années n'avaient point flétrie."

The last years of her life were spent in retirement, and in a penitence which we may hope to be sincere. She died at Paris in 1734, in her eighty-seventh year.

The Duchess of Portsmouth had a younger sister, Henriette de Quérouaille, whom she invited over to England, and married to Philip seventh Earl of Pembroke. He was a man of violent and eccentric temper; she lived most unhappily with him, and he treated her so ill, that the duchess threatened to make the King interfere. The earl made a brutal reply, which silenced her, and his death soon after, (in 1683), relieved his wife from his tyranny. This Countess of Pembroke had a daughter married to the son of the infamous Judge Jefferies.

It is, perhaps, worth remarking, that the first company of French actors who ever appeared in England, came over for the amusement of the Duchess of Portsmouth; and, through her patronage were for a time so followed by the court and the public, as to excite the envy and despair of the English players, and call down a bitter satire from Dryden, who wrote one of his Prologues expressly to turn them into ridicule.

The pictures of the Duchess of Portsmouth are very numerous, and easily recognized; for though her face had not much expression, its extreme loveliness, the peculiar beauty of the full lips, and a childish sweetness and simplicity in the look, give to all her pictures a very distinct character. There is a splendid full-length of her at Dunham Massey, the seat of the Earl of Stamford: another, equally fine, at Blenheim. The picture of her at Hampton Court is by Gascar, a French painter, whom she brought over and patronised; that at Goodwood, in the possession of her descendant the Duke of Richmond, I presume to be by the same artist. At Kensington there is a portrait of her by Verelst, holding a wreath of flowers. There is a picture of her at Holland-House, and two at Strawberry-hill.

Lely painted a picture representing Charles and the Duchess of Portsmouth as Cymon and Iphigenia.

> " Along the margin of the fount was laid,
> Attended by her nymphs, a sleeping maid.
> * * *
> The fool of nature stood with stupid eyes,
> And gaping mouth that testified surprise,
> Fix'd on her face, nor could remove his sight,
> New as he was to love, and novice in delight.
> Long mute he stood ———"

This picture is mentioned by Horace Walpole as being missed or lost from the royal collection. Either the original, or a most admirable copy, is in the possession of Sir Gerard Noel. It is the only known picture of the duchess in which the face is represented in profile, and nothing can exceed it in voluptuous beauty.

There was another picture representing the duchess and her

son as the Madonna and Child, which was painted for a rich convent in France, and used as an altar-piece. It may account for this *not* singular piece of profaneness to remark, that the duchess was regarded at one time by the most bigoted party in France, as a chosen instrument of Heaven for the conversion of the King of England and his people.

The engraving is from the celebrated picture at Althorpe, one of the finest of all. It was painted by Lely soon after her arrival in England: it represents her as an Arcadian Bergère—

> ——" A peeress there in ermined pride,
> Is here Pastora by a fountain's side."

In the original there is an emblematical lamb, which is omitted in the engraving for want of space; the same style of beauty, striking, and perfect in its way, without being intellectual or interesting, prevails through all the known portraits of this " très puissante maîtresse."

[It is said that, after having created her Duchess of Portsmouth, the King, in order to gratify her pride and quiet her pretended scruples, was married to his new mistress at the house of the Earl of Arlington,—a ceremony quite superfluous, to say nothing worse of it, as his Queen was yet living; and upon the very day of this pretended marriage, he dined with her according to the ceremony of the court, and *supped below stairs*. The duchess required this mock celebration to *save her conscience,* (!) and when she proclaimed her marriage to the courtiers, which was on a Lord Mayor's day, at Mr. Easton's in Cheapside, where the King and his attendants usually stood, some one having said something to her discredit, she prefaced it by exclaiming in broken English, " Me no ——— ! if me thought me were, me would cut mine own throat!"

During the reigns of the two last Stuarts, we are constantly meeting with rumours of poisoning: it was a practice then fashionable in France, and the good people of England, seeing so many new fashions come in, probably thought that this fashion must also have come along with the others. We are inclined to believe in very few of the stories of this kind which contemporary, or nearly contemporary, writers have handed down to us, because, in the violent and bitter party feelings which then existed, the sudden death of a partisan was too severely felt by his friends to allow them to judge deliberately or impartially. After the death of King Charles, it was confidently reported by many that he was taken off by poison, and popular clamour accused the Duchess of Portsmouth of being implicated in the crime. Bishop Burnet reports a conversation between the duchess and a Mr. Henly of Hampshire, wherein the duchess confessed that the King had been murdered by the Popish party, and Harris,* to whom we refer our readers for further information on the subject, endeavours to show that the story was not improbable.

The story of the poisoning of Charles's sister is, unhappily, far more authentic, and our readers, will, perhaps, not grudge the space occupied by the following letters of a person of quality who witnessed her death, as they give some curious details relating to the fate of Madame Henriette d'Angleterre.

Never, perhaps, was there a family so stained with a long series of crimes, and so severely punished for them in all its members, as that of the Stuarts. "Though it was notorious," says the Editor of the *Secret History of Charles the Second*,† "that she died in excruciating agonies; though it was notorious she fell a victim to her husband's jealousy; yet Charles, on receiving the news, only shed a few tears, and gave Monsieur a hard name; but desired the messenger not to divulge the secret, before a formal account was sent from France of the subject. The English ministers were directed to notify to foreign courts, that Madame did not die a violent death; and the Marshal de Bellefond, who was sent over to remove the King's suspicions, was received with singular marks

---

* Hist. of Charles II., vol. ii. p. 372.
† Secret Hist., Suppl., p. 24.

of civility. It is not, perhaps, the least odious feature in Charles's portrait, that neither the fullest proofs of his sister's untimely end, nor the expressions of tenderness uttered with her dying breath, in which she declared that her only regret in leaving the world was because she left him, had the smallest effect on his callous feelings to rouse him to a returning sense of national interest, family honour, or brotherly affection."

"PARIS, JUNE 30, 1670,
Four in the Morning.

" My Lord,

" I am sorry to be obliged, by my employment, to give you an account of the saddest story in the world, and which I have hardly the courage to write. Madam, on Sunday the 29th of this instant, being at St. Clou, with a great deal of company, about five o'clock in the afternoon called for a glass of *chicory* water, that was prescribed her to drink, she having for two or three days after bathing found herself indisposed; she had no sooner drank this, but she cried out she was dead, and fell into Madam Mascbourgh's arms, and desired to be put to bed, and have a confessor. She continued in the greatest tortures imaginable till three o'clock in the morning, when she dyed: the King, the Queen, and all the court being there till about an hour before.

" God send the King our master patience and constancy to bear so great an affliction. Madam declared she had no reluctancy to die, but out of the grief she thought it would be to the King her brother; and when she was in any ease, from the torture she was in, which the physicians call *Colich Bileuse*, she asked for me, and it was to charge me to say all the kind things from her to her brothers, the King and the duke. I did not leave her till she expired, and hapned to come to St. Clou an hour after she fell ill. Never any body died with that piety and resolution, and kept her senses to the last. Excuse this imperfect relation for the grief I am in. I am sure all that had the honour to know her, will have their share for so great and general a loss.

I am, my Lord,
Yours," &c.

"Paris, July 6, 1670.

"My Lord,

"This acknowledgeth two of your lordship's, the one of June 17th by Sir Henry Jones, the other of the 23rd by the post. I suppose by this time you may have with you the Marshal de Bellefond, who, besides his condolence, will endeavour, I believe, to disabuse our court of what the court and people here will never be disabused of, which is Madam's being poisoned. Which, having so good an authority as her own saying it several times in her great pains, makes the report much more credited. But to me in particular, when I asked her several times whether she thought herself poisoned, she would answer nothing; I believe being willing to spare the addition of so great a trouble to the King our master; which was the reason why, in my first letter, I made no mention of it: neither am I physician good enough to say she was poisoned or she was not. They are willing, in this countrey, to make me the author of the report, I mean Monsieur, who says, I do it to break the good intelligence between the two crowns.

"The King and ministers here seem extremely affected with the loss of Madam, and I do not doubt but they are, for they hoped, upon her consideration, to bring the King our master to condescend to things, and enter into a friendship with this crown, stricter, perhaps, than they think he will now she is no more. What was begun, or what was intended, I will not presume to search into, since your lordship did not think fit to communicate the least part of it to me; but I cannot help knowing the town talk, and I dare answer that all that the King our master can propose will be granted here, to have his friendship; and there is nothing, on the other side, the Dutch will not do to hinder our joining with the French. All I desire to know, my lord, is, that whilst I am here, I may know what language to hold in conversation with the other ministers, that I may not be ridiculous with the character I have upon me. Whilst Madam was alive, she did me the honour to trust me enough to hinder me from being exposed to that misfortune.

"I am sure, for the little time you knew her in England, you could not but know her enough to regret her as long as you live; as I am sure you have reason; for I never knew any body kinder, nor have a better opinion of another, in all kinds, than she had of you. And I believe she loved the King her brother too well, if she had not been persuaded how well and faithfully you served him, to have been so really concerned for you, as I have observed her to be, upon all occasions, since there has been a good understanding between you. As for my own particular, I have had so great a loss, that I have no joy in this country, nor hopes of any in another. Madam, after several discourses with me in her illness, which was nothing but kind expressions of the King our master, at last told me she was extremely sorry she had done nothing for me before she died, in return of all the zeal and affection with which I had served her, since my being here. She told me that there were six thousand pistoles of hers in several places: she bid me take them for her sake. I told her she had many poor servants that wanted more than I; that I never served out of interest, and that absolutely I would not take it; but, if she pleased to tell which of them I should give it to, I would dispose of it according to her pleasure. She had so much presence of mind as to name them to me by their names: but the breath was no sooner out of her body, but Monsieur seized all her keys and cabinets. I enquired, next day, where the money was; one of the women said it was in such a place, which hapned to be the first six thousand pistoles the King our master sent her. For just as that money came, it was designed to unpawn some jewels, upon which she had already taken up some money; but two days before, the King of France gave her money, with which she unpawned them, so the money came clear in to her.

"I demanded the money upon this from Monsieur, as money of mine that was borrowed for Madam, it having been delivered by my servant to two of her women, who assured him, as they could not do otherways, that that money came from me, for they never knew that the King our master sent it her. Monsieur had in this time got away above half of the money; the rest I had delivered me, which I did, to the utmost farthing, in the presence of my Lord Abbot Montague and two other witnesses, dispose to Madam's servants equally, as she directed. Monsieur has promised me the rest, which they are to have in the same manner; but if they are not wise enough to keep their councel, he will certainly take it from them. I could not have got it for the poor people any other way, and I believe the King will be gladder they have it, than Monsieur. I desire you will let the King know this for my discharge, and let it go no further. Sir George Hamilton was a witness of the thing, with my Lord Abbot Montague. I thought fit to trouble your lordship with this account, which is all at present from,

My Lord,
Yours."

"P.S. Since the writing of this, I am told, from very good hands, and one that Monsieur trusts, that he being desired by the King to deliver up all Madam's papers, before he would do it, he first sent for my Lord Abbot Montague to read them, and interpret them to him; but not trusting enough to him, he employed other persons that understood the language to do it, amongst which Madam de Fienne was one; so that most of the private things between the King and Madam are and will be very publick; there were some things in cyphers, which trouble him extremely, of the King our master, for having a confidence with Madam, and treating things with her, without his knowledge. My Lord Abbot Montague will, I hope, give you a larger account of this matter than I can; for tho' Monsieur enjoined him secrecy to all the world, it cannot extend to you, if there be any thing that concerns the King our master's affairs."

To the King.

"Paris, July 15, 1670.

"Sir,

"I ought to begin with begging your majesty's pardon for saying any thing to you upon so sad a subject, and where I had the misfortune to be a witness of the cruellest and most generous end any person in the world ever made. I had the honour, on the Saturday, which was the day before Madam dyed, to entertain conversation with her a great while; the most of her discourse being concerning Monsieur, and how impossible she saw it was for her to live happily with him, for he was fallen out with her worse than ever, because that two days before she had been at Versailles, and there he found her talking privately with the King, about affairs which were not fit to be communicated to him. She told me your majesty and the King here were both resolved upon a war with Holland, as soon as you could be agreed on the manner of it. These were the last words I had the honour to have from her till she fell ill, for Monsieur came in and interrupted her, and I returned to Paris the next day. When she fell ill, she called for me two or three times: Madam de Mechelburgh sent for me; as soon as I came in, she told me, 'You see the sad condition I am in; I am going to die; how I pity the King my brother! for I am sure he loses the person in the world that loves him best.' A little while after she called me again, bidding me be sure to say all the kind things in the world from her to the King her brother, and thank him for all his kindness and care of me. Then she asked me if I remembered what she had said to me, the night before, of your majesty's intentions to joyn with France against Holland. I told her, yes; 'Pray then, said she, tell my brother I never persuaded him to it out of my own interest, or to be more considered in this countrey; but because I thought it for his honour and advantage: for I always loved him above all things in the world, and have no regret to leave it, but because I leave him.' She called to me several times to be sure to say this to you, and spoke to me in English. I asked her then if she believed herself poisoned: her confessor that was by, understood that word, and told her, 'Madam, you must accuse nobody, but offer up your death to God as a sacrifice;' so she would never answer me to that question, tho' I asked her several times, but would only shrink up her shoulders. I asked for her casket, where all her letters were

to send them to your majesty: she bid me take it from Madam
de Borde; but she was swounding and dying to see her mistress
in that condition, and before she came to herself, Monsieur had
seized on them. She recommended to you to help, as much as you
could, all her poor servants: she bid me write to my Lord
Arlington, to put you in mind of it, 'and tell the King my brother,
I hope he will, for my sake, do for him what he promised; *car
c'est un home qui l'ayme, et qui le sert bien.*' She spoke afterwards
a great deal in French aloud, bemoaning and lamenting the condition she knew your majesty would be in, when you heard the
news of her death. I humbly beg again your majesty's pardon
for having been the unfortunate teller of so bad news; there being
none of your servants that wishes your content and happiness with
more zeal and truth, than

     Sir,
      Your Majesty's."

"Paris, July 15, 1670.

"My Lord,

"I have, according to your lordship's directions, sent
you here inclosed the ring, which Madam had on her finger when
she dyed; which your lordship will be pleased to present to his
majesty. I have taken the liberty myself to give him an account
of some things that Madam gave me in charge, presuming your
lordship would, out of modesty, be glad to be spared the telling his
majesty them yourself; there being some things that concern you.
There has been ever since Madam's death, as you may imagine
upon these occasions, various reports, that of her being poisoned
prevailing above all the rest, which has disordered the ministers
here, as well as the King, to the greatest degree that can be. For
my own particular, I have been so struck with it, that I have
hardly had the heart to stir out since; which joined with the
reports of the town, how much the King our master resented so
horrid a fact, that he would not receive Monsieur's letter, and that
he had commanded me home, made them conclude that the King
our master was dissatisfied with this court, to the degree it was

reported. So that to-day, when I was at St. Germains, from whence I am newly returned, to make those compliments you ordered me to do, I am not able to express the satisfaction that the King and everybody had to know that the King our master was a little appeased, and that those reports had made no impression in his mind to the disadvantage of the French. I give you this account, my lord, that you may judge how much, in this conjuncture, they value the friendship of England, and how necessary our master's kindness is to all their designs. I do not doubt but there will be that use made of it, as may be most for the honour of the King and the good of the nation, which is the chief desire of him, who is, with all truth and sincerity,

Yours."

"My Lord,

"I am not able to write to you in my own hand, being so lame, with a fall I had in coming, that I can hardly stir either hand or arm; however, I hope in a day or two to go to St. Germains.

* "This is only to give your lordship an account, of what I believe you know already, of the Chevalier de Lorain's being permitted to come to court, and to serve in the army as a Marshal-de-Camp to the King.

"If Madam were poisoned, as few people doubt, he is looked upon by all France to have done it; and it is wondered at by all France, that that King should have so little regard for the King of England our master, considering how insolently he always carried himself to her when she was alive, as to permit his return. It is my duty to let you know this, to tell his majesty; and if he thinks fit to speak to the French ambassador of it, to do it vigorously; for I assure you it reflects here much upon him to suffer it."

* This paragraph is in cypher in the original.

Charles Lennox, Duke of Richmond, was son to King Charles the Second, by the Duchess of Portsmouth; he was carried by his mother into France, in the reign of James, and returned to England in that of William, when he declared himself for the religion and constitution of his country.

Spring Macky describes him as "a gentleman good-natured to a fault, very well bred," with "many good things in him; an enemy to business, very credulous, well shaped, black complexion, much like King Charles:" to which Dean Swift adds, that he was "a shallow coxcomb."—ED.]

ments, as she was for beauty, gentleness, and modesty. Carte, the prolix but faithful historian of the Ormond family, pauses in his narrative of great events and political revolutions, to dwell for a moment on these auspicious nuptials. He tells us that " it were more easy to imagine than to describe the vast resort of persons of distinction, especially of the relations of the family, which were drawn together by this solemnity, and the glee and satisfaction which appeared in all faces upon so joyful an occasion and so happy a change of fortune; after so many dreary years of banishment, dispersion, and confusion."

If there was one clouded brow in the chapel of Kilkenny Castle, when Lady Mary gave her hand to the young heir of the Cavendishes, it must have been that of poor Lady Chesterfield or her moody lord. Their domestic felicity was at this time not quite perfect; but the occasion on which they were assembled, the presence of the Duchess of Ormond, who had lately taken pains to reconcile her charming but giddy daughter with her "mari loup-garou," prevented any display of temper beyond a frown or a pout, and all was splendid hilarity and genuine Irish hospitality. The Duke of Ormond kept open house till Christmas, and the bridal party did not return to England till the following summer.

After her marriage, Lady Mary bore the title of Lady Cavendish during the whole of the reign of Charles II., as her husband did not succeed to the Earldom till 1686.[*]

This noble, beautiful, and virtuous lady, as she is styled by her lord's biographers, appears to have resembled her lovely sister-in-law, Lady Ossory, in disposition as in destiny. She was united to one of the most illustrious characters of the age; but in herself of so gentle and unobtrusive a temper, so little formed for ambition or display, that she is principally interesting from the extraordinary

[*] In the present time she would have been entitled Lady Mary Cavendish, being the daughter of a duke, wedded to the son of an earl.

endowments and splendid career of her husband. Lord Cavendish appears to have possessed every quality which could excite the affection and admiration of his youthful bride, and every propensity that could militate against her happiness. If it be true, as all *his* biographers assert, that they lived in uninterrupted harmony,* it is the strongest and most comprehensive eulogium that could be pronounced on *her* temper and character. We do not hear much of the lady during the first years of her marriage; but a glance at Lord Cavendish's known character and pursuits will show, that he must frequently have tried her forbearance, alarmed her affection, and pained her heart. He was uncommonly handsome and graceful, brave even to rashness; magnificent to profusion in his habits and expenditure; witty, and yet never, even in that licentious age, "forgot the distinction between the profane wit and the gentleman;"† he united an inflexible temper with an exceeding softness of manner and suavity of deportment; so that while his friends could not presume on his courtesy, his enemies could not resist the attraction of his manner. Perhaps he was married too young, for we find him leading, *after* his marriage, the life which a dissipated young noble now leads before he has made up his mind to settle down into matrimony. His love of pleasure, his passion for gambling and the race-course, and other extravagancies, appear to have frequently enraged the old earl, his father, and plunged him into difficulties. Moreover (and this looks ill for poor Lady Cavendish's domestic happiness,) we find that the King forbade him the house of Nell Gwynn, or rather forbade Nell to see him; and he was in strict intimacy with the Duke of Monmouth, Tom Thynne, Lord Dorset, and other distinguished *roués* of that time, although he does not figure in De Grammont's Memoirs; and yet, in the midst of these follies, he had qualities which must have rendered him as interesting and beloved in private, as his public career was historically glorious. His chival-

---

* Dr. Kippis in the Biogr. Brit., and Dr. Kennet's Memoirs of the Cavendishes.
† This was said of him by Dryden.

rous gallantry often gave his wife occasion to tremble for his life. About six years after his marriage, when Montagu was appointed ambassador to France, Lord Cavendish accompanied him to Paris; while there, he was one evening on the stage of the Opera* when some young officers of the royal guard came on, flushed with wine and insolence: one of them addressed to him an insulting question, which Lord Cavendish immediately answered with a blow: the whole party then drew their swords, and rushed upon him; he set his back against one of the side-scenes, and defended himself for some time with the utmost bravery, but after receiving several wounds, he must have been overpowered by numbers, and probably murdered on the spot, if a Swiss in Montagu's service, a man of uncommon strength and stature, had not suddenly caught him in his arms and flung him into the pit:—he was thus saved; but in the fall one of the iron spikes caught his arm, and tore it severely. His conduct on this occasion, which was quite that of a hero of romance, gave him considerable éclat, not only at Paris, but through all Europe; and when Louis XIV. ordered his cowardly assailants to be put under arrest, Cavendish crowned his exploit by generously interceding for their pardon.†

His challenge to Count Koningsmark, who had been acquitted, (in defiance of the most damning proofs,) of the murder of his friend Thynne, was in the same spirit. He offered to meet the count in any part of the world, charge the guilt of blood upon him,

* Both in the English and the French theatres, a part of the audience were at this time admitted on the stage, and sometimes mingled pell-mell with the players.

† *Vide* Sir William Temple's Letters to him, and Kennet's Memoirs of the Cavendishes. Sir William thus writes: "I can assure your lordship, all that can be said to your advantage upon this occasion is the common discourse here, and not disputed by the French themselves; who say you have been as generous in excusing your enemies, as brave in defending yourself. The Dutch will have it, that you have been the first in excess; and say, that such a thing as seven or eight falling upon one, would never have been done in any other place but France, nor suffered neither by the rest of the company."—*Sir William Temple's Letters*, vol. i. p. 70.

and prove it with his sword; but that libertine and fanfaron avoided the encounter.*

To the valour and bearing of a paladin of old romance, Lord Cavendish added the spirit of an ancient Roman. While his gallantry and love of pleasure brought him into constant association with some of the wildest profligates of the court, his ardent love of liberty, his enlightened views of policy, his lofty principles of honour and patriotism, kept him constantly in opposition to the crooked and despotic measures of the government.†

He and Lord Russell were considered as leaders of the Whig party; and when his heroic friend was persecuted to death by a venal and dissolute court, Cavendish, with his characteristic gallantry, was ready to run all risks for his deliverance: he offered to change clothes with him in prison, and thus effect his escape; and when this was declined, it was his intention to have waylaid the cavalcade on the road to execution with a troop of armed friends, and to have rescued Lord Russell by open force. But Lord Russell declared, that he would not suffer his friends to risk their lives for his sake; and that having submitted to the decision of the laws, he was ready to endure the penalty. Lord Cavendish took leave of his friend as he was led out to death, and Lord Russell, after bidding him farewell, turned back, and in a few energetic words, entreated him to reform his libertine course of life, and reflect ere it was too late. Lord Cavendish made no answer, but wrung his hand, and burst into a flood of tears.

* See page 169, of this work.
† Lord Cavendish would have been esteemed a *liberal* even in these liberal days, and considering the times in which he lived, we must wonder at the boldness of some of the articles of his political creed; he was of opinion that Parliament should be triennial, and openly complained (when in the House of Peers) that "a little dirty borough might be bought for a certain price, as easily as a bullock at Smithfield!" He desired they would inscribe on his tomb, "Here lies William Cavendish, the loyal subject of good princes, a hater of tyrants, and by them hated."

These last words of his noble friend probably made a salutary impression on the mind and character of Lord Cavendish. We find him thenceforward more retired from the court, living a good deal on his estates, and devoting much of his time to state affairs: he is one of the very few public characters of Charles's time who can be contemplated with unmingled satisfaction. And while "our youth, all livery'd o'er with foreign gold," were contending for the notice and favour of an arrogant mistress, and our statesmen were selling themselves and betraying each other, Cavendish recalls us to the spirit of classic times:—" It had been as easy to turn the sun from his course, as Fabricius from the path of honour!"*

These things are matters of history, and are only mentioned here to give some idea of what the wife of such a man ought to have been, and ought to have felt. It is mortifying that we know so little relating to her personal habits; that there is so little mention made of her in the panegyrics on her husband; and that the epithets, noble, beautiful, and virtuous, must comprise all that can be said concerning her.† Yet this is perhaps the most significant praise of her character, as well as the most satisfactory evidence of her general contented and tranquil existence. The crimes or miseries of women make a noise in the world; their virtues and their happiness alike seek the shade. From the few allusions to Lady Cavendish, we may judge that she had sense enough to be proud of her husband, and affection enough to pardon his follies; that she was domestic, of a most affectionate disposition, attached to her own family, and tenderly devoted to her children. In the first years of her marriage, when she appeared at court so very young, and with all the advantages of birth and beauty, a safeguard was formed around her in the virtues of her nearest connexions. Her own admirable mother, the Duchess of Ormond, and her aunt, Lady Hamilton, lived

* The celebrated exclamation of King Pyrrhus.
† See Lady Russell's Letters.

revered and respected in the court. Her lovely sister-in-law, Lady Ossory, and her cousin, Miss Hamilton, were among its chief ornaments. The catastrophe of her sister, Lady Chesterfield, though not necessary as a warning, probably contributed, with other causes, to render her guarded in her conduct. Her mother-in-law, the Countess of Devonshire,* with whom she chiefly resided when in the country, seldom came to London; she was an excellent and amiable woman, and had been a celebrated beauty in her day:—while Lord Cavendish's grandmother, the Countess-dowager,† who lived for fourteen years after his marriage, was really one of the most extraordinary and celebrated women of the time. She preserved in her old age the talents, vivacity, and active habits of business which had distinguished her youth, resided almost constantly in or near London,‡ and her house was the resort of wits, poets, statesmen,— in short, it was the Holland-House of that day. The King frequently dined with her in the beginning of his reign; and her exertions in the royal cause, her correctness of conduct, and her commanding intellect, rendered her an object of general respect. Among these family connexions, Lady Cavendish must have passed many years of her life, fulfilling her various duties with a blameless dignity. Her

---

* Lady Elizabeth Cecil, daughter of the Earl of Exeter. There is a lovely picture of her by Vandyke at Burleigh-House; and another, either a duplicate or a good copy, at Hardwick. When her son, Lord Devonshire, was fined thirty thousand pounds for pulling Colonel Culpeper's nose within the verge of the court, "his mother, the countess, who had long absented herself from court, made her appearance in the circle, and saying she was come to discharge her son' fine, humbly desired that his majesty would accept of her delivering up bonds ar other acknowledgments for above sixty thousand pounds, lent by her husband and his mother to his royal father and brother in their greatest extremities." This was refused, but the decree was afterwards reversed as illegal and unjust.

† Christian Bruce, daughter of Edward Lord Bruce. It has been the destiny of the noble house of Cavendish to be allied almost from generation to generation to remarkable women; and of these, Christian, second countess, was one of the most remarkable: she had all the good qualities of the celebrated Bess of Hardwick, of Elizabeth's time, and none of her failings.

‡ At Roehampton.

eldest son, William, was born in 1672; her second son, Henry, in 1673, and she had a daughter and another son born previous to 1680.* In 1684, Lord Cavendish succeeded to his father's titles and estates, and became fourth Earl of Devonshire; and, during the reign of James, both he and the countess absented themselves almost entirely from court. The earl was deeply involved in all the secret measures which led to the Revolution. Yet, in the midst of these plots, and while his liberty and even his head were in danger, he amused himself with building and improving his noble seat at Chatsworth, the principal front of which was erected by him as it now stands. In the beginning of the eventful year 1688, he came up to London to complete the arrangements for the marriage of his eldest son with the eldest daughter of his friend Lord Russell. Lord Cavendish was not then quite seventeen, and the bride about fifteen. Within two months after their nuptials, in August 1688, he sent his son abroad to travel for his improvement, perhaps also to be out of the way of the approaching troubles. The bride remained at Woburn, under the care of her mother, Lady Russell; and Lady Devonshire retired to Chatsworth, while the Revolution was effected, in which the earl took so distinguished a share.

In February 1689, when William and Mary were proclaimed King and Queen, we find the Countess of Devonshire present at their first drawing-room, when she presented her daughter-in-law to the Queen. The lively and *naïve* letter of the young Lady Cavendish on this occasion, addressed to her "*beloved Sylvia,*"† gives the following account of her reception at court:—"You may imagine I was very much pleased to see Ormanzor and Phenixana, (*i. e.* William and Mary), proclaimed King and Queen of England,

* The dates of their birth do not appear. See one of Lady Russell's letters, written in 1685, in which she mentions that on occasion of a fire, (at Montagu-House,) Lady Devonshire's youngest boy was brought by his nurse, wrapt up in a blanket, and put to bed with her own son.—Letters, p. 89.

† These sentimental designations, taken from the French romances, were fashionable at the time and long afterwards.—See the *Spectator* in many places.

in the room of King James, my father's murderer. There was wonderful acclamations of joy, which, though they were very pleasing to me, yet frightened me too; for I could not but think what a dreadful thing it is to fall into the hands of the rabble,— they are such a strange sort of people. At night I went to court with my Lady Devonshire, and kissed the Queen's hands and the King's also," &c.: in another part of the letter she says, with amusing *naïveté*, that when the deputation from Parliament waited on William and Mary to offer the crown, "the Prince answered them in a few words, and the Princess made curtsies."* In truth it was rather an embarrassing situation for the daughter, who had come over to ascend her father's throne. But in this case, as in others, " silence spoke consent."

After the Revolution, the Earl of Devonshire was, in consideration of his great services, created Duke of Devonshire and Marquis of Hartington; and after filling some of the highest offices in the state, he died in 1707. The duchess survived him about three years; and having lived to see around her a numerous family of hopeful grandchildren, she died at Devonshire-House, July 31, 1710, at the age of sixty-eight, and was buried near her father in Westminster Abbey.

William, her eldest son, was the second Duke of Devonshire; her second son, Lord Henry Cavendish, a young man of uncommon talents and merit, and infinitely beloved by his family, died in the life-time of his mother, in his twenty-seventh year. He left one daughter, who was married to the seventh Earl of Westmoreland.

---

* See the whole letter, printed in the Life of Lady Russell, prefixed to the letters of her husband. There is a lovely picture of young Lady Cavendish, the writer of the above letter, in the gallery at Hardwick; the lips are full and red and a little pouting; there is something very fine and patrician-like in the turn of the head, and the whole air and expression. She was afterwards the second Duchess of Devonshire. Her young husband returned from his travels in the beginning of the year 1690; they afterwards lived happily together, and she became the mother of nine children.

The Duchess of Devonshire's third son, Lord James Cavendish, of Stayley Park, died in 1751. Her only daughter, Lady Elizabeth, married Sir John Wentworth, of Broadsworth, in Yorkshire.

The accompanying portrait has been engraved after the original picture in the gallery at Hardwick, where there are also several portraits of her gallant, accomplished, and illustrious husband; one of these, which represents him on horseback in full dress *à la Louis Quatorze*, is a confused but imposing mass of wig and embroidery; but all the portraits, however various in merit or costume, agree in one point,—they are all eminently handsome and dignified—in the noblest style of manly beauty.

MISS JENNINGS.

AFTERWARDS DUCHESS OF TYRCONNEL.

> "Say, why are Beauties praised and honour'd most?
> The wise man's passion, and the vain man's toast?
> Why deck'd with all that land or sea afford?
> Why angels called, and angel-like adored?
> How vain are all these glories, all our pains,
> Unless good sense preserve what Beauty gains!"
>
> POPE.

WHEN the Duchess of York found herself under the necessity of reforming her establishment of honourable handmaidens, she was resolved not to leave the selection of her new attendants to chance or interest, but to depend on her own taste alone, and listen to no recommendations which were not presented in person. Her choice fell on Miss Temple, Miss Jennings, and Miss Churchill: we will discuss the last-mentioned first.

Hamilton, who has done for the court of Charles II. what Ovid did for that of Olympus,—revealed to mocking mortals "all the laughing scandal of the lower sky," has treated Miss Churchill with peculiar malice, and even denied her any pretensions to that beauty which she certainly did possess, if her portraits may be trusted. She was the eldest sister of him who was afterwards the GREAT Duke of Marlborough, but at this time merely an ensign in the Guards, and page of honour to the Duke of York. When they were first introduced to the court, about the year 1664, Arabella Churchill was sixteen, and her brother about fourteen years old; and certain scandal-mongers affirm, that young Churchill's rapid promotion was owing to his sister's *promotion* in a different sense. She captivated the Duke of York more by the charms of her figure and manner, than her face; and she had not virtue enough to resist his importunities, or wit enough to make the best conditions for herself; but having, unhappily, forfeited her place and title of Maid of Honour, did not seek to parade or ennoble her degradation. She was the mother of four children by the duke; her eldest son, James Fitz-James, was the famous Marshal Duc de Berwick, one of the greatest military characters of the last century; and one of her daughters married the first Earl of Waldegrave. Arabella Churchill afterwards married Colonel Godfrey of the Jewel-office, with whom she lived in the utmost harmony, and was respected for the correctness of her conduct and her domestic virtues.

She died in 1730, at the great age of eighty-two, having survived her lover, husband, and her children. The feelings and situation of this woman, about the beginning of the last century when the sovereign who had loved her had been tumbled from his throne, and was living a poor exile,—when her husband was serving against him,—when her brother was opposed to the armies of Louis XIV., and her not less illustrious son defending the interests of that monarch in Spain,—must have been strange and interesting.

> "Which is the side that I must go withal?
> I am with all: each army hath a hand—
> Whoever wins on that side shall I lose—
> Assured loss before the match be played!"

Miss Temple and Miss Jennings were of different metal,—metal purer as well as more attractive. Anne Temple, the eldest of the two, was the daughter of a Warwickshire gentleman of ancient family; she was beautiful, something of a brunette in complexion, had a slight graceful figure, fine teeth, with a peculiar softness in her eye and smile. Her disposition was gentle and confiding, but vain and credulous; in short, Miss Temple, thrown among the shoals and quicksands of the court, seemed destined either to sink ingloriously, or make an illustrious shipwreck of her maiden honour.

> "How each pirate eyes
> So weak a vessel and so rich a prize!"

But she is a proof that simplicity and purity of mind are, in certain cases, a better safeguard than pride, or wit, or cunning; in spite of the predictions of those who had watched her *début* and knew something of her character; in spite of the machinations of Rochester, who laid siege to her with equal art and audacity, Miss Temple came off victorious; for in this case escape was victory. After being in the service of the Duchess of York for about two years, she married Sir Charles Lyttelton, who had lately returned from the government of Jamaica, and had greatly distinguished himself during the civil wars by his loyalty and military talents. Sir Charles was nearly forty, the lady not more than eighteen; yet the union proved in all respects happy. She was the mother of thirteen children: the rest of her life was spent almost entirely at Hagley, where she died in 1718. It is curious that her son Sir Thomas Lyttelton also married a Miss Temple, who was a Maid of Honour,* but no relation to his mother's family; and her grandson was the first and celebrated Lord Lyttelton.

Last came the heroine of our last memoir,—the fair, the elegant, the fascinating Frances Jennings; she who moved through the glittering court "in unblenched majesty;" who robbed the men of their hearts, the women of their lovers, and never lost herself! The very model of an intellectual coquette; perhaps a little too wilful, a little too wary for a perfect woman; but in the flush and

---

* Christian Temple, daughter of Sir Richard Temple of Stow, ancestor to the Duke of Buckingham.

bloom of early youth, and in the dangerous situation in which she was now placed, the first of these qualities was only an additional charm, the last a necessary safeguard. As to hearts and such things,—to bring them to Charles's court was mere work of supererogation; it was like trading to the South-sea islands with diamonds and ingots of gold, where glass beads and tinfoil bear just the same value, and answered quite as well.

Frances Jennings was the eldest of the three daughters, coheirs, of Richard Jennings, Esq. of Sunbridge, near St. Albans: her mother was Frances Thornhurst, daughter of Sir Gifford Thornhurst, a Kentish baronet. If we may give any credit whatever to the *on dits* of that time, the mother of Miss Jennings was more remarkable for her beauty than her discretion. Of the two other daughters, Barbara became the wife of Mr. Griffiths, a man of large fortune, and of her we hear no more. Sarah, who was younger than Frances by twelve or fourteen years, became the famous Duchess of Marlborough.

Miss Jennings was about sixteen when she was appointed Maid of Honour to the Duchess of York. She had no sooner made her appearance in the court circle, than she was at once proclaimed "oltre le belle, bella!" Over Miss Hamilton and Miss Stewart she had the advantage of youth and novelty, and over the others every advantage of mind and person. Her form was that of a young Aurora, newly descended to the earth; she never moved without discovering some new charm, or developing some new grace. Her eyes and hair were light, and her complexion transcendently fair; but the rich profusion of her long tresses, the animated bloom upon her cheek, and the varying expression of her countenance and smile, left her nothing of that *fadeur* which often accompanies exceeding fairness of complexion. Her mouth, as Hamilton tells us, was not perhaps the smallest, but was certainly the loveliest mouth in the world. But Nature, in forming this exquisite *chef d'œuvre*, had in mercy to mankind left part of her handiwork imperfect. Some critics declared that the tip of her nose was not *de la dernière délicatesse;* that her hands and arms were not quite worthy of the small foot and delicate ankle; and it was admitted that her eyes were not quite as perfect as her mouth. To her external attractions, Miss Jennings added what was rarely met with in the court of Charles,—all the witchery of mind, and all the dignity of virtue. Her conversation and deportment were alike irresistible, from a just and delightful mixture of softness and sprightliness. A little petulance and caprice of temper; a little heedlessness of manner; a good deal of her sex's pride, yet more vanity; a quickness of imagination which sometimes hurried her to the very verge of an imprudence, and a natural acuteness and readiness of wit which as often extricated her,—

"Yielding by nature, stubborn but for fame;"

such, in early youth, was the character of La Belle Jennings.

No sooner had the Duke of York beheld this fair frigate sailing in the wake of his consort, than he regarded her, as did others, as his predestinate and lawful prize, upon the principle which his brother Charles had created into "a right divine," viz.—that his wife's Maids of Honour were bound to *his* service as well as hers. The duke preferred his suit, and found, to his unspeakable surprise, that Miss Jennings did not subscribe to his favourite doctrine of non-resistance. His Highness, who seems to have made love " avec toute la grâce d'une chénille qui se traine sur les roses," paraded his awkward devotion without scruple or disguise. He began by opening a battery of glances,—Miss Jennings looked another way. He next found words of pretty plain import,—Miss Jennings was either deaf, or most respectfully slow of comprehension. His presents were as ill received as his protestations, and his magnificent promises excited only a smile,—beautiful indeed, but without even an accompanying blush to soften its provoking—its poignant significancy.

The duke could not believe in his own defeat. It is true, he had lately brooked a repulse from the high-born, high-minded Miss

Hamilton, who had the blood of half the nobility in her veins; but the spirit of this daughter of a country squire was an unheard-of assumption. "Que faire pour apprivoiser une impertinente vertu qui ne voulait point entendre raison?" He next tried the effect of billets-doux; and finding there was no other way to ensure their reception, he became his own Mercury. Day after day he contrived to insinuate into the fair lady's pocket, or into her muff, notes in the usual style,—prodigal of oaths, vows, promises. As etiquette did not allow Miss Jennings to fling them back in his highness's face, she affected perfect unconsciousness, and only waiting till he turned away, carelessly drew out her handkerchief, or shook her muff, and, lo! a shower of royal billets-doux; which fell around her for the edification of whoever might choose to pick them up.* The gentlemen wondered; the ladies tittered; the poor duchess,† who, in her adventitious elevation, sighed, and " was no duchess at her heart," could not but forgive an impertinence which avenged her. The duke, angry and disconcerted, but too cold and proud to persist in a suit which only rendered him ridiculous, carried his "lourds hommages" to the feet of Miss Churchill, and found that she at least was inclined "to listen to reason."

The fame of Miss Jennings now spread from St. James's to Whitehall;‡ so much beauty, so much vivacity, and so much discretion, appeared incomprehensible. The King himself was piqued to enter the lists, merely, as he said, to convince himself that it was to the unskilful tactics of the gentleman, not to the virtue of the lady, that this marvel was to be attributed. He set himself,

---

* Miss Jennings here recalls to mind a story told, I believe, by Madame de Sévigné. One of the French princes of the blood having addressed a pretty *bourgeoise* rather disrespectfully, she replied with indignation, "Pour Dieu! Monseigneur, votre Altesse a la bonté d'être trop insolente!"

† Anne Hyde.

‡ At this time St. James's Palace was the residence of the Duke and Duchess of York: the King held his court at Whitehall.

therefore, first half seriously, and then in very resolute earnest, to study Miss Jennings's fortifications. What might have been the event, history does not presume to guess; but, apparently, his progress was not encouraging, and Miss Stewart, who was then at the height of her power, was not inclined to give way to this new rival. She was seized with a fit of pouting and penitence,—dropped some hints about the Duke of Richmond, or a convent, which brought the volatile monarch back to his allegiance, and all the honours of his supposed discomfiture rested with Miss Jennings. Scandal was silenced by a triumph which confounded all the calculations of the most knowing in these matters. Those who had ever entertained hopes or designs unworthy of their object now shrunk aloof, despairing to succeed where a King and a Prince had failed; and honourable suitors flocked around her.

Just at this crisis, Richard Talbot returned from Ireland, whither he had gone to forget Miss Hamilton's charms and cruelty, but apparently without success. On his arrival in the court, he found Miss Jennings the last new topic of discourse. All voices were raised in admiration of her charms, and wonder at her prudence,—a prudence which so little accorded with the lively and almost too unguarded frankness of her manner.

Dick Talbot, for so he was familiarly designated, was descended from a younger branch of the Talbots of Malahide, who had been settled in Ireland since the days of Henry II. He had attended on the royal brothers in their exile, and to the Duke of York he was devotedly and blindly attached, partly from a principle of loyalty, and partly from a feeling of gratitude.

He was accounted the finest figure and the tallest man in the kingdom, and set off his noble form by a peculiar loftiness in his deportment. For his character, it seems to have combined extremes of good and ill. He was dissipated, rapacious, boastful, overbearing; loving bold ends for the sake of their boldness;

witty, generous, devoted to his friends; of great talents, headlong passions, and reckless valour.*

It had been suspected, before Talbot's departure for Ireland, that Miss Boynton, one of Queen Catherine's Maids of Honour, had indulged for him some partial and fond regards; and on his re-appearance at court, before he was introduced to Miss Jennings, the love-lorn nymph signalized her tenderness by fainting away. Talbot, as a man and an Irishman, could not behold a lady in such a pitiful case without feeling a wish to console her, particularly as Miss Boynton was really very pretty and elegant, though on the smallest and most fairy-like scale of beauty; he therefore began to pay her some attentions. Before he had proceeded beyond a few tender glances and equivocal compliments, the destinies placed Miss Jennings before him in all her unrivalled attractions; Miss Boynton was forgotten, and Miss Hamilton no longer regretted; and as modesty was not among Talbot's qualifications, he at once threw himself at her feet, and tendered himself to her acceptance.

We have reason to suppose that Miss Jennings, though something of a coquette, was *coquette par calcul*, rather than by instinct. She had no desire to extend her conquests, nor to remain in a court, the dangers of which she began to comprehend; she wished to surrender honourably, and to secure a good establishment. But though the fine exterior and imposing manners of Talbot could not be disregarded, and his fortune and favour at court had due influence, his self-sufficiency seems to have a little shocked her high spirit: he was more favourably received than any former suitor, but he was not at once accepted. Talbot, who rightly thought that a woman who hesitates may be considered as won,

* The unfavourable character which Clarendon has drawn of Richard Talbot should be taken with much reservation, when we remember that the Chancellor *allows*, in so many words, that he was noted for having a prejudice against all the Talbots.

pressed his suit with all the impetuosity of his character. The court considered them all but affianced, when a trifling circumstance destroyed his hopes when nearest their completion, and to all human probability for ever.

Miss Price, who has already been mentioned, still resided in the court; but from being a Maid of Honour, had sunk into the office of bedchamber woman to the Duchess of Cleveland. The worse than equivocal character of Miss Price was perhaps unknown to Miss Jennings, while her wit, good-humour, and conversational powers captivated her, particularly as she took every opportunity of cultivating her good graces. At that time the multifarious occupations and amusements, which women of moderate fortune and comparatively confined education now command, were unknown; and we can scarcely, in these days, estimate the value of an entertaining companion to those who had few resources and lively spirits; to those who had no taste for the *fadeurs* of the eternal French romances; as little for the excitements of hunt-the-slipper and blind-man's-buff, and still less for the mysteries of chain-point and cross-stitch.*

* "Women in those days," says a lively writer, "possessed few of the means of self-amusement now in the hands of almost all the world. Music was cultivated by none but those whose strong natural taste and talent for it made them overcome all obstacles in its pursuit; drawing, or any taste for the fine arts, seems never to have been thought of, either as an employment of the hands, or a cultivation of the mind. In spite, therefore, of the numberless tapestry chairs, carpets, beds, and hangings, now, for the most part, discarded in rags from the garrets of their grand-daughters, an unsatisfied curiosity yet remains as to the amusements of the younger women, whose fortune and rank elevated them above the common every-day household cares of existence."

The following entry in Pepys' Diary, is extremely amusing and characteristic of the manners of the times. "We found them (the Duke and Duchess of York) at dinner in the great room, unhung; and there was with them my Lady Duchess of Monmouth, the Countess of Falmouth, Castlemaine, Henrietta Hide, my Lady Hinchingbroke's sister, and my Lady Peterborough; and, after dinner, Sir James Smith and I were invited down to dinner with some of the Maids of Honour; namely, Mrs. Ogle, Blake, and Howard, (which did me good to have the honour to dine with and look on), and the mother of the maids, and Mrs. Howard, the

But while Miss Jennings encouraged Miss Price's visits as a cordial against *ennui*, and became every day fonder of her society, Talbot viewed this intimacy with deep and well-founded disgust. He ventured to remonstrate, but in doing so, assumed a tone which Miss Jennings thought more suitable to a husband of ten years' standing, than a lover not yet accepted. Her high spirit was up in arms, and she received his interference with such pointed displeasure, and replied with such stinging raillery, that Talbot for awhile stood aloof in all the sullenness of offended pride. Miss Jennings, who was not very deeply in love, contrived to console herself; and poor Talbot, unable to carry on his assumed coldness, was again at her feet, all penitence and submission, but was received with such a scornful air, that he suspected a rival in the heart of his imperious mistress, and discovered him at last where he would least have expected to find him.

Le Petit Jermyn, who had been banished from the court on account of the Duchess of Cleveland, had lately re-appeared, and absence had not dissipated the dazzling halo with which fashion and fancy had arrayed his empty head and insignificant person.

This prince of coxcombs cast his eyes on Miss Jennings. She was young, with little experience, and much vanity: to bring to her feet a man who was *le terreur des maris, et le fléau des amans*,—the desperation of men and the perdition of women,—seemed a conquest worthy of her; and in the effort to fix this formidable rake, her own feelings became entangled before she was aware. The thinking part of the court, (if indeed there were any who thought,) wondered to see the proud, the fair, the elegant Frances

---

mother of the Maid of Honour of that name, and the duke's housekeeper here. * * * Having dined very merrily, we went up, and there I did find the Duke of York and Duchesse, with all the great ladies, sitting upon a carpet on the ground, there being no chairs, playing at 'I love my love with an A, because he is so and so; and I hate him with an A, because this and that;' and some of them, but particularly the Duchesse herself and my Lady Castlemaine, were very witty."

Jennings caught in so flimsy a net; and Jermyn plumed himself, as he justly might, on the preference of one so lovely, and hitherto so circumspect. Meantime the Duchess of York began to feel a real and affectionate interest for Miss Jennings; and as she had refused the protection of the duke, her own, in the fullest sense of the word, she was now resolved to extend to her. She spoke to Jermyn herself, who declared that his intentions towards Miss Jennings were strictly honourable. The duchess failed not to publish his reply; and Miss Jennings was congratulated on having reduced the invincible Jermyn to matrimony and good behaviour. Talbot, enraged at the levity of his mistress, yet more enraged by the contemptible rival she had given him, withdrew, after an ineffectual attempt to win back her heart: in a moment of pique he offered himself to the languishing Miss Boynton, and was accepted.

Whether Miss Jennings heard of this with perfect indifference may be doubted; but Jermyn was heir to an earldom, and twenty thousand a-year,* and moreover was very much in love — or seemed so: she therefore consoled herself; only she wondered not a little why the gentleman did not press for the possession of a hand which waited but the formal question to be bestowed on him, in her heart contrasting his nonchalance with the ardour and assurance of Talbot. Still, as day after day passed, her wonder grew; and as her wonder grew her love declined.

It was now that Rochester put in practice that celebrated frolic so amusingly related in De Grammont, and so gravely recorded by his biographer Bishop Burnet.† Being forbidden the court, he assumed the disguise of a German astrologer and physician, and undertook to reveal the past and future to all whom curiosity or credulity might lead to his enchanted den, somewhere near the

* He was heir to his uncle, the rich old Earl of St. Albans.
† *Vide* Life and Death of Wilmot, Earl of Rochester. The same freak was played by Sir Francis Delaval in the last century.—See the Life of Mr. Edgeworth.

precincts of Drury-lane.* Rochester's wit and self-possession, and his knowledge of all the private scandal of the town, gave him an advantage over all the conjurors before or since. The fame of his extraordinary revelations reached the court, and spread astonishment and consternation through the whole tribe of abigails: even the Maids of Honour began to flutter with wonder, curiosity, and apprehension. Miss Price failed not to entertain her young friend with all the gossip concerning this astrologer; and as she talked, Miss Jennings grew pensive. She was seized with a violent inclination to consult this wonderful man, who might, perhaps, be able to explain what appeared so inexplicable in the conduct of her lover. Her precious confidante assured her that nothing was more easy; and, after some consultation, they agreed to dress themselves up as orange-girls, in hoods and serge petticoats, and each a basket under her arm, and thus proceed to the den of the magician. To disguise the round vulgar figure of Miss Price was not difficult; but the distinguished air of Miss Jennings, whose figure and step were those of a young wood-nymph, could scarcely be concealed by any costume. Like the goddess in the Eneid, whose gait betrayed her through her mortal guise, so this "fair young celestial" stood revealed through her homely attire. Though perfectly conscious of her own attractions, of this natural consequence of superior beauty, she was unhappily unconscious, and the two damsels errant set forth boldly. They made their way from St. James's, through the Park, to Charing-cross, got into a hackney-coach, and desired the man to drive to the residence of the conjuror.

On their way they passed the theatre, called then the Duke's House, where the Queen and the Duchess of York were seated in

* The neighbourhood of Drury-lane was then the fashionable part of the town, and Bow-street, Covent-garden, was the Bond-street of that day, the lounge and resort of all the wits and the beaux. Dryden somewhere mentions a lady as overwhelmed with billets-doux from Bow-street; on which Sir Walter Scott observes, that, in these latter times, a billet-doux from Bow-street would be much more alarming than flattering.

state. Miss Price, whose spirits were raised to a wild pitch of extravagance, was of opinion that it would infinitely add to the jest of their escapade, if they were to alight, and offer their oranges for sale under the Duchess of York's box. To this Miss Jennings consented; but just at the entrance of the lobby they encountered Le Beau Sydney, who was hastening to pay his court to the duchess.* He passed them, humming an air and combing his voluminous wig, too much occupied with his own graces to notice those which lurked under the little hood, and were now averted from his gaze. Not so Killigrew, who next advanced: he was struck at once by the nymph-like gait and air which broke through all disguise, and accosted the pretended orange-girl with a freedom which at once offended and terrified her. She began to think that she might sell her oranges too dear; and Miss Price, observing that her indignation would betray her if her fears did not, drew her away in haste. They escaped through the crowd; and calling another hackney-coach, they again set forward, like Britomart and Glaucé of old,† " disguised in base attire," to seek the cave of Merlin.

Miss Jennings, whose courage was by this time oozing from the tips of her pretty fingers, still trembled with recent agitation when the coach stopped. Miss Price, whose mind was rather more disengaged, beheld, as she looked up, a pair of eyes fixed on them with a sort of exulting and malignant leer which made her blood run cold: they were the very last she would have chosen to meet on such an occasion,—those of the witty, insolent, cynical, profligate Brounker; who, being one of the Duke of York's equerries, was perfectly well acquainted with them both. Miss Price, in her fright, desired the coachman to drive on, and set them down a few yards in advance. Brounker, whose curiosity was strongly excited, followed with the perseverance of a sleuth-hound. The coach door opened. Miss Jennings first stepped out; and, to his

* He was said at the time to be in love with the Duchess of York, or she with him.—See Pepys.

† Faerie Queene, book iii. canto iii.

astonishment, an exquisite little foot, in an embroidered slipper, was disclosed from beneath the coarse serge petticoat. They now stood completely betrayed, and the cynical Brounker was enchanted by the discovery. He entertained the most degrading opinion of the sex generally; and in proportion as the modesty and prudence of Miss Jennings had hitherto disconcerted all his preconceived notions on the subject, was his delight to find her (as he supposed) "no better than one of those to whom the vulgar give bold titles." He addressed them, therefore, in their assumed characters with so much freedom and insolence, that Miss Jennings lost the little self-possession which remained to her, and Miss Price herself knew not which way to look. While Brounker enjoyed and prolonged their embarrassment, some little blackguards in the street began to steal their oranges; the hackney-coachman thought it incumbent on him to protect his fare, and a squabble ensued. A crowd collected; and the hateful Brounker, having just waited to see them in almost inextricable distress and confusion, and without an attempt to rescue them, glided away through the crowd, exulting in the idea of the exposure he anticipated. The terrified damsels, abandoning their oranges to the enemy, scrambled into their coach and returned to the palace; Miss Jennings lamenting her imprudence, and declaring that nothing should induce her to proceed, and Miss Price reviling the stars, as "more in fault than they."

The malice of Brounker was so far disappointed, that though the story got abroad, and was related with the usual malicious exaggeration, it fixed no stigma on Miss Jennings; who, probably, on seeing the dilemma in which she was placed, had sense enough and wit enough to join in the laugh at her own folly. It appears that the duchess pardoned her *étourderie*.* We hear no more of Miss Price and her dangerous visits, and Jermyn continued his attentions in a manner which kept all competitors at a

---

* This adventure occurred about the beginning of February 1665, as appears from Pepys' Diary, where it is mentioned incidentally among the gossip of the day. Vol. i. p. 331.

distance, but still without proposing that critical and definitive question which his impatient mistress longed to hear.

While week after week thus passed, and Miss Jennings fretted at her lover's unaccountable and capricious delays, the government planned an expedition to the coast of Guinea, and the command was given to Prince Rupert. The fame of the leader, and the dangers of the expedition, fired the imagination of the young cavaliers; and all who wished to give themselves *éclat* in the eyes of the public or their mistresses, volunteered to follow the prince. Amongst others, to the astonishment of the whole court, Jermyn asked and obtained permission to serve in this expedition. Such a step, taken at such a time, without the slightest reference to her wishes, or any explanation on his part, appeared to Miss Jennings equally ridiculous and insulting. It at once dissipated all illusion, and cured her of a passion which was more a fancy than a feeling. Jermyn, whose heartless coxcombry could not estimate the value of the heart with which he trifled, and who enjoyed the idea of calling up some tender tears of regret into the eyes of his fair one, waited on her to impart his warlike projects, and had prepared himself to resist, most heroically, her despair and her terrors at the dangers to which he was about to expose his valuable person; but, instead of finding a dishevelled Ariadne, he was much surprised when the high-spirited Jennings received him with a smile, rallied him with the most poignant wit on his sudden love of glory, and then giving him to understand that she considered this as a final farewell, and had not the slightest wish to see him again, she civilly wished him *bon voyage,* and curtsied him out of the room.

Not satisfied with this private vengeance, she composed a ludicrous parody on one of Ovid's Epistles, addressed to Jermyn; some copies of which were dispersed through the court, and covered him with ridicule. It happened, after all, that Jermyn did not sail with the Guinea fleet; but Miss Jennings never gave him another opportunity of pretending to her hand. All his attempts to reinstate himself in her good graces were treated with scorn. She would not even listen to him; and after awhile, felt that to be rid of such a pitiful lover, was not so much a loss, as an escape.

She was in temper as little inclined to indulge eternal regrets, as Jermyn was formed to inspire them; and soon she shone forth afresh in all the lustre of her beauty. The proof she had just given, that where pride and feeling were touched she could rise superior to vanity and interest, lent to her character a higher value, and to her youth and loveliness an additional charm. Numberless suitors now pressed around her: among them George Hamilton, (the younger brother of Miss Hamilton,) who has been so frequently mentioned.* He was young, noble, handsome, brave, good-natured — in short, he had but one fault; he had the trick of falling sincerely and desperately in love with every beautiful face that smiled upon him. His heart was a perfect furnace, which never lacked fuel. He had lately been jilted by Lady Chesterfield, and entangled by the coquetry of Miss Stewart; but again free, the sparkling graces of Miss Jennings were not likely to be lost on such an inflammable subject. He was captivated at once, and though he was not "*du bois dont on fait de grandes passions,*" he was for this time very seriously and sighingly in love.

Hamilton's gay inconstancy was very different from levity, he was not a man who would lightly trust his honour to the keeping of a woman who could lightly esteem her own. He was but a younger brother, with a younger brother's portion; and Miss Jennings, in frankly accepting his addresses, gave the best proof that the insinuation conveyed in De Grammont, of her being cold and self-interested, is altogether unfounded.

They were married in the year 1665. Hamilton soon after accepted military rank in the French service; and after receiving the honour of knighthood from Charles II., went over to France,

* See the Memoirs of Lady Chesterfield and Miss Stewart.

accompanied by his wife. It appears that he greatly distinguished himself abroad; though for what particular exploits he was soon after created by Louis XIV. Count and Mareschal-de-Camp, does not appear. He was unfortunately killed in Flanders within a few years after his marriage.*

It is to be regretted that the personal notices of Lady Hamilton —or the Countess Hamilton, as she is generally styled — are henceforth extremely confused and obscure: to connect these, and to reconcile various and opposing dates, has been a matter of some difficulty. She could not have been more than two-and-twenty when she was left a beautiful widow with three infant daughters; and, it appears, that after her husband's death she had a pension from France, and returned to England, where her daughters were certainly educated.

The next notice I find of her is in Evelyn's Diary: he notes that when the Earl of Berkeley was appointed Ambassador Extraordinary to Paris in 1675 (for the arrangement of the treaty of Nimeguen,) he accompanied the earl and his suite as far as Dover. "There was," he adds, "in the company of my Lady Ambassadress, my Lady Hamilton, a sprightly young lady, much in the good graces of the family, wife of that valiant and worthy gentleman, George Hamilton, not long afterwards slain in the wars.†

---

* It is difficult to reconcile the dates in the peerages with the occurrences: the death of Sir George Hamilton was placed in 1667, and it is said that he left three daughters. Now it is clear from Pepys' Diary, that Miss Jennings was still unmarried in the beginning of the year 1665; and from a passage in Evelyn, hereafter quoted, I am inclined to place his death much later. In the notes to the Life of Lady Russell, this Sir George Hamilton is confounded with the Colonel Hamilton (his younger brother, I believe), who was taken prisoner at the battle of the Boyne.

† *Query*—Not long after his marriage, or not long after the date of this memorandum? Evelyn is frequently careless and obscure in the arrangement of his sentences, else we might presume with certainty that Sir George Hamilton was at this time (1675) living.

She had been Maid of Honour to the duchess, and now turned Papist."

The conversion of Lady Hamilton to the Roman Catholic faith, appears a very natural consequence of her feelings and position, both before and after her marriage: the Duchess of York, her patroness, had formally renounced Protestantism, to the horror of her father Lord Clarendon, and the consternation of Dr. Burnet, who had previously had the charge of her conscience. All the Hamiltons were Catholics; and, whatever were the motives, whether feeling, or conviction, or expediency, which induced Lady Hamilton to change her religion, such change was in the sequel sincere, and adhered to with constancy and fervour.

It must have been within the next two years, and while abroad with the Countess of Berkeley, that she again met Talbot, who was residing in France, an exile,—not by the course of justice, but certainly not voluntarily, from his own country. He had always been distinguished as a bigoted Papist, and a devoted adherent of the Duke of York; and while the Popish plot and the Exclusion Bill inflamed the public mind, his master had insisted on his absence as a means of personal safety. The lovers met again, thus unexpectedly, after a separation of many years, each freed from all former ties, for Talbot was now a widower without children. In her, time and sorrow had subdued the petulance of early feelings; but still young and not less beautiful than ever, Talbot could not behold her without acknowledging at once "*il segno del antica fiamma.*" And, in short, they were married at Paris about the year 1679.

They were again in England in 1683 and 1684.* Talbot still held his office of groom of the chamber to the Duke of York, and

* It should seem that Talbot was enabled to return to England through the mediation of the Duke of Ormond, whom he is said to have requited very ungratefully, by plotting the duke's recall from the Irish government in 1684.— *Vide* Diary and Correspondence of Henry Earl of Clarendon.

still kept his place in his favour and confidence; while his beautiful wife became as great a favourite with the new Duchess of York, (Maria d'Este,) as she had been with the former one. On the death of Charles II. and the accession of the duke, in 1685, he rewarded the steady and devoted attachment of Talbot by creating him Earl of Tyrconnel; and he was sent to take the command of the King's forces, and support the Roman Catholic interest in Ireland, whither Lady Tyrconnel accompanied him.

The Earl of Clarendon, son of the great Chancellor, was Lord-Lieutenant. The military and civil government were thus divided; and the continual disagreement between Clarendon and Tyrconnel, opposed as they were in religion, politics, temper, and character, kept Ireland in a state of distraction for the next few years. It must be allowed, that while Talbot possessed many splendid qualities, his manners were ill calculated to conciliate exasperated minds. He was insolent and violent, even to the verge of brutality; and when under the slightest excitation, every second word was a tremendous oath.* The spirit and temper of his wife were of a more intellectual order, and she is said to have ruled him without much effort; but, as all her prejudices and passions held the same direction, she on many occasions only added the fuel of her feminine impatience to his headlong self-will.

* The "swaggering" deportment of Talbot is very graphically described in some of Clarendon's letters; but we must recollect that all the usual authorities on the subject of Talbot's character and government are liable to suspicion, as proceeding from party animosity. Clarendon had inherited his father's hatred of the Talbots; and Talbot, who knew but one means to a given end, the short cut of violence, detested the slow, temporizing, insinuating policy of Clarendon. "Two qualities Talbot possessed in an eminent degree—wit and valour: and if to gifts so brilliant and so Irish be joined devotion to his country, and fidelity to the unfortunate and fated family with whose exile he began life, and with whose ruin he finished it, it cannot be denied that in his character the elements of evil were mixed with much great and striking good. Under happier circumstances, the good might have predominated; and he whose deeds are held, even by his own family, in such right estimation, might have shed a lustre on his race by those talents and heroism, which gave force to his passions and celebrity to his errors."
—Lady Morgan.

Lord Melfort, one of James's accredited agents in Ireland, speaks of Lady Tyrconnel's influence over her husband;* complains in his letters of her dissimulation and her intriguing propensities; and asserts that the King's affairs will never go well till she is persuaded to leave Ireland, and return to France. But before we attach too much importance to Lord Melfort's opinion, we should consider that he hated Lady Tyrconnel, and was himself of a temper so impatient, officious, and meddling, that he became insupportable even to those whom he most wished to serve: he is accused of embroiling the King's affairs both in Ireland and at St. Germain's, and was at length sent out of the way, under the pretence of a mission to Rome. It is also observable that, though we have few particulars of the conduct of Lady Tyrconnel during this eventful period, the terms in which she is alluded to are generally favourable to her character, and leave a strong impression of her talents and her prudence, as well as of her influence.

At the Revolution, Tyrconnel, faithful to the interest of his old master, refused to take the oath of allegiance to William III., and placed himself at the head of King James's party in Ireland; and James rewarded his fidelity by sending him over the patent of Viceroy, and appointing him Commander-in-Chief. Lady Tyrconnel, from this time, resided in Dublin Castle with her three beautiful daughters, now growing into womanhood. She held her state as Vice-queen with much grace and magnificence; and while her sister, Lady Churchill, threw all the weight of her influence, talents, and spirit into the opposite party, she supported with yet more enthusiasm the interests of the exiled family, in which all the Hamiltons and all the Talbots were engaged heart and soul.

It was during her reign in Ireland,—for such it might truly be called,—that Lady Tyrconnel married her three daughters by

---

* In allusion to some measures they were then contemplating, he says pointedly, "This will draw in my lady, and consequently my lord," &c.—*Vide* Macpherson's State Papers.

Hamilton to three of the wealthiest and most powerful among the Irish nobles. Elizabeth, the eldest, became the wife of Laurence, first Viscount Rosse; Frances, the second and most beautiful of the three, married Henry, eighth Viscount Dillon; and Mary, the youngest, married Nicholas Viscount Kingsland. They have since been distinguished as "the three Viscountesses."

In 1689, when James II. had resolved to try his fortune in Ireland, he was met by Tyrconnel and a numerous train of gallant and devoted followers, and conducted to Dublin Castle, where Lady Tyrconnel entertained him and his foreign and Irish adherents with French urbanity and Irish hospitality. On this occasion Tyrconnel was advanced to the dignity of Marquis and Duke of Tyrconnel, and received from the King every mark of affection and confidence. Six months afterwards the battle of the Boyne was fought, in which fifteen Talbots of Tyrconnel's family were slain, and he himself fought like a hero of romance. After that memorable defeat, King James and Tyrconnel reached Dublin on the evening of the same day. The duchess, who had been left in the castle, had passed four-and-twenty hours in all the agonies of suspense; but when the worst was known, she showed that the spirit and strength of mind which had distinguished her in her early days was not all extinguished. When the King and her husband arrived as fugitives from the lost battle, on which her fortunes and her hopes had depended, harassed, faint, and so covered with mud that their persons could scarcely be distinguished, she, hearing of their plight, assembled all her household in state, dressed herself richly, and received the fugitive King and his dispirited friends with all the splendour of court etiquette. Advancing to the head of the grand staircase with all her attendants, she kneeled on one knee, congratulated him on his safety, and invited him to a banquet; respectfully inquiring what refreshment he would be pleased to take at the moment. James answered, sadly, that he had but little stomach for supper, considering the sorry breakfast he had made that morning. She, however, led the way to a banquet already prepared; and did the honours with as

much self-possession and dignity as Lady Macbeth, though racked
at the moment with equal terror and anxiety.

The next day a council was held, when, in spite of the advice of
the Duke and Duchess of Tyrconnel, James acceded to the wishes
of Lauzun and his French followers, who were panic-struck, and
determined on flying to France. In the confused accounts of the
movements of the two parties at this time, we find no farther
mention made of the Duchess of Tyrconnel, whose situation must
have been in the highest degree interesting and agitating: it
appears, however, that she and her husband quitted Ireland, either
in company with the King, or immediately after him, leaving her
three married daughters, and taking with her her two children by
Tyrconnel. She joined the exiled court at St. Germain's, where
she remained for several years.

In the troublesome times which ensued, Tyrconnel continued
to maintain the cause of James II. in Ireland with unshaken
loyalty and courage, through evil repute and good repute: he
was destined, however, to exhibit another proof of that ingratitude which has been the stigma of the whole race of Stuart, and
the curse of those who were devoted to its fortunes. Talbot, who
hated the French party, and was disgusted by their insolence and
exactions, threw himself into the Irish party; and it is even said
that his first wish (so changed was he now by time, and cares, and
calamity,) was to give peace to his own wretched country by
acting as moderator between all the factions.* However this
may be, King James became mistrustful of his old and faithful
servant; and, with a thankless duplicity, sent over a commission,
superseding Tyrconnel in all his governments and the chief command: but so loved as well as feared was Tyrconnel throughout
the whole country, that it was deemed necessary to keep this commission and his disgrace a profound secret. At length, in 1691,
when preparing to defend Limerick for the second time against
William III., Tyrconnel died suddenly by poison administered in

* Harris's Life of William III.

a cup of ratafia. The times were so critical, his enemies were so numerous and bitter, and his friends so divided and so wrong-headed, that his death caused only a temporary excitement: the siege went on, and the celebrated Sarsfield succeeded Talbot in the chief command.*

After the death of her husband, the Duchess of Tyrconnel continued to reside abroad till the dispersion of the court of St. Germain's, and the marriage of her daughters by Talbot. During this time she appears to have been reduced to great distress and poverty, for she is mentioned among the poor Jacobites who were assisted out of the pension which James II. received from the Pope. She received on this occasion three thousand crowns, (about four hundred pounds), but it was only temporary relief. In 1705 she was in England, and had a private interview with her brother-in-law, the Duke of Marlborough, then at the height of his power. Respecting her visit to England, Horace Walpole relates a singular anecdote, for which he does not give his authority; but he was personally acquainted with so many of the family, that his own authority, as the very prince of biographical gossip, may be considered all-sufficient.

At that time, part of the Royal Exchange was let out in small stalls or shops, perhaps something like a modern bazaar, and was a favourite and fashionable resort of women of the highest rank. It is said that the Duchess of Tyrconnel, being reduced to absolute want on her arrival in England, and unable for some time to procure secret access to her family, hired one of the stalls under the Royal Exchange, and maintained herself by the sale of small articles of haberdashery. She wore a white dress wrapping her

* Limerick surrendered on the 13th of October, 1691. The first siege of Limerick, in August 1690, when Tyrconnel and the Duke de Lauzun nobly defended it, and obliged William III. to raise the siege, is famous in the military history of Ireland; and the second siege, which ended in the surrender of the city, is yet more fatally celebrated in the political annals of that miserable country.

whole person, and a white mask, which she never removed, and excited much interest and curiosity.

It is now very well known, that the Duke of Marlborough was at this time carrying on some intrigues with the exiled court and the leading Jacobites; and it is possible, and very probable, that his interview with the Duchess of Tyrconnel was partly of a political nature: this, however, can only be presumed. The more apparent result of this visit was, that she obtained the restoration of a small part of her husband's property, with permission to reside in Dublin. To that city, perhaps endeared to her as the scene of past happiness, and power, and splendour, she returned in 1706, a widow, poor, proscribed, and broken-hearted. The account of the last years of this celebrated beauty, and really admirable and distinguished woman, cannot be contemplated without a sad and serious feeling. While her high-spirited sister, the Duchess of Marlborough, was ruling the councils of England, or playing a desperate and contemptible game for power,—the sport of her own turbulent passions, and the victim of the perfidy and the artifices of others,—the Duchess of Tyrconnel withdrew from the world: she established on the site of her husband's house, in King-street, a nunnery of the order of Poor Clares, and she passed, in retreat and the practice of the most austere devotion, the rest of her varied life. Her death was miserable: one cold wintry night, during an intense frost, she fell out of her bed; and being too feeble to rise or call for assistance, she was discovered next morning lying on the floor in a state of insensibility. It was found impossible to restore warmth or motion to her frozen limbs; and after lingering a few hours in a half lethargic state, she gradually sank into death. She expired on the 20th of February, 1730, in her eighty-second year; and on the 9th of March following, she was interred in the cathedral church of St. Patrick.

Her eldest daughter by the Duke of Tyrconnel, Lady Charlotte Talbot, was married to the Prince de Vintimiglia, and left two daughters: the eldest married the Comte de Verac, and the other the Neapolitan Prince Belmonte; but both died without leaving any offspring. Of the youngest Lady Talbot, I find no account.

Of the "three Viscountesses," Lady Dillon appears to have been the most remarkable, and to have inherited, with the high blood of the Hamiltons, no small share of that lively and wilful temper which distinguished her mother's family. There is a curious tradition respecting her still preserved among the peasantry of the country in which she resided. It is related that, on the death of Lord Dillon, she inhabited Laughlin Castle, then only one of the numerous castles and palaces possessed by the Irish Dillons. This princely feudal edifice covered two acres of land; and, with the estate round it, was assigned to her as her jointure, but with the proviso, that she should reside during her life in the castle. The lady, in her widowhood, was seized with a passion for a young Englishman; and being unable to detain him with her, or to follow him to England as long as her castle existed, she determined on the wildest and boldest project that ever entered the head of an impetuous woman borne away by the violence of passion: she ordered a banquet to be spread in her garden, then fired the castle, and feasted by the light of the blazing pile. After supper, and while the towers were yet burning, she set off for England with her lover.

Such is the tale of the peasantry round Laughlin Castle; and it must be allowed that there are few anecdotes more striking and picturesque to be found in the chronicles of romance.

The present Viscount Dillon is the lineal descendant of La Belle Jennings. Arthur Dillon, who was guillotined during the French Revolution, was her great-great-great-grandson; his daughter, Fanny Dillon, married General Count Bertrand, celebrated for his fidelity to Napoleon, and his long residence at St. Helena.

Portraits of the Duchess of Tyrconnel are extremely rare, and those engraved for the various editions of De Grammont are all fictitious. The engraving, which forms the frontispiece to this work, is from an original picture in the possession of Earl Spencer.

[It seems not to have been in 1705, but in 1708, that Lady Tyrconnel visited England. The correspondence of her sister, the Duchess of Marlborough, lately published by Mr. Colburn, seems to set at least the manner of her visit, and the conduct of the Duke of Marlborough, in a light entirely different from that in which it appears in the foregoing narrative. The Duke was in Flanders, occupied in the movements which preceded the battle of Oudenarde. On the 14th of May, he writes to the duchess, from Brussels, " I went yesterday to wait upon Lady Tyrconnel, who I think is grown very old, and her hoarseness much worse than when I saw her last." Three days after, May 17, he again writes, " I was yesterday a long while with Lady Tyrconnel, who complains very much of the non-payment of their rents; by what they say, I am afraid they are very unjustly dealt with." On the 24th of the same month, the duke says, " When I took leave of Lady Tyrconnel, she told me that her jointure in Ireland was in such disorder, that there was an absolute necessity for her going for two or three months for the better settling of it. As the climate of Ireland will not permit her being there in the winter, she should begin her journey about ten days hence: she said that she did not intend to go to London, but hoped she might have the pleasure of seeing you at St. Albans. I have offered her all that might be in my power to make her journey to Holland and England easy. As also, that if she cared to stay at St. Albans, either at her going or return, you would offer it her with good heart. You will find her face a good deal changed, but in the discourse I have had with her, she seems to be very reasonable and kind." On the 31st, " I had a letter yesterday from your sister Lady Tyrconnel, in which she tells me that she leaves Brussels in two or three days, and that her stay in Holland will be no longer than by going by the first safe opportunity, so that you will hear very quickly from her."—ED.]

INDEX.

Admirals, Gallery of, 48.
Althorpe, Earl Spencer's mansion, described, 243, 246, 294.
Anne, Queen, 211, 247.
Arlington, Earl of, 90, 276, 277, 284, 294.
Arran, Earl of, 194, 195.
———, Countess of, [Anne Spencer] 244, 247.
Aubrey, the antiquarian, his account of Sir John Denham, 139, 141, 142.
Audley-End, a fair there, visited by Catherine and her court, 70.

Bagot, Miss Elizabeth, 212, 214; beauty of, 215; her happy union with the Earl of Falmouth, 216; her subsequent marriage with the Earl of Dorset, 218; portrait of, by Lely, 219.
———, Colonel Hervey, a royalist, 215.
Bastide, the French envoy, 57.
Beauclerc, Lord Vere, 159.
———, Lord Sidney, (father of Topham Beauclerc,) 159.
———, Lord James, 159.
Beauties of Charles II.'s court, 28; painted by Lely, 41; of 'Hampton Court,' painted by Kneller, 45; of 'the time of George III.,' painted by Reynolds, 49; of 'the Regency,' painted by Lawrence, ib.
Bellasys, Lady, her splendid portrait, 230, 235; particulars relative to her husband, 232; who was killed in a duel with Tom Porter, 233; the Duke of York's marriage contract with, 233, 234; created a Baroness, 235; marries Mr. Fortrey, 235; her son Henry, Lord Bellasys, ib.; she is well received by Queen Anne, ib.; her death, ib.
Blague, Miss, 43, 111, 214.
Blenheim Gallery, the, 26.
Boynton, Miss, 43, 321.
Bridgewater, Countess of, her personal attractions, 26, 48.
Bristol, Earl of, [George Digby] his advice to Charles II., 55, 72; court

intrigue of, 138; his daughter, Lady Sunderland, 238; his extraordinary caprices, ib.; ingratiates himself into the King's favour, ib.; his eloquence when called to the bar of the Commons, 239.
Brooke, Sir William, 138.
Brounker, Lord, a famous chess-player, 140; alluded to, 141, 326.
Buckingham, Duke of, a mad proposal of, 70, 72; disgrace of, 87; his power at Court, 94, 120; his dispute with Ossory, 130; attracted by Miss Stewart's fascinations, 176; and deceived by her, 177; his inconsistencies, 275.
———, Duchess of, 70.
Bulkeley, Lady, [Sophia Stewart] 185.
Burlington, Richard, Earl of, [Cork and] 201.
Burnet, Gilbert, Bishop of Salisbury, anecdote of, 70; employed to write in favour of a royal divorce, 72; his style, 84; allusion to, 97; speaks of Nell Gwynn, 154, 157; of Lord Clarendon's disgrace, &c. 183, 208; various allusions to, 236, 276, 295.
Butler, satires of, 37, 141; neglect of this witty and original poet, 164.
Byron, Lord, quoted, 27; stanza of, 167.
———, Lady, [Elinor Needham] 230.

Carnegie, family of, 225; their misfortunes, 228.
Castlemaine, Lady: see Duchess of Cleveland.
———, Earl of, [Roger Palmer, Esq. so created] 80, 81, 89, 91.
Catherine of Braganza: the Duke John, her father, secures the crown of Portugal, 53; the princess's education, ib.; overtures to Charles II. relative to her, 54; her dowry, 55; the portion in money left unpaid, 59; her nuptials, 60; her beauty and manners, 61; costume of, ib.; her ladies sent back to Portugal, 62; she refuses Lady Castlemaine's appointment, ib.; faints on an unexpected interview with her, 63; neg-

lected by the King, 66; her shrewd reply to Lady Castlemaine, 67; her anxiety to have children, ib.; latent affection and respect shown by the King towards her, 68; does not interfere in politics, 69; recovers her gaiety, ib.; libels and satires on, 71; accused of designs against the King, 72; but is exonerated by the monarch, 73; his death, 74; the Queen-dowager's mode of life at Somerset-house, ib.; her death at Lisbon, 75; portrait of, by Lely, ib.; character of, by Clarendon, 76; reconciled to Lady Castlemaine, ib.; her religious devotion, 93; her masked ball described, 108; letter of, 135; her reception of Miss Stewart, 182; her forbearance towards the Duchess of Portsmouth, 282.

Cavendish, Lady, [daughter of William Lord Russell] 311; letter from her, ib.; portrait of, 313.

———, Lord, 305; his extraordinary affray at Paris, 307; his parting with his friend Lord Russell, 308; his high principles of honour, 309; succeeds his father, 311; takes part in the Revolution, ib.; is created a Duke, 312.

Charles I., his portrait at Sion-house, 41; good morals and example of, 64; his ward, Lady Elizabeth Desmond, 120.

Charles II., beauty and gallantry at his Court, 28; represses luxury of dress, 31; but perseveres not in that reform, 32; a patron of music and operas, 38; portraits of, 45; obtains Bombay and Tangier, 55; said to be a Catholic, 56; political intrigue of, ib.; indignant at the presumption of Louis de Haro, the Spanish ambassador, 57; resolves on his marriage, ib.; disappointed of the Queen's dowry, 59; celebration of his marriage, 60; writes to Clarendon relative to the Queen, 61; his neglect of the Queen, 66; his attentions to her during her illness, 67; declines the proposed divorce, 70; exculpates the Queen from the accusations against her, 73; particulars relative to, 74; clandestinely visits Mrs. Palmer, 80; creates her husband an Earl, and appoints her to be one of the Queen's ladies, 81; parallel between the King and Henri Quatre, 82; his lavish grants to Lady Castlemaine, 84, 93; her violent temper, 85, 87; rivals of the King in her good graces, 88; confers new titles on her, 89; his children by her, and their titles, 90; receives a letter from her from Paris in her disgrace, 96—101; banishes her the country, 101; his conversation with the Chevalier de Grammont, 110; his letter respecting Miss Hamilton, 113; captivated by Nell Gwynn, 153, 163; how recalled by her to attendance at Council, 164; his love for Miss Stewart, 173, 178, 180; detects the Duke of Richmond with her, 181; his temporary reconciliation with her, 182; his indignation on her marriage with the Duke, 183; offers her no further molestation, 184; his dislike of the Earl of Chesterfield, 191; his grief for the death of the gallant Falmouth, 217; desires Montagu at Paris to consult a famous astrologer, 265; shameful treaty effected with, by the Duchess of Orleans, 274; is fascinated with the beauty of Mlle. de Quérouaille, 275; has a son by that lady, 277; narrowly escapes the snares of the Duchess of Mazarin, 279; jewels for his niece [Queen of Spain] intercepted by De Quérouaille, 281; becomes the slave of his mistresses, 282; obtains the sobriquet of 'Old Rowley,' 283; his treaty with Louis XIV., ib., 287; his abandonment of the national interests, 285; venality of his courtiers, 284, 285; measures of the Whigs, 285; calls no parliament, 283, 287; vexation arising to him from the treaty with France, 288; he becomes jealous of a French nobleman, 289; dies a Catholic, 290; anecdotes of, 294; death of his sister, Henrietta, by poison, 295—302; rumours as to the cause of his death, 295.

Châtillon, Chevalier de, letter from the Duchess of Cleveland respecting him, 96, 99, 100.

Chatsworth, Derbyshire, the splendid mansion of the Duke of Devonshire, 311.

Chelsea Hospital, its institution how promoted, 155, 164.

Chesterfield, Countess of, [Elizabeth Butler, daughter of the Duke of Ormond] green stockings of, 31, 195; guitar played by, 40; her talents, 175; her marriage, 190; indifference of the earl to her, 191; yet he becomes enamoured of her, 192; jealousy ensues, 192, 193; he forcibly carries her from court to his country-house, 195; she signalizes her vengeance on George Hamilton, the adviser of her abduction, 196; her daughter, Elizabeth Stanhope, becomes Countess of Strathmore, 197; her death, ib.; the earl suspected of poisoning her, 198; her portrait by Lely, ib.; allusion to, 305.

Chesterfield, Philip, Earl of, his marriage, 189; temper and character of, 190; his unhappy union, 190—195; his second Countess, 197; frightful tradition relative to, 198; his general character, 200, 305.

Churchill, Arabella, [sister of Marlborough] 314; her eldest son James Fitz-James, Duke of Berwick, 315; her union with Colonel Godfrey, ib.; her curious political position, ib.

Cibber, Colley, anecdote related by, 157.

Clancarty, Earl of, [Donogh Macarty] 244.

Clarendon, Lord Chancellor; 55; his account of the Earl of Sandwich, 58; he is ordered to reconcile Catherine of Braganza to Lady Castlemaine, 63; his diplomacy to that effect, 64; character of the Queen given by, 76; disgraced and banished from Court, 83, 183; his children, 202, 203; passages of his history, 107, 176, 210.

————, Countess of, [Theodosia Capel] 43.

————, Earl of, [son of the great Chancellor] 202, 203, 332.

"Clarendon Papers," the, 204, 332.

Cleveland, Duchess of, moral to be derived from her history, 29; appointed a lady to Queen Catherine, 62; scene at Court in consequence, 63; at length received by the Queen, 67; is familiarly treated by her, 76; her father and family, 79; her husband created Earl of Castlemaine, 80, 81; the declared mistress of Charles II. immediately after the Restoration, 80; their early correspondence, ib.; quits her husband, 82; causes the downfall of Clarendon, 83; her rapacity and extravagance, 84; her tyrannical dominion over Charles, and his submissiveness, 85, 138, &c.; resents the disgrace of Buckingham, 87; her anger renewed, the King makes his peace with her by patents of nobility, 88, 89; her notice of Wycherly, 87; confers favours on young Churchill, [Marlborough] ib.; marries Beau Fielding, 89; dies of dropsy, 90; titles of Charles II.'s descendants by this lady, ib.; her great beauty, 91, 92; visits Bartholomew Fair, 92; her portrait, ib.; resumé of her history, ib.; her influence renewed, 94; dismissed by the King into France, ib.; her extraordinary letter to Charles, 96—101; her banishment, 101; her contests with Miss Stewart, 174, 181; her spies and perfidy, 181, 265; some allusions to, 190, 192.

————, Dukes of, [an extinct peerage] 90.

Cleveland-row, Berkshire-House in, 85.

Coffee-houses, establishment of, 37.

Colbert, the French ambassador, 277.

Commons, proceedings of the House of, on the Popish plot, 73.

Cornbury, Lord, his marriage with Theodosia Capel, 183, 202.

Costume in the reign of Charles II. 29; locks flowing down the shoulders, 30; dress of the ladies, ib.; patches, 31; riding habits, 32; cocked hats, ib.; perukes, ib.; painting and rougeing, 33; hoods and trains, ib.; neck and shoulders displayed, ib.; coiffure, ib.; high boddices, ruffs, and farthingales of the Portuguese ladies of Queen Catherine, 61, 62.

Court, costume at, 29; scandal at, 37; music and the Opera, 38; painters at, 41, &c.; beautiful women composing, ib. &c.; reception of the Infanta Catherine at, 54, 61; contest regarding Lady Castlemaine at, 62; the Queen's masked ball at, 108; Nell Gwynn at, 153; Miss Stewart, Maid of Honour, 174; pastimes at, 176; Miss Stewart's retirement from and return to, 184; the Duchess of Portsmouth's power at, 277—290.

Cromwell, hypocrisy in his Court, 78; his fear of the Duke and Duchess of Ormond, 123, 124; facetious idea of bringing him back, 165.

Dahl, the Swedish portrait painter, 48.

Danby, Lord Treasurer, 266.

Dangeau, Marquis de, 116.

Davenant, Sir William, operas of, 38; curious apology made by, 150.

INDEX.

Denham, Sir John, the poet, 139; insanity of, 141; Aubrey's Life of, 142; his works, 143.
———, Lady, history of, 138; surmises respecting her death, 141; her portrait, 142.
Devonshire, [Christian Bruce] second Countess of, 310.
———, [Elizabeth Cecil] Countess of, 310.
———, William, Duke of, 304.
———, Duchess of, [Lady Mary Butler] 191; life of, 304; her family much respected, 309; her son William espouses the daughter of Lord Russell, who was attainted, 311; history of the family, 312; her portrait, 313.
De Witt, 119, 127.
Digby, Sir Kenelm, 27, 222.
———, George, see Earl of Bristol.
———, Francis, [son of the Earl of Bristol] 178.
———, Lady Venetia, beauty of, 27, 222.
Dillon, Viscount, 338.
———, Viscountess, [Frances Hamilton] 334, 338; tradition of her castle of Laughlin, 338.
———, Arthur, guillotined, 338; his daughter, Countess Bertrand, ib.
Dorchester, Countess of, 291.
Dorset, Earl of, [Lord Buckhurst] resigns Nell Gwynn for his earldom, 152, 153; marries the Countess of Falmouth, [Elizabeth Bagot] 218; and secondly, Lady Mary Compton, 219.
Dryden, characters of his plays, 34; genius of, 37; his Monody on the death of Charles II., 74; his "Conquest of Granada," 152; his interests recommended to Rochester, 162; poetry of, 84, 129, 132, 151, 178, 293, 325.
Dutch, their action off Southwold-bay with the Earl of Sandwich, 58; actions at sea, 129; resist the power of Louis XIV., 273.

Evelyn, his Diary, 30, 31, 34, 90, 214, 237, 242, 254, 276, 330; singular adventure of, 123; his account of Lord Ossory, 131, 132; of the Countess of Sunderland, 241, 247; letter from him to that lady, 242; visits the Duchess of Portsmouth, 278.

Falmouth, Berkeley Earl of, 107, 113; married to Miss Bagot, 215, 216; killed in action, 217.
Fielding, Beau, marries the Duchess of Cleveland, 89; is prosecuted for bigamy, ib.
Fontenelle, his censorship of the press, 115.
Fountaine, Sir Andrew, 223.
Fox, Sir Stephen, 242, 270.
French language fashionable at the English Court, 34.
——— intrigue, treaties, &c. 57, 97, 99, 266, 267, 273, 277, 281, 283, 287.

Gainsborough, truth and vigour of his portraits, 49.
Grafton, Duke of, [Henry Fitzroy] valour of, 90; killed at the siege of Cork, 91; his Duchess, [Isabella, daughter of Harry Bennett, Earl of Arlington] 90.
Grammont, Chevalier de, quotations from the "Memoirs" of the, 28, 31, 114, 138; describes Catherine and her Portuguese ladies, 62; mediates between the King and Lady Castlemaine, 88; his courtship of Elizabeth Hamilton, 104; his rivals described, 106, 107, 112; his predictions fulfilled, 113, 114; recalled from exile, 113; succeeds his brother as Count de Grammont, 114; particulars relative to, 114, 115; his interview with Fontenelle, 115; his illness, 116; his death, ib.; poetical epistle of St. Evremond to, 118; various allusions to, 178, 180, 195, 196, 202, 212, 223; pays his addresses to Mrs. Middleton, 254.
———, Elizabeth, Countess de, [La Belle Hamilton] her high character, 28, 41, 102; in great favour at Court, 103; described by De Grammont, 104; letter of Charles II., relative to, 113; appointed Dame du Palais at Versailles, 114; her influence with her husband, 116; account of her daughters, ib.; portrait of, 117; allusions to, 317, 319, &c.
Guitar much in fashion, 40.
Gwynn, Nell, recollections of, 146; her frankness, 148; ill education of, ib.; her character its own apology, 146—148; her birth, 149; brought on the stage by Lacy and Hart, 150; her popularity, ib.; her dramatic characters, 151; her intimacy with Lord Buckhurst, 152; her performance of "Alma-

hide," ib.; Charles II. becomes enamoured of her, 153; appointed a lady to the Queen, ib.; her wit and gaiety, 154; disinterestedness and generosity of, 155; a favourite of the people, ib.; example of vivacity in the King's presence, 157; good conduct after his death, ib.; her children named Beauclerc, 158; anecdote of, ib.; family history of, 159; her goodness of heart and beauty, ib.; her portrait by Lely, 160; further remarks on her life, ib.; anecdotes of her and Charles II., 162, 163; her charity, 164; her patriotic persuasions, ib.; held in contempt at Court, not having a title like other favourites, 280.

Hamilton, James, first Duke, beheaded, 224.

———, William, second Duke, mortally wounded at Worcester, 224.

———, Sir George, a distinguished partisan of Charles I., 103, 299; his sons and daughters, 103.

———, La Belle: see De Grammont.

———, Count Anthony, facts recorded by him in the Memoirs of De Grammont, 113, 176, 190, 193, 314, 317, &c.

———, his younger brother George, 177; his admiration of Lady Chesterfield, 192, 194; advises the Earl to remove her from Court, 195; her revenge, 196; marries Frances Jennings, 329; is knighted by Charles II., ib.; created a Count by Louis XIV.; and slain in his wars, 330; his children, 334, 338.

Hampton Court gallery of Beauties, 45.

Haro, Don Louis de, gives offence to Charles II., who dismisses this Spanish ambassador, 56, 57.

Hart, the celebrated actor, 88, 149, 151.

Herbert, Lord, quotation from, 104.

Hertford, Algernon, Earl of, 170.

Hewit, Sir George, 110.

Hobart, Miss, 214.

Holland, Earl of, 121.

Hollis, Lord, high character of, 284.

Howard, Miss, visit of the King to, 283, 322.

Hudson, stiffness and insipidity of his portraits, 48, 49.

Huysman, John, the eminent portrait-painter, 44, 236.

Hyde, Anne: see Duchess of York, and her father Lord Clarendon.

———, Henry, [Lord Cornbury and Earl of Clarendon] 202, 208.

———, Laurence, Earl of Rochester, 202, 203.

———, Lady Catherine, [Duchess of Queensbury] 209.

James II. when Duke of York, 32, 143, &c.; his admiration of Miss Hamilton, 106; his affection for Lady Denham, 138, 140; his attentions to Lady Chesterfield, 192; Philip Earl of Chesterfield's jealousy of, 195; his union with Anne Hyde recognized, 41, 55, 202, 212; defeats the Dutch off Harwich, 217; his love for the beautiful Countess of Southesk, 227; affair of the Duke and Lady Bellasys, 231, 233; his contract handed to that lady, 234; his taste superior to that of Charles II. 233; his accession, 291; his early care of Miss Churchill, 314; his son the Duke of Berwick, ib.; his courtship of Miss Jennings, 318; his consort Maria d'Este, or Maria of Modena, 208, 332; rise and progress of the Revolution during his reign, 183, 208, 210, 241, 244, 286, 288, 289, 311, 312.

Jennings, Miss Frances: see Duchess of Tyrconnel.

———, Miss Sarah: see Duchess of Marlborough.

Jermyn, Henry, 88, 107, 218; his duel, 187; his loss of Frances Jennings, 323—329; his family prospects, 324.

Jervas, the court-painter, 47.

Killigrew, Italian singers imported by, 38, 39; a companion to the King, 60; amusing anecdote of, 165; other jests, 177, 326.

Kneller, Sir Godfrey, style of, 42; the competitor of Lely, 44; distinctions conferred on him, 45; portraits by, ib.; wit and vanity of, 46; death and monument to, 47.

Koningsmark, Count, crime of, 169; challenged by Cavendish, 307.

Lacy, comedian, and Nell Gwynn, 149.

Lawrence, Sir Thomas, peculiar merit of his style, 49; chef d'œuvres of, 50.

Lawson, Mrs., account of, 186; her connexions, 187; portrait of, 188.
———, Admiral Sir John, 146.
———, Sir John, of Brough, 187.
Lee, Nathaniel, the dramatic poet, 148, 179.
Lely, Sir Peter, 27; account of, 41; painted the Windsor Beauties, 41, 142; his style defended, 42; historical paintings by, 43; crayons, ib.; his marriage and knighthood, ib.; his death, ib.; his portraits of Queen Catherine, 75; of Miss Hamilton, 117; of the Duchess of Somerset, 167; of Lady Chesterfield, 198; of Lady Rochester, 209; of Miss Bagot, 219; of Lady Sunderland, 251; of Mrs. Middleton, 258; of the Duchess of Portsmouth and Charles II., 293.
Limerick, William III. raises the siege of, 336; its capitulation, ib.
Lichfield, Countess of, [Charlotte Fitzroy] 91.
Louis XIV., 57; illness of, 97; his policy, 99; why he banished De Grammont, 113; his message to him when ill, 116; his overture to Lord Ossory, 129; bribes Montague, 266; his revocation of the Edict of Nantes, 267; his project against Holland, 273; grants the duchy of Aubigny to Charles II.'s French mistress, 277; allusion to, 281; his treaty with Charles II., 283; his design on the Duchy of Luxembourg, 287; threatens to betray Charles II., 288; his conduct on the death of Henrietta, Duchess of Orleans, 297, 299.
Lyttelton, Lady, 316.
———, the celebrated Lord, 316.

Macky, Spring, extracts from his 'Memoirs,' 186, 171, 200, 303.
Maria d'Este, Queen of James II., 208, 332.
Marlborough, Duke of, his obligations to Lady Castlemaine, 87; his ingratitude to her while in disgrace, ib.; his friendship for the Earl of Sunderland, 240; marriage of his daughter Anne Churchill to Lord Spencer, ib.; his sister Arabella Churchill, 314, 315; he marries Sarah Jennings, 317; his interview with Frances Jennings, the widow of the Duke of Tyrconnel, 337.
———, Sarah, Duchess of, 211; friendship of Queen Anne for, 248; ambitious career of, 337.

Marriage à la Mode, Dryden's comedy of, 34.
Martial, French glover, alluded to by Molière, 105, 214.
Marvel, Andrew, verses by, 34; letter of, 84; satire by, 280.
Mary II., Queen, 158, 247, 312.
Mazarin, Duchess of, [Hortense Mancini] portrait of, 26; her house at Chelsea, 255; her views with regard to Charles II., 279; her love for the Prince of Monaco, 280.
———, Cardinal, 279.
Melfort, Lord, letters from, 333.
Melo, Don Francisco de, ambassador from Portugal, 54.
Middleton, Mrs., 43; portraits of, by Lely, 252, 257; her father, Sir Roger Needham, 252; receives billets from De Grammont, 253; sarcastic verses of St. Evremond relative to, 256.
Monmouth, Duke of, 290, 306; portrait of, 45.
Montagu, Edward, 69.
Montague, Ralph, ambassador at Paris, [afterwards Duke of] 95; complained of, 96; intrigue of, 254; personal description of, 262; his courtship of Lady Northumberland, ib.; their marriage, 264; builds Montague-House, [the British Museum] 265; politics of, 266; his perfidy against Danby, ib.; promotes the Revolution, 268; created an Earl, ib.; his mansion at Boughton, 269; his marriage with Lady Elizabeth Cavendish, 270; curious anecdotes relative to, 270, 276, 284, 307.
Montespan, Madame de, her elevation, 274, 281, 285.
Morland, Sir Samuel, his house at Vauxhall, 80.
Muskerry, Lady, her eccentric character, 103, 108, 112.
———, Lord, 108, 111; killed in action off Harwich, 217.

Nassau, Louis of, titles and posterity of, 119.
Newcastle, Duchess of, 108, 111.
Ninon de l'Enclos, 116; parallel of her humour with that of Nell Gwynn, 148.
Nokes, the stage buffoon, 153.
Norfolk, Duke of, 107, 113.
Northumberland, Joseeline, Earl of, 168.
———, Countess of, [Elizabeth Howard] 168.

INDEX. 347

Northumberland, Countess of, [Elizabeth Wriothesley] 28, 259; her family connexions, ib.; her marriage, 260; accompanies the Earl to France, 261; John Locke her physician, ib.; takes the title of Countess of Montague, 268; dies at Boughton, 269; her son John Duke of Montague, ib.; her portrait, 270: *see* Montague.

————, Duke of, [George Fitzroy] an extinct peerage, 91.

————, estates and title of, their descent, 171.

Nott, Mrs., portrait of, 220; her family, 222.

Oates and Bedloe accuse Queen Catherine of a participation in the Popish plot, 72.

Opera, Italian, introduced, 38.

Orleans, Duke of, 205, 207, 301.

————, Henrietta, Duchess of, [Madame d'Angleterre] letter from Charles II. to her, 113; escorted to Dunkirk by Louis XIV. and his Court, 274; her interview at Dover with Charles II., ib.; her treaty with Louis XIV. ib.; her death by poison, 275; like fate of her daughter, the Queen of Spain, 281; her affection for Charles II., 296; letters relative to her death, 296—302.

Orleans, Mademoiselle d', 100.

Ormond, Earl of, his dispute with the Earl of Leicester, 131.

————, James, the great Duke of, offends Lady Castlemaine, 83; his sister, 103; family connections of the Butlers, 119; his high character, 120; his union with the heiress of the house of Desmond, ib.; his many adventures, ib.; his fortune, 120, 126; Colonel Blood's attempt on his life, 130; his admirable letters on his son Lord Ossory's death, 132, 134; on his daughter's, 199; on Lady Ossory's, 206; his daughter Mary, Duchess of Devonshire, 304; he was Lord-Lieutenant of Ireland, ib.; his palace of Kilkenny-Castle, 305.

————, Duchess of, her family, 120; her union with Duke James, 122; generous temper of, 123, 126; her interview with Cromwell, 124; her daughter Elizabeth, Countess of Chesterfield, 180.

————, James, Duke of, grandson of the great Duke, history and impeachment of, 133, 136.

Ossory, Earl of, his marriage, 119, 126; committed to the Tower by Cromwell, 124; set at liberty, 125; anecdote of him by Evelyn, 124; portraiture of, 125; his return to England, 127; his valour, 128; public services of, ib.; his quarrel with Buckingham, 130; his death, 132; his children, 133; allusions to him, 281, &c.

Ossory, Countess of, [Emilie of Nassau] 28, 119; her marriage, ib.; her sweetness of temper, 127; her's and the Earl's history, 128, 129.

————; Earl of, (grandson to the great Duke of Ormond,) marries Lady Anne Hyde, 205; her death, ib.; his second Countess, 206.

Painting, art of, 25, 27, 41; Sir P. Lely, 41; Wissing, 44; Kneller, ib.; Huysman, ib.; Jervas, 47; Dahl, 48; Richardson and Hudson, ib.; Gainsborough, 49; Sir Joshua Reynolds, ib.; Hoppner, ib.; Sir Thomas Lawrence, ib.

Pembroke, Philip Earl of, 292.

Penalva, Countess of, 62.

Pepys, 'Diary' of, 30, 31, 61, 69, 70, 72, 81, 83, 89, 92, 94, 139, 150, 152, 183, 195, 217, 228, 239, 322, 327.

Peveril of the Peak, by Sir W. Scott, 283.

Pope, his flattery of Sir Godfrey Kneller, 46; of Jervas, 47, 48; illustration of a verse of, 185, 209.

Popish Plot, the, 72, 286.

Portsmouth, Duchess of, her power over Charles II., 89, 155; letter concerning, 97, 98; De Sévigné contrasts her with Nell Gwynn, 156; her son created Duke of Richmond, 179; her character and political influence, 271, 277; her maiden name, 272; her reception at Court, 276; her son, 277; her titles of nobility, ib.; well received by the court ladies, 280; her jewels, 281; her insolent behaviour, 282; intrigues in favour of the designs of Louis XIV., 283, 287; her mind and disposition, 285; advice given to by the Earl of Sunderland, 289; her behaviour on the King's death, 290; retires to France, 291; revisits England, ib.; dies at an advanced age in Paris, 292; her sister the Countess of Pembroke, ib.; portraits of, 293; her pretended marriage, 294.

Portugal, John Duke of Braganza, 53; menaced by Spain, 56; Alphonso VI. deposed by his brother Pedro, 72.
Price, Miss, 112, 213, 322, 325, 327.

Ranelagh, Lord, [Richard Jones] 254.
Raphael, epitaph by Cardinal Bembo on, 47.
Reynolds, Sir Joshua, 49.
Rich, Lady Isabella, 121, 123.
Richmond, Duchess of, her sarcasm on Lady Castlemaine, 89.
———, Duchess of, [Mary Villiers] 187.
———, Duchess of, [Anne Brudenell] 235.
———, Duchess of, [Miss Frances Stewart] affection of Charles II. for her, 69, 70; court intrigues to favour her, 70; her influence with the merry monarch, 88; her charms, 93, 175; her character portrayed, 173; friendship for, and subsequent rivality with Lady Castlemaine, 174; her many admirers, Buckingham, Digby, Hamilton, the Duke of Richmond, 176—179; also the King, 180; marries the Duke of Richmond, 181—183; quits the Court, 184; illness of, ib.; returns to Court, ib.; her will, 185; her estates, ib.; portrait of, at Windsor, ib.; further allusions to, 317, 320.
———, Charles Duke of, 93; his proposal to Miss Hamilton, 106; of the house of Stewart, 179; his adventure at Miss Stewart's, 181; his marriage with that lady, 181—183; his death, 277.
———, Duke of, [Charles Lennox] created Duke by Charles II. 179, 277; changes the mode of wearing the ribbon of the order of the Garter, 286; his Duchess and their children, 291; he declares for the religion and constitution of England, 303.
Rochester, Earl of, [John Wilmot] and Nell Gwynn, 162, 203; pretends to be an astrologer, and is much consulted, 324—327.
———, Earl of, [Laurence Hyde] 202; his honours, 203; his meditations on his daughter's death, 206; his politics, 208; his death, ib.; further account of, 210; his letter to Ormond, 211.
———, Countess of, [Lady Henrietta Boyle] her ancestry, 201; her marriage, 202; her domestic character, 203; delicate health of, 204; she laments her daughter's death, 206; her speech to Queen Maria, 208; her death, ib.; portrait of, 209.
Roos, Lord, divorce-bill of, 72.
Rotier, Philippe, the medallist, 179.
Rupert, Prince, his expedition to Guinea, 328.
Russell, Lord, execution of, 243; attainder reversed, 268; the Earl of Bedford's endeavour to save his son, 286; his advice to Cavendish, 308; letter of his daughter, 311.
———, Lady, character of, 126, 237; her life and correspondence, 248, 264, 267; her sister the Countess of Northumberland, 259, 260, 268, 269.

St. Albans, Charles first Duke of, his bravery, 158; his children, 159.
———, Duchess of, Diana de Vere, daughter of Aubrey, Earl of Oxford, 159.
Sandwich, Earl of, 40, 57; high character of, 58; his victories and death, ib.; his account of the nuptials of Charles II., 60; withdraws from the Queen's interests, 69.
Sedley, love songs of, 37.
Sévigné, Madame de, 114, 156, 276, 319.
Shakspeare, sonnet of, 146; his great nephew, Hart, the comedian, 149.
Sheldon, Dr., Bishop of London, 60.
Shrewsbury, Countess of, 284.
Somerset, Duke of, [Charles Seymour] 'the Proud,' 169—172.
———, Elizabeth, Duchess of, her marriages, 168, 169; her children, 170, 171; portrait of, 43, 171.
Sourches, Marquis de, Memoirs of, 291.
Southampton, Lord Treasurer, 260; his opposition to Lady Castlemaine, 89.
Southesk, Robert Earl of, 225; character of, 226; his unhappy marriage, ib.
———, Countess of, her portrait, 223; severe censure of, ib.; her father slain in Charles II.'s service, 224; her acquaintance with Lady Castlemaine, 225; her marriage with Lord Carnegie, [Earl of Southesk] 226; her ill conduct at court, ib.; her lord's jealousy, ib.; her sons, 228.
Spencer, Lord, [son of the Earl of Sunderland] 244, 249; his marriage with

INDEX.   349

Lady Anne Churchill, 250; their sons, 251.
St. Evremond, observations, verses, &c. by, 26, 105, 107, 112, 118, 255—257, 276.
Stewart, Walter, Esq., loyalty of, 173; his daughter, Miss Stewart, *see* Frances, Duchess of Richmond.
Sunderland, Henry first Earl of, killed at Newbury, 239.
———, second Earl of, [Robert Spencer] unhappy career of, 238—241; his marriage, 240; his children, 242; the ancestor of the Duke of Marlborough and Earl Spencer, ib.; proscribed and in misfortune, 244; his discontent and death, 251; political measures of, 288.
———, third Earl of, and Secretary of State, 251; his patriotism and integrity, ib.
———, Countess of, [Dorothy Sidney] 26, 237, 255.
———, Countess of, [Anne Digby] her character, 237; her family connexions, 238; charity of, 241; her filial piety, 243; her letter to William III., 245; to Evelyn, 246; other letters of, 249, 250; her death, 251; portrait of, by Lely, ib.
Sussex, Countess of, [Anne Palmer Fitzroy] 91, 96, 99, 100.
Swift, Dean, 89, 172, 200, 235, 303.
Sydney, Algernon, execution of, 243.

Tangier, acquisition of, by Charles II. 55; affair of, 131.
Tatler, the, 89.
Temple, Sir William, 95, 98, 307.
———, Miss, 315, 316.
Tennison, Archbishop, 157.
Test Act, its proviso in favour of Queen Catherine, 282.
Theatre;—actresses that first appeared on the London Stage, 150; Nell Gwynn, 150, 151, 153; French company imported, 292; Drury-lane, and Bow-street, 325; the Duke's House, ib.
Thornhurst, Sir Gifford, Bart., 317.
Thynne, Thomas, Esq., murder of, 169, 306, 307.
Tyrconnel, Duke of, [Richard Talbot] his untoward meeting with Lord Southesk, 227; a steady adherent to the Stuarts, 320; valour and eminent qualities of, ib.; his courtship of Frances Jennings, 321; his sudden jealousy and temporary loss of her, 322; he meets her in France, 331; his marriage, ib.; commands for James II. in Ireland before and after the downfall of that monarch, 332; viceroy, 333; is defeated at the river Boyne, 334; wounded, ib.; he still maintains the Stuart cause, 335; dies by poison, ib.; succeeded by Sarsfield in his command, 336.
Tyrconnel, Duchess of, [daughter of Richard Jennings, Esq.] 314, 316; repulses the suit of James, Duke of York, 318; her fame attracts the notice of Charles II., 319; courted by Richard Talbot, 320; and by Jermyn, 323; wishes to consult a very clever astrologer, 325—327; dismisses the suit of Jermyn, 328; marries George Hamilton, 329; becomes a widow, 330, 331; turns Catholic, 331; marriages of her daughters by Hamilton, 333, 338; accompanies Tyrconnel to Ireland, 332—334; her dignified reception [as vice-queen] in Dublin, of the defeated James, 334; her poverty after the dispersion of the court of St. Germain's, 336; her milliner's shop at the Royal Exchange, London, ib.; her white mask, 337; establishes a convent of Poor Clares in Dublin, ib.; her miserable death, ib.; her daughter the Princess of Vintimiglia, ib.; her daughter Lady Dillon, 338; her portrait, ib.

Vandyke, portrait by, 26; his marriage, 43; his style, 117.
Vendôme, the Grand-Prieur de, 289.
Villiers, Sir William, [Viscount Grandison] mortally wounded at Bristol, 79; his beautiful daughter Barbara Villiers, *see* Duchess of Cleveland.
Virtue, female, the court a test of, 29.

Wakeman, Sir George, physician to Charles II., 73.
Waller, poetry of, 68, 143, 237.
Walpole, Horace, observations and anecdotes by, 27, 42, 48, 209, 223, 230, 231, 235, 293, 336.
Warton, remark of, 185.
Wells, Miss, a favourite at court, 88.
Whigs, power of the, 285, 308.
William III., a patron of Kneller, 45; and of Dahl, the painter, 48; allusions

to, 133, 136; the English Revolution in his reign, 172, 208, 210, 244, 249, 311, 333; he besieges Limerick, 335.
Windsor Castle, the Gallery of Beauties in, 27, 92, 117, 134, 142, 185, 186, 188, 209, 221, 223, 230, 235, 251, 254, 270.
Wissing, the Dutch painter, 41, 44, 134, 188.
Withers, George, the poet, 145.
Women, occupations and amusements worthy their attention, 322.

Wycherly, the dramatic writer, 87.

Yarborough, Sir Thomas, and his lady, 214.
York, Duchess of, [Anne Hyde] particulars of her union with James, Duke of York, 41, 55, 103, 141, 202, 212, 314, 317, 319, 322, 324, 325; turns Catholic, 331.
Young, Dr. Edward, Author of the 'Night Thoughts,' marries a grand-daughter of Charles II., 91.

THE END.

G. NORMAN, PRINTER, MAIDEN LANE, COVENT GARDEN.

www.ingramcontent.com/pod-product-compliance
Lightning Source LLC
Chambersburg PA
CBHW032141010526
44111CB00035B/857